Lecture Notes in Business Information Processing   **470**

LNBIP reports state-of-the-art results in areas related to business information systems and industrial application software development – timely, at a high level, and in both printed and electronic form.

The type of material published includes

- Proceedings (published in time for the respective event)
- Postproceedings (consisting of thoroughly revised and/or extended final papers)
- Other edited monographs (such as, for example, project reports or invited volumes)
- Tutorials (coherently integrated collections of lectures given at advanced courses, seminars, schools, etc.)
- Award-winning or exceptional theses

LNBIP is abstracted/indexed in DBLP, EI and Scopus. LNBIP volumes are also submitted for the inclusion in ISI Proceedings.

Alessandro Gianola

Verification of Data-Aware Processes via Satisfiability Modulo Theories

 Springer

Alessandro Gianola
Free University of Bozen-Bolzano
Bolzano, Italy

ISSN 1865-1348   ISSN 1865-1356 (electronic)
Lecture Notes in Business Information Processing
ISBN 978-3-031-42745-9   ISBN 978-3-031-42746-6 (eBook)
https://doi.org/10.1007/978-3-031-42746-6

This Springer imprint is published by the registered company Springer Nature Switzerland AG
The registered company address is: Gewerbestrasse 11, 6330 Cham, Switzerland

Paper in this product is recyclable.

To all my friends.

Preface

"When I was a student, even the topologists regarded mathematical logicians as living in outer space. Today the connections between logic and computers are a matter of engineering practice at every level of computer organization."

– Martin Davis, *Influences of Mathematical Logic on Computer Science*

Contemporary organizations are complex organisms involving multiple actors that use multiple resources to perform activities, interact with data objects and take decisions based on this interaction. Due to this high complexity, it is becoming more and more important to model and analyze business processes by relying on modern and efficient techniques coming from several area of computer science, and to regulate and automatize their internal work by exploiting Artificial Intelligence (AI) methods. Business process management (BPM) is now a well-established research field and industry-oriented area of study that stands at the intersection of operations management, computer science, data science, and software and systems engineering. Its principal aim is to help managers, analysts, ICT professionals and domain experts in the design, deployment, enactment and continuous improvement of processes, toward the desired goals and the predetermined objectives of the company. In order to achieve this aim, the intrinsic complexity of modern business processes needs to be handled in its full generality, so as to devise *safe and trustworthy systems* on which stakeholders and BPM practitioners can rely. This poses several challenges for both modeling and analysis tasks, challenges that can only be tackled by relying on mature and well-established AI and formal methods approaches.

The problem becomes even more complicated if business processes are not only studied from the perspective of their control flow, but considering also their interaction with data. The data dimension can be of several kinds, such as case variables carrying data objects, or more complex persistent storage like relational databases. Indeed, a huge body of research has been recently devoted to the problem of integrating *data* and *processes* to achieve a more comprehensive understanding of their concrete interplay within BPM. This requires investigation of how data influence the process behavior, and how the control flow of the process impacts on the data it queries and manipulates.

The development of trustworthy and safe BPM systems that also incorporate the data component is a challenging, open problem in BPM. In fact, the interaction with data causes the resulting process to have *infinitely many states* even when its control flow is bounded. This calls for developing and combining sophisticated techniques and methods coming from different fields like symbolic AI, information systems, formal methods and automated reasoning.

The development of theoretical frameworks for the formalization and the verification of such Data-Aware Processes (DAPs) has consequently flourished. These frameworks present two main drawbacks: first, the results obtained are usually achieved at a quite abstract level, with strong assumptions on the underlying model that do not match those of front-end languages used in practice; second, the studied verification techniques, when concretely implemented, are developed *ad hoc*, without appealing to well-established tools and techniques.

In this book, we tackle this twofold problem by attacking the verification of DAPs with solid techniques for the verification of infinite-state systems. To do so, we start from the observation that many approaches to symbolic reasoning for infinite-state systems have been developed in the realm of model checking, providing not only solid foundations to the verification tasks of interest, but also highly efficient technologies. This is, in particular, the case of Satisfiability Modulo Theory (SMT) solving, which provides a powerful setting for infinite-state verification, and supports well-performing tools, called SMT solvers.

In this respect, this work aims at bridging the gap existing between DAP verification and SMT-based infinite-state model checking, focusing in particular on the *safety* problem. This problem amounts to establishing whether a system can reach an undesired, unsafe configuration starting from its initial states.

In order to attack this problem, we introduce a general framework for DAP verification based on SMT. We study and develop new algorithmic techniques and methods in the context of automated reasoning: specifically, our DAP verification machinery strongly relies on the notion of *uniform interpolant* modulo a first-order theory, which has strict connections with well-studied concepts from mathematical logic and model theory. Thus, a substantial portion of this book is devoted to presenting theoretical results on interpolation that not only are essential for DAP verification, but are of independent interest. This framework is shown to be effectively applicable for verifying real-world data-aware business processes modeled using extensions and combinations of standard languages: this is also supported by our experimental validation on a concrete DAP benchmark.

For all these reasons, this book addresses both the BPM and the automated reasoning communities. The two spirits of the book are the core of what we believe is the main contribution of this work: to build a bridge between mathematical logic and automated reasoning on one side, and the modeling and analysis of business processes on the other. We hope that the reader will appreciate the result of this unusual but effective combination.

Contributions

This book presents a new approach to safety verification of a particular class of infinite-state systems, called Data-Aware Processes (DAPs). To do so, the developed technical machinery requires to devise novel results for uniform interpolation and its combination in the context of automated reasoning. These results are then applied to the analysis of concrete business processes enriched with real data. To be more precise, there are three main contributions that are at the core of this book.

- First, *we propose a general framework for modeling and verifying DAPs that relies on mathematical logic* (specifically, model-theoretic algebra) *and on SMT solving*. Within this framework, we first introduce an algebraic formalization of database schemas, called DB (extended-)schemas, that is essential for exploiting model-theoretic properties. Then, building on top of DB schemas, we define some variants of artifact systems (SASs, RASs, U-RASs) with different expressiveness. These systems are the foundational representation of DAPs on which we focus in this work. For such systems, we study SMT-based verification techniques that make use of *model completions*, the central model-theoretic notion: specifically, we introduce a novel version of the SMT-based backward search that can deal with the database-driven setting of artifact systems. This setting requires handling of quantified 'data' variables by exploiting quantifier elimination features provided by model completions. Finally, we provide sufficient conditions for guaranteeing the termination of the verification techniques.
- Second, to make our verification machinery efficient, *we develop sophisticated algorithmic techniques that build on and extend well-established automated reasoning methods*. These methods are based on the crucial concept of *uniform interpolant*, which is strictly related to model completions studied in the first part. One of the main results is to show that computing (quantifier-free) uniform interpolants in a first-order theory is equivalent to eliminating quantifiers in the model completion of that theory. Then, building on top of well-established first-order calculi, we study sophisticated algorithms for computing uniform interpolants for uninterpreted functions and relations of any arity: this contribution is of general interest for automated reasoning. We also specialize these algorithms to the case of significant DB theories, showing that computing uniform interpolants is computationally tractable. Moreover, we study combination of uniform interpolants, both from the theoretical and algorithmic points of view, and we discuss applications to DAP verification. At the end of the second part of the book, we demonstrate the feasibility of our approach by showing its implementation in the state-of-the-art MCMT model checker: we provide an experimental evaluation by testing the MCMT capabilities against a DAP benchmark.
- Finally, as a last crucial contribution, *we apply our general framework to business process management*. We introduce formal and operational settings that are based on standard languages and/or can capture advanced modeling capabilities. Specifically, we first propose a general model of data-aware business processes, called DAB, that builds on top of RASs, one of the artifact systems from the

first part of the book. Differently from artifact systems, DABs provide a clear representation of the control flow, since its process schema employs the BPMN constructs. The data layer of DABs comprises both volatile data variables and persistent storage in the form of read-only and read-write relational databases. The data manipulation layer of DABs still presents a quite abstract update specification language. For this reason, we then introduce another framework, called delta-BPMN, which is the operational and implemented counterpart of DABs: in delta-BPMN, the data manipulation layer is formalized via a suitable SQL dialect. Finally, we propose a Petri-net based formalism, called COA-nets, which is a data-aware extension of Colored Petri nets. COA-nets can query a relational database, in the same spirit of artifact systems. COA-nets present expressive modeling features: for instance, they are an object-centric model, since they provide the ability to track the co-evolution of different objects and to represent their parent-child relationships. We study the safety problem for DABs, delta-BPMN and COA-nets: we show that they can all be encoded into the artifact systems studied in the first part, and we assess safety by applying to them the SMT-based backward reachability procedure for artifact systems.

Book Structure

The book is organized in 14 chapters: the first one provides an overview of motivations and contributions, and a detailed introduction of the content, whereas the remaining 13 chapters are divided in 3 parts. In the first part, we present the general foundational framework for DAP verification, and we discuss theoretical guarantees of the technical machinery. In the second part, we focus on the algorithmic techniques based on uniform interpolation that are needed for the verification machinery, and we present the implementation and experiments. The third part introduces the application of DAP verification to business process models of different types.

More specifically, this is the content of the chapters:

- In Part I we pave the way for SMT-based safety verification of DAPs.
  - In Chapter 2, we introduce basic logical and model-theoretic notions, and preliminaries on the SMT problem and on (typed) relational databases.
  - In Chapter 3, we present the general framework of Array-Based Artifact Systems, by first introducing DB schemas, DB extended-schemas and then the SAS and (Universal) RAS models. Examples of these notions that are inspired by concrete business processes are given.
  - In Chapter 4, we present our DAP verification machinery based on our SMT-based backward search. We discuss model-theoretic properties needed for the machinery, we prove that such properties are satisfied in interesting cases for our applications and we prove (partial) correctness of the procedure for several classes of Array-Based Artifact Systems.
  - In Chapter 5, we describe some decidable classes of Array-Based Artifact Systems, by proving termination of backward reachability. Verifying Array-

Based Artifact Systems is a challenging task, hence termination cannot be guaranteed in general.

- In Part II we develop algorithmic techniques, based on automated reasoning, that are instrumental for our verification machinery.
  - In Chapter 6, we introduce some preliminaries on interpolants, uniform interpolants (or, equivalenty speaking, covers) and their theory combinations, which are needed for the following chapters.
  - In Chapter 7, we focus on the problem of computing covers/uniform interpolants: we show its relevance to the verification problem for Array-Based Artifact Systems, and we study efficient algorithmic techniques for computing covers in cases interesting for our applications. These cases comprise the one where the studied theory is provided by basic but significant DB schemas.
  - Chapter 8 studies the problem of computing covers/uniform interpolants in theory combinations: we study this problem from the theoretical and the algorithmic perspectives, pointing out how it can be applied to DAP verification.
  - In Chapter 9, we describe the database-driven mode of MCMT and we show an experimental evaluation of our approach to DAP verification against a benchmark of concrete business processes enriched with data.

- In Part III we apply the general framework from Part I to interesting models of (concrete) business processes enriched with data.
  - In Chapter 10, we present some preliminaries on BPM basic notions and Colored Petri Nets.
  - Chapter 11 presents a theoretical framework for modeling and verifying business processes enriched with data, called DABs. The process schema of DABs is represented using the BPMN standard language. We provide theoretical guarantees for the approach.
  - Chapter 12 presents delta-BPMN, the operational and implemented counterpart of DABs. This operational framework makes uses of standard languages such as BPMN for the process layer and SQL dialects for the data manipulation layer.
  - Chapter 13 introduces a Petri net-based model enriched with data, called COA-nets, studying its modeling capabilities and its safety verification.
  - Chapter 14 concludes the book and discusses the relevant future work.

The present book is strongly based on my PhD dissertation, submitted to the Free University of Bozen-Bolzano in November 2022 and defended in March 2023.

In the figure below, we provide a road map of the book and the possible paths that the reader can follow. The numbers in the nodes of the graph stand for Chapters, Sections or Subsections. Blue paths are suggested for the reader who is interested in the mathematical details of the framework and in model-theoretic proofs; red paths are suggested for the reader who is interested in the techniques based on automated reasoning methods; green paths are suggested for the reader who is interested in

BPM and Petri net-based applications. Black arrows are more 'neutral' and may be followed by any reader. Every possible path is, to some extent, self-contained.

Bolzano,   *Alessandro Gianola*
July 2023

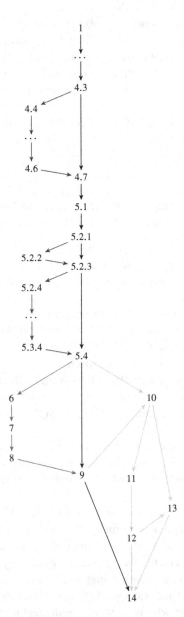

Road map of the book

Detailed Index of Main Notions

Chapter 2

- **Quantifier Elimination Procedure**: important technique used in automated reasoning
- **Model Completion** (Definition 2.2): crucial notion at the core of the verification machinery presented in the book
- **SMT problem**: the most important type of decision problem considered in this work

Chapter 3

- **DB schema** (Definition 3.1): formalization of a read-only relational database schema (one of the contributions of the book)
- **DB instance** (Definition 3.2): formalization of a read-only relational database instance
- **DB extended-schema** (Definition 3.3): formalization of a richer form of read-only database schema, involving arithmetics (one of the contributions of the book)
- **DB extended-instance** (Definition 3.4): formalization of a richer form of read-only database instance, involving arithmetics
- **SAS** (Definition 3.5): Simple Artifact System, one of the main models, involving only artifact variables
- **RAS** (Definition 3.7): Relational Artifact System, one of the main models, involving also artifact relations
- **U-RAS** (Definition 3.6): Universal Relational Artifact System, the most expressive model of this work, involving also artifact relations and universal guards

Chapter 4

- **Finite Model Property**: one of the ingredients of our verification machinery that the DB schema must satisfy
- **BReach$_{SAS}$**(Algorithm 1): SMT-based backward reachability procedure for verifying SASs (one of the main verification procedures)
- **BReach$_{RAS}$** (Algorithm 2): SMT-based backward reachability procedure for verifying RASs (one of the main verification procedures)
- **ApproxBReach$_{U-RAS}$**(Algorithm 3): SMT-based backward reachability procedure for verifying U-RASs (one of the main verification procedures)
- **Partial Soundness**: meta-property of a verification procedure
- **Soundness**: meta-property of a verification procedure
- **Completeness**: meta-property of a verification procedure
- **Effectiveness**: meta-property of a verification procedure
- **Termination**: meta-property of a verification procedure

Chapter 5

- **Well Quasi Order (wqo)**: one of the main mathematical ingredients for proving termination of notable classes of models
- **Acyclic SASs**: one of the decidable classes
- **RASs with Local Updates** or **Local RASs**: one of the decidable classes
- **RASs with Tree-like Signatures** or **Tree-like RASs**: : one of the decidable classes
- **Freshness**: important modeling feature that U-RASs can partially address

Chapter 6

- **Ordinary Interpolant** (Definition 6.1): useful notion in logic and automated reasoning
- **Uniform Interpolant** (Definition 6.2) or **Cover** (Definition 6.3): useful notion in logic and automated reasoning, crucial for our verification machinery
- **Equality Interpolating Property** (Definition 6.4): useful notion in automated reasoning and essential condition for theory combination in our context
- **Beth Definability Property**: useful logical notion, employed in our combination method

Chapter 7

- **Declarative Transition Systems** (Definition 7.1): generic transition systems comprising SASs, where model checking requires computing covers
- **BReach$_{DTS}$**: SMT-based backward reachability procedure for verifying Declarative Transition Systems
- $\mathcal{EUF}$: theory of equality and uninterpreted symbols, particularly useful for formalizing significant DB schemas
- **SuperCover**: Constrained Superposition Calculus for computing covers in $\mathcal{EUF}$

Chapter 8

- $\mathcal{LIA}$: theory of linear integer arithmetic, useful for formalizing arithmetic datatypes in U-RASs
- $\mathcal{LRA}$: theory of linear real arithmetic, useful for formalizing arithmetic datatypes in U-RASs
- **ConvexCombCover**: algorithm for computing combined covers in the convex case
- **TameCombCover**: algorithm for computing combined covers for tame combinations

Chapter 9

- **MCMT**: model checker for verifying safety of infinite-state transition systems
- **Database Driven Module**: specific module extending traditional MCMT capabilities so as to formally verify U-RASs

Chapter 10

- **BPMN**: standard language for modeling business processes
- **Colored Petri Nets** (Definition 10.1): well-known extension of classical place/-transition (or Petri) nets

Chapter 11

- **DAB** (Definition 11.9): Data-Aware BPMN, a formal framework for modeling and verifying data-aware processes
- **DAB schema** (Definition 11.2): read-only database of DABs
- **DAB repository**: read-write database of DABs
- **DAB data schema**: DAB Catalog + DAB Repository
- **DAB Updates (insert&set, delete&set, condition update)** (Definition 11.8): update specifications in DABs
- **DAB process schema**: process component of DABs based on the BPMN standard language
- **BReach$_{DAB}$**: SMT-based backward reachability procedure for verifying DABs
- **Acyclic DABs**: notable decidable case for DABs
- **Local DABs**: notable decidable case for DABs

Chapter 12

- **delta-BPMN**: operational and implemented framework for modeling and verifying DABs
- **PDMML**: Process Data Modeling and Manipulation Language for delta-BPMN
- **Camunda**: graphical editor for representing delta-BPMN models

Chapter 13

- **COA-net** (Definition 13.1): Catalog and Object-Aware nets, a data-aware extension of Petri nets for capturing sophisticated model capabilities and supporting local freshness
- **COA-net Catalog**: read-only database of COA-nets

- **Bounded COA-nets** (Definition 13.4): a notable (decidable) class of COA-nets, such that every reachable marking of each net does not assign more than a bounded number of tokens to every place of the net
- **Object Creation Patterns**: modeling feature of COA-nets
- **Object Relationship Patterns**: modeling feature of COA-nets, for representing many-to-many relations
- **Conservative COA-nets**: a notable class of COA-nets not supporting fresh variables

Conceptual Map of the Book

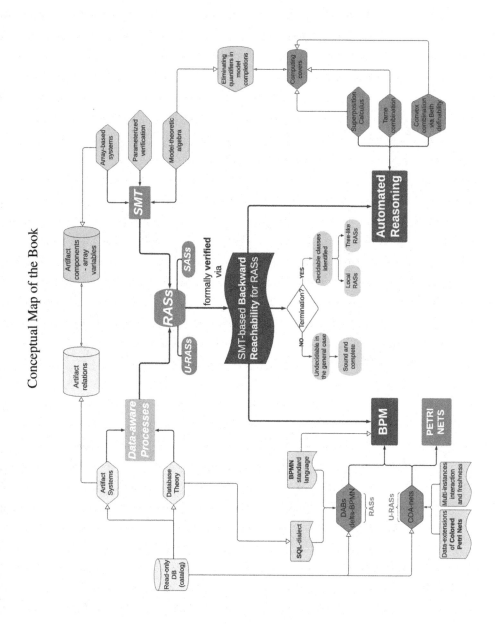

The online version of this book has been revised after publication: The abstracts have been updated to match the ones originally submitted by the author. A correction to the book can be found at https://doi.org/10.1007/978-3-031-42746-6_15

Acknowledgements

This book is strongly based on my PhD dissertation. I am grateful to many people who were key in my path, only some of whom I can acknowledge here.

First, I express my special gratitude to my PhD supervisor, Marco Montali, and to my PhD co-supervisor, Silvio Ghilardi. I would like to thank Marco for his endless patience and continuous support, which were crucial for me to approach research in Computer Science. Special thanks to Silvio, a mentor since my Master's Degree, for introducing me to research and for the long and rich collaboration. All my academic achievements I owe to Marco and Silvio.

I would also like to thank the reviewers of my PhD dissertation, Cesare Tinelli and Dirk Fahland, for the time and effort dedicated to provide a careful and scrupulous review. Their insightful, constructive and meticulous comments have strongly contributed to improving my work, rendering it more insightful and accessible.

Regarding UNIBZ, I would like to sincerely thank my friends Andy and Paolo and my 'moral' co-supervisor Diego, for the fruitful collaboration and for the nice atmosphere at work. I would also like to thank Sarah, Nicola, Luca, Alessandro, Davide, Julien, Gabriele, Eftychia and all the other colleagues from the Faculty of Computer Science.

I am also deeply grateful to the friends who encouraged me throughout my PhD: Marco, Andrea and Joana. They have been fundamental and always present in this long journey. The last years would not have been the same without their constant support and affection.

I would like to thank also my 'pre-PhD' friends, with whom I built so many great memories in Milan: Fabio, Matteo, Andrea and Francesco. Warm thanks to my long-standing 'historical' friends: Francesco, Lorenzo, Stefano, Gabriele, Davide, Simone and Marco. They are the strong foundation that sustains me. I would also like to thank Stefano and Nicoletta: our collaboration and friendship have been an important inspiration and support.

Last but not least, I am grateful to my parents, Daria and Vincenzo, for the unconditional and loving support, and for having made all of this possible.

Contents

Acronyms

BALSA	Business Artifacts, Lifecycles, Services and Associations
BAUML	BALSA UML
BPM	Business Process Management
BPMN	Business Process Model and Notation
COA	Catalog and Object-Aware
CQ	Conjunctive Queries
CPN	Colored Petri Net
CTL	Computational Tree Logic
dapSL	data-aware process Specification Language
DAB	Data-Aware BPMN
DAG	Directed Acyclic Graphs
DAP	Data-Aware Process
DB	Database
DCDS	Data-centric Dynamic System
EUF	Equality and Uninterpreted Functions
FO	First Order
FOL	First-Order Logic
FM-QE	Fourier-Motzkin Quantifier Elimination
GSM	Guard-Stage-Milestone
HAS	Hierarchical Artifact Systems
IDL	Integer Difference Logic
ISML	Information Systems Modeling
LIA	Linear Integer Arithmetic
LQA	Linear Rational Arithmetic
LRA	Linear Real Arithmetic
LTL	Linear Temporal Logic
MCMT	Model Checker Modulo Theories
MDM	Master Data Management
OCL	Object Constraint Language
PDMML	Process Data Modeling and Manipulation Language
PN	Petri Net

PNID	Petri Nets with Identifiers
QE	Quantifier Elimination
RAB	Relational Action Base
RAS	Relational Artifact Systems
SAS	Simple Artifact Systems
SAT	(Boolean) Satisfiability
SMT	Satisfiability Modulo Theories
SQL	Structured Query Language
TS	Transition System
UCQ	Union of Conjunctive Queries
UML	Unified Modeling Language
U-RAS	Universal Relational Artifact Systems
WQO	Well Quasi-Order

Chapter 1
Introduction

In this first chapter, we provide an overview of the motivations and the contributions presented in this book, and a detailed introduction of its content. We introduce verification of data-aware processes and we show how this problem can be successfully attacked by exploiting Satisfiability Modulo Theories (SMT).

1.1 Overview

The thesis brought forward in this book is that:

> Principles, methods and techniques from automated reasoning and Satisfiability Modulo Theories can be effectively employed to lay solid foundations and to develop concrete tools for the formalization and verification of infinite-state systems arising from the interplay between the control flow of a (business) process and the data it queries and manipulates.

Designing agents that are trustworthy is central in general artificial intelligence (AI). In the context of business process management (BPM), the choice of the right symbolic models employed for formalizing the systems is fundamental to specify how the agents should act according to the process under study. In this case, developing techniques for the formal analysis of these symbolic models allows us to verify exactly whether the involved agents follow legitimate behaviors.

Integrating data and processes to understand their concrete interplay is a long-standing problem at the intersection of AI, information systems and BPM. In the last two decades, the increasing demand for process modeling languages in industry and for AI-driven automatic analysis techniques for formally checking them has moved from considering only the control flow dimension of a (business) process, to more integrated models encompassing also the data dimension [104, 221]. We call such combined systems *Data-Aware Processes* (DAPs): due to the presence of unbounded data, e.g., taken from arbitrary databases whose size is unknown a priori or from infinite value domains, these systems are intrinsically *infinite-state*, making automated analysis particularly complicated [47]. Few approaches have been proposed so far to rigorously analyze data-aware processes, especially when they are

A. Gianola: *Verification of Data-Aware Processes via Satisfiability Modulo Theories*, LNBIP 470, pp. 1–32, 2023.
https://doi.org/10.1007/978-3-031-42746-6_1

expressive enough to track the co-evolution of different objects. There is a huge body of foundational, abstract results that do not lend themselves to be implemented, nor to be linked to concrete languages and methods used in practice. This is a serious limitation for applications in real-world scenarios. Moreover, well-established formal methods techniques can be directly applied to verify process control-flows, but cannot be applied off-the-shelf when data are also taken into account.

The goal of this book is to investigate general-purpose and expressive frameworks for **the automated verification of complex dynamic systems enriched with real data capabilities**, that support practice-oriented standard modeling languages employed in the industry, and rely on industry-strength technologies for their automated analysis. To achieve this goal, we investigate and further extend approaches based on symbolic reasoning developed in the realm of infinite-state model checking, providing at once novel foundational results coupled with actual verification technologies, such as those stemming from SAT/SMT solvers and contemporary model checkers.

In this section, we give an overview of the safety verification problem for data-aware processes, starting from classical model checking to the infinite-state one, and, then, we state the main goals of the book. In the next sections, we will first enter into more details about the related literature (Section 1.2) and, finally, we will present thoroughly the contributions we provide (Section 1.3).

1.1.1 Finite-State Model Checking

Formal verification is one of the most studied and prolific research fields at the intersection of computer science, artificial intelligence and mathematics: its goal is to provide automated techniques and methods for analyzing and verifying complex systems against some property of interest. Since the eighties, several approaches to formal verification have been introduced and developed: thanks to its successful applications to hardware and software systems, *model checking* [74, 75], based on the use of mathematical logic for representing models and properties, has gained increasing attention, becoming one of the most famous and celebrated approaches. After the seminal work by Pnueli [216] in the context of temporal logic specifications, and the pioneering study carried out by Clarke, Emerson [70, 71] and Sifakis [219], a plethora of different frameworks and techniques has been introduced in the context of model checking, depending on the specific domain under investigation and the type of specification language employed. In most cases, the aim of these verification approaches is to exhaustively and automatically check whether the hardware or software models to verify meet some given specification represented by formulae expressed in a suitable formal language.

Traditional model checking techniques focus on assessing whether some temporal properties are satisfied in *intrinsically finite-state* systems [219, 69]. This approach relies on the assumption that in most cases the systems to verify can be abstractly described by means of *finite-state* transition systems. Finite-state models allow one to employ *explicit* search procedures in the space of all configurations (which is *finite*) in order to detect if, for example, some *unsafe* state can be reached starting from some initial state of the system. Naively, since the state space is finite, this exploration can be performed via explicit graph search. More practically, in many software contexts, where the executions of the systems are only considered from the point of view of their control flows and, hence, they can be represented via finite flowcharts, sophisticated techniques for a smart and exhaustive exploration of the state space are sufficient to guarantee that these approaches are successful [72, 46, 73].

1.1.2 Verification of Data-Aware Processes

In recent years, a growing number of application domains asks for automated verification techniques that do not just consider the control flow dimension, but also take into consideration the manipulation of data along the system executions and how data influence them. From a *theoretical perspective*, the development of formal, abstract frameworks for attacking the problem of verifying so-called *Data-Aware Processes* has consequently flourished [28, 167, 250, 89, 47, 99], leading to a wide plethora of formal models depending on how the data and process components, as well as their interplay, is actually represented. What all these frameworks have in common is that they strive to focus on very general DAP models that formalize abstract dynamic systems (i.e., the *process* component) interacting with data persistent storage (i.e., the *data* component): in these models, the concept of "process" should be interpreted in an abstract sense, as a (possibly undetermined) mechanism that guides the evolution of a dynamic system.

We discussed already how traditional model checking can successfully attack the problem of verifying finite-state systems. One may wonder whether formal frameworks for verifying DAPs can employ the same techniques. Comprehensive approaches that aim at applying model checking techniques to the formal verification of DAPs should then reflect the possibility of expressing and verifying properties that simultaneously account for the data and the process perspectives, and most importantly for their interaction. However, due to the presence of data, DAP models are *intrinsically infinite-state*: the content of a relational database is typically *finite* but its size is *unbounded* and *unknown* (since a new tuple can always be added to some relation using data elements taken from infinite domains) and its size cannot be foreseen a priory; in addition, many real-world scenarios often require the presence of possibly fresh data values (e.g., string, new identifiers, integer or real numbers) injected into the process by external users. In such sophisticated settings, *explicit* model checking is not possible anymore: exhaustive search and graph exploration-based procedures cannot be applied, since they need to visit an infinite state space. Also traditional approaches in data management and ontologies do not help here, since they typically investigate *static*, structural aspects of a domain of interest, disregarding dynamic aspects [11, 22]. In the line of research of DAP verification, the results obtained for the formal verification of such integrated systems are still quite fragmented, since they consider a variety of different assumptions on the model and on the static analysis tasks [47, 99]. In many cases, these assumptions are quite strong when compared with both concrete business process and data management models.

During the last two decades, while theoretical frameworks for DAPs were studied, a huge body of research has been dedicated to the challenging problem of reconciling data and business process management within contemporary organizations [224, 104, 221]. More specifically, in the context of BPM it has become more and more important to study multi-perspective models that do not just conceptually account for the control-flow dimension of the concrete business process of interest, but also consider the interplay with data [47]: in contrast with abstract DAPs, these models are more focused on concrete processes as they are interpreted by stakeholders and BPM practitioners in real companies. Business processes can be defined as a set of logically related tasks performed within an organization to jointly realize a business goal for a particular customer or market [105]. Traditionally, BPM models are also formalized using pure control-flow models, ignoring the effects that data can cause to the evolution of the process, i.e., neglecting how data are manipulated during the execution of tasks, and how the executability of tasks is affected by data-related conditions. To overcome this fundamental limitation, in the last decade many concrete languages and corresponding formalisms have been proposed to represent business processes where the data and the control-flow dimension are both considered as first-class citizens. One important challenge that naturally arises is how to formally verify such business processes enriched with data: in this respect, it seems natural to employ the abstract frameworks developed for DAPs, and to try to adapt these frameworks to the desired BPM-based application domains (see for some attempts in this direction, e.g., [100, 88, 241, 12]). However, this adaption is quite challenging because of the lack of a comprehensive framework for the verification of DAPs that is able to capture most of the essential features of business process (BP) data-aware extensions. Moreover, one should also consider that currently there are few theoretical frameworks that also support an implemented tool for concrete verification, which is one of the desiderata for every model checking application domain. Finally, an orthogonal challenging dimension regards the abstract flavor of these frameworks and their modeling constructs, which often depart from those offered by process and data modeling standard languages used by BPM practitioners, e.g., the Business Process Model and Notation (BPMN), and data management masters, e.g., the Structured Query Language (SQL). In fact, it is essential to rely on the standard languages used in practice when dealing with real applications, given the assumption that model checking should have a big impact in guaranteeing the correctness and trustworthiness of concrete systems.

1.1.3 Infinite-State Model Checking: from Parameterized Systems to SMT Verification

In parallel, in the nineties, a completely separated line of research in formal verification started to investigate how to attack the problem of verifying *infinite-state systems* in general, disregarding the data perspective. A particularly interesting class of infinite-state systems is given by *parameterized* systems [7]. Such systems can be seen as transition systems that are *parametric* in the number n of components (these components are called *parameters*): such components can behave independently of each other or interact among them following the system topology. In this context, the main goal of parameterized verification is to provide automatic verification methods to prove trustworthiness of these parametric transition systems regardless of the number of their components: these systems are considered trustworthy if they conform to some given formal specification, which is usually expressed, as in traditional model checking, via temporal properties written in a suitable logical language. Contrary to what happens in finite-state model checking, parameterized verification is undecidable in general. The verification problem for parameterized systems has been studied extensively, and a number of decidability results are known for various kinds of specifications. For example, it is decidable for forms of regular specifications [112] but undecidable even for stuttering-insensitive properties such as LTL\X formulae [108] if asynchronous rendezvous is allowed. As summarized in [36], decidability results for the verification of parameterized systems are based on reduction to finite-state model checking via abstraction [217, 172, 9, 8], *cutoff* computations (a bound on the number of instances that need to be verified [109, 10]), or by proving that they can be represented as well-structured transition systems [122, 6].

Another successful way for tackling infinite-state model checking consists of providing a *symbolic setting* [193] where to verify properties: the main idea is to represent infinitely many states in a symbolic way, i.e., using logical formulae. Thanks to this representation, the exploration of the state space does not need to be explicitly carried out, but it can be performed *symbolically*.

One of the most studied techniques for exploring the state space and verifying symbolic systems is *interpolation* [194, 196]. Although this notion has a long-standing tradition in the mathematical logic literature [85], symbolic model checking via interpolation was only introduced by McMillan in his seminal paper in 2003 [194]. In this paper, McMillan provides a fully SAT-based method for performing *unbounded* symbolic model checking tasks. This method consists of computing interpolants for exploring the state space: indeed, interpolants are used to over-approximate the symbolic sets of reachable states through transitions from the initial configurations. In the last fifteen years, interpolation has been well-studied for proving correctness of programs in the context of Satisfiability Modulo Theories [32], an emerging area in computational logic: the SMT problem consists of deciding the satisfiability of logical formulae with respect to combinations of relevant background first-order logic (FOL) theories. Indeed, it is possible to translate preconditions, postconditions, loop conditions, and assertions of software programs into suitable logical formulae modulo specific (combinations of) theories, so as to reduce to SMT the problem of assessing the correctness of such programs.

SMT-based model checking has been proved to be particularly successful for verifying infinite-state systems. Besides interpolation, the state of the art of SMT-based model checking includes a wide range of methods, whose implementations use SMT solvers as their underlying engine. In this book, we will focus only on one of these methods, i.e., the backward reachability procedure, where the exploration of the state space is performed by iteratively regressing the bad states of the system (i.e., exploring *backward* the state space starting from the bad states). Nevertheless, we remark that there is a plethora of other prominent methods that are based on *forward* reachability, such as K-induction [236] and IC3 [38].

In order to verify DAPs, we will consider the SMT-based formal framework of *array-based* systems [143, 146], where infinite-state transition systems are implicitly specified using a declarative, logic-based formalism, where arrays are the central notion. The technique employed to verify such systems is based on an SMT-based version of the backward reachability procedure, and it was successfully applied to a vast class of infinite-state and parameterized systems, such as mutual exclusions protocols [146], timed [61] and fault-tolerant [17] distributed systems, and imperative programs [20].

1.1.4 Main Goal of the Book

As argued before, the verification problem for Data-Aware Processes has recently gained increasing attention, also motivated by BPM applications. Several approaches have been proposed for attacking this problem, but they usually present two significant limitations. First, the employed verification techniques are developed *ad hoc*, and do not rely on *well-established methods* and *already implemented and state-of-the-art technologies*. Second, these frameworks are usually studied at a quite abstract level, which makes it challenging to connect them to the standard front-end languages used in practice. To summarize, there is the lack of a *universal* and *comprehensive* approach to verify DAPs via a sufficiently expressive formalism that natively supports effective techniques and can encode "front-end" languages and models.

At the same time, many approaches to symbolic reasoning for *infinite-state systems* have been successfully applied to different classes of models, such as parameterized systems. Most of these approaches provide not only a solid theoretical framework, but also the support of computationally efficient and highly engineered tools, like state-of-the-art solvers and model checkers. This is the case of SMT solvers and model checkers based on them. Nevertheless, importing SMT-based model checking in the context of DAP verification is extremely challenging and cannot be done *as is*: as it will be discussed in the following sections, it requires carrying out genuinely novel research for handling the data perspective, and to develop corresponding algorithmic techniques.

In this book, we bridge the gap between DAP verification and infinite-state model checking, by introducing for the first time a general model-theoretic framework for automated safety verification of DAPs based on SMT solving. Our approach relies on array-based systems: we extend their underlying theory so as to incorporate the needed capabilities to formalize and reason about relational databases. Specifically, we exhibit how arrays are useful for representing read-write database relations that can be queried and updated during the evolution of the system, and how the standard verification machinery usually used in that context can be suitably extended for verifying safety of DAPs. For this purpose, we develop sophisticated algorithmic techniques building on top of well-known methods in automated reasoning. We also demonstrate the feasibility of our approach by showing these techniques in action thanks to the implementation in the state-of-the-art MCMT model checker, testing it against a concrete DAP benchmark: in this respect, we provide a first experimental evaluation of our verification machinery. Finally, within our general framework, we introduce a theoretical formalism, inspired by Colored Petri Nets, that is able to capture expressive modeling capabilities (such as the co-evolution of different objects), and also we propose more practice-oriented models, based on standard languages used in the BPM literature. For these models, we also provide a proof-of-concept implementation of an operational framework for modeling and verifying concrete business processes enriched with data management features.

The contributions and the content of this book stem directly from my PhD dissertation [154].

We devote the rest of this introductory chapter to analyzing in detail the verification problem we are interested in and to exhaustively presenting the technical contributions of this book.

1.2 Related Literature

The works that are related to the topic of this book involve different research areas within both computer science, business process management and mathematical logic. We first briefly discuss some formal models for Data-aware Processes that have been introduced recently. We then introduce the verification problem for such systems. We finally give a high-level overview of array-based systems and of the SMT-based methods used for verifying them. SMT provides a powerful, yet unexplored setting for tackling the verification of Data-Aware Processes.

1.2.1 Formal Models for Data-Aware (Business) Processes

In Section 1.1 we shortly commented on the separation between traditional process and data modeling.

Traditional data modeling focuses on *entities*, *relationships* and *static constraints* that are relevant for the domain of interest. The dynamic aspects of the systems are usually not considered. Instead, traditional process modeling focuses on the *control-flow* created by the activities that realize the goals of an organization. This approach does not take into account how to evaluate conditions over data, how data are manipulated and how data influence the evolution of the system [221, 105].

This separation is due to the inadequacy of formalizing abstract models able to interconnect the two components. In fact, this problem is usually solved at the technological level, where relationships between data and processes are considered in practice, and tackled at the implementation level: indeed, several well-established suites (e.g. Bizagi BPM Suite, Bonita BPM, Camunda and YAWL) are able to express both the process control-flow and relevant data [95]. Nevertheless, recently a few more systematic but still practice-oriented approaches [200, 117, 86], mainly from the modeling perspective, have been proposed to integrate data and processes, within a system engineering setting, in the scope of business process applications.

Business Process Management (BPM) [105] requires handling this significant connection at the conceptual level. BPM can be seen as a collection of concepts and methods used to help humans in modeling, administration, configuration, execution, analysis, and continuous improvement of *business processes*. Business processes can be thought of as a collection of tasks and activities that take one or more kinds of input and create an output that is of value to the customer: they are performed in order to achieve some specific business outcome.

From a theoretical point of view, the attempt of finding a *coherent* and *holistic* conceptual view has been carried out by several authors in the last decades. They have been studying formal models accounting for the interconnection of processes and data. We informally give a brief description of two of the most significant models [47]: Artifact-Centric Systems [102, 186] and DCDS [28].

1.2.1.1 Artifact-Centric Systems

The Artifact-Centric approach to business process modeling was triggered by IBM Research in the late nineties [214], and it is based on the notion of *business artifact*. A business artifact (or, simply, an *artifact*) is a business entity that merges an *information model*, which represents the business-relevant data of a business object (such as an order or a loan request), and a *lifecycle model*, which involves dynamic aspects of the artifact progression. The information model contains the current state of data, possibly stored in some relational storage, and/or in a set of variables, which may refer either to a primitive value or to some other artifact instance. It evolves over time according to its lifecycle.

In various artifact models, lifecycles have a procedural flavor since they are based on finite state machines whose transitions either create a new artifact, or modify/eliminate an existing one. These transitions can be fired by *actions* (also called *services*), that are usually described in terms of preconditions (and, sometimes, postconditions) and nondeterministic effects related to the creation, manipulation and elimination of artifacts.

More formally, following the representation of artifact systems since their initial versions (e.g., in [100]), we can summarize their essential features by considering three main components: *(i) a read-only database*, storing background information that does *not* change during the system evolution; *(ii) an artifact working memory*, storing data and lifecycle information about artifact(s), which *does* change during the system evolution; *(iii) actions/services* that access the read-only database and the working memory, and determine how the working memory itself has to be updated.

Different variants of this framework have been considered toward decidability of verification, by carefully tuning the expressive power of the three components. For instance, for the working memory, radically different models are obtained depending on whether only a single artifact instance is evolved, or whether instead the co-evolution of multiple instances of possibly different artifacts is supported. In particular, early formal models for artifact systems merely considered a fixed set of so-called *artifact variables*, altogether instantiated into a single tuple of data. This, in turn, allows one to capture the evolution of a single artifact instance [100]. Instead, more sophisticated types of artifact systems have been studied recently in [102, 186, 103]. Here, the working memory is not only equipped with artifact variables, but also with so-called *artifact relations*, which supports storing arbitrarily many tuples, each accounting for a different artifact instance that can be separately evolved on its own.

Actions are usually specified using logical formulae relating the content of the read-only database as well as the current configuration of the working memory to (possibly different) next configurations. An applicable action may be executed, nondeterministically transforming the current configuration of working memory in one of such next configurations.

As for illustration, we give a brief presentation of the Artifact-Centric model called *HAS**, presented in [186]. This model is a variant of another system, *HAS*, introduced by the same authors in [102]. Differently from *HAS*, we will see that a procedure for verifying *HAS** systems have been implemented (in a tool called VERIFAS [186]). A *HAS** system comes with a fixed *database schema* (i.e. a finite set of relation symbols), whose concrete instance is not updated along a run of the system (thus accounting for *persistent, read-only data*), and some *tasks T* with its *artifacts* (the working memory) and its *internal services*, which account for the *dynamics* of the system. Tasks are organized in a *Hierarchy H*, capturing units of work at different granularities.

Artifacts and Internal Services are associated with tasks T:

(i) Artifacts are divided into *artifact variables* and *artifact relations*. These are dynamic entities which can be modified during a run of the system.

(ii) Internal Services formalize the *actions* that can be fired internally to the task T if some (pre- and post-)conditions over the artifact variables of T are satisfied in the instance of the read-only database. They produce an update of the artifact variables and of the artifact relations.

Every task T provides also a pair of *opening* and *closing* services, which allow the activation of parent or children tasks of the hierarchy H.

Thanks to the presence of (unbounded) data, this system is infinite-state. In fact, the initial read-only database instance is not fixed a priory, since only its schema is relevant: this means that unbounded information can be represented by considering different instances of the same database schema. Furthermore, during the run of a system it is possible to introduce (potentially new) data values (for example strings, numbers etc.) that can be thought of as the effects of nondeterministic external functions (such as user interactions).

A similar setting, where only artifact variables are considered but with some applications to XML and tree-automata, is provided in [37].

1.2.1.2 Data-Centric Dynamic Systems

Data-Centric Dynamic Systems (DCDSs) were introduced in [28] and further studied in [48, 204]. They provide a powerful framework for the combination of data and processes, so as to guarantee sufficient expressiveness and significant decidability results for verification. Sufficient expressiveness means that this formalism is able to represent several types of interesting scenarios, e.g., web applications.

The model of *DCDS* consists of two main components: a *data layer* and a *process layer*. The data layer supplies the storage of persistent data and captures the static aspects of system, whereas the process layer provides declarative specifications of system dynamics. The data layer is defined in a full-fledged relational flavor: it can be thought of as a relational schema $\mathcal{R}$ (as in database theory) endowed with integrity constraints (which are, as customary, domain-independent first-order sentences). The process layer provides a set of *actions*, whose execution can modify and update the data layer. It may involve external *service calls* (not to be confused with services of artifact systems): they are functions representing the interface to external services that compute output results in an "unknown" (i.e., nondeterministic) way.

The execution semantics of such a system can be intuitively described as follows. A DCDS is initialized with I_0, which is a database instance of the relational schema $\mathcal{R}$ and satisfies all the constraints. Then, this database instance is evolved by the process layer via applications of actions, which have as effects the modification of the database instance. After a transition, the new obtained database has to be still an instance of $\mathcal{R}$ and must satisfy again the constraints. An action can fire a transition after querying the content of the database instance at the current state, and the update can introduce new values (taken from an infinite countable domain) into the database instance by means of external services. Since these systems have the possibility of introducing new values taken from an infinite domain, their execution runs are infinite and can use an unbounded quantity of information: hence, they are infinite-state.

1.2.2 Verification of Data-Aware Processes

The goal of formal verification is to provide an automated analysis of a formal model against a *property* of interest, considering all possible system behaviors. In the context of DAPs, the analysis of correctness of processes at design time needs to be carried out by taking into account the data component and by checking all the executions (infinitely many, in general).

In the formal verification literature, formal models are verified against several kinds of interesting properties: general, domain-independent properties such as safety, liveness, and fairness [29], reachability of the final state and deadlock freedom, or sophisticated, domain-specific properties such as the following: "in every state of the system, it is always possible to eventually reach a state where all pending orders are delivered". The distinction between general and domain-specific properties is sometimes blurred, since, as it happens in traditional model checking, all these properties can be expressed by temporal/dynamic logics, like:

- *Branching-time logics*: μ-calculus, CTL— Computation Tree Logic—;
- *Linear-time logics*: LTL — Linear Temporal Logic.

We briefly review the traditional model checking perspective.

1.2.2.1 Traditional finite-state Model Checking

Since Pnueli, Clarke, Emerson, Sifakis et al. first introduced the basis of model checking [216, 70, 219], transition systems have been investigated from a temporal logic perspective, where properties to be verified are represented by using logical languages able to express dynamic aspects of models. Since these models are usually *abstractions* formalizing only the control-flow of the system, they can have just a finite number of states. Thus, these systems can be represented as finite labeled graphs: vertices are states labeled by atomic propositions (i.e., atomic properties that hold in that specific state) and arcs are transitions. These systems can be interpreted as Kripke structures [74], as defined in classical temporal (modal) logic: therefore, the usage of temporal logic formalisms turns out to be significantly fruitful in this context.

There are various types of properties that traditionally are verified in transition systems: two of them that are particularly interesting are *safety* and *liveness*. Intuitively, a system is said to be safe if "nothing bad ever happens", whereas a liveness property holds whenever "something desirable will eventually happen".

In this book, we focus our attention just on safety problems: we leave the study of liveness for future work. We now give an informal presentation of the safety problem, which will be the main topic of this work.

Given an unwanted condition of the system (which can be expressed using a formula ϕ in some unspecified logical formalism), we say that there exists an *unsafe* path that leads to ϕ if there is a finite sequence of states such that each state is connected to the other by "legal" transitions (i.e., transitions that can be fired) in the system, the first state of this sequence is one of the *initial states* of the system, and the last state makes ϕ true. This means that there is an unwanted (i.e., *unsafe*) possible configuration of the system which is reachable starting from an initial configuration. In this sense, the safety problem can be cast as a *reachability* question: starting from a set of initial states I, is it possible to reach, exploring the run of the systems, states that satisfy ϕ?

We give an informal example of a simple safety property.

Example 1.1 Suppose to have a system formed by two concurrent processes that share a critical section C, and suppose to have the following requirement: one thread of execution can never enter the critical section at the same time that another concurrent thread of execution enters it (for instance, this critical section could be a portion of the memory where only one process at a time can access). Let ϕ be the temporal formula that states "sometimes the two processes can access C at the same time", which represents an unwanted configuration: if the system is *safe*, then this configuration can never be reached.

1.2.2.2 Abstract DAP Verification in the Literature

Turning to formalisms for Data-Aware Processes, we underlined in the previous section that Artifacts-Centric Systems and DCDSs are intrinsically infinite-state due to the presence of data: hence, in this context it is not possible to directly build a faithful finite-state abstraction (in general), since such an abstraction could not exhaustively account for all the system behaviors. Thus, traditional model checking is not applicable. In addition, because of the presence of data, it is crucial to express properties that take into consideration data and their evolution, hence it is needed to combine temporal logics (for the system dynamics) and first-order logic (in order to express conditions over data).

In [102] the authors develop a complex machinery based on symbolic representation of infinite runs of tasks in *HAS* in order to verify restricted forms of *first-order temporal properties*, like:

"If an order is taken and the ordered item is out of stock, then the item must be restocked before it is shipped".

In order to specify such temporal properties, they use an extension of LTL, called *H-LTL-FO*, in which atoms are *quantifier-free* first-order formulae. The presence of data is witnessed by first-order variables in quantifier-free formulae (that substitute propositional formulae). Using the technical notion of *isomorphism types*, they reduce their verification problem to *repeated state reachability* in VASS (Vector Addition Systems with States), which is a well-known mathematical modeling language for the description of distributed systems [176, 164]. Exploiting this reduction, they show the decidability of verifying whether, given a *HAS* model M and a *H-LTL-FO* formula ϕ, M satisfies ϕ. In [186] the same authors provide an implementation of the machinery studied in [102] in a tool called VERIFAS. In order to do so, they slightly modify the *HAS* model, introducing the variant called *HAS** presented above. In that paper, they introduce some technical heuristics (Karp-Miller algorithm, pruning coverability etc.) for improving the performance of their model checker.

Similar results are presented in [37]. In this setting the authors show, using model-theoretic notions like amalgamation and Fraissè classes, the decidability of the *(non-)emptiness problem*, which can be equivalently reformulated as a reachability (i.e., safety) problem.

We underline that both the approaches from [102] and from [37] propose quite abstract mathematical models that, despite being very expressive and suitable for verification, are far from adopting standard languages that can be used in practice and in industrial applications.

A very different approach to DAP verification is given in [28], where the DCDS model is considered. Since for the activation of actions the data layer is queried through domain-independent FO-formulae, and since the systems evolve along time, the combination of temporal and first-order logic components is necessary. The authors show the undecidability of verification in the general case: in order to guarantee decidability, they also study expressiveness restrictions to the models (e.g., *state-boundedness*) and to the specification logics. The machinery employed involves variants of bisimulations preserving the validity of μ-calculus formulae.

We remark that DCDSs are abstract models for which powerful verification techniques are available but for which practice-oriented modeling languages are *not* employed, neither for the process nor the data layer.

There is a substantial difference between HAS* and DCDS concerning the studied verification problem:

1. in the first case, the verification is "parametric on" (or, "parameterized by") a class of read-only databases, which means that the property of interest is verified for an infinite class of read-only databases that are not modified during a run of the system;
2. in the second case, an *initial* database instance is fixed from the beginning, and this instance is modified during a run of the system thanks to the (unbounded) effects of external services.

1.2.2.3 Practice-oriented models of DAPs

So far, we mainly focused our attention on the most expressive theoretical frameworks (such as DCDS and HAS) for modeling and verifying data-aware processes. These frameworks are defined using an abstract, mathematical syntax, even for approaches like that in [186], which adopts a language inspired by artifact-centric models and supports concrete tools for verification. We now discuss more practice-oriented models for DAPs that have been introduced in the literature.

It is important to mention here that there is a wide range of other approaches falling into the artifact-/data-/object-centric spectrum. As for illustration, we provide a non-exhaustive list of examples of such approaches: the Guard-Stage-Milestone (GSM) language [90], the object-aware business process management framework of PHILharmonic Flows [183], the declarative data-centric process language RESEDA based on term rewriting systems [233]. In a nutshell, these approaches combine the data and process components, but largely focus on modeling, with few exceptions offering runtime verification of *specific* properties (e.g., RESEDA allows for a specific form of liveness checking). For this reason, we will not consider these approaches anymore.

There exists a huge literature devoted to investigating DAPs formalisms based on standard/end user-oriented languages. Specifically, there are important related works that investigate the integration of data and processes with a system engineering setting [200, 117, 86] that are tailored to modeling and enactment.

In [200] the authors study the problem of modeling processes with complex data dependencies, such as many-to-many relationships, and provide an implementation for their automatic enactment from process models. Specifically, this work has the merit of exploiting standard languages for modeling processes and data. Indeed, it introduces an extensions of BPMN data objects that use annotations supporting sophisticated features such as management of data dependencies and differentiation of data instances. In addition, SQL-queries are derived from process models thanks to a pattern-based approach. Of particular relevance is ADEPT [86], which permits to combine fragments of an ad-hoc process modeling language with SQL statements that interact with an underlying relational storage, with the goal of providing execution and analytic services. However, all these approaches do not focus on verification and do not provide automatic techniques for assessing safety of data-aware processes.

Other works that are worth mentioning are [84, 165]. In the first one, the authors address the problem of modeling BPMN collaborations taking into account different perspectives, such as the interaction with data and the co-evolution of multiple instances. They do not only study the formal semantics of these models, but also implement an animator tool for the representation and visualization of their execution semantics. In the second one, a first attempt toward verification of BPMN collaboration models is presented, although in this case the data perspective is abstracted away.

Since the focus of this book is on verification of business processes enriched with data, we now circumscribe the discussion of the relevant related works to those dealing with the formal verification of complex processes enriched with data. This point is particularly significant in view of the general goal of this work, because the choice of language constructs is affected by the verification task one needs to solve - indeed, verifying sophisticated models supporting expressive constructs requires suitably controling the data and control-flow components as well as their interaction [47, 99].

The vast majority of the contributions in the line of research on verification provides foundational results, but does not come with corresponding operational tools for verification. Hence, we conclude the subsection by *briefly presenting only those approaches for the integration of data and processes that come with verification tool support*. We already briefly presented VERIFAS, so we will focus now on other tools relying on practice-oriented models.

In [114], the authors present an approach for automatically verifying and validating the correctness of artifact-centric business processes that are defined by means of BAUML models. One of the great advantages of BAUML models lies in the fact they are based on practice-oriented languages, since they rely on a combination of UML/OCL-based models to specify the various process components: UML (Unified Modeling Language) and OCL (Object Constraint Language) are approved ISO standard language, the first one is used to model and visualize the design of a system, whereas the second one is used to describe in a declarative way rules. The approach of [114] translates the verification task into first-order satisfiability tests over the flow of time, via the definition of a fixed set of *test cases* expressing properties that are checked as derived predicates.

In [218], the authors present a framework for modeling and verifying information systems combining information models and process models. To do so, they propose the Information Systems Modeling Language (ISML). ISML models can express static, information aspects by exploiting first-order logic with finite sets and equality, and dynamic aspects by exploiting Petri Nets with Identifiers (PNIDs [249]). The verification machinery relies on state-space construction techniques for Colored Petri Nets, assuming that the data domains are all bounded; no specific verification language is employed, leaving to the user the decision on how to explore the state space. Although ISML, from the process-centric of view, adopts a Petri Net-based perspective that is in line with the modeling conventions used in the literature, it employs data definition and manipulation languages specified in an ad-hoc way.

In [60], the dapSL approach is proposed: it is a declarative language, built on top of the SQL standard, that supports modeling, enactment and verification of data-aware processes. dapSL defines the control-flow implicitly via condition-action rules, and uses a language grounded in the SQL standard for querying and updating the data. Its verification engine relies on an ad-hoc state-space construction that, under suitable restrictions, faithfully represents in a finite-state way the infinite state space induced by the data-aware process under analysis; however, no additional techniques are defined to explore the state space or verify temporal properties of interest.

Since, in general, verifying data-aware processes is highly undecidable [47, 99], it is crucial to investigate the key meta-properties (such as soundness, completeness, and termination) of the employed algorithmic techniques. In this respect, all the practice-oriented approaches presented in this paragraph lack a precise and detailed meta-analysis, as it will be carefully discussed in Chapter 12.

There is a final consideration that is worth highlighting, which regards the type of verification problem addressed by the aforementioned approaches. Indeed, the problem and the employed verification techniques are strongly affected by whether persistent data are managed under a unique access policy, or instead there is a fine-grained distinction based on how the process can access them [47, 99]. On the one hand, the approaches presented in this paragraph (i.e., BAUML, dapSL, and ISML) do not distinguish read-only from updatable persistent data. They require to fully fix the initial configuration of data: hence, they perform verification tasks by considering all possible evolutions of the process starting from the fixed initial configuration. Differently, approaches like VERIFAS distinguish read-write from read-only data, in turn focusing on forms of parameterized verification where the properties of interest are studied for every possible configuration of the read-only data, assessing whether the process correctly works regardless of which specific read-only data are retrieved. In this book, we will study the latter: in the settings we are interested in, the language separates read-only persistent data from persistent data that are updated during the execution.

A more detailed discussion on the related works that propose practice-oriented frameworks for modeling and verifying Data-Aware Processes is carried out in Chapter 12, where the existing approaches are carefully compared with the one proposed in this book.

1.2.3 Model Checking for Infinite-State Systems using SMT-based Techniques

SMT-based infinite-state model checking has a long tradition, as witnessed by several papers like [142, 146, 34]. Other approaches on symbolic model checking that are worth mentioning, but that we are not going to use in this book, are [193, 161, 195, 194].

Since an exhaustive exploration in the space of configurations is not possible when the states are infinitely many, a symbolic representation is needed. Instead of describing all the states of the system explicitly, states are represented symbolically using individual and/or function variables, called "state variables": these variables can change their value during the evolution of the system, and their content in every moment is supposed to determine the current state of the system. The current values of all the state variables of the system identify a *configuration*. States are not always considered separately: in fact, in transition systems described symbolically, there could be a set of (possibly infinitely many) states that induce the same behavior. Hence, (possibly infinite) sets of states can be characterized via logical formulae involving the state variables: all the states satisfying the same formulae need to be thought, to some extent, as indistinguishable.

Besides sets of states, also the transitions of the system can be formalized by using logical formulae: given a symbolic configuration represented by a state variable x (identifying the current state of the system), a transition t between two configurations is represented by means of a formula $T(x, x')$, where the variable x' is a renamed copy of x that represents the next state of the variable x, obtained after applying t. Symbolic formalisms are powerful enough to formulate the safety verification problem: intuitively, establishing if there exists a model, taken from a specific class of models, and a path inside it leading to the satisfaction of the property of interest, is in some sense reduced to deciding through logical mechanisms and reasoning tasks (e.g., satisfiability and logical implication) the existence of some relations among symbolic representations of states and transitions.

We restrict our attention to symbolic formalisms that use SMT solving as its underlying logical reasoning task, and in particular on array-based systems [143, 146]. We first provide some intuitions on the SMT problem and SMT-based model checking in general.

1.2.3.1 SMT problem and SMT-based model checking

The *Satisfiability Modulo Theories* (SMT) problem is a decision problem that extends propositional satisfiability to satisfiability of first-order formulae with respect to combinations of background theories such as arithmetic, bit-vectors, arrays, uninterpreted functions. There exists a family of tools for attacking this problem, called *SMT solvers*: a non-comprehensive list of SMT solvers contains Yices [4, 106], Z3 [201, 96], CVC5 [2, 30], MathSAT5 [3, 68]. They extend SAT solvers with specific decision procedures customized for significant (and useful in practice) first-order theories.

The SMT-LIB project[1] [31] (started in 2003) aims at bringing together people interested in developing powerful tools combining sophisticated techniques in SAT solving with dedicated decision procedures involving specific theories used in applications (especially in software verification). All in all, SMT solving relies on a *universal, flexible* and *largely expressive* approach that allows us to exploit a full-fledged declarative framework where SMT solvers are highly competitive.

SMT tools are at the heart of declarative approaches to model checking, both in the bounded and in the unbounded case: they are employed in many advanced techniques, for instance in interpolation-based [196]. Specifically, SMT solving can be employed to attack the verification of infinite-state systems expressed by means of symbolic models. Several different methods have been successfully studied in this respect: for the purpose of this work, the *backward reachability* procedure plays a crucial role, which we will discuss better in the following paragraph.

Other important methods that have been investigated for the verification of infinite-state systems are based on *forward reachability*, which means that the state space is explored, starting from the initial configurations, via an iterative computation of direct images of state, i.e. the set of states reachable through transitions of the system under analysis. Some well-known methods of this type are K-induction [236] and IC3 [38]. There exist various SMT-based model checkers that implement these methods: as for illustration (and by no means with the intention of providing a complete list), we briefly report three of them.

nuXmv [64] is a symbolic model checker for the formal verification of synchronous infinite-state systems that extends the nuSMV model checker [67]. It employs SMT-based techniques that are implemented building on top of the MathSAT5 SMT solver [68]. nuXmv implements the interpolation-based method by McMillan [194], which is integrated with other techniques based on K-induction and on IC3.

KIND 2 [65] is a multi-engine infinite-state model checker for assessing safety properties of synchronous reactive systems, based on SMT solving. Its input language relies on an extension of Lustre, a declarative language for programming synchronous systems introduced in [63]. Kind 2 employs various SMT-based techniques that are executed concurrently and in strict cooperation: specifically, it combines induction-based engines such as K-induction, IC3 and additional invariant generation methods.

---

[1] http://smtlib.cs.uiowa.edu/

Finally, JKind [123] is an SMT-based inductive model checker for safety checking of infinite-state systems. Analogously to Kind 2, in JKind models and properties are specified by using the Lustre language too. JKind exploits multiple parallel engines and is used as the back-end for several industrial applications. By building on top of several SMT solvers, it proves or falsifies safety properties by employing K-induction and IC3 methods.

We will not enter into a deeper analysis of these approaches since in this work, in order to formally verify DAPs, we will only focus on backward reachability techniques and on the MCMT model checker implementing them.

1.2.3.2 Array-based Systems: an Informal Overview

In [143], Ghilardi et al. introduced for the first time a declarative method, based on SMT solving, for the verification of infinite-state systems formalized using *arrays*. Arrays were originally introduced to provide a declarative framework for verifying distributed systems. Distributed systems are parameterized in their essence: the number N of interacting processes within a distributed system is unbounded, and the challenge is that of supplying certifications that are valid for all possible values of the parameter N. The overall state of the system is typically described by means of arrays indexed by process identifiers, and used to store the content of process variables like locations and clocks.

In array-based systems, transitions manipulate arrays via logical formulae. This formalism provides two theories, needed to capture the main idea behind arrays: the theory of indexes, which describe the topology of the system (e.g., the network of distributed or concurrent processes), and the theory of the elements that are stored in the components of the arrays (i.e., data element). The theory of arrays is given by the theory of total functions that map indexes to elements. Formally, arrays are genuine *second-order variables* and are interpreted as these total functions. Arrays can change their content and evolve over time. States and transitions are represented by using logical formulae. For instance, given a tuple of arrays $\underline{a}$, we represent the transitions as a formula $\tau(\underline{a}, \underline{a}')$, where $\underline{a}'$ is equal to $\underline{a}$ up to a renaming of the variables of $\underline{a}$. A state of the system is given by the evaluation (or interpretation) of all the array variables $\underline{a}$.

Also initial and unsafe states are represented using formulae, called *initial* and *unsafe* formulae respectively. In this context, the *(un)safety problem* becomes the problem of detecting a path in an array-based model such that the initial evaluation of the arrays satisfies the initial formulae and, after a finite sequence of states that satisfy the transition formula, we reach an evaluation of the arrays that satisfies the unsafe formula.

Ghilardi et al. have developed an SMT-based version of the *backward reachability* procedure [143, 146], and implemented it into a model checker, called *Model Checker Modulo Theories (MCMT)* [147]. Another model checker employing backward reachability for array-based systems is called CUBICLE [80].

There is a historical reason for choosing backward reachability: it was known since the seminal paper of Abdulla et al. [6] that backward search decides safety problems for a large class of systems, called *well-structured transition systems*. What backward search in array-based systems is meant to achieve is precisely to reproduce the results of [6] in a declarative, SMT-based setting: in such a declarative setting, the abstract *well quasi order* (wqo) underlying well-structured transitions systems is replaced by the standard model-theoretic notion of an *embedding* between finitely generated models (in many practical cases, in fact, such embeddability relation can be proved to be a wqo, using a suitable version of Dickson or of Higman lemma, as shown in Chapter 5 below).

We give an informal presentation on how the backward reachability procedure works. Starting from the symbolic representation of unsafe states provided by a formula K, the procedure computes step by step the *preimages* $Pre(\tau, K)$, $Pre(\tau, Pre(\tau, K))$, ... through the transitions τ. These preimages are logical formulae of the form $Pre(\tau, B)$ (for some formula B) that intuitively represent the (possibly infinite) set of states that can reach B in one step by applying τ. The iterated computation of these preimages is done at a purely symbolic level via satisfiability tests supplied by the backend SMT solver: MCMT uses Yices and Z3 as backend SMT solvers.

If the unsafe condition is reachable from the initial states after a finite number of preimage computations, the system is proved to be *unsafe*; otherwise, if the procedure *terminates* reaching a *fixed point*, the system is proved to be *safe*. In general, since these systems are intrinsically infinite-state, the procedure may not terminate in case the system is safe, whereas it always terminates when it is unsafe.

In the next sections, we present the main contributions provided by this book.

1.3 Contributions of the Book

In this section, we describe in detail the main contributions presented in this work. We first discuss the content of the first part of the book, which is about a general framework for DAP safety verification. We then comment on the sophisticated automated reasoning techniques requested for efficiently performing verification in such a framework, also showing the promising results obtained with a first experimental evaluation. Finally, we present two relevant applications of our general framework in the context of business processes.

1.3.1 Contributions of the First Part

The main contribution of the first part of the book comes from a rather surprising confluence of two well-established research traditions: *model-theoretic algebra* from mathematical logic and *Satisfiability Modulo Theories*. We show that such seemingly very different scientific paradigms can indeed cooperate in formal verification and we shall supply evidence for this claim by developing an innovative application to DAP verification. We briefly explain how the above-mentioned ingredients fit together.

1.3.1.1 Model-Theoretic Algebra

Finding solutions to equations is a challenge at the heart of both mathematics and computer science. Model-theoretic algebra, originating with the ground-breaking work of Robinson [225, 226], cast the problem of solving equations in a logical form, and used this setting to solve algebraic problems via model theory. The central notions are those of *existentially closed models* and *model completions*, which we explain in the following paragraph. In order to be sufficiently informative, this explanation, although presented at a high level, requires some notions that are defined in Chapter 2. The non-interested reader can ignore the details of this paragraph.

Call a quantifier-free formula with parameters in a model M *solvable* if there is an extension M' of M where the formula is satisfied. A model M is *existentially closed* if any solvable quantifier-free formula already has a solution in M itself. This notion is not first-order definable in general. However, in fortunate and important cases, the class of existentially closed models of T are exactly the models of another first-order theory T^*. In this case, the theory T^* can be characterized abstractly as the *model companion* of T. Model companions become *model completions* in interesting cases (formally, universal theories with the amalgamation property); in such model completions, quantifier elimination holds, unlike in the original theory T. The model companion/model completion of a theory identifies the class of those models where *all satisfiable existential statements can be satisfied*.

In declarative approaches to (infinite-state) model-checking, the runs of a system are identified with certain definable paths in the models of a suitable theory T: we will show in Chapter 4 that, without loss of generality, one may *restrict to paths within existentially closed models*, thus taking profit from the properties enjoyed by the model completion T^* (quantifier elimination being the key property to be carefully exploited).

Interestingly, model completeness has other well-known applications in computer science. It has been applied: *(i)* to reveal interesting connections between temporal logic and monadic second-order logic [148, 149]; *(ii)* in automated reasoning to design complete algorithms for constraint satisfiability in combined theories over non-disjoint signatures [128, 23, 144, 210, 209]; *(iii)* again in automated reasoning in relationship with interpolation and symbol elimination [239, 240]; *(iv)* in modal logic and in software verification theories [129, 130], to obtain combined interpolation results.

1.3.1.2 SMT solving: the Problem of Quantifiers

Specifically, our approach to DAP verification is grounded in array-based systems. First of all, notice that the term "array-based systems" is an umbrella term generically referring to transition systems specified with logical formulae using arrays. The precise formal notion depends on the application and is defined on the spot. In fact, in this book we will introduce a specific instance of array-based systems for verifying generic DAP models whose transitions are expressed by means of logical formulae containing existential quantifiers ranging over specific 'data domains': this attempt requires genuinely novel research because we need to solve sophisticated problems originated by the presence of these quantifiers.

As already mentioned in the previous section, the safety problem is handled via *backward reachability*: this procedure needs to iteratively *regress* bad states by computing their predecessors, the predecessors of the predecessors, etc., until a fixpoint is reached or the initial state(s) are intersected. This is done symbolically by manipulating *quantifier-free* logical formulae that describe sets of *states*. In general, *first-order quantifiers* (usually, *existential* quantifiers) are introduced to represent the sets of *reachable states* computed through preimages: sometimes, such quantifiers are introduced by transitions, e.g., in case their guards are existential queries over a relational database. Depending on the specific features of the array-based system, to guarantee the regressability of such formulae the procedure may require eliminating *existentially* quantified variables present in the formula: indeed, preimages are intended to describe sets of states, and as such, they should be *quantifier-free*.

Backward search, once done in a declarative symbolic setting, requires discharging proof obligations that can be reduced to satisfiability tests for quantified formulae, albeit of a restricted syntactic shape. This raises the question of how to handle such (first-order) quantifiers. In the original papers [143, 146] first-order quantifiers were handled in satisfiability tests by *instantiation*, whereas in successive applications [61, 15] *quantifier elimination* was also used to handle quantifiers ranging over specific data structures (typically, real-valued clocks). In that context, the existential quantifiers to eliminate involved only arithmetic variables, and the corresponding quantifier elimination procedures were consequently the standard ones studied for arithmetic theories (such as Fourier-Motzkin and Presburger): indeed, the theories axiomatizing such data structures were limited to *light versions* of arithmetic (mostly even included in what is called 'difference logic' in the SMT terminology), and at least in the examples arising from benchmarks quantifier elimination was not as harmful as in the general arithmetic case. However, quantifier elimination is not available for generic first-order theories. Suitable combinations of quantifier instantiations and quantifier eliminations are needed at the foundational level to design complete algorithms for the satisfiability tests that a model checker for array-based systems has to discharge during the search: specific forms of this combination will be developed in this work too. By means of such combinations, *satisfiability tests involving quantified formulae of special shape are reduced to satisfiability tests at quantifier-free level*, to be very efficiently discharged to existing SMT solvers (as confirmed in Chapter 9).

1.3.1.3 Bringing all the Ingredients Together

To capture DAPs, we follow the traditional line of research focused on the formal representation of artifact systems [167, 250, 100, 89, 47, 99]. As remarked in Section 1.2, different variants of this framework have been studied in the literature, by carefully tuning the expressive power of the three components. In this work, we are mostly interested in two types of artifact systems: those where the working memory consists of only a fixed set of artifact variables, and those where the working memory also contains artifact relations. The latter naturally fit the paradigm of array-based systems: the read-only database is axiomatized by a suitable universal first-order theory T and the artifact variables and relations are modeled by second-order variables (i.e., array variables): we will explain in detail in Chapter 3 how artifact relations can be formalized using array variables. Here, we just mention that tuple identifiers (i.e., the "entries") of the artifact relations play the same role played by process identifiers in distributed systems: formally, in both cases, they are just sorted first-order variables whose sort is the domain sort (i.e., an index sort) of an array variable.

The resulting framework, however, requires novel and non-trivial extensions of the array-based technology to make it operational. In fact, as we saw, quantifiers are handled in array-based systems both by quantifier instantiation and by quantifier elimination. Quantifier instantiation can be transposed to the new framework, whereas quantifier elimination becomes problematic. Since we focus on DAP models, quantifier elimination should be applied to data variables, which do not simply range over data types (like integers, reals, or enumerated sets) as in standard array-based systems, but instead point to the content of a whole, full-fledged (read-only) relational database and it could be the case that the theory T axiomatizing it does *not* enjoy quantifier elimination. In general, as we will see below, theories formalizing relational databases *do not* admit quantifier elimination. Here, model-theoretic algebra comes into the picture: we show that, without loss of generality, we can assume that system runs take place in existentially closed structures, so that we can exploit quantifier elimination, *provided T has a model completion.*

The question of whether T admits or not a model completion is related to the way we represent the read-only database. Model completions exist in case the read-only database is represented in the most simple way, as consisting of free n-ary relations, not subject to any kind of constraint. However, applications require the introduction of at least some minimal integrity constraints, like *primary* and *foreign* keys. Naive declarative modeling of such requirements (for instance, via relations that are partially functional) would compromise the existence of model completions (because amalgamation is destroyed, see Chapter 4). Instead, we propose a "functional view" of relations, where the read-only database and the artifact relations forming the working memory are represented with *sorted unary function symbols.*

1.3.1.4 Overview of the Contributions of the First Part

By exploiting the above-explained machinery and its model-theoretic properties, we provide a fourfold contribution.

Our first contribution is provided in Chapter 3, and consists in defining a general framework for *Array-Based Artifact Systems*, in which artifacts are formalized in the spirit of array-based systems. In this setting, we define the Simple Artifact System (SAS) model and the (Universal) Relational Artifact System (RAS) model. SASs are a particular class of (Universal) RASs, where only artifact variables are allowed; RASs are specific Universal RASs whose working memory also contains artifact relations; Universal RASs are the most expressive model, where guards of transitions can contain some form of universal quantification over the content of artifact relations. Universal RASs employ arrays to capture a very rich working memory that simultaneously accounts for artifact variables storing single data elements, and full-fledged artifact relations storing unboundedly many tuples. Each artifact relation is captured using a collection of arrays, so that a tuple in the relation can be retrieved by inspecting the content of the arrays with a given index. The elements stored therein may be fresh values injected into the Universal RAS, or data elements extracted from the read-only DB, whose relations are subject to key and foreign key constraints.

To attack this modeling complexity within array-based systems, Universal RASs encode the read-only database (the *DB schema*) using a functional, algebraic view, where relations and constraints are captured using multiple sorts and unary functions. To the best of our knowledge, this encoding has never been explored in the past, but is essential in our context. In fact, more direct attempts to encode the read-only DB into standard array-based systems would fail.

Our resulting RAS model captures the essential features of [186], which in turn is tightly related (though incomparable) to one of the most sophisticated formal models for Artifact-Centric Systems [102, 103] (cf. Subsection 1.2.1 for details on these models). We discuss the relationships between RASs and the frameworks of [186, 102, 103] in Section 5.4.

Our second contribution is about safety verification of Universal RASs, which is done *irrespective of the content of the read-only database*. In this sense, our verification problem is *parametric* on the specific database instances, so as to ensure that the process works as desired irrespectively of the specific read-only data stored therein. We develop a new version of the backward reachability algorithm employed in traditional array-based systems [143, 146], making it able to verify unsafety of RASs (and consequently SASs) in a sound and complete way (we will see later that for Universal RASs we can only guarantee a waker result). As already briefly mentioned, the main technical difficulty, which makes the original algorithm not applicable anymore, is that transition formulae in Universal RASs, in RASs and in SASs contain special existentially quantified *"data" variables* pointing to the read-only DB, which, in turn, stores data elements possibly constrained by primary keys and foreign keys. Such data variables are central in our approach as they are needed:

- from the modeling point of view, to equip array-based systems with the ability to query the read-only DB;
- again for modeling reasons, to express nondeterministic inputs from the external environment, such as users (a feature that is customary in business processes);
- to encode typical forms of updates employed in the artifact-centric literature [102, 186].

The presence of these quantified data variables constitutes a big leap from traditional array-based systems: due to the peculiar nature of data variables pointing to the read-only DB, the standard techniques studied for arithmetic do not carry over. Hence, genuinely novel research is needed in order to eliminate new existentially quantified data variables that are introduced during the computation of predecessors in the backward reachability procedure, so as to guarantee its regressability.

From a theoretical point of view, we solve this problem by introducing a dedicated machinery based on model completions. While in the case of arithmetic variables the corresponding theories admit themselves quantifier elimination, this is not the case anymore for our data variables. However, we show that quantifier elimination for data variables that is available in the model completion of their theory can actually be safely employed in the context of backward reachability, retaining soundness and completeness when checking safety of RASs. This requires *modifying significantly* the original procedure and the original proofs.

We get a similar (but weaker) result for Universal RASs: because of the difficulties created by universal quantifiers in guards, in order to apply again backward reachability, we need to get rid of them so as to deal with plain RASs. This is possible but requires to *approximate* the behavior of the original system: if after this approximation a safe outcome is obtained, then the original system is safe; however, spurious unsafe traces can be introduced during the approximation, so an unsafe outcome returned by backward reachability may be wrong. This implies that for Universal RASs we can only partially retain the meta-properties we are able to prove for RASs.

In the general case, backward reachability is not guaranteed to terminate when checking safety of SASs and RASs. As a third contribution, we consequently isolate three notable classes of RASs for which backward reachability is guaranteed to terminate, in turn witnessing decidability of safety. The first class restricts the working memory to variables only, i.e., focuses on SAS. The second class focuses on RASs operating under the restrictions imposed in [186]: it requires acyclicity of foreign keys and requires a sort of locality principle in the action guards, ensuring that different artifact tuples are not compared. Consequently, it reconstructs in our setting the essence of the decidability result exploited in [186] if one restricts the verification logic used there to safety properties only. In addition, our second class supports full-fledged bulk updates, which greatly increase the expressive power of dynamic systems [231] and, in our setting, witness the incomparability of our results and those in [186]. The third class is genuinely novel, and while it further restricts foreign keys to form a tree-shaped structure, it does not impose any restriction on the shape of updates, consequently supporting not only bulk updates, but also comparisons between artifact tuples. To prove termination of backward reachability for the second and the third classes, we resort to techniques based on well-quasi orders (the relation shown to be a wqo is the embeddability relation between database instances): for the third class in particular, we make use of a non-trivial application of Kruskal's Tree Theorem [182].

1.3.2 Contributions of the Second Part

The problem of eliminating quantifiers in model completions during backward search is strictly related to another well-studied problem in the automated reasoning literature: the one of computing uniform interpolants, or, equivalently, covers. We first give an overview of uniform interpolants. This subsection, although providing a high-level presentation of the results of the second part of the book, is quite technical and addresses those who are mainly interested in automated reasoning.

1.3.2.1 Uniform Interpolant: an Overview

We summarize the two main (quite independent) research lines that investigated uniform interpolants in the last three decades.

We briefly recall what uniform interpolants are. We fix a logic or a theory T and a suitable fragment L (propositional, first-order quantifier-free, etc.) of its language. Given an L-formula $\phi(\underline{x}, \underline{y})$ (where $\underline{x}, \underline{y}$ are the variables occurring free in ϕ), a *uniform interpolant* of ϕ (w.r.t. $\underline{y}$) is an L-formula $\phi'(\underline{x})$ where only variables $\underline{x}$ occur free, and that satisfies the following two properties: *(i)* $\phi(\underline{x}, \underline{y}) \vdash_T \phi'(\underline{x})$; *(ii)* for any further L-formula $\psi(\underline{x}, \underline{z})$ such that $\phi(\underline{x}, \underline{y}) \vdash_T \psi(\underline{x}, \underline{z})$, we have $\phi'(\underline{x}) \vdash_T \psi(\underline{x}, \underline{z})$. In other words, whenever uniform interpolants exist, one can compute an interpolant for an entailment like $\phi(\underline{x}, \underline{y}) \vdash_T \psi(\underline{x}, \underline{z})$ in such a way that this interpolant is *independent* of ψ.

Uniform interpolants were originally studied in the context of non-classical logics, starting from the pioneering work by Pitts [215]. Uniform interpolants have in such non-classical logics context a 'local' and a 'global' version, depending on how the entailment $\vdash_T$ is interpreted: in the local version it is interpreted as 'provability of implication', whereas in the global version is interpreted as 'provability under assumption' (the two versions coincide for intuitionistic logic, but not for modal logics). Uniform interpolants can be semantically connected to some appropriate notion of bisimulation at the level of Kripke models [87].

The existence of uniform interpolants is an exceptional phenomenon, which is however not so infrequent; it has been extensively studied in non-classical logics starting from the nineties, as witnessed by a large literature, including for instance [235, 251, 150, 152, 151, 127, 35, 248, 181, 197]). The main results from the above papers are that uniform interpolants exist for intuitionistic logic and for some modal systems (like the Gödel-Löb system and the S4.Grz system); they do not exist for instance in modal systems $S4$ and $K4$, whereas for the basic modal system K they exist for the local consequence relation but not for the global consequence relation (the opposite situation is also well-possible, already in the locally finite case, as a consequence of Maksimova's results on amalgamation and super-amalgamation [190, 191]).

In the last decade, the automated reasoning community developed an increasing interest in uniform interpolants as well, with a particular focus on quantifier-free fragments of first-order theories. This is witnessed by various talks and drafts by Kapur presented in many conferences and workshops (FloC 2010, ISCAS 2013-14, SCS 2017 [174]), as well as by the paper presented in ESOP 2008 authored by Gulwani and Musuvathi [157]. In this last paper uniform interpolants were renamed as *covers*, a terminology we shall adopt in this work too. In these contributions, examples of cover computations were supplied and also some algorithms were sketched (but no formal proof of correctness was provided).

As discussed several times, declarative approaches to infinite-state model checking like [230] and [146] need to manipulate logical formulae in order to represent sets of reachable states. To prevent divergence, various abstraction strategies have been adopted, ranging from interpolation-based [196] to sophisticated search via counterexample elimination [163]. Precise computations of the set of reachable states require some form of quantifier elimination and hence are subject to two problems, namely that quantifier elimination might not be available at all and that, when available, it is computationally very expensive. To cope with the first problem, Gulwani and Musuvathi [157] introduced the notion of *cover* and showed that covers can be used as an alternative to quantifier elimination and yield a precise computation of reachable states. Concerning the second problem, again in [157] it was observed (as a side remark) that computing the cover of a conjunction of literals becomes tractable when only free unary function symbols occur in the signature: we will show in Section 7.4 that the same observation applies when also free relational symbols occur.

The usefulness of covers in model checking was firstly stressed in [157]. By showing its connections with quantifier elimination in model completions, we will discuss also its importance in DAP verification.

1.3.2.2 Overview of the Contributions of the Second Part

1) Cover Computation.

Chapter 7 is devoted to studying efficient techniques for computing covers.

The use of cover is motived by our techniques for the verification of DAPs. In such a context, we apply model completeness techniques for verifying transition systems based on read-only databases, in a framework where such systems employ both individual and higher-order variables.

We first show that covers are strictly related to *model completions*, thus creating a bridge that links different research areas. In particular, we prove that computing covers for a theory is *equivalent* to eliminating quantifiers in its model completion. This connection reproduces, in a first-order setting, an analogous well-known connection for propositional logics: the connection between propositional uniform interpolants and model completions of equational theories axiomatizing the varieties corresponding to propositional logics, which was first stated in [153] and further developed in [150, 248, 181, 197].

We provide the *first formal proof* about the existence of covers in $\mathcal{EUF}$: such a proof is equipped with powerful semantic tools (see the Cover-by-Extensions Lemma 7.1 below) obtained thanks to interesting connections with model completeness [225], and comes with an algorithm for computing covers that is based on a constrained variant of the Superposition Calculus [213], equipped with appropriate settings and reduction strategies. The related completeness proof requires a careful analysis of the constrained literals generated during the saturation process. Complexity bounds for the fragment used for representing DB schemas in DAP verification, i.e., where only free unary function and n-are relation symbols occur in the signature, are also investigated: we show that computing covers for such fragment is a computationally tractable problem, i.e. it has a quadratic upper bound in time.

An extension of our constrained Superposition Calculus that handles a schema of additional constraints (useful for our applications) is provided in Section 7.5. Notably, computing covers in this extended case is also operationally mirrored in the MCMT model checker starting from version 2.8: we give some details about this implementation.

2) Cover Combination.

Chapter 8 is dedicated to studying the problem of computing covers (or, uniform interpolants) in *theory combinations*. Theory combination is a classical problem in the automated reasoning and SMT literature: it consists of transferring properties and methods to the union (i.e., the combination) of theories, making use of the methods and properties of the component theories. In this case, the property of interest is admitting covers and the method investigated is how to compute covers.

Indeed, the cover transfer problem for combined theories is an important question that is also suggested by the applications to DAP verification: for instance, when modeling and verifying DAPs, it is natural to consider the combination of different theories, such as the theories accounting for the read-write and read-only data storage of the process as well as those for the elements stored therein. Formally, the cover transfer problem can be stated as follows: *by supposing that covers exist in theories T_1, T_2, under which conditions do they exist also in the combined theory $T_1 \cup T_2$?* We show that the answer is affirmative in the disjoint signatures convex case, using the same hypothesis (that is, the *equality interpolating condition*) under which quantifier-free interpolation transfers (for this result, see [45]). Thus, for convex theories we essentially obtain a necessary and sufficient condition, in the precise sense captured by Theorem 8.4. We also provide for the first time a *formal proof* of the correctness of a combined cover algorithm (the proof for the sketched combined cover algorithm in [157] is missing). We also prove that if convexity does not hold (e.g., for integer difference logic $\mathcal{IDL}$), the non-convex equality interpolating property [45] may not be sufficient to ensure the cover transfer property. As a witness for this, we show that $\mathcal{EUF}$ combined with integer difference logic or with linear integer arithmetic constitutes a counterexample.

The main tool employed in our combination result is the *Beth definability theorem for primitive formulae* (this theorem has been shown to be equivalent to the equality interpolating condition in [45]). In order to design a combined cover algorithm, we exploit the equivalence between implicit and explicit definability that is supplied by the Beth theorem. Thus, the combined cover algorithm guesses the implicitly definable variables, then eliminates them via explicit definability, and finally uses the component-wise input cover algorithms to eliminate the remaining (not implicitly definable) variables. The identification and the elimination of the implicitly defined variables via explicitly defining terms is an essential step toward the correctness of the combined cover algorithm: when computing a cover of a formula $\phi(\underline{x}, \underline{y})$ (w.r.t. $\underline{y}$), the variables $\underline{x}$ are (non-eliminable) parameters, and those variables among the $\underline{y}$ that are implicitly definable *need to be discovered and treated in the same way as the parameters $\underline{x}$*. Only after this preliminary step (Lemma 8.5 below), the input cover algorithms can be suitably exploited (Proposition 8.1 below).

The combination result we obtain is quite strong, as it is a typical 'black box' combination result: it applies not only to theories used in verification (like the combination of real arithmetic with $\mathcal{EUF}$), but also in other contexts. For instance, since the theory $\mathcal{B}$ of Boolean algebras satisfies our hypotheses (being model completable and strongly amalgamable [130]), we get that uniform interpolants exist in the combination of $\mathcal{B}$ with $\mathcal{EUF}$. The latter is the equational theory algebraizing the basic non-normal classical modal logic system **E** from [234] (extended to n-ary modalities).

At the end of Chapter 8, we also prove that for *tame* multi-sorted (i.e., not 'completely' disjoint) theory combinations used for formalizing complex database schemas extended with "data values" (see Section 3.1.2 for details), the existence of covers transfers to the combined theory under only the stable infiniteness requirement for the shared sorts: we also provide an algorithm for computing such combined covers.

3) MCMT: the Database-driven Module.

The last contribution of the second part of the book is the first experimental evaluation of the new version of backward reachability required to handle the verification of RASs. This procedure has been implemented in MCMT starting from version 2.8. Versions 2.8 and following of MCMT provide a fully operational counterpart to all the foundational results presented in Part I and Part II: the capability of formalizing DB schemas and U-RASs is implemented in the "databased-driven" mode of MCMT, together with the algorithms for computing covers both in the standard artifact model and in the one enriched with arithmetic theories.

Even though implementation and experimental evaluation are not the central goals of our work, we point out that MCMT correctly handles the examples produced to test VERIFAS [186], as well as additional examples that go beyond the verification capabilities of VERIFAS. The performance of MCMT to conduct verification of these examples is very encouraging, and indeed provides the first stepping stone toward effective, SMT-based verification techniques for artifact-centric systems.

1.3.3 Contributions of the Third Part

As discussed in Section 1.2, increasing attention has been given in recent years to multi-perspective models of business processes to capture the interplay between the process and data dimensions [221]. In the last part of the book, we focus on BPM-oriented applications of our formal framework based on Array-Based Artifact Systems. In Chapters 11 and 12, we present a theoretical and operational framework for modeling and verifying business processes enriched with data that are formalized using the BPMN standard language. In Chapter 13, we introduce a Petri net-based model enriched with relational data that natively supports significant modeling capabilities for object creations and co-evolution tracking. This subsection mainly addresses those who are interested in BPM applications.

1.3.3.1 Data-Aware Extensions of BPMN models and Verification

Recent results in the literature on DAP verification, as witnessed by [102, 186] or by the artifact framework that we present in this book, come with two strong advantages. First, they consider the relevant setting where the running process evolves a set of relations —henceforth called a data *repository* — containing data objects that may have been injected from the external environment (e.g., due to user interaction), or borrowed from a read-only relational database with constraints — henceforth called *catalog*. The catalog stores background, contextual facts that are not updated during the process execution, whereas the repository acts as a working memory and a log for the process. The second main advantage is that they employ a symbolic approach for verification, in turn paving the way for the development of feasible implementations [186, 101], or for the exploitation of state-of-the-art symbolic model checkers (e.g., MCMT).

At the same time, several formalisms have been brought forward to capture multi-perspective processes based on Petri nets enriched with various forms of data: from data items locally carried by tokens [228, 184], to case data with different data types [94], and/or persistent relational data manipulated with the full power of FOL/SQL [95, 205], and finally fresh case objects created and (co-)evolved during the execution of the process [116, 218]. While these formalisms qualify well to capture data-aware extensions of business processes, they suffer from the main limitation that, on the foundational side, they require to specify the data present in the read-only storage, and only allow boundedly many tuples (with an apriori known bound) to be stored in the read-write ones. A last critical problem is that they mainly provide foundational results that have not yet led to the development of actual verifiers.

A common limitation of all the formalisms mentioned in this paragraph concerns the choice of modeling constructs, which often depart from those offered by process and data modeling standards such as BPMN and SQL, in turn hampering the adoption of the resulting frameworks. "Verifiability" of models is thus typically obtained by using abstract languages that do not adhere to well-established standards when it comes to the data and/or process component: either the control-flow backbone of the process is captured using Petri nets or other mathematical formalisms for dynamic systems that cannot be directly understood using front-end notations such as BPMN, or the data manipulation part is expressed using abstract, logical operations that cannot be easily represented in concrete data manipulation languages such as SQL. At the same time, the repertoire of constructs used to model data-aware processes cannot cover these languages in their full generality, as verification becomes immediately undecidable if they are not suitably controlled [47].

We remark here that in a parallel research line process modeling standards have been adopted: for instance, in [200, 93, 77] conventional, activity-centric approaches, such as the de-facto standard BPMN, have been extended toward data support, mainly focusing on conceptual modeling and enactment. However, these works do not address the problem of verification, nor the more complex one of *parameterized verification*. Since the main focus of this work is on parameterized verification of DAPs and on the usage of concrete verifiers for assessing safety in particular, in the rest of the book we will not discuss in more detail the formalisms that only address the problems of modeling and enactments. From now on, we will focus only on works that deal with the formal verification of data-aware processes.

1.3.3.2 DABs: a theoretical framework

This leads us to the main question tackled by the third part of the book: *how to extend the BPMN standard language towards data support, guaranteeing the applicability of the existing parameterized verification techniques and the corresponding actual verifiers, so far studied only in the artifact-centric setting?* We answer this question by considering the theoretical framework presented in the first part of the book and the verification of safety properties (i.e., properties that must hold in every state of the analyzed system). Specifically, our *first contribution* is a data-aware extension of BPMN called DAB, which supports case data, as well as persistent relational data partitioned into a read-only catalog and a read-write repository. Case and persistent data are used to express conditions in the process as well as task preconditions; tasks, in turn, change the values of the case variables and insert/update/delete tuples into/from the repository.

The resulting framework is similar, in spirit, to the BAUML approach [113], which relies on UML and OCL instead of BPMN as we do here. While [113] approaches verification via a translation to first-order logic with time, we follow a different route, by encoding DABs into the array-based artifact system framework of RASs.

The *second contribution* relies on the use the backward reachability procedure studied for RASs: we show that it is sound and complete when it comes to checking safety of DABs.

The fact that the procedure is sound and complete does not guarantee that it will always terminate. This brings us to our *third contribution*: we introduce further conditions that, by carefully controlling the interplay between the process and data components, guarantee the termination of the procedure. Such conditions are expressed as syntactic restrictions over the DAB under study, thus providing a concrete, BPMN-grounded counterpart of the conditions imposed to RASs (and based on wqos) to enforce termination. By exploiting the encoding from DABs to array-based artifact systems, and the soundness and completeness of backward reachability, we derive that checking safety for the class of DABs satisfying these conditions is decidable.

To show that our approach goes end-to-end from theory to actual verification, as a *fourth contribution* we report some preliminary experiments demonstrating how MCMT checks safety of DABs.

All in all, DABs provide a powerful framework for modeling and verifying data-aware extensions of business processes. However, DAB models are still too abstract to cope with the common limitation on the choice of modeling constructs: although they employ the BPMN standard language for representing the process, the data component and its query language are formulated in a logical way and are closely related to formal DB schemas and the query language of RASs. We solve this limitation by introducing the operational counterpart of DABs, i.e., delta-BPMN.

1.3.3.3 delta-BPMN: an operational and implemented framework

We address the common limitation on the lack of supported standard languages by proposing delta-BPMN, an operational framework supporting both modeling and verification of BPMN enriched with data management capabilities. The *first contribution* that we provide in this chapter is the introduction of the front-end data modeling and manipulation language PDMML, supported by delta-BPMN, which instantiates the data-related aspects of the abstract modeling language of DABs by using a SQL-based dialect to represent as well as manipulate volatile and persistent data, and show how it can be embedded into a fragment of BPMN for its process backbone. Our *second contribution* is how the delta-BPMN front-end can be realized in actual business process management systems, considering in particular Camunda, one of the most popular BPMN environments. Finally, as the last contribution of Chapter 12, we report on the implementation of a translator that takes a delta-BPMN model created in Camunda and transforms it into the syntax of MCMT.

1.3.3.4   COA-nets: Catalog and Object-Aware Nets

When dealing with DAPs, one particularly important point is the capability of the used approaches to flexibly accommodate processes with multiple case objects that need to co-evolve [116, 21]. Several modeling paradigms have tackled this and other important features: data-/artifact-centric approaches [167, 47], declarative languages based on temporal constraints [21], and imperative, Petri net-based notations [205, 116, 218]. With an interest in (formal) modeling and verification, in the last chapter of the book we concentrate on the latter stream, taking advantage of the long-standing tradition of adopting Petri nets as the main backbone to formalize processes expressed in front-end notations such as BPMN, EPCs, and UML activity diagrams. In particular, we investigate the combination of two different, key requirements in the modeling and analysis of data-aware processes. On the one hand, we support the creation of fresh (case) objects during the execution of the process, and the ability to model their (co-)evolution using guards and updates. On the other hand, we handle read-only, persistent data that can be accessed and injected into the objects manipulated by the process. Importantly, read-only data have to be considered in a *parameterized* way. This means that the overall process is expected to operate as desired in a robust way, irrespectively of the actual configuration of such data.

While the first requirement is commonly tackled by the most recent and sophisticated approaches for integrating data within Petri nets [205, 116, 218], the latter has been extensively investigated in the context of artifact systems [102], and in particular in the first part of the book.

As *the first contribution* of the last chapter, we reconcile these two themes in an extension of Colored Petri Nets (CPNs) called *Catalog and Object-Aware nets* (COA-nets). On the one hand, COA-net transitions are equipped with guards that simultaneously inspect the content of tokens and query facts stored in a read-only, persistent database. On the other hand, such transitions can inject data into tokens by extracting relevant values from the database or by generating genuinely fresh ones. We provide a set of modeling guidelines to highlight these features in a practical spectrum. The *second contribution* that we provide is to study the parameterized safety verification problem for COA-nets, in which one can check correctness of various properties for any possible catalog instance. To attack this problem, we systematically encode COA-nets into the database-driven mode of MCMT. Moreover, we demonstrate an application of the aforementioned encoding to a simple COA-net. Our *last contribution* is to obtain some meta-properties on the verification machinery applied to COA-nets and its relation to the decidability of the verification problem. We then stress that, thanks to the encoding into MCMT, a relevant fragment of the model can be readily verified using MCMT, and that verification of the whole model is within reach. Finally, we discuss how COA-nets provide a unifying approach for some of the most sophisticated formalisms in this area, highlighting differences and commonalities.

Part I
Foundations of SMT-based Safety Verification of Artifact Systems

Chapter 2
Preliminaries from Model Theory and Logic

In this chapter, we provide the basic preliminaries from first-order logic that are needed for the first part of the book. We also present some notations employed in this work and some notions from model theory that will be extensively used for the technical treatment. Finally, we summarize basic notions on classical relational databases.

2.1 Preliminaries

We adopt the usual first-order (FO) syntactic notions of signature, term, atom, (ground) formula, and so on; our signatures are multi-sorted and include equality for every sort. This implies that variables are sorted as well. For simplicity, most basic definitions in this section will be supplied for single-sorted languages only (the adaptation to multi-sorted languages is straightforward). However, we assume that in general we are in a multi-sorted setting. We compactly represent a tuple $\langle x_1, \ldots, x_n \rangle$ of variables as $\underline{x}$. The notation $t(\underline{x}), \phi(\underline{x})$ means that the term t, the formula ϕ has free variables included in the tuple $\underline{x}$. The notions of bound and free occurrences of variables employed along the book is the standard one used in first-order logic.

We assume that a function arity can be deduced from the context. Whenever we build terms and formulae, we always assume that they are well-typed, in the sense that the sorts of variables, constants, and function sources/targets match. A formula is said to be *universal* (resp., *existential*) if it has the form $\forall \underline{x}(\phi(\underline{x}))$ (resp., $\exists \underline{x}(\phi(\underline{x}))$), where ϕ is a quantifier-free formula. Formulae with no free variables are called *sentences*.

From the semantic side, we use the standard notion of a Σ-structure $\mathcal{M}$ and of truth of a formula ϕ in a Σ-structure $\mathcal{M}$ under a free variables assignment α (in symbols, $\mathcal{M}, \alpha \models \phi$).

A (FO) Σ-*theory* T is a set of Σ-sentences; a *model* of T is a Σ-structure $\mathcal{M}$ where all sentences in T are true. We use the standard notation $T \models \phi$ ('φ *is a logical consequence of T*') to say that ϕ is true in all models of T for every assignment to the

A. Gianola: *Verification of Data-Aware Processes via Satisfiability Modulo Theories*, LNBIP 470, pp. 35–44, 2023. https://doi.org/10.1007/978-3-031-42746-6_2

variables occurring free in ϕ. We say that ϕ is *T-satisfiable* iff there is a model $\mathcal{M}$ of T and an assignment to the variables occurring free in ϕ making ϕ true in $\mathcal{M}$. Thus, according to this definition, ϕ is T-satisfiable iff its *existential closure* is true in a model of T (notice that this convention might not be uniform in the literature). A Σ-theory T is *complete* iff for every Σ-sentence φ, either φ or $\neg\varphi$ is a logical consequence of T. Given a Σ_1-theory T_1 and a Σ_2-theory T_2, we call *(theory) combination of T_1 and T_2* the $\Sigma_1 \cup \Sigma_2$-theory $T_1 \cup T_2$. In the mono-sorted case, we say that this combination is a *(signature-)disjoint combination* (or that it has *disjoint* signatures) when Σ_1 and Σ_2 do not have any symbol in common, apart from the equality symbol. In the multi-sorted case, we say that the combination is a *(signature-)disjoint combination* (or that it has *disjoint* signatures) when Σ_1 and Σ_2 do not have any symbol or sort in common, apart from the equality symbol. In the multi-sorted case, we also say that a combination is *almost disjoint* (or that it has *almost disjoint* signatures) if the only function or relation symbols in $\Sigma_1 \cap \Sigma_2$ are the equality predicates over the sorts in $\Sigma_1 \cap \Sigma_2$ (if any sort in $\Sigma_1 \cap \Sigma_2$ exists). Differently from what the nomenclature seems to suggest, it follows from the definitions that (multi-sorted) disjoint combinations are a particular case of almost disjoint combinations.

A Σ-formula ϕ is a *Σ-constraint* (or just a constraint) iff it is a conjunction of literals. The constraint satisfiability problem for T is the following: given an existential formula $\exists \underline{y}\, \phi(\underline{x}, \underline{y})$ (with ϕ a constraint, but, for the purposes of this definition, we may equivalently take ϕ to be any quantifier-free formula), to establish whether there exist a model $\mathcal{M}$ of T and an assignment α to the free variables $\underline{x}$ such that $\mathcal{M}, \alpha \models \exists \underline{y}\, \phi(\underline{x}, \underline{y})$.

We say that a theory T has the *strong finite model property* (for constraint satisfiability) iff every constraint ϕ that is satisfiable in a model of T is satisfiable in a finite model of T.

A theory T has *quantifier elimination* iff for every formula $\phi(\underline{x})$ in the signature of T there is a quantifier-free formula $\phi'(\underline{x})$ such that $T \models \phi(\underline{x}) \leftrightarrow \phi'(\underline{x})$. It is well-known (and easily seen) that quantifier elimination holds in case we can eliminate quantifiers from *primitive* formulae, i.e. from formulae of the kind $\exists \underline{y}\, \phi(\underline{x}, \underline{y})$, where ϕ is a conjunction of literals (i.e. of atomic formulae and their negations). Since we are interested in effective computability, we consider in this book only the cases where *effective* quantifier elimination procedures are available: from now on, *whenever* we talk about quantifier elimination, an *effective procedure* for eliminating quantifiers needs to be given.

2.2 Substructures and Embeddings

Let Σ be a first-order signature. The signature obtained from Σ by adding to it a set $\underline{a}$ of new constants (i.e., 0-ary function symbols) is denoted by $\Sigma^{\underline{a}}$. Analogously, given a Σ-structure $\mathcal{A}$, the signature Σ can be expanded to a new signature $\Sigma^{|\mathcal{A}|} := \Sigma \cup \{\bar{a} \mid a \in |\mathcal{A}|\}$ by by adding a constant $\bar{a}$ (the name for a) for each element $a \in |\mathcal{A}|$, with the convention that two distinct elements are denoted by different "name" constants (we use $|\mathcal{A}|$ to denote the support of the structure $\mathcal{A}$). $\mathcal{A}$ can be expanded to a $\Sigma^{|\mathcal{A}|}$-structure $\mathcal{A}' := (\mathcal{A}, a)_{a \in |\mathcal{A}|}$ just interpreting the additional constants over the corresponding elements. From now on, when the meaning is clear from the context, we will freely use the notation $\mathcal{A}$ and $\mathcal{A}'$ interchangeably: in particular, given a Σ-structure $\mathcal{A}$, a Σ-formula $\phi(\underline{x})$ and elements $\underline{a}$ from $|\mathcal{A}|$, we will write, by abuse of notation, $\mathcal{A} \models \phi(\underline{a})$ instead of $\mathcal{A}' \models \phi(\bar{a})$.

A Σ-*homomorphism* (or, simply, a homomorphism) between two Σ-structures $\mathcal{A}$ and $\mathcal{B}$ is any mapping $\mu : |\mathcal{A}| \longrightarrow |\mathcal{B}|$ among the support sets $|\mathcal{A}|$ of $\mathcal{A}$ and $|\mathcal{B}|$ of $\mathcal{B}$ satisfying the condition

$$\mathcal{A} \models \varphi \quad \Rightarrow \quad \mathcal{B} \models \varphi \tag{2.1}$$

for all $\Sigma^{|\mathcal{A}|}$-atoms φ (here - as above - $\mathcal{A}$ is regarded as a $\Sigma^{|\mathcal{A}|}$-structure, by interpreting each additional constant $a \in |\mathcal{A}|$ into itself and $\mathcal{B}$ is regarded as a $\Sigma^{|\mathcal{A}|}$-structure by interpreting each additional constant $a \in |\mathcal{A}|$ into $\mu(a)$). In case condition (2.1) holds for all $\Sigma^{|\mathcal{A}|}$-literals, the homomorphism μ is said to be an *embedding* (denoted by $\mu : \mathcal{A} \hookrightarrow \mathcal{B}$) and if it holds for all first-order formulae, the embedding μ is said to be *elementary*. Notice the following facts:

(a)   since we have equality in the signature, an embedding is an injective function;
(b)   an embedding $\mu : M \longrightarrow N$ must be an algebraic homomorphism, that is for every n-ary function symbol f and for every $m_1, ..., m_n$ in $|M|$, we must have $f^N(\mu(m_1), ..., \mu(m_n)) = \mu(f^M(m_1, ..., m_n))$;
(c)   for an n-ary predicate symbol P we must have $(m_1, ..., m_n) \in P^M$ iff $(\mu(m_1), ..., \mu(m_n)) \in P^N$.

It can be easily seen that an embedding $\mu : M \longrightarrow N$ can be equivalently defined as a map $\mu : |M| \longrightarrow |N|$ satisfying the conditions (a)-(b)-(c) above. If $\mu : \mathcal{A} \longrightarrow \mathcal{B}$ is an embedding which is just the identity inclusion $|\mathcal{A}| \subseteq |\mathcal{B}|$, we say that $\mathcal{A}$ is a *substructure* of $\mathcal{B}$ or that $\mathcal{B}$ is an *extension* of $\mathcal{A}$. A Σ-structure $\mathcal{A}$ is said to be *generated by* a set X included in its support $|\mathcal{A}|$ iff there are no proper substructures of $\mathcal{A}$ including X.

We recall that a substructure *preserves* and *reflects* the validity of ground formulae, in the following sense: given a Σ-substructure $\mathcal{A}_1$ of a Σ-structure $\mathcal{A}_2$, a ground $\Sigma^{|\mathcal{A}_1|}$-sentence θ is true in $\mathcal{A}_1$ iff θ is true in $\mathcal{A}_2$.

2.3 Robinson Diagrams and Amalgamation

Let $\mathcal{A}$ be a Σ-structure. The *diagram* of $\mathcal{A}$, denoted by $\Delta_\Sigma(\mathcal{A})$, is defined as the set of ground $\Sigma^{|\mathcal{A}|}$-literals (i.e. atomic formulae and negations of atomic formulae) that are true in $\mathcal{A}$. For the sake of simplicity, once again by abuse of notation, we will freely say that $\Delta_\Sigma(\mathcal{A})$ is the set of $\Sigma^{|\mathcal{A}|}$-literals which are true in $\mathcal{A}$.

An easy but nevertheless important basic result, called *Robinson Diagram Lemma* [66], says that, given any Σ-structure $\mathcal{B}$, the embeddings $\mu : \mathcal{A} \longrightarrow \mathcal{B}$ are in bijective correspondence with expansions of $\mathcal{B}$ to $\Sigma^{|\mathcal{A}|}$-structures which are models of $\Delta_\Sigma(\mathcal{A})$. The expansions and the embeddings are related in the obvious way: $\bar{a}$ is interpreted as $\mu(a)$. The typical use of the Robinson Diagram Lemma is the following: suppose we want to show that some structure $\mathcal{M}$ can be embedded into a structure $\mathcal{N}$ in such a way that some set of sentences Θ are true. Then, by the Lemma, this turns out to be equivalent to the fact that the set of sentences $\Delta(\mathcal{M}) \cup \Theta$ is consistent: thus, the Diagram Lemma can be used to transform an *embeddability* problem into a *consistency* problem (the latter is a problem of a logical nature, to be solved for instance by making use of the compactness theorem for first-order logic).

Amalgamation is a classical algebraic concept. We give the formal definition of this notion.

Definition 2.1 (Amalgamation) A theory T has the *amalgamation property* if for every couple of embeddings $\mu_1 : \mathcal{M}_0 \longrightarrow \mathcal{M}_1$, $\mu_2 : \mathcal{M}_0 \longrightarrow \mathcal{M}_2$ among models of T, there exists a model $\mathcal{M}$ of T endowed with embeddings $\nu_1 : \mathcal{M}_1 \longrightarrow \mathcal{M}$ and $\nu_2 : \mathcal{M}_2 \longrightarrow \mathcal{M}$ such that $\nu_1 \circ \mu_1 = \nu_2 \circ \mu_2$

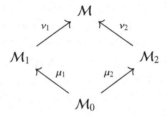

The triple $(\mathcal{M}, \mu_1, \mu_2)$ (or, by abuse, $\mathcal{M}$ itself) is said to be a T-amalgam of $\mathcal{M}_1, \mathcal{M}_2$ over $\mathcal{M}_0$

2.4 Model Completions

We recall a standard notion in model theory, namely the notion of a *model completion* of a first-order theory [66] (we limit the definition to universal theories, because we shall consider only this case):

Definition 2.2 (Model Completion) Let T be a universal Σ-theory and let $T^\star \supseteq T$ be a further Σ-theory; we say that $T^\star$ is a model completion of T iff: (i) every model of T can be embedded into a model of $T^\star$; (ii) for every model $\mathcal{M}$ of T, we have that $T^\star \cup \Delta_\Sigma(\mathcal{M})$ is a complete theory in the signature $\Sigma^{|\mathcal{M}|}$.

Since T is universal, condition (ii) is equivalent to the fact that $T^\star$ *has quantifier elimination*; on the other hand, a standard argument (based on diagrams and compactness) shows that condition (i) is the same as asking that T and $T^\star$ have the same universal consequences. Thus we have an equivalent definition [128] (to be used in the following):

Proposition 2.1 *Let T be a universal Σ-theory and let $T^\star \supseteq T$ be a further Σ-theory; $T^\star$ is a model completion of T iff: (i) every Σ-constraint satisfiable in a model of T is also satisfiable in a model of T^*; (ii) T^* has quantifier elimination.*

As stated before, for the purposes of this work we only consider theories with a model completion that has an *effective procedure* for eliminating quantifiers in it. We recall also that the model completion $T^\star$ of a theory T is unique, if it exists (see [66] for these results and for examples). It is well-known that a universal theory T which admits a model completion is also amalgamable [66]. The other way around holds in case T is also *locally finite*. For our purpose, we define a theory T to be *locally finite* iff for every finite tuple of variables $\underline{x}$ there are only finitely many T-equivalence classes of atoms $A(\underline{x})$ involving only the variables $\underline{x}$: the remarkable fact is that a universal, locally finite theory T having the amalgamation property admits a model completion.

Example 2.1 The theory of undirected graphs admits a model completion (and, hence, is amalgamable); this is the theory T whose signature Σ contains only a binary relational symbol R, and whose axioms are specified as follows

$$T := \{\forall x \neg R(x,x), \forall x \forall y \, (R(x,y) \rightarrow R(y,x))\} \ .$$

Indeed, it is folklore that the model completion of T is the theory of the *Rado graph* [220]: a Rado (also called *random*) graph is a countably infinite graph in which, given any non-empty sets $X = \{x_0, ..., x_m\}$ and $Y = \{y_0, ..., y_n\}$ of nodes with $X \cap Y = \emptyset$, there is a node z (with $z \notin X \cup Y$) such that there is an edge between z and all elements of X and there is no edge between z and any element of Y. This theory is first-order definable [115].

2.5 Satisfiability Modulo Theories (SMT)

In this section, we say that a term, an atom, a literal, or a formula is an *expression*. Let $\underline{x}$ be a finite tuple of variables and Σ an FO signature; a $\Sigma(\underline{x})$-expression is an expression built out of the symbols in Σ where only (some of) the variables in $\underline{x}$ may occur free (we write $E(\underline{x})$ to emphasize that E is a $\Sigma(\underline{x})$-expression).

According to the current practice in the SMT literature [31], an SMT-theory $\mathcal{T}$ is a pair (Σ, Z), where Σ is a signature and Z is a class of Σ-structures; the structures in Z are the models of T. We assume $\mathcal{T} = (\Sigma, Z)$. A Σ-formula ϕ is T-satisfiable in the SMT sense if there exists a Σ-structure M in Z such that ϕ is true in M under a suitable assignment a to the free variables of ϕ (in symbols, $(M, a) \models \phi$); it is $\mathcal{T}$-valid in the SMT-sense (in symbols, $T \vdash \phi$) if its negation is $\mathcal{T}$-unsatisfiable in the SMT-sense. Two formulae ϕ_1 and ϕ_2 are $\mathcal{T}$-equivalent in the SMT-sense if $\phi_1 \leftrightarrow \phi_2$ is $\mathcal{T}$-valid in the SMT-sense. The problem of (quantifier-free) *satisfiability modulo the theory* $\mathcal{T}$ $(SMT(\mathcal{T}))$ amounts to establishing the $\mathcal{T}$-satisfiability in the SMT-sense of quantifier-free Σ-formulae. Notice that in case the SMT-theory T is first-order definable via a set of sentences (i.e., a FO theory in the classical sense), then the previous definitions are equivalent to the corresponding classical first-order ones given in the previous sections.

Intuitively, the *Satisfiability Modulo Theories* (SMT) problem is a decision problem for the satisfiability of quantifier-free first-order formulae that extends the problem of propositional (boolean) satisfiability (SAT) by taking into account (the combination of) background first-order theories (e.g., arithmetics, bit-vectors, arrays, uninterpreted functions). There exists a plethora of solvers, called *SMT solvers*, able to solve the SMT problem: they extend SAT solvers with specific decision procedures customized for the specific theories involved. SMT solvers are useful both for computer-aided verification, to prove the correctness of software programs against some property of interest, and for synthesis, to generate candidate program fragments. Examples of well-studied SMT theories are the theory of uninterpreted functions $\mathcal{EUF}$, the theory of bitvectors $\mathcal{BV}$ and the theory of arrays $\mathcal{AX}$. All these theories are usually employed in applications to program verification. SMT solvers also support different types of arithmetics for which specific decision procedures are available, like difference logic $\mathcal{IDL}$ (whose atoms are of the form $x - y \leq c$ for some integer constant c), or linear arithmetics ($\mathcal{LIA}$ for integers and $\mathcal{LQA}$ for rationals).

SMT-LIB [31] is an international initiative with the aims of providing an extensive on-line library of benchmarks and of promoting the adoption of common languages and interfaces for SMT solvers. For the purpose of this book, we make use of the SMT solvers that are supported by the MCMT model checker, i.e., Yices [4, 106] and Z3 [96, 201].

2.6 Definable Extensions and λ-Notations

In the following, we specify transitions of artifact-centric systems using first-order formulae. To obtain a more compact representation, we make use of definable extensions as a means to introduce case-defined functions, abbreviating more complicated (still first-order) expressions. Let us fix a signature Σ and a Σ-theory T; a T-*partition* is a finite set $\kappa_1(\underline{x}), \ldots, \kappa_n(\underline{x})$ of quantifier-free formulae such that $T \models \forall \underline{x} \bigvee_{i=1}^{n} \kappa_i(\underline{x})$ and $T \models \bigwedge_{i \neq j} \forall \underline{x} \neg(\kappa_i(\underline{x}) \wedge \kappa_j(\underline{x}))$. Given such a T-partition $\kappa_1(\underline{x}), \ldots, \kappa_n(\underline{x})$ together with Σ-terms $t_1(\underline{x}), \ldots, t_n(\underline{x})$ (all of the same target sort), a *case-definable extension* is the Σ'-theory T', where $\Sigma' = \Sigma \cup \{F\}$, with F a "fresh" function symbol (i.e., $F \notin \Sigma$), and $T' = T \cup \bigcup_{i=1}^{n} \{\forall \underline{x} \ (\kappa_i(\underline{x}) \rightarrow F(\underline{x}) = t_i(\underline{x}))\}$. Arity, source sorts, and target sort for F can be deduced from the context (considering that everything is well-typed).

Intuitively, F represents a case-defined function, which can be reformulated using nested if-then-else expressions and can be written as

$$F(\underline{x}) := \mathsf{case\ of}\ \{\kappa_1(\underline{x}) : t_1; \cdots ; \kappa_n(\underline{x}) : t_n\}.$$

By abuse of notation, we shall identify T with any of its case-definable extensions T'. In fact, it is easy to produce from a Σ'-formula ϕ' a Σ-formula ϕ that is equivalent to

ϕ' in all models of T': just remove (in the appropriate order) every occurrence $F(\underline{v})$ of the new symbol F in an atomic formula A, by replacing A with $\bigvee_{i=1}^{n}(\kappa_i(\underline{v}) \wedge A(t_i(\underline{v})))$.

We also exploit λ-abstractions (see, e.g., formula (3.7) below) for more "compact" representation of some complex expressions, and always use them in atoms like $b = \lambda y.F(y,\underline{z})$ as abbreviations of $\forall y.\ b(y) = F(y,\underline{z})$ (where, typically, F is a symbol introduced in a case-defined extension as above). Thus, also our formulae containing lambda abstractions, can be converted into plain first-order formulae.

2.7 Typed Relational Databases with Constraints

In this section, we give a brief introduction on relational databases with key dependencies. In order to do that, we take inspiration from the traditional formalization of relational databases [11], but we enrich our databases with a basic notion of *types*: every attribute is associated to a corresponding type.

Definition 2.3 A *type* is a pair $S = \langle \Delta_S, =_S \rangle$, where Δ_S is a set (called *domain* of values), and $=_S$ is the equality predicate interpreted in Δ_S.

Sometimes, more sophisticated kinds of data types are considered in the literature, where Δ_S is an interpreted structure over some non-trivial first-order signature, i.e., involving (interpreted) functions and relations. For the sake of simplicity, we here consider only the case where the domain of values is a pure set equipped with the equality operator.

Definition 2.4 A *type set* S is a finite set of types with pairwise disjoint domains of values. We set $\Delta_S = \bigcup_{S \in \mathcal{S}} \Delta_S$.

Note that the pairwise disjointness is set so as to assure that for all types in S respective domains do not intersect.

For the sake of the book, we restrict our attention on *abstract* types, i.e., disjoint types each of them providing only a domain and an equality attribute. This is sufficient to create a correspondence with DB schemas of our Data-Aware Processes introduced in Section 3.1, where interpretation of sorts of DB instances are sets endowed with equalities. We will see that this framework can be enriched with more complex data types (e.g., arithmetics) when considering the *value sorts* of DB extended-schemas (see Section 3.1.2).

We provide now the definition of typed relation schema.

Definition 2.5 (Typed Relation Schema) Let $\mathfrak{R}$ be a countably infinite set of relation names. By $R(\underline{att}_S)$ we define an (n-ary) *(S-typed) relation schema*, where R is a relation name from $\mathfrak{R}$, and $\underline{att}_S$ is an n-tuple of elements $(att_{S_1}, \ldots, att_{S_n})$ such that every component att_{S_i} is associated to a type S_i in S. Every component att_{S_i} is called an *attribute* of R.

Consider, for example, a typed relational schema $Emp(id_{\texttt{Eid}}, name_{\texttt{string}})$ denoting a binary relation for employees, where the first component is the id of the employee of type $\texttt{Eid}$ and the second component is the employee name of type $\texttt{string}$. When the types are not relevant, we denote the relation schema simply as R or R/n, where n is the arity of R.

Definition 2.6 (Typed Classical Database Schema) A *(S-typed) classical database schema* $\mathcal{R}$ is a finite set of *(S-typed) relation schemas*.

Definition 2.6 allows us to specify the logical structure of a database. We now provide a mechanism that allows to concretely instantiate typed relational schemas, so as to assign actual content to them.

Definition 2.7 A *(S-typed) relation instance* i for a relation schema $R(att_{S_1}, \ldots, att_{S_n})$ is a *finite* set of *facts* $R(o_1, \ldots, o_n)$ such that $o_i \in \Delta_{S_i}$, for $i = 1, \ldots, n$.

For example, consider the previously mentioned relation Emp. Then, a fact $Emp(\texttt{emp127}, \texttt{John Doe})$ is denoting that employee with id $\texttt{emp127}$ is called John Doe.

Definition 2.8 (Typed Active Domain) Given a type $S \in \mathcal{S}$, and a relation instance i, the *(S-)active domain of* i is the set $Adom_S(i) = \{o \in \Delta_S \mid$ there is $R(o_1, \ldots, o_m) \in$ i s.t. $o_i = o$ for some $i = 1, \ldots, m\}$. We define the *active domain* of i as $Adom_S(i) = \bigcup_{S \in \mathcal{S}} Adom_S(i)$.

We now briefly discuss queries. As query language, we resort to standard first-order logic (FOL) and interpreted under the *active-domain semantics* [187, 110]. This means that quantifiers are relativized to the active domain of the database instance of interest, guaranteeing that queries are domain-independent (actually, safe–range): their evaluation only depends on the values explicitly appearing in the database instance over which they are applied. Notice that this query language is equivalent to the well-known SQL standard [11].

Let us fix a countably infinite set V_S of *typed* variables with a *variable typing function* $\texttt{type} : V_S \rightarrow \mathcal{S}$, stipulating that a variable x ranges only over $\Delta_{\texttt{type}(x)}$. For conciseness, we write $x : S$ for $\texttt{type}(x) = S$ and omit the variable type when irrelevant or clear from the context.

Definition 2.9 ((FO(S)) query) A *(FO(S)) query* Q over a *(S-typed) database schema* $\mathcal{R}$ has the form $\{\underline{x} \mid \varphi(\underline{x})\}$, where $\underline{x}$ is the tuple of answer variables of Q, and φ is a FO formula defined as follows:

$$\varphi ::= y_1 =_S y_2 \mid R(\underline{z}) \mid \neg\varphi \mid \varphi \wedge \varphi \mid \exists y.\varphi,$$

where
- every variable y_i ($i = 1, 2$) is either an element of Δ_S or a S-typed variable from V_S with $\texttt{type}(y_i) = S$, for some $S \in \mathcal{S}$, and $=_S$ is the equality predicate from S;
- for $\underline{z} = \langle z_1, \ldots, z_n \rangle$, $R(S_1, \ldots, S_n) \in \mathcal{R}$, and every variable z_i is either an element of Δ_{S_i} or a S-typed variable from V_S with $\texttt{type}(z_i) = S_i$.

- $\underline{x}$ contains all and only those variables appearing in Q and not belonging to scope of a quantifier.

A variable $x \in V_S$ occurring in a FO(S) query Q is *free* if it does not appear in the scope of a quantifier: all the answer variables are free. This definition of *free occurrence* of a variable is not the standard one used in first-order logic: it is only instrumental to the presentation of the current section. In the following chapters we will instead make use of the standard one employed in classical first-order logic. We use $Q(\underline{x})$ to make the answer variables $\underline{x}$ of Q explicit, and denote the set of such variables as *Free*(Q). We use standard abbreviations $\texttt{true}$, $\texttt{false}$, $Q_1 \vee Q_2 = \neg(\neg Q_1 \wedge \neg Q_2)$, and $\forall x.Q = \neg\exists x.\neg Q$.

Definition 2.10 (Boolean query) A query Q is called *boolean* if it has no free variables (i.e., *Free*(Q) = $\emptyset$).

Note that boolean queries are nothing but closed FOL formulae whose terms are either constants from $Adom_S(\mathrm{i})$ or quantified variables.

Definition 2.11 (Substitution) Given a set $X = \{x_1, \ldots, x_n\}$ of typed variables, a *substitution* for X is a function $\theta : X \rightarrow \Delta_S$ mapping variables from X into values, such that for every $x \in X$, we have $\theta(x) \in \Delta_{\mathsf{type}(x)}$. A *substitution θ for a* FO(S) *query Q* is a substitution for the free variables of Q.

We denote by $Q\theta$ the boolean query obtained from Q by replacing each occurrence of a free variable $x \in Free(Q)$ with the value $\theta(x)$. In this case we sometimes say that Q is *instantiated* by θ.

We now provide the definition of query entailment employing the active domain semantics (i.e, the range of values that quantified variables can be instantiated with is restricted to the active domain of a given relation instance i).

Definition 2.12 (Query entailment) Given an S-typed database schema $\mathcal{R}$, an S-typed instance i over $\mathcal{R}$, a FO(S) query Q over $\mathcal{R}$, and a substitution θ for Q, we inductively define when i *entails* Q *under* θ, written i, $\theta \models Q$, as follows:

$$
\begin{aligned}
&\mathrm{i}, \theta \models R(\mathbf{x}) &&\text{if } R(\mathbf{x})\theta \in \mathrm{i} \\
&\mathrm{i}, \theta \models \neg Q &&\text{if } \mathrm{i}, \theta \not\models Q \\
&\mathrm{i}, \theta \models Q_1 \wedge Q_2 &&\text{if } \mathrm{i}, \theta \models Q_1 \text{ and } \mathrm{i}, \theta \models Q_2 \\
&\mathrm{i}, \theta \models \exists x.Q &&\text{if there exists o} \in Adom_{\mathsf{type}(x)}(\mathrm{i}) \text{ such that } \mathrm{i}, \theta[x/\mathrm{o}] \models Q
\end{aligned}
$$

where $\theta[x/\mathrm{o}]$ denotes the substitution obtained from θ by assigning o to x.

Definition 2.13 (Query answers) Given a S-typed database schema $\mathcal{R}$, a S-typed instance i over $\mathcal{R}$, and a FO(S) query Q over $\mathcal{R}$, the set of *answers* to Q in i is defined as $ans(Q, \mathrm{i}) = \{\theta : Free(Q) \rightarrow Adom_S(\mathrm{i}) \mid \mathrm{i}, \theta \models Q\}$.

When Q is boolean, we write $ans(Q, \mathrm{i}) \equiv \texttt{true}$ if $ans(Q, \mathrm{i})$ consists only of the empty substitution (denoted $\langle\rangle$), and $ans(Q, \mathrm{i}) \equiv \texttt{false}$ if $ans(Q, \mathrm{i}) = \emptyset$.

We now fix the classical database schema $\mathcal{R}$ for the rest of the section. Boolean queries can be employed to express *constraints* over $\mathcal{R}$. We use constraints in the context of relational databases to impose an additional structure over their database instances: in fact, given a constraint Φ, we would like to require that each database instance satisfies it. Formally, a *database instance* i *satisfies a constraint* Φ *(or that* Φ *holds in* i if $ans(\Phi, i) \equiv$ `true`. We introduce explicitly two common types of constraints that are the only ones that will be used in this work: primary keys and foreign keys. We focus on *primary* keys and not keys because we will define one and only one (primary) key per relation.

Definition 2.14 (Primary Keys) Given a relation R/n and a set of attributes N' of R (with $|N'| = n' < n$), which we suppose w.l.o.g. to be the first n' attributes of R, we say that N is a *primary key* for R, or that *the constraint* $PK(R) = N'$ *holds* (and *it expresses that the projection* $R[N']$ *of R on N' is a primary key for R*), if every database instance i satisfies the following formula

$$\forall x_1, \ldots, x_{n'}, y_1 \ldots, y_{n-n'}, y_1' \ldots, y_{n-n'}', R(x_1, \ldots, x_{n'}, y_1, \ldots, y_{n-n'}) \wedge$$
$$\wedge R(x_1, \ldots, x_{n'}, y_1', \ldots, y_{n-n'}') \rightarrow \bigwedge_{i=1}^{n-n'} y_i = y_i'.$$

For the sake of simplicity, we restrict our definition of foreign keys to the case where a relation R refers only a unique relation S: this definition can be easily generalized to the case that the foreign keys dependencies starting from R are more than one (the notation to employ in the general case would be tedious).

Definition 2.15 (Foreign Keys) Given a relation R/n and S/m, let N' be a set of attributes of R (with $|N'| = n' < n$), which we suppose w.l.o.g. to be the last n' attributes of R, and let M' be a set of attributes of S (with $|M'| = m' < m, m' = n'$), which we suppose w.l.o.g. to be the first m' attributes of S. We say that N is a *foreign key for R pointing to S*, or that *the constraint* $R[N'] \subseteq S[M']$, *or* $R[N'] \rightarrow S[M']$, *holds* (and *it expresses that the projection* $R[N']$ *of R on N' refers the projection* $S[M']$ *of S on M', which has to be a key for S*), if every database instance i satisfies the following formula:

$$\forall x_1, \ldots, x_{n-n'}, y_1 \ldots, y_{n'}.R(x_1, \ldots, x_{n-n'}, y_1, \ldots, y_{n'}) \rightarrow$$
$$\exists z_1 \ldots, z_{m-m'}.S(y_1, \ldots, y_{n'}, z_1 \ldots z_{m-m'});$$

and i satisfies the constraint $PK(S) = M'$, i.e.

$$\forall y_1, \ldots, y_{m'}, z_1 \ldots, z_{m-m'}, z_1' \ldots, z_{m-m'}', S(y_1, \ldots, y_{m'}, z_1, \ldots, y_{m-m'}) \wedge$$
$$\wedge S(y_1, \ldots, y_{m'}, z_1', \ldots, z_{m-m'}') \rightarrow \bigwedge_{i=1}^{m-m'} z_i = z_i'.$$

Chapter 3
Array-Based Artifact Systems: General Framework

In this chapter, we introduce *Array-based Artifact Systems* – a rich and powerful theoretical framework for the formal specification and verification of Data-Aware Processes (DAPs). In the following, for the sake of conciseness, we will sometimes leave the nomenclature 'Array-based' implicit.

DAPs can be generally thought of as dynamic systems whose execution is guided by *processes* that can interact via queries and updates with a full-fledged relational database. As the reader can expect, the concept of DAP is quite generic and embraces a plethora of different formalisms, each of them with different features and assumptions on the concrete behavior it is supposed to model. In this context, one of the most famous and studied classes of formalisms is given by artifact systems. As already mentioned in the introduction, artifact systems are traditionally formalized using three components: *(i) a read-only database (DB)*, storing background information that does *not* change during the system evolution; *(ii) an artifact working memory*, storing data and lifecycle information about artifact(s) that *does* change during the evolution; *(iii) actions* (also called *services*) that access the read-only database and the working memory, and determine how the working memory itself has to be updated.

In this chapter, we adopt this setting too. In the first section we define DB schemas, which formalize the read-only database component of our Artifact Systems, and then DB extended schemas, which enrich DB schemas with additional constrained datatypes such as arithmetic values. DB schemata exploit an algebraic, functional representation of relations and of their (primary and foreign) key dependencies: this representation is necessary in order to make our verification machinery (presented in the next chapter) fully operational. Nevertheless, we will show in Subsection 3.1.1 that DB schemas can be interpreted in the standard relational model.

Different models of artifact systems have been considered in the literature, depending in particular on the assumptions made over the shape of the working memory. In the course of this chapter (Section 3.2), we introduce two different well-studied variants of Artifact Systems and formulate them in the array-based setting. Both variants assume a read-only database storage that is formalized by a DB schema; they differ in the type of working memory used by the process.

A. Gianola: *Verification of Data-Aware Processes via Satisfiability Modulo Theories*, LNBIP 470, pp. 45–67, 2023. https://doi.org/10.1007/978-3-031-42746-6_3

The first variant works over a fixed set of so-called *artifact variables*, altogether instantiated into a single tuple of data. In this respect, in Subsection 3.2.1 we introduce the formal model of *Simple Artifact Systems (SASs)*. There, we also give two concrete examples of SAS, one simpler and the other more complex.

More recently (e.g. [102, 186, 103]), more sophisticated types of artifact systems have been considered, where the working memory is not only equipped with artifact variables as in SASs, but also with so-called *artifact relations*. These relations change over time and can store arbitrarily many tuples, each accounting for a different artifact instance that can be separately evolved on its own. In this respect, in Subsection 3.2.2 we define the formal model of *Universal Relational Artifact Systems (Universal RASs*, or, simply, *U-RASs)*, and then a slightly weaker variant of U-RASs called *(plain) RASs*. In that subsection, we also provide two sophisticated examples of (Universal) RASs inspired by a concrete job hiring process within a company and by a visa application process, respectively. The difference between U-RASs and RASs lies in the fact that the transitions of the former contain, besides standard (existential) guards, also *universal* guards (i.e., they use a universal quantification over tuples of artifact relations), whereas the latter can only use (existential) guards.

Both SASs and (Universal) RASs are formalized in the spirit of array-based systems [146], a formalism that provides a theoretical framework for assessing safety of infinite-state systems. The main intuitions behind array-based systems are briefly recalled at the beginning of Section 3.2. For both SASs and (Universal) RASs we will study the problem of parameterized safety verification in the next chapter: the goal of performing SMT-based safety verification motivates by itself the choice of employing array-based systems.

The content of this chapter mainly stems from [55, 51].

3.1 Read-Only DB Schemas

We now provide a formal definition of (read-only) DB schemas by relying on an algebraic, functional characterization. In the next chapter, we will argue why we need this functional representation for verifying Artifact Systems and we will derive some key model-theoretic properties instrumental to the technical treatment of our verification machinery. In the following, we sometimes refer to the setting of DB schemas as the "database-driven setting" of our Artifact Systems.

Definition 3.1 (DB schema) A *DB schema* is a pair $\langle \Sigma, T \rangle$, where: *(i)* Σ is a *DB signature*, that is, a finite multi-sorted signature whose only symbols are equality, unary functions, and constants; *(ii)* T is a *DB theory*, that is, a set of universal Σ-sentences.

Next, we refer to a DB schema simply through its (DB) signature Σ and (DB) theory T. Given a DB signature Σ, we denote by Σ_{srt} the set of sorts and by Σ_{fun} the set of functions in Σ. Since Σ contains only unary function symbols and equality, all

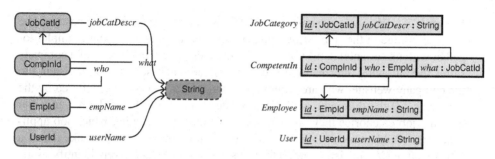

Fig. 3.1: On the left: characteristic graph of the human resources DB signature from Example 3.6. On the right: relational view of the DB signature; each cell denotes an attribute with its type, underlined attributes denote primary keys, and directed edges capture foreign keys.

atomic Σ-formulae are of the form $t_1(v_1) = t_2(v_2)$, where t_1, t_2 are possibly complex terms, and v_1, v_2 are either variables or constants.

We associate to a DB signature Σ a characteristic (directed) graph $G(\Sigma)$ capturing the dependencies induced by functions over sorts. Specifically, $G(\Sigma)$ is an edge-labeled graph whose set of nodes is Σ_{srt}, and with a labeled edge $S \xrightarrow{f} S'$ for each $f : S \longrightarrow S'$ in Σ_{fun}. We say that Σ is *acyclic* if $G(\Sigma)$ is so. The *leaves* of Σ are the nodes of $G(\Sigma)$ without outgoing edges. These terminal sorts are divided in two subsets, respectively representing *unary relations* and *value sorts*. Non-value sorts (i.e., unary relations and non-leaf sorts) are called *id sorts*, and are conceptually used to represent (identifiers of) different kinds of objects. Value sorts, instead, represent datatypes such as strings, numbers, clock values, etc. We denote the set of id sorts in Σ by Σ_{ids}, and that of value sorts by Σ_{val}, hence $\Sigma_{srt} = \Sigma_{ids} \uplus \Sigma_{val}$.

We now consider extensional data.

Definition 3.2 (DB instance) A *DB instance* of DB schema $\langle \Sigma, T \rangle$ is a Σ-structure $\mathcal{M}$ that is a model of T and such that every id sort of Σ is interpreted in $\mathcal{M}$ on a *finite* set.

Contrast this to arbitrary *models* of T, where no finiteness assumption is made. What may appear as not customary in Definition 3.2 is the fact that value sorts can be interpreted on infinite sets. This allows us, at once, to reconstruct the classical notion of DB instance as a finite model (since only finitely many values can be pointed from id sorts using functions), at the same time supplying a potentially infinite set of fresh values to be dynamically introduced in the working memory during the evolution of the artifact system. More details on this will be given in Section 3.1.1.

We respectively denote by $S^{\mathcal{M}}$, $f^{\mathcal{M}}$, and $c^{\mathcal{M}}$ the interpretation in $\mathcal{M}$ of the sort S (this is a set), of the function symbol f (this is a set-theoretic function), and of the constant c (this is an element of the interpretation of the corresponding sort). Obviously, $f^{\mathcal{M}}$ and $c^{\mathcal{M}}$ must match the sorts in Σ. E.g., if f has source S and target U, then $f^{\mathcal{M}}$ has domain $S^{\mathcal{M}}$ and range $U^{\mathcal{M}}$.

Example 3.1 We give an example of a DB schema: this read-only database will be the data storage of the 'job hiring' business process used as a running example (together with its variants) in the book. The human resource (HR) branch of a company stores the following information inside a relational database: *(i)* users registered to the company website, who are potentially interested in job positions offered by the company; *(ii)* the different, available job categories; *(iii)* HR employees, together with the job categories they are competent in (in turn indicating which job applicants they could interview). To formalize these different aspects, we make use of a DB signature Σ_{hr} consisting of: *(i)* four id sorts, used to respectively identify users, employees, job categories, and the competence relationship connecting employees to job categories; *(ii)* one value sort containing strings used to name users and employees, and describe job categories. In addition, Σ_{hr} contains five function symbols mapping: *(i)* user identifiers to their corresponding names; *(ii)* employee identifiers to their corresponding names; *(iii)* job category identifiers to their corresponding descriptions; *(iv)* competence identifiers to their corresponding employees and job categories. The characteristic graph of Σ_{hr} is shown in Figure 3.1 (left part).   ◄

We close the formalization of DB schemas by discussing DB theories. The role of a DB theory is to encode background axioms to express constraints on the different elements of the corresponding signature. We illustrate a typical background axiom, required to handle the possible presence of *undefined identifiers/values* in the different sorts. This, in turn, is essential to capture artifact systems whose working memory is initially undefined, in the style of [102, 186]. To accommodate this, to specify an undefined value we add to every sort S of Σ a constant undef_S (written from now on, by abuse of notation, just as undef, used also to indicate a tuple). Then, for each function symbol f of Σ, we add the following axiom to the DB theory:

$$\forall x \ (x = \mathsf{undef} \leftrightarrow f(x) = \mathsf{undef}) \tag{3.1}$$

This axiom states that the application of f to the undefined value produces an undefined value, and it is the only situation for which f is undefined.

Remark 3.1 In the artifact-centric model in the style of [102, 186] that we intend to capture, the DB theory consists of Axioms (3.1) only. However, our technical results do not require this specific choice, and more general sufficient conditions will be discussed in Section 4.6.

3.1.1 Relational View of DB Schemas

One might be surprised by the fact that signatures in our DB schemas contain unary function symbols, instead of relational symbols. The algebraic, functional characterization of DB schema and instance presented above can be actually reinterpreted in the classical, relational model (see Section 2.7 for preliminaries on classical relational databases), so as to reconstruct the requirements posed in [186]. In this last work, the schema of the *read-only* database must satisfy the following conditions: *(i)* each relation schema has a single-attribute primary key; *(ii)* attributes are typed; *(iii)* attributes may be foreign keys referencing other relation schemas; *(iv)* the primary keys of different relation schemas are pairwise disjoint. We now discuss why these requirements are matched by DB schemas. Definition 3.1 naturally corresponds to the definition of relational database schemas equipped with single-attribute *primary keys* and *foreign keys* (plus a reformulation of constraint (3.1)). To technically explain the correspondence, we adopt the *named perspective*, where each relation schema is defined by a signature containing a *relation name* and a set of *typed attribute names*. Let $\langle \Sigma, T \rangle$ be a DB schema. Each id sort $S \in \Sigma_{ids}$ corresponds to a dedicated relation R_S with the following attributes: *(i)* one identifier attribute id_S with type S; *(ii)* one dedicated attribute a_f with type S' for every function symbol $f \in \Sigma_{fun}$ of the form $f : S \longrightarrow S'$.

The fact that R_S is built starting from functions in Σ naturally induces different database dependencies in R_S. In particular, for each non-id attribute a_f of R_S, we get a *functional dependency* from id_S to a_f; altogether, such dependencies in turn witness that id_S is the *(primary) key* of R_S. In addition, for each non-id attribute a_f of R_S whose corresponding function symbol f has id sort S' as image, we get an *inclusion dependency* from a_f to the id attribute $id_{S'}$ of $R_{S'}$; this captures that a_f is a *foreign key* referencing $R_{S'}$. For details on the general definitions of primary and foreign keys, see Section 2.7.

Example 3.2 The diagram on the right in Figure 3.1 graphically depicts the relational view corresponding to the DB signature of Example 3.6. ◂

Given a DB instance $\mathcal{M}$ of $\langle \Sigma, T \rangle$, its corresponding relational instance $\mathcal{R}[\mathcal{M}]$ (or i) is the minimal set satisfying the following property: for every id sort $S \in \Sigma_{ids}$, let $f_1, \ldots, f_n$ be all functions in Σ with domain S; then, for every identifier $o^{\mathcal{M}} \in S^{\mathcal{M}}$, $\mathcal{R}[\mathcal{M}]$ contains a *labeled fact* of the form $R_S(id_S : o^{\mathcal{M}}, a_{f_1} : f_1(o)^{\mathcal{M}}, \ldots, a_{f_n} : f_n(o)^{\mathcal{M}})$, where $attr : c^{\mathcal{M}}$ means that the element $c^{\mathcal{M}}$ corresponds to the attribute $attr$ of the relation R_S.

With this interpretation, the *active domain of $\mathcal{R}[\mathcal{M}]$ (or of i)*, denoted with $Adom_{\Sigma_{ids}}(\mathcal{R}[\mathcal{M}])$ (or $Adom_{\Sigma_{ids}}(i)$), is the set

$$\bigcup_{S \in \Sigma_{ids}} (S^{\mathcal{M}} \setminus \{undef^{\mathcal{M}}\})$$

$$\cup \left\{ v \in \bigcup_{V \in \Sigma_{val}} V^{\mathcal{M}} \;\middle|\; \begin{array}{l} v \neq undef^{\mathcal{M}} \text{ and there exist } f \in \Sigma_{fun} \\ \text{and } o^{\mathcal{M}} \in dom(f^{\mathcal{M}}) \text{ s.t. } f(o)^{\mathcal{M}} = v \end{array} \right\}$$

consisting of all (proper) identifiers assigned by $\mathcal{M}$ to id sorts, as well as all values obtained in $\mathcal{M}$ via the application of some function. Since such values are necessarily *finitely many*, one may wonder why in Definition 3.2 we allow for interpreting value sorts over infinite sets. The reason is that, in our framework, an evolving artifact system may use such infinite provision to inject and manipulate new values into the working memory. From the definition of active domain above, exploiting Axioms (3.1) we get that the membership of a tuple $(x_0, \ldots, x_n)$ to a generic $n+1$-ary relation R_S with key dependencies (corresponding to an id sort S) can be expressed in our setting by using just unary function symbols and equality:

$$R_S(x_0, \ldots, x_n) \text{ iff } x_0 \neq \textsf{undef} \land x_1 = f_1(x_0) \land \cdots \land x_n = f_n(x_0) \qquad (3.2)$$

where f_i is as defined above (i.e., the unary function that has as domain the id sort S and as image the sort S' corresponding to the attribute a_{f_i} of R_S).

Hence, the representation of negated atoms is the one that directly follows from negating (3.2):

$$\neg R_S(x_0, \ldots, x_n) \text{ iff } x_0 = \textsf{undef} \lor x_1 \neq f_1(x_0) \lor \cdots \lor x_n \neq f_n(x_0) \qquad (3.3)$$

This relational interpretation of DB schemas exactly reconstructs all the requirements posed by [102, 186] on the schema of the *read-only* database presented at the beginning of this Section.

We stress that all such requirements are natively captured in our functional definition of a DB signature, and do not need to be formulated as axioms in the DB theory. The DB theory is used to express additional constraints, like that in Axiom (3.1). In the following chapter, we will thoroughly discuss which properties must be respected by signatures and theories to guarantee that our verification machinery is well-behaved.

One may wonder why we have not directly adopted a relational view for DB schemas. This will become clear during the technical development. We anticipate the main, intuitive reasons. First, our functional view allows us to guarantee that our framework remains well-behaved even in the presence of key dependencies, since our DB theories *do* enjoy the crucial condition of Assumption 4.1 introduced below (i.e., that the DB theories admit a model completion), whereas relational structures with key constraints *do not*. Second, our functional view makes the dependencies among different types explicit. In fact, our notion of characteristic graph, which is readily computed from a DB signature, exactly reconstructs the central notion of foreign key graph used in [102] towards the main decidability results.

3.1.2 DB Extended-Schemas

If desired, we can freely extend DB schemas by adding arbitrary n-ary relation symbols to the signature Σ, or by combining DB schemas with an additional theory T' constraining value sorts. For this purpose, we give the following definition.

Definition 3.3 (DB extended-schema) A *DB extended-schema* is a pair $\langle \Sigma \cup \Sigma', T \cup T' \rangle$, where:
  (i) Σ (called *strong DB signature*) is a *DB signature* plus n-ary relations;
  (ii) T (called *strong DB theory*) is a set of universal Σ-sentences.
  (iii) Σ' (called *value signature*) is a finite multi-sorted signature, s.t. the only function or relation symbols in $\Sigma \cap \Sigma'$ are the equality predicates over the common sorts

in $\Sigma \cap \Sigma'$ and the sorts in $\Sigma \cap \Sigma'$ *can only be the codomain sort* (and not a domain sort) of a symbol from Σ other than an equality predicate.

(iv) T' (called *value theory*) is a set of universal Σ'-sentences.

We respectively call $\Sigma \cup \Sigma'$ and $T \cup T'$ the *DB extended-signature* and the *DB extended-theory* of the DB extended-schema.

Intuitively, DB extended-schemas are combinations of a DB schema possibly extended with n-ary relations (supposed to formalize the read-only database) *and* another theory T' in another language Σ' (supposed to formalize other data/value domains, possibly completely disjoint from the read-only DB). This combination is what in Section 8.5 we call *tame combination*, i.e. an 'almost disjoint' combination in which if a relation or a function symbol has as among its domain sorts a sort from $\Sigma \cap \Sigma'$, then this symbol is from Σ' (and not from Σ, unless it is the equality predicate). The (multi-sorted) disjoint signature combination is contemplated since it is a particular case of tame combination.

All the sorts from Σ' are called *value sorts* as well as the value sorts from the (strong) DB signature Σ. The intuition behind tame combinations is that, since the sorts of Σ' are interpreted as value sorts, there cannot be a function from the DB signature Σ (i.e., formalizing a key dependency) that has a sort of Σ' as its domain, otherwise this sort should be interpreted as an id sort. An example of DB extended-schema is given by the combination of a (ordinary) DB schema with an arithmetic theory T' as linear integer arithmetic ($\mathcal{LIA}$) or linear real arithmetic ($\mathcal{LRA}$). T' itself can be the (mono-sorted) disjoint-signature combination of different theories, e.g., $\mathcal{LRA}$ and $\mathcal{EUF}$, or $\mathcal{LRA}$ and suitable data structures.

Definition 3.4 (DB extended-instance) A *DB extended-instance* of a DB extended-schema $\langle \Sigma \cup \Sigma', T \cup T' \rangle$ is a $\Sigma \cup \Sigma'$-structure M that is a model of $T \cup T'$ and such that every id sort of Σ is interpreted in M on a *finite* set.

Remark 3.2 (Relational view of DB extended-schemas) If we consider a DB extended-schema obtained by adding "free" relations to a pre-existing DB schema, we keep the natural interpretation for these relations. Formally, the relational instance $\mathcal{R}[M]$ (defined in Subsection 3.1.1) contains also the tuples from r^M, for every relational symbol r from Σ (these relational symbols represent plain relations, i.e. those not possessing a key).

For simplicity, even if our implementation takes into account also the case of DB schemas extended with "free" relations, i.e. without key dependencies, we restrict our focus on DB schemas, which are sufficient to capture those constraints (as explained in the following subsection). The extension is straightforward and left to the reader. In fact, we can give in an analogous way the definitions of the characteristic graph $G(\Sigma)$ and of acyclicity for extended DB schemas. We notice that, in case Assumption 4.1 discussed below holds for DB extended-theories, all the results presented in Chapter 4 still hold even considering DB extended-schemas instead of DB schemas.

Example 3.3 We give an example of a DB extended-schema that will be used in the following as background knowledge for a variant of the job hiring process, where the job position is offered in academia.

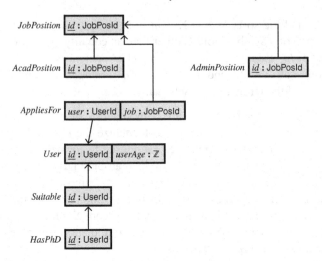

Fig. 3.2: Relational view of the DB extended signature; each cell denotes an attribute with its type, underlined attributes denote primary keys, and directed edges capture inclusion dependencies.

We define $\langle \Sigma \cup \Sigma', T \cup T' \rangle$. The strong DB signature Σ contains:

- two id sorts JobPosId and UserId, to denote the ids of job positions and of the users may want to apply, respectively;
- four unary relations *AcadPosition*(JobPosId), *AdminPosition*(JobPosId), *Suitable*(UserId), *HasPhD*(UserId), respectively for academic job positions, for administrative job positions, for users that are suitable to work in academia and for users that hold a PhD degree;
- one binary relation *AppliesFor*(UserId, JobPosId), which keeps the information of the users that applied for some position;
- one function symbol *userAge* : UserId $\rightarrow \mathbb{Z}$, giving information about the age of users.

Since the unique attribute of *AcadPosition*, *AdminPosition* is *JobPosId*, both academic and administrative positions are also job positions.

The strong DB theory is given by the following set of universal sentences:

$$T := \{ \ \forall x(AcadPosition(x) \rightarrow \neg AdminPosition(x))$$
$$\forall x(HasPhD(x) \rightarrow Suitable(x))\}$$

The first axiom states that academic positions and administrative positions are disjoint, whereas the second axiom states that the interpretation of the relation *HasPhD* is always a subset of the interpretation of the relation *Suitable*.

The value signature Σ' is given by the signature of $\mathcal{LIA}$ with the single sort $\mathbb{Z}$ (which is used as codomain of the unary function *userAge*). The value theory T' is given by $\mathcal{LIA}$ itself.

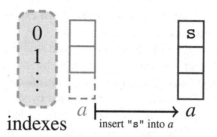

indexes a insert "s" into a a

Fig. 3.3: Graphical intuition showing the evolution of an array-based system. The current state of the array is represented in green, whereas consequent states resulting from updates are shown in blue: the shown update corresponds to the insertion of value "s" into an "empty" array whose elements have string type. Empty cells implicitly hold the undefined string.

Notice that the strong DB signature Σ contains unary and binary relation symbols and the value signature contains an arithmetical domain constrained by the $\mathcal{LIA}$ theory.

3.2 Array-Based Artifact Systems

Since SASs and U-RASs are formalized in the spirit of array-based systems, we start by recalling the intuition behind them.

In general terms, an array-based system logically describes the evolution of array data structures of unbounded size. Figure 3.3 intuitively shows a simple array-based system consisting of a single array storing strings. The logical representation of array-based systems relies on a multi-sorted theory that contains two types of sorts, one accounting for the array indexes, and the other for the elements stored in the array cells. The system variables changing over time are both individual first-order variables for data and second-order variables for arrays. Since the content of an array changes over time, it is referred to using a (second-order) *function* variable, called *array state variable*, whose interpretation in a state is that of a total function mapping indexes to elements (so that applying the function to an index denotes the classical *read* operation for arrays): for each index, this function returns the element stored by the array in that index. In the initial green state of Figure 3.3, the array a is interpreted as a total function mapping every index to the undefined string.

Starting from an initial configuration, the interpretation changes when moving from one state to another, reflecting the intended manipulation on the array. Hence, the definition of an array-based system with array state variable a always requires (*i*) a state formula $I(a)$ describing the *initial configuration(s)* of the array a; (*ii*) a formula $\tau(a, a')$ describing the *transitions* that transform the content of the array from a to a'. By suitably using logical operators, τ can express in a single formula a repertoire of different updates over a.

In such a setting, one of the most fundamental, and studied, verification problem is that of checking whether the evolution induced by τ over a starting from a configuration in $I(a)$ eventually *reaches* one of the *unsafe* configurations described by a state formula $K(a)$. This, in turn, can be tackled by showing that the formula $I(a_0) \wedge \tau(a_0, a_1) \wedge \cdots \wedge \tau(a_{n-1}, a_n) \wedge K(a_n)$ is satisfiable for some n. If no such n exists, then no finite run of the system can reach the undesired configurations, and hence the system is safe. Several mature model checkers exist to ascertain (un)safety of these type of systems, such as MCMT [147] and CUBICLE [80].

In the following sections, we make these ideas formally precise by grounding array-based systems in the artifact-centric setting. We will first consider the simpler case of SASs, where we only have individual variables for data, and then we pass to the complete framework of U-RASs where we also have second order variables formalizing artifact relations (that is, relations which are mutable during system evolution), and universal guards (employing universal quantifiers) in transitions.

3.2.1 Simple Artifact Systems

The SAS Formal Model. In this subsection we consider systems manipulating only individual variables and reading data from a given database instance. In order to introduce verification problems in a symbolic setting, one first has to specify which formulae are used to represent sets of states, the system initializations, and system evolution. Given a DB schema $\langle \Sigma, T \rangle$ and a tuple $\underline{x} = x_1, \ldots, x_n$ of variables, we introduce the following classes of Σ-formulae:

- a *state formula* is a quantifier-free Σ-formula $\phi(\underline{x})$;
- an *initial formula* is a conjunction of equalities of the form $\bigwedge_{i=1}^{n} x_i = c_i$, where each c_i is a constant (typically, c_i is an undef constant mentioned in Section 3.1 above);
- a *transition formula* tr is an existential formula

$$\exists \underline{y} \left(G(\underline{x}, \underline{y}) \wedge \bigwedge_{i=1}^{n} x'_i = F_i(\underline{x}, \underline{y}) \right) \tag{3.4}$$

where $\underline{x}'$ are renamed copies of $\underline{x}$, G is quantifier-free and $F_1, \ldots, F_n$ are case-defined functions. We call G the *guard* and F_i the *updates* of Formula (3.4).

As discussed in Subsection 1.3.1, the existentially quantified "data" variables $\underline{y}$ that appear in transitions are a distinctive and essential feature of Artifact Systems: they are crucial to express existential queries over the DB schema, to retrieve data elements from it and also to represent (non-deterministic) external user inputs.

Definition 3.5 (SAS) A *Simple Artifact System* (SAS) has the form

$$S = \langle \Sigma, T, \underline{x}, \iota(\underline{x}), \tau(\underline{x}, \underline{x}') \rangle$$

where: *(i)* $\langle \Sigma, T \rangle$ is a DB schema, *(ii)* $\underline{x} = x_1, \ldots, x_n$ are variables (called *artifact variables*), *(iii)* ι is an initial formula, and *(iv)* τ is a disjunction of transition formulae of the type (3.4).

A formula tr of the kind (3.4) is a *single* transition formula, where τ from Definition 3.5 is a disjunction of formulae of the kind (3.4); hence, such τ symbolically represents the union of all the possible transitions of the system. The formula τ is very general, so it allows to formalize expressive features such as nondeterminism: this is essential for modeling, e.g., the behavior of an external user that interacts with the system in a nondeterministic way. We will omit the dependence of ι (and τ) from $\underline{x}$ (and $\underline{x}, \underline{x}'$, respectively) when clear from the context.

In SASs, the DB schema $\langle \Sigma, T \rangle$ is intended to formalize the read-only database. The working memory, formalized by the tuple of artifact variables $\underline{x}$, interacts with the read-only database via the transitions τ. As noticed in Subsection 3.1.2, the DB schema $\langle \Sigma, T \rangle$ can be substituted with a generic DB extended-schema $\langle \Sigma \cup \Sigma', T \cup T' \rangle$, for example with $T' := \mathcal{LRA}$ (linear real arithmetic).

Example 3.4 We consider a very basic SAS working over the DB schema of Example 3.1. It captures a global, single-instance artifact tracking the main, overall phases of a hiring process. The job hiring artifact employs a dedicated *pState* variable to store the current process state. Initially, hiring is disabled, which is captured by setting the *pState* variable to undef. A transition of the process from disabled to *enabled* may occur provided that the read-only HR DB contains at least one registered user (who, in turn, may decide to apply for a job). Technically, we introduce a dedicated artifact variable *uId* initialized to undef, and used to load the identifier of such a registered user, if (s)he exists. The enabling action is then captured by the following transition formula:

$$\exists y : \mathsf{UserId} \left(\begin{array}{l} pState = \mathsf{undef} \wedge y \neq \mathsf{undef} \wedge uId = \mathsf{undef} \\ \wedge\, pState' = \mathtt{enabled} \wedge uId' = y \end{array} \right)$$

The existential quantified variable $y : \mathsf{UserId}$ is a data variable pointing to the read-only DB and is used to represent an external user input. Notice in particular how the existence of a user is checked using the typed variable y, checking that it is not undef and correspondingly assigning it to *uId*.

If the selected user is (non-deterministically) assessed as eligible, then (s)he is immediately declared as winner by the commission. This is formalized via the following two transitions. In the first one, the *pState* variable is set to eligible-found, stating that an eligible candidate has been found.

$$pState = \mathtt{enabled} \wedge uId \neq \mathsf{undef} \wedge pState' = \mathtt{eligible\text{-}found}$$

In the second one, the eligible candidate is declared the winner of the competition by assigning his/her identifier to an artifact variable *uwinner*, and is notified about the decision.

$$pState = \mathtt{eligible\text{-}found} \wedge pState' = \mathtt{notified} \wedge uwinner \neq uId$$

If the selected user is not assessed as eligible, the process goes back to the previous phase and selects a new user. This is formalized via two transitions as follows. In the first one, the user is assessed as non-eligible:

$$pState = \texttt{enabled} \wedge uId \neq \textsf{undef} \wedge pState' = \texttt{not-eligible}$$

In the second one, a new process instance is initialized by setting the artifact variables to undef:

$$pState = \texttt{not-eligible} \wedge uId \neq \textsf{undef} \wedge pState' = \textsf{undef} \wedge uId' = \textsf{undef}$$

◁

Example 3.5 We now consider a variant of the job hiring process that is modeled as a SAS working over a DB extended-schema that captures the background information of the process.

In order to do so, we present a SAS $S = \langle \Sigma \cup \Sigma', T \cup T', \underline{x}, \iota(\underline{x}), \tau(\underline{x}, \underline{x}') \rangle$, whose components are defined in the following.

First, $\langle \Sigma \cup \Sigma', T \cup T' \rangle$ is the DB extended schema presented in Example 3.3.

Differently from the previous example, the DB extended-schema employed here makes use of features not supported by DB schemas, such as free binary relations (*AppliesFor*), arithmetical value sorts like integers, a non-empty DB theory T as in Example 3.3 and $T' := \mathcal{LIA}$.

The artifact variables $\underline{x}$ of the system are:

$$\underline{x} = (x_{\text{status}}, x_{\text{appl}}, x_{\text{job}}, x_{\text{elig}}, x_{\text{wnr}}),$$

, where x_{status} keeps track of the current status of process and of its phases, x_{job} contains the id of the opened (either academic or administrative) job position, x_{appl} records the user id of the applicant currently evaluated, x_{elig} is intended to bring the id of the user eligible for the job and x_{wnr} is assigned at the end of the process when the winner user is selected.

At the beginning, all artifact variables are set to an undefined value undef. This is expressed through the following initial formula:

$$\iota = \bigwedge\nolimits_{x_i \in \underline{x}} x_i = \textsf{undef},$$

We now formally define the transitions of the system. In the following, artifact variables that are not explicitly mentioned in the transitions are assumed to be propagated from the current to the next state, keeping their values unaltered.

The process case is triggered by the selection of a job position, which is retrieved from the relation *JobPos* and assigned to the case variable x_{job}:

$$\tau_1 = \exists z_1 : \textsf{JobPosId}(x_{\text{status}} = \textsf{undef} \wedge z_1 \neq \textsf{undef} \wedge x'_{\text{job}} = z_1 \wedge x'_{\text{status}} = \texttt{phase1});$$

Then, a user nondeterministically applies to the selected job position. This is formalized by retrieving the id of a user from the relation *User* such that (s)he satisfies the binary relation *AppliesFor* together with the selected job position; this id is assigned to the artifact variable x_{appl}:

$$\tau_2 = \exists y_1 : \text{UserId}(x_{\text{status}} = \text{phase1} \wedge y_1 \neq \text{undef} \wedge x_{\text{job}} \neq \text{undef}$$
$$\wedge \, AppliesFor(y_1, x_{\text{job}}) \wedge x'_{\text{appl}} = y_1 \wedge x'_{\text{status}} = \text{phase2});$$

At this point, a new phase of the process starts: the evaluation of the current applicant. This phase distinguished the case where the job position is an academic position from the case where it is an administrative position. In the former case, if the applicant holds a PhD and is suitable for working in academia (i.e., (s)he is in the relation *Suitable*), then (s)he is declared as eligible for the position. Formally:

$$\tau_3 = x_{\text{status}} = \text{phase2} \wedge x_{\text{elig}} = \text{undef} \wedge AcadPos(x_{\text{job}}) \wedge$$
$$\wedge \, Suitable(x_{\text{appl}}) \wedge HasPhD(x_{\text{appl}}) \wedge x'_{\text{elig}} = x_{\text{appl}} \wedge x'_{\text{status}} = \text{phase3};$$

Otherwise, the applicant is discarded and the process case is reset to the first phase, so that a new candidate can be evaluated:

$$\tau_4 = x_{\text{status}} = \text{phase2} \wedge x_{\text{elig}} = \text{undef} \wedge AcadPos(x_{\text{job}})$$
$$\wedge \neg HasPhD(x_{\text{appl}}) \wedge x'_{\text{appl}} = \text{undef} \wedge x'_{\text{status}} = \text{phase1}$$

In the latter case, if the applicant is suitable for working in academia (i.e., (s)he is in the relation *Suitable*), then (s)he is declared as eligible for the position. Formally:

$$\tau_5 = x_{\text{status}} = \text{phase2} \wedge x_{\text{elig}} = \text{undef} \wedge AdminPos(x_{\text{job}}) \wedge$$
$$\wedge \, Suitable(x_{\text{appl}}) \wedge x'_{\text{elig}} = x_{\text{appl}} \wedge x'_{\text{status}} = \text{phase3}.$$

Otherwise, the applicant is discarded and the process case is reset to the first phase, so that a new candidate can be evaluated:

$$\tau_6 = x_{\text{status}} = \text{phase2} \wedge x_{\text{elig}} = \text{undef} \wedge AdminPos(x_{\text{job}})$$
$$\wedge \neg Suitable(x_{\text{appl}}) \wedge x'_{\text{job}} = \text{undef} \wedge x'_{\text{appl}} = \text{undef} \wedge x'_{\text{status}} = \text{undef},$$

In the final phase of the process, the winner of the selection is (nondeterministically) declared. If the eligible applicant that is currently under evaluation is declared as winner, her/his id is assigned to the artifact variable x_{wnr}:

$$\tau_7 = x_{\text{status}} = \text{phase3} \wedge x_{\text{elig}} \neq \text{undef} \wedge x_{\text{wnr}} = \text{undef} \wedge x'_{\text{wnr}} = x_{\text{elig}} \wedge x_{\text{status}} = \text{end}$$

Otherwise, the eligible candidate is not chosen and the process goes back to phase1 where a new applicant is selected:

$$\tau_8 = x_{\text{status}} = \text{phase3} \wedge x_{\text{elig}} \neq \text{undef} \wedge x_{\text{wnr}} = \text{undef} \wedge x'_{\text{elig}} = \text{undef}$$
$$\wedge x'_{\text{appl}} = \text{undef} \wedge \wedge x_{\text{status}} = \text{phase1},$$

3.2.2 Universal Relational Artifact Systems

The U-RAS Formal Model. Following the tradition of artifact-centric systems [100, 102], a Universal Relational Artifact System (U-RAS) consists of a read-only database, a read-write working memory for artifacts, and a finite set of actions (also called services) that inspect the relational database and the working memory, and determine the new configuration of the working memory. In a U-RAS, the working memory consists of *individual* and *higher order* variables. These higher order variables (usually called *arrays*) are supposed to model evolving relations, so-called *artifact relations* in [102, 186]. The idea is to treat artifact relations in a uniform way as we did for the read-only database: we need extra sort symbols (recall that each sort symbol corresponds to a database relation symbol) and extra unary function symbols, the latter being treated as second-order variables.

Given a DB signature Σ, an *artifact extension* of Σ is a signature Σ_{ext} obtained from Σ by adding to it some extra sort symbols[1]. These new sorts (usually indicated with $E, E_1, E_2 \dots$) are called *artifact sorts* (or *artifact relations* by some abuse of terminology), whereas the old sorts from Σ are called *basic sorts*. In U-RAS, artifacts and basic sorts correspond, respectively, to the index and the elements sorts mentioned in the literature on array-based systems. Below, given $\langle \Sigma, T \rangle$ and an artifact extension Σ_{ext} of Σ, when we speak of a Σ_{ext}-model of T, a DB instance of $\langle \Sigma_{ext}, T \rangle$, or a Σ_{ext}-model of T^*, we mean a Σ_{ext}-structure $\mathcal{M}$ whose reduct to Σ respectively is a model of T, a DB instance of $\langle \Sigma, T \rangle$, or a model of T^*.

An *artifact setting* over Σ_{ext} is a pair $(\underline{x}, \underline{a})$ given by a finite set $\underline{x}$ of individual variables and a finite set $\underline{a}$ of unary function variables: *the latter are required to have an artifact sort as source sort and a basic sort as target sort.* Variables in $\underline{x}$ are called (as before) *artifact variables*, and variables in $\underline{a}$ *artifact components*. Given a DB instance $\mathcal{M}$ of Σ_{ext}, an *assignment* to an artifact setting $(\underline{x}, \underline{a})$ over Σ_{ext} is a map α assigning to every artifact variable $x_i \in \underline{x}$ of sort S_i an element $x^\alpha \in S_i^\mathcal{M}$ and to every artifact component $a_j : E_j \longrightarrow U_j$ (with $a_j \in \underline{a}$) a set-theoretic function $a_j^\alpha : E_j^\mathcal{M} \longrightarrow U_j^\mathcal{M}$.

We can view an assignment to an artifact setting $(\underline{x}, \underline{a})$ as a DB instance *extending* the DB instance $\mathcal{M}$ as follows. Let all the artifact components in $(\underline{x}, \underline{a})$ having source E be $a_{i_1} : E \longrightarrow S_1, \cdots, a_{i_n} : E \longrightarrow S_n$. Viewed as a relation in the artifact assignment $(\mathcal{M}, \alpha)$, the artifact relation E "consists" of the set of tuples

$$\{\langle e, a_{i_1}^\alpha(e), \dots, a_{i_n}^\alpha(e) \rangle \mid e \in E^\mathcal{M}\}$$

Thus each element of E is formed by an "entry" $e \in E^\mathcal{M}$ (uniquely identifying the tuple) and by "data" $\underline{a}_i^\alpha(e)$ taken from the read-only database $\mathcal{M}$. When the system evolves, the set $E^\mathcal{M}$ of entries remains fixed, whereas the components $\underline{a}_i^\alpha(e)$ may change: typically, we initially have $\underline{a}_i^\alpha(e) = \mathsf{undef}$, but these values are changed when some defined values are inserted into the relation modeled by E; the values are

---

[1] By 'signature' we always mean 'signature with equality', so as, soon as new sorts are added, the corresponding equality predicates are added too.

then repeatedly modified (and possibly also reset to undef, if the tuple is removed and e is re-set to point to undefined values). In accordance with MCMT conventions, we denote the application of an artifact component a to a term (i.e., constant or variable) v also as $a[v]$ (standard notation for arrays), instead of $a(v)$.

To introduce U-RASs, we discuss the kind of formulae we use. In such formulae, we use notations like $\phi(\underline{z}, \underline{b})$ to mean that ϕ is a formula whose free individual variables are among the $\underline{z}$ and whose free unary function variables are among the $\underline{b}$.

Let $(\underline{x}, \underline{a})$ be an artifact setting over Σ_{ext}, where $\underline{x} = x_1, \ldots, x_n$ are the artifact variables and $\underline{a} = a_1, \ldots, a_m$ are the artifact components (their source and target sorts are left implicitly specified). We list the kind of formulae we shall use:

- An *initial formula* is a formula $\iota(\underline{x}, \underline{a})$ of the form

$$(\textstyle\bigwedge_{i=1}^{n} x_i = c_i) \wedge (\textstyle\bigwedge_{j=1}^{m} a_j = \lambda y.d_j) \tag{3.5}$$

where c_i, d_j are constants from Σ (typically, c_i and d_j are undef). Recall that $a_j = \lambda y.d_j$ abbreviates $\forall y\, a_j(y) = d_j$.
- A *state formula* has the form

$$\exists \underline{e}\, \phi(\underline{e}, \underline{x}, \underline{a}) \tag{3.6}$$

where ϕ is quantifier-free and the $\underline{e}$ are individual variables of artifact sorts.
- A *transition formula* tr has the form

$$\exists \underline{e} \left(\begin{aligned} \gamma(\underline{e}, \underline{x}, \underline{a}) \wedge (\forall \underline{k}\, \gamma_u(\underline{k}, \underline{e}, \underline{x}, \underline{a})) \wedge \textstyle\bigwedge_i x_i' = F_i(\underline{e}, \underline{x}, \underline{a}) \\ \wedge \textstyle\bigwedge_j a_j' = \lambda y.G_j(y, \underline{e}, \underline{x}, \underline{a}) \end{aligned} \right) \tag{3.7}$$

where the $\underline{e}$ are individual variables (of *both* basic and artifact sorts), $\underline{k}$ are individual variables of artifact sort, γ (the '(plain) guard') and γ_u (the 'universal guard') are quantifier-free, $\underline{x}', \underline{a}'$ are renamed copies of $\underline{x}, \underline{a}$, and the F_i, G_j (the 'updates') are case-defined functions. Sometimes, when we need to explicitly distinguish variables of basic sorts from variables of artifact sort, we will use the following equivalent but slightly different notation:

$$\exists \underline{e}, \underline{d} \left(\begin{aligned} \gamma(\underline{e}, \underline{d}, \underline{x}, \underline{a}) \wedge (\forall \underline{k}\, \gamma_u(\underline{k}, \underline{e}, \underline{d}, \underline{x}, \underline{a})) \wedge \textstyle\bigwedge_i x_i' = F_i(\underline{e}, \underline{d}, \underline{x}, \underline{a}) \\ \wedge \textstyle\bigwedge_j a_j' = \lambda y.G_j(y, \underline{e}, \underline{d}, \underline{x}, \underline{a}) \end{aligned} \right)$$
$$(3.8)$$

where everything is as before, apart from $\underline{e}$ that are individual variables of artifact sorts and $\underline{d}$ that are individual variables of basic sorts.

As discussed in Subsection 1.3.1 and noticed also for SASs, the existentially quantified "data" variables $\underline{d}$ (i.e., of basic sort) that appear in transitions are a distinctive and essential feature of Artifact Systems: they are crucial to express existential queries over the DB schema, to retrieve data elements from it and also to represent (non-deterministic) external user inputs.

Note that transition formulae as above can express, e.g., *(i)* insertion (with/without duplicates) of a tuple in an artifact relation, *(ii)* removal of a tuple from an artifact relation, *(iii)* transfer of a tuple from an artifact relation to artifact variables (and vice-versa), and *(iv)* removal/modification of *all* the tuples satisfying a certain condition from an artifact relation. All the above operations can also be constrained. The formalization of the above operations in the formalism of our transitions is not difficult: some of these operations are described in more details in Section 5.3, where a comparison with the transitions of [102, 186] is also presented. Moreover, in that section a proper discussion on the conditions to impose to the format of transition formulae tr and which operations are allowed in order to guarantee the decidability of our verification machinery is extensively carried out.

We now give the most important definition of this work: the definition of Universal Relational Artifact System, i.e. the most general model of DAPs that we employ in this work. Every other formalism introduced in the course of this book is an instance or can be translated into Universal Relational Artifact SystemS.

Definition 3.6 (U-RAS) A *Universal Relational Artifact System* (Universal RAS, or, simply, U-RAS) has the form

$$S = \langle \Sigma, T, \Sigma_{ext}, \underline{x}, \underline{a}, \iota(\underline{x}, \underline{a}), \tau(\underline{x}, \underline{a}, \underline{x}', \underline{a}') \rangle$$

where: *(i)* $\langle \Sigma, T \rangle$ is a DB schema, *(ii)* Σ_{ext} is an artifact extension of Σ, *(iii)* $(\underline{x}, \underline{a})$ is an artifact setting over Σ_{ext}, *(iv)* ι is an initial formula, and *(v)* τ is a disjunction of transition formulae tr of the type (3.7).

A formula tr of the kind (3.7) is a *single* transition formula, where τ from Definition 3.6 is a disjunction of formulae of the kind (3.7); hence, such τ symbolically represents the union of all the possible transitions of the system. We will omit the dependence of ι (and τ) from $\underline{x}, \underline{a}$ (and $\underline{x}, \underline{a}, \underline{x}', \underline{a}'$, respectively) when clear from the context.

In U-RASs, the DB schema $\langle \Sigma, T \rangle$ is intended to formalize the read-only database. The working memory, formalized by the artifact setting $(\underline{x}, \underline{a})$ and containing both artifact variables and artifact relations, interacts with the read-only database via the transitions τ. As noticed in Subsection 3.1.2, the DB schema $\langle \Sigma, T \rangle$ can be substituted with a generic DB extended-schema $\langle \Sigma \cup \Sigma', T \cup T' \rangle$, for example with $T' := \mathcal{LRA}$ (linear real arithmetic).

U-RASs are difficult to manage, not only because of the presence of artifact relations, but especially because their transitions contain universally quantified guards (i.e., universal guards). However, in most practical cases universal guards are not needed, and it is convenient to define a slightly weaker version of U-RAS that does not use universal guards. This version of U-RASs are called Relational Artifact Systems (RASs).

Definition 3.7 (RAS) A *Relational Artifact System* (RAS) has the form

$$S = \langle \Sigma, T, \Sigma_{ext}, \underline{x}, \underline{a}, \iota(\underline{x}, \underline{a}), \tau(\underline{x}, \underline{a}, \underline{x}', \underline{a}') \rangle$$

where: *(i)* $\langle \Sigma, T \rangle$ is a DB schema, *(ii)* Σ_{ext} is an artifact extension of Σ, *(iii)* $(\underline{x}, \underline{a})$ is an artifact setting over Σ_{ext}, *(iv)* ι is an initial formula, and *(v)* τ is a disjunction of transition formulae tr of the type (3.7) where γ_u is substituted with the tautological formula $\top$.

As it is clear from the definition, RASs are a special case of U-RASs; SASs are a particular class of RASs where the working memory consists *only* of artifact variables (without artifact relations).

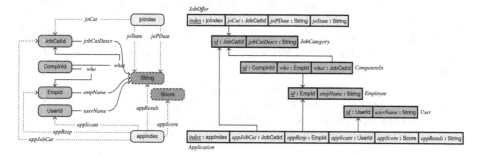

Fig. 3.4: On the left: characteristic graph of the human resources DB signature from Example 3.6, augmented with the signature of the artifact extension for the job hiring process; value sorts are shown in pink, basic id sorts in blue, and artifact id sorts in yellow. On the right: relational view of the DB signature and the corresponding artifact relations; each cell denotes an attribute with its type, underlined attributes denote primary keys, and directed edges capture foreign keys.

Example 3.6 We continue our running example, presenting a RAS S_{hr} capturing a job hiring process where multiple job categories may be turned into actual job offers, each one receiving many applications from registered users. Such applications are then evaluated, finally deciding which are accepted and which are rejected. The example is inspired by the job hiring process presented in [237] to show the intrinsic difficulties of capturing real-life processes with many-to-many interacting business entities using conventional process modeling notations (such as BPMN). Note that this example is also demonstrating the co-evolution of multiple instances of two different artifacts (namely, job offer and application). At the end of this paragraph, we will add an additional (final) transition containing a universal guard so as to transform S_{hr} into a Universal RAS.

As for the read-only DB, S_{hr} works over the DB schema of Example 3.1, extended with a further value sort Score used to score the applications sent for job offerings. Score contains 102 different values, intuitively corresponding to the integer numbers from -1 to 100 (included), where -1 denotes that the application is considered to be not eligible, while a score between 0 and 100 indicates the actual score assigned after evaluating the application. For the sake of readability, we make use of the usual integer comparison predicates to compare variables of type Score. This is simply syntactic sugar and does not require the introduction of rigid predicates in our framework. In fact, given two variables x and y of type Score, $x < y$ is a shortcut for the finitary disjunction testing that x is one of the scores that are "less than" y (similarly for the other comparison predicates).

As for the working memory, S_{hr} consists of three artifacts: a single-instance *job hiring* artifact tracking the three main phases of the overall process, and two multi-instance artifacts accounting for the evolution of *job offers*, and that of corresponding *user applications*. The job hiring artifact simply requires a dedicated *pState* variable to store the current process state. The job offer and user application multi-instance artifacts are instead modeled by enriching the DB signature Σ_{hr} of the read-only database of human resources. In particular, an artifact extension is added containing two artifact sorts JobIndex and AppIndex used to respectively *index* (i.e., *"internally" identify*) job offers and applications. The management of job offers and applications is then modeled by a full-fledged artifact setting that adopts:

- artifact components with domains JobIndex and AppIndex to capture the artifact relations storing multiple instances of job offers and applications;
- individual variables used as temporary memory to manipulate the artifact relations.

The actual components of such an artifact setting will be introduced when needed.

We now describe how the process works, step by step. When writing transition formulae, we make the following assumption: if an artifact variable/component is not mentioned at all, it is meant that it is updated identically; otherwise, the relevant update function will specify how it is updated. Notice that, as mentioned also in the introduction, nondeterministic updates can be formalized using existentially quantified variables in the transition.

Initially, hiring is disabled, which is captured by initially setting the *pState* variable to undef. A transition of the process from disabled to *enabled* may occur provided that the read-only HR DB contains at least one registered user (who, in turn, may decide to apply for job offers created during this phase). Technically, we introduce a dedicated artifact variable *uId* initialized to undef, and used to load the identifier of such a registered user, if (s)he exists. The enablement task is then captured by the following transition formula:

$$\exists y : \mathsf{UserId}\ (pState = \mathsf{undef} \wedge y \neq \mathsf{undef} \wedge pState' = \mathtt{enabled} \wedge uId' = y)$$

We now focus on the creation of a job offer. When the overall hiring process is enabled, some job categories present in the read-only DB may be published into a corresponding job offer, consequently becoming ready to receive applications. This is done in two steps. In the first step, we transfer the id of the job category to be published to the artifact variable *jId*, and the string representing the publishing date to the artifact variable *pubDate*. Thus, *jId* is filled with the identifier of a job category picked from JobCatId (modeling a nondeterministic choice of category), while *pubDate* is filled with a String (modeling a *user input* where one of the infinitely many strings is injected into *pubDate*).

In addition, the transition interacts with a further artifact variable *pubState* capturing the publishing state of offers, and consequently used to synchronize the two steps for publishing a job offer. In particular, this first step can be executed only if *pubState* is *not* in state publishing, and has the effect of setting it to such a value, thus preventing the first step to be executed twice in a row (which would actually overwrite what has been stored in *jId* and *pubDate*). Technically, we have:

$$\exists j{:}\text{JobCatId}, d{:}\text{String} \begin{pmatrix} pState = \texttt{enabled} \land pubState \neq \texttt{publishing} \land j \neq \text{undef} \\ \land\, pState' = \texttt{enabled} \land pubState' = \texttt{publishing} \\ \land\, jId' = j \land pubDate' = d \end{pmatrix}$$

The second step consists in transferring the content of these three variables into corresponding artifact components that keep track of all active job offers, at the same time resetting the content of the artifact variables to undef. This is done by introducing three function variables with domain joIndex, respectively keeping track of the category, publishing date, and state of job offers:

$$
\begin{aligned}
joCat \quad &: \text{joIndex} \longrightarrow \text{JobCatId} \\
joPDate \quad &: \text{joIndex} \longrightarrow \text{String} \\
joState \quad &: \text{joIndex} \longrightarrow \text{String}
\end{aligned}
$$

With these artifact components at hand, the second step is then realized as follows:

$$\exists i{:}\text{joIndex}$$
$$\begin{pmatrix} pState = \texttt{enabled} \land pubState = \texttt{publishing} \land joPDate[i] = \text{undef} \\ \land\, joCat[i] = \text{undef} \land joState[i] = \text{undef} \\ \land\, aState' = \text{undef} \land pState' = \texttt{enabled} \land pubState' = \texttt{published} \\ \land\, joCat' = \lambda j. \begin{pmatrix} \text{if } j = i \text{ then } jId \\ \text{else if } joCat[j] = jId \text{ then undef} \\ \text{else } joCat[j] \end{pmatrix} \\ \land\, joPDate' = \lambda j. \begin{pmatrix} \text{if } j = i \text{ then } pubDate \\ \text{else if } joCat[j] = jId \text{ then undef} \\ \text{else } joPDate[j] \end{pmatrix} \\ \land\, joState' = \lambda j. \begin{pmatrix} \text{if } j = i \text{ then } \texttt{open} \\ \text{else if } joCat[j] = jId \text{ then undef} \\ \text{else } joState[j] \end{pmatrix} \\ \land\, uId' = \text{undef} \land eId' = \text{undef} \land jId' = \text{undef} \\ \land\, pubDate' = \text{undef} \land cId' = \text{undef} \end{pmatrix}$$

The "if-then-else" pattern is used to create an entry for the job offer artifact relation containing the information stored into the artifact variables populated in the first step, at the same time *making sure that only one entry exists for a given job category.* This is done by picking a job offer index i that is not already pointing to an actual job offer, i.e., such that the i-th element of *joCat* is undef. Then, the transition updates the whole content of the three artifact components *joCat*, *joPDate*, and *joState* as follows:

- The i-th entry of such variables is respectively assigned to the job category stored in JobCatId, the string stored in *pubDate*, and the constant open (signifying that this entry is ready to receive applications).
- All other entries are kept unaltered, with the exception of a possibly existing entry j with $j \neq i$ that points to the same job category contained in JobCatId. If such an entry j exists, its content is reset, by assigning to the j-th component of all three artifact components the value undef. Obviously, other strategies to resolve this possible conflict can be seamlessly captured in our framework.

A similar conflict resolution strategy will be used in the other transitions of this example.

We now focus on the evolution of applications to job offers. Each application consists of a job category, the identifier of the applicant user, the identifier of an employee from human resources who is responsible for the application, the score assigned to the application, and the application final result (indicating whether the application is among the winners or the losers for the job offer). These five information types are encapsulated into five dedicated function variables with domain appIndex, collectively realizing the application artifact relation:

$$
\begin{aligned}
appJobCat &: \text{appIndex} \longrightarrow \text{JobCatId} \\
applicant &: \text{appIndex} \longrightarrow \text{UserId} \\
appResp &: \text{appIndex} \longrightarrow \text{EmpId} \\
appScore &: \text{appIndex} \longrightarrow \text{Score} \\
appResult &: \text{appIndex} \longrightarrow \text{String}
\end{aligned}
$$

With these function variables at hand, we discuss the insertion of an application into the system for an open job offer. This is again managed in multiple steps, first loading the necessary information into dedicated artifact variables, and finally transferring them into the function variables that collectively realize the application artifact relation. To synchronize these multiple steps and define which step is applicable in a given state, we make use of a string artifact variable called *aState*. The first step to insert an application is executed when *aState* is undef, and has the effect of loading into *jId* the identifier of a job category that has a corresponding open job offer, while at the same time putting *aState* in state joSelected.

$$
\exists i{:}\text{joIndex}
$$
$$
\begin{pmatrix}
pState = \text{enabled} \wedge aState = \text{undef} \wedge joCat[i] \neq \text{undef} \wedge joState[i] = \text{open} \\
\wedge\, pState' = \text{enabled} \wedge aState' = \text{joSelected} \wedge jId' = joCat[i] \\
\wedge\, joCat' = joCat \wedge uId' = \text{undef} \wedge eId' = \text{undef} \wedge jId' = \text{undef} \\
\wedge\, pubDate' = \text{undef} \wedge cId' = \text{undef}
\end{pmatrix}
$$

The last row of the transition resets the content of all artifact variables, cleaning the working memory for the forthcoming steps (avoiding that stale values are present there). This is also useful from the technical point of view, as it guarantees that the transition is *strongly local* (this notion will be introduced in Section 5.2.1; see also the discussion in Subsection 5.3.1).

The second step has a twofold purpose: picking the identifier of the user who wants to submit an application for the selected job offer, and assigning to its application an employee of human resources who is competent in the category of the job offer. This also results in an update of variable *aState*:

$$
\exists u{:}\text{UserId},\, e{:}\text{EmpId},\, c{:}\text{CompInId}
$$
$$
\begin{pmatrix}
pState = \text{enabled} \wedge aState = \text{joSelected} \wedge who(c) = e \wedge what(c) = jId \\
\wedge\, jId \neq \text{undef} \wedge u \neq \text{undef} \wedge c \neq \text{undef} \wedge pState' = \text{enabled} \\
\wedge\, aState' = \text{received} \wedge jId' = jId \wedge uId' = u \wedge eId' = e \wedge cId' = c
\end{pmatrix}
$$

The last step transfers the application data into the application artifact relation, making sure that no two applications exist for the same user and the same job category. The transfer is done by assigning the artifact variables to corresponding components of the application artifact relation, at the same resetting all application-related artifact variables to undef (including *aState*, so that new applications can be inserted). For the insertion, a "free" index (i.e., an index pointing to an undefined applicant, with an undefined job category and an undefined responsible) is picked. The newly inserted application gets a default score of -1 (thus initializing it to "not eligible"), while the final result is undef:

$$\exists i:\text{appIndex}$$
$$\begin{pmatrix} pState = \texttt{enabled} \land aState = \texttt{received} \\ \land\, appJobCat[i] = \textsf{undef} \land applicant[i] = \textsf{undef} \land appResp[i] = \textsf{undef} \\ \land pState' = \texttt{enabled} \land aState' = \textsf{undef} \\ \land\, appJobCat' = \lambda j. \begin{pmatrix} \text{if } j = i \text{ then } jId \\ \text{else if } (applicant[j] = uId \land appResp[j] = eId) \text{ then undef} \\ \qquad\text{else } appJobCat[j] \end{pmatrix} \\ \land\, applicant' = \lambda j. \begin{pmatrix} \text{if } j = i \text{ then } uId \\ \text{else if } (applicant[j] = uId \land appResp[j] = eId) \text{ then undef} \\ \qquad\text{else } applicant[j] \end{pmatrix} \\ \land\, appResp' = \lambda j. \begin{pmatrix} \text{if } j = i \text{ then } eId \\ \text{else if } (applicant[j] = uId \land appResp[j] = eId) \text{ then undef} \\ \qquad\text{else } appResp[j] \end{pmatrix} \\ \land\, appScore' = \lambda j. \begin{pmatrix} \text{if } j = i \text{ then } -1 \\ \text{else if } (applicant[j] = uId \land appResp[j] = eId) \text{ then undef} \\ \qquad\text{else } appScore[j] \end{pmatrix} \\ \land\, appResult' = \lambda j. \begin{pmatrix} \text{if } j = i \lor (applicant[j] = uId \land appResp[j] = eId) \text{ then undef} \\ \text{else } appResult[j] \end{pmatrix} \\ \land\, uId' = \textsf{undef} \land eId' = \textsf{undef} \land jId' = \textsf{undef} \land pubDate' = \textsf{undef} \land cId' = \textsf{undef} \end{pmatrix}$$

Each single application that is currently considered as not eligible can be made eligible by carrying out an evaluation that assigns a proper score to it. This is managed by the following transition:

$$\exists i:\text{appIndex},\, s:\text{Score} \begin{pmatrix} pState = \texttt{enabled} \land applicant[i] \neq \textsf{undef} \land appScore[i] = -1 \\ \land\, s \geq 0 \land pState' = \texttt{enabled} \land appScore'[i] = s \end{pmatrix}$$

Evaluations are only possible as long as the process is in the `enabled` state. The process moves from enabled to *final* once the deadline for receiving applications to job offers is actually reached. This event is captured with pure nondeterminism, and has the additional *bulk* effect of turning all open job offers to *closed*:

$$pState = \texttt{enabled} \land pState' = \texttt{final}$$
$$\land\, joState' = \lambda j. \begin{pmatrix} \text{if } joState[j] = \texttt{open then closed} \\ \text{else } joState[j] \end{pmatrix}$$

Finally, we consider the determination of winners and losers, which is carried out when the overall hiring process moves from final to *notified*. This is captured by the following *bulk* transition, which declares all applications with a score above 80 as winning, and all the others as losing:

$$pState = \texttt{final} \wedge pState' = \texttt{notified}$$
$$\wedge\ appResult' = \lambda j. \begin{pmatrix} \text{if } appScore[j] > 80 \text{ then } \texttt{winner} \\ \text{else } \texttt{loser} \end{pmatrix}$$

So far, none of the transitions contain universal guards. Hence, the system described above is a plain RAS. We now transform it into a Universal RAS by adding a final transition containing a universal guard. This final transition checks (using a universal guard) whether no winner can be determined since *all* the applicants received a score below 80: if this is the case, the transition changes that state of *pState* to no-winner.

$$pState = \texttt{final} \wedge \forall k\ (appScore[k] < 80) \wedge pState' = \texttt{no-winner}$$

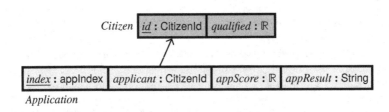

Fig. 3.5: Relational view of the DB signature and the corresponding artifact relations for the visa application process; each cell denotes an attribute with its type, underlined attributes denote primary keys, and directed edges capture foreign keys.

Example 3.7 We now provide the formalization of a visa application process by introducing a U-RAS over a DB extended-schema that employs both universal guards and proper arithmetical operations in updates, such as the sum of terms in linear real arithmetics.

Consider a visa application center, with a read-only DB storing information critical to the application process. We formalize this in a DB signature Σ_v with: *(i)* one id sort CitizenId to identify citizens; *(ii)* two value sorts $\mathbb{R}$ and String, used for evaluating applications (e.g., by giving scores); *(iii)* one unary function symbol *citizenQualif* : CitizenId $\rightarrow \mathbb{R}$. The value signature Σ' contains real constants and linear arithmetical operations.

Consider a U-RAS $\mathcal{S}_{va}$ capturing a process for evaluating visa applications and informing the applicants about the visa decisions. $\mathcal{S}_{va}$ works over the DB extended-schema from Figure 3.5. The working memory of $\mathcal{S}_{va}$ consists of artifact variables capturing the main process phases (*pState*), the citizen's visa status (*visaStat*) and ID used to notify about the application result (*toNotify*), and a multi-instance artifact for managing visa applications. The latter is formalized by adding to DB signature Σ_v a memory sort appIndex (to "internally" identify the applications), and by adding a memory schema with the applicant's ID *applicant* : appIndex $\longrightarrow$ CitizenId, evaluation score *appScore* : applndex $\longrightarrow$ Int, and application results *appResult* : applndex $\longrightarrow$ String.

We now showcase a few t-formulae for managing visa applications. We assume that if a memory variable/component is not mentioned in a t-formula, then its values remain unchanged. To insert an application into the system, the process has to be enabled. The corresponding update simultaneously *(i)* selects the applicant's ID and inserts it into the memory component *applicant*, *(ii)* evaluates the visa application and inserts a non-negative score into the memory component *appScore*. Since memory tuples must have implicit identifiers, the above insertion requires a "free" index (i.e., an index pointing to an undefined applicant) to be selected:

$$\exists i\text{:applndex},\ \exists a\text{:Citizenld},\ d\text{:}\mathbb{R},\ s\text{:}\mathbb{R}$$
$$\begin{pmatrix} pState = \text{enabled} \land a \neq \text{undef} \land citizenQualif(a) = d \land s \geq 0 \\ \land\ 0 \leq d \leq 1 \land pState' = \text{enabled} \\ \land\ applicant' = \lambda j.\ (\text{if } j = i \text{ then } a \text{ else } applicant[j]) \\ \land\ appScore' = \lambda j.\ (\text{if } j = i \text{ then } s + 20d \text{ else } appScore[j]) \end{pmatrix}$$

Notice that in the update of the artifact component *appScore* we used the $\mathcal{LRA}$ term $s + 20d$. Applications can be nondeterministically evaluated (by assigning evaluation to *pState*), resulting in highly evaluated ones being approved and others rejected:

$$pState = \text{evaluation} \land pState' = \text{evaluated}$$
$$\land appResult' = \lambda j.\ \begin{pmatrix} \text{if } appScore[j] > 60 \text{ then approved} \\ \text{else rejected} \end{pmatrix}$$

If there is at least one approved application, a nondeterministically selected applicant is getting notified:

$$\exists i\text{:applndex}$$
$$\begin{pmatrix} pState = \text{evaluated} \land pState' = \text{notified} \\ \land\ applicant[i] \neq \text{undef} \land appResult[i] = \text{approved} \\ \land\ toNotify' = applicant[i] \land visaStat' = appResult[i] \end{pmatrix}$$

Finally, we demonstrate a transition with a *universal guard* checking whether no application has been approved and, if so, changes the process state to no-visa:
$$pState = \text{evaluated} \land \forall k\ (appResult[k] \neq \text{approved})$$
$$\land pState' = \text{no-visa}$$

Chapter 4
Safety Verification of Artifact Systems

In this chapter, we introduce the safety verification problem for SASs and (Universal) RASs. In general, the safety problem accounts for establishing the non-existence of an "unsafe trace", i.e., a system run that, starting from the initial configuration of the system, leads to an "unsafe" configuration violating a desired property of interest that the system is supposed to satisfy. In the case that, considering all executions, it is impossible that the system leads to such an unsafe configuration, the system is said to be *safe* with respect to the unsafe configuration. Usually, the safety problem is stated dually, in the terms of a *reachability problem*: the last problem amounts to establishing whether the given property, called *unsafe formula* – expressed in a symbolic way and intended to formalize the undesired, unsafe states – can be *reached*. In this respect, the safety problem is about deciding if there does *not* exist a system run from an initial state that can reach one of the states satisfying the unsafe formula. The array-based setting of our Artifact Systems provides a natural formalism for expressing safety problems. We will make these intuitions precise in the following, by defining the notions of unsafe formula, symbolic unsafe trace and safety problem for both SASs and (Universal) RASs.

The main focus of this chapter is on the verification machinery we employ to assess safety of our Artifact Systems. For both SASs and (Universal) RASs we make use of a powerful and non-trivial extension of the *backward reachability procedure* studied in the context of array-based systems [143, 146]: this procedure was presented there as a *declarative version*, based on SMT solving, of the standard backward reachability procedure introduced by Abdullah et al. [6]. This declarative version is not sufficient to attack the safety problem of our Artifact Systems, because of the presence of "the database-driven setting": transitions contain queries over the read-only DB, and queries are existential formulae that can retrieve "data" elements from the DB or the working memory through existentially quantified variables. As explained in the introduction and as it will be clear in the following, these variables need to be eliminated at every iteration of the main loop of the backward reachability procedure, since their presence would break the format of the allowed formulae, compromising correctness. The growth in the number of existentially quantified variables would also affect the performance of the backward search. This issue is solved by studying

A. Gianola: *Verification of Data-Aware Processes via Satisfiability Modulo Theories*,
LNBIP 470, pp. 69–96, 2023.
https://doi.org/10.1007/978-3-031-42746-6_4

a suitable machinery for eliminating these variables at each iteration of the main loop of the procedure. This is achieved by exploiting the model-theoretic notion of model completion for the DB theories used by Artifact Systems.

The chapter is organized as follows: in Section 4.1, we first state the model-theoretic properties for DB schemas that are needed in order to make our machinery work. Then, in Section 4.2 we define the safety problem for SASs and we provide BReach_{SAS}, i.e., our extended version of the SMT-based backward reachability procedure for verifying SASs: we also prove some useful meta-properties (e.g., correctness) of BReach_{SAS}. In Section 4.3 we introduce the safety problem for Universal RASs and plain RASs, and we describe BReach_{RAS}, i.e., our extended version of the SMT-based backward reachability procedure for verifying *plain* RASs. For both SASs and (Universal) RASs, we give examples of safety problems. We then show how BReach_{RAS} can be employed/adapted to (partially) verify Universal RASs as well (Section 4.4). In Section 4.5, we prove some interesting meta-properties (like correctness) of BReach_{RAS}. In Section 4.6, we provide examples of DB schemas for which the described machinery concretely works. Finally, we conclude by discussing two important topics emerging from this chapter: the use of quantifier elimination in model completions for model checking (Subsection 4.7.1) and the notion of freshness supported by Universal RASs and in other approaches (Subsection 4.7.2).

The technical content of this chapter is based on [55, 141].

4.1 Model-Theoretic Requirements of DB Schemas

The theory T from Definition 3.1 must satisfy few crucial model-theoretic requirements for our approach to work. In this section, we define such requirements: we will see at the end of chapter that, even if these requirements seem too abstract, they are matched in concrete and useful cases, e.g., when we are concerned with an acyclic signature Σ and with key dependencies, i.e., the setting presented in [186]). Actually, acyclicity is a stronger requirement than needed, which, however, simplifies our exposition.

4.1.1 Finite Model Property

We remark that a DB (extended)-theory T *as a first-order theory* has the *strong finite model property* (for constraint satisfiability) iff every constraint ϕ that is satisfiable in a model of T is satisfiable in a DB instance interpreting also the value sorts into finite sets. This assumption is usually *too strong*, especially for DB extended-schemas. That is why we introduce a slightly weaker version: a DB (extended)-theory T has the finite model property (for constraint satisfiability) iff every constraint ϕ is satisfiable in a (generic) DB instance (whose value sorts can be infinite sets). It can be easily seen that, in case of DB schemas, the strong finite model property is equivalent to the finite model property.

4.1.2 The Constraint Satisfiabilty Problem Is Decidable

We recall from the preliminaries that the constraint satisfiability problem for T is to establish whether, for an existential formula $\exists \underline{y}\, \phi(\underline{x}, \underline{y})$ (with ϕ a constraint) there exist a model $\mathcal{M}$ of T and an assignment α to the free variables $\underline{x}$ such that $\mathcal{M}, \alpha \models \exists \underline{y}\, \phi(\underline{x}, \underline{y})$. The finite model property implies decidability of the constraint satisfiability problem in case T is recursively axiomatized. Indeed, in this case it is possible to enumerate unsatisfiable constraints via a logical calculus and this enumeration can be interleaved with the enumeration of finite models, thus supplying a full decision procedure.

4.1.3 Model Completion of DB Theories

A DB theory T does not necessarily have quantifier elimination; however, it is often possible to strengthen T in a conservative way (with respect to constraint satisfiability) and get quantifier elimination (cf. Proposition 2.1). In order to do that, we require that the model completion T^* of T exists and effective algorithms for eliminating quantifiers in T^* are available. We will show in the next sections that model completions turn out to be successful to attack the verification of dynamic systems operating over relational databases.

4.1.4 Assumption for the Technical Machinery

Hereafter, we make the following assumption:

Assumption 4.1 The DB theories we consider have decidable constraint satisfiability problem, finite model property, and admit a model completion (for which an effective algorithm for quantifier elimination is available).

We disclose now (but we will discuss again on this at the end of the chapter, arguing why it is true) that this assumption is matched, for instance, in the following three cases: *(i)* when T is empty; *(ii)* when T is axiomatized by Axioms (3.1); *(iii)* when Σ is acyclic and T is axiomatized by universal one-variable formulae (such as Axioms (3.1)).

Hence, thanks in particular to case *(ii)*, the artifact-centric model in the style of [102, 186] (see Section 3.1.1 for recalling the requirements over the read-only database from their setting) that we intend to capture *matches* Assumption 4.1.

Moreover, in case we consider DB extended-schemas obtained by adding "free" relations to the DB schemas of *(i)*, *(ii)*, *(iii)* above, or by combining them with linear real arithmetic as T' (cf. Subsection 3.1.2), we still satisfy Assumption 4.1.

4.2 Parameterized Safety via Backward Reachability for SASs

An *unsafe* formula for a SAS S is a state formula $\upsilon(\underline{x})$ describing undesired states of S. By adopting a customary terminology for array-based systems, we say that S is *safe with respect to* υ if intuitively the system has no finite run leading from ι to υ. Formally, there is no DB-instance $\mathcal{M}$ of $\langle \Sigma, T \rangle$, no $k \geq 0$, and no assignment in $\mathcal{M}$ to the variables $\underline{x}^0, \ldots, \underline{x}^k$ such that the formula

$$\iota(\underline{x}^0) \wedge \tau(\underline{x}^0, \underline{x}^1) \wedge \cdots \wedge \tau(\underline{x}^{k-1}, \underline{x}^k) \wedge \upsilon(\underline{x}^k) \tag{4.1}$$

is true in $\mathcal{M}$ (here $\underline{x}^i$'s are renamed copies of $\underline{x}$). Formula (4.1) is sometimes called *symbolic unsafe trace*. The *safety problem* for S w.r.t. to υ is the following: *given an unsafe formula υ decide whether S is safe with respect to υ*. We sometimes call *safety problem* (S, υ) the safety problem for S w.r.t. to υ.

Example 4.2 We provide an example of an unsafe formula for Example 3.4. Consider the *unsafe* configuration where the process is enabled but the identifier of the registered user loaded into *uId* is undef. Formally, this can be represented by the following state formula:

$$pState = \texttt{enabled} \wedge uId = \texttt{undef}$$

Notice that the following formula

$$\exists y \, (pState = \texttt{enabled} \wedge y \neq \texttt{undef} \wedge uId = y)$$

is *not* an unsafe formula, because of the existential quantified data variable y, but it is equivalent to

$$pState = \texttt{enabled} \wedge uId \neq \texttt{undef}$$

which is an unsafe formula. We will see in Lemma 4.2 that this equivalence (in some sense) holds in the general case of RASs (which SASs are a specific case of).

Example 4.3 Referring to Example 3.5, an undesired situation of the system is the one where an applicant registered user is declared winner even if they were not 'suitable'. This situation is formally described by the following safety formula:

$$\upsilon = x_{\text{wnr}} \neq \texttt{undef} \wedge \neg Suitable(x_{\text{wnr}}).$$

Algorithm 1 shows the *modified/extended version of the SMT-based backward reachability procedure* BReach$_{SAS}$ (sometimes called *backward reachability* or *backward search* in the following when clear from the context) for handling the safety

---

Algorithm 1: BReach$_{SAS}$

Function BReach(v)

1    $\phi \longleftarrow v; B \longleftarrow \bot;$

2   **while** $\phi \wedge \neg B$ is T-satisfiable **do**

3   **if** $\iota \wedge \phi$ is T-satisfiable **then**

       $\lfloor$ **return** (UNSAFE, *unsafe trace* witness)

4      $B \longleftarrow \phi \vee B;$

5      $\phi \longleftarrow Pre(\tau, \phi);$

6      $\lfloor \phi \longleftarrow \mathsf{QE_{SAS}}(T^*, \phi);$

   $\lfloor$ **return** SAFE;

---

problem for a SAS S (the original version of the SMT-based backward reachability procedure can be found in [143, 146]). An integral part of the algorithm is to compute *symbolic* preimages (Line 5). The intuition behind the algorithm is to execute a loop (sometimes called *main loop* or *while loop* of the procedure) where, starting from the undesired states of the system (described by the unsafe formula $v(\underline{x})$), the state space of the system is explored *backward*: in every iteration of the while loop (Line 2), the current set of states is *regressed* through transitions thanks to the preimage computation. For that purpose, for any $\tau(\underline{z}, \underline{z}')$ and $\phi(\underline{z})$ (where $\underline{z}'$ are renamed copies of $\underline{z}$), we define $Pre(\tau, \phi)$ as the formula $\exists \underline{z}'(\tau(\underline{z}, \underline{z}') \wedge \phi(\underline{z}'))$. Let $\phi(\underline{x})$ be a state formula, describing the state of the artifact variables $\underline{x}$. The *preimage* of the set of states described by the formula $\phi(\underline{x})$ is the set of states described by $Pre(\tau, \phi)$ (notice that, when $\tau = \bigvee_i \mathrm{tr}_i$, then $Pre(\tau, \phi) = \bigvee_i Pre(\mathrm{tr}_i, \phi))$. We recall that a state formula for a SAS is a quantifier-free Σ-formula (cf. Chapter 3). Unfortunately, because of the presence of the existentially quantified variables $\underline{y}$ in τ, $Pre(\tau, \phi)$ is *not* a state formula, in general. If the quantified variables were not *eliminated*, we would break the *regressability* of the procedure: indeed, the states reached by computing preimages, intuitively described by $Pre(\tau, \phi)$, need to be represented by a state formula ϕ' in the new iteration of the while loop. In addition, the increase of the number of variables due to the iteration of the preimage computation would affect the performance of the satisfiability tests described below, in case the loop is executed many times. In order to solve these issues, it is essential to introduce the subprocedure $\mathsf{QE_{SAS}}(T^*, \phi)$ in Line 6.

The main modification of the original SMT-based backward reachability procedure lies exactly in the new subprocedure $\mathsf{QE_{SAS}}(T^*, \phi)$ in Line 6 for computing quantifier elimination in the model completion T^*.

$\mathsf{QE_{SAS}}(T^*, \phi)$ in Line 6 is a subprocedure that implements the quantifier elimination algorithm of T^* and that converts the preimage $Pre(\tau, \phi)$ of a state formula ϕ into a state formula (equivalent to it modulo the axioms of T^*), so as to guarantee the regressability of the procedure: this conversion is possible since T^* eliminates from tr the existentially quantified variables $\underline{y}$. Backward search computes iterated preimages of the unsafe formula v, until a fixpoint is reached (in that case, the SAS S is *safe* w.r.t. v) or until a set intersecting the initial states (i.e., satisfying ι) is found (in that case, the SAS S is *unsafe* w.r.t. v). *Inclusion* (Line 2) and *disjointness*

(Line 3) tests can be discharged via proof obligations to be handled by SMT solvers. The fixpoint is reached when the test in Line 2 returns *unsat*: the preimage of the set of the current states is included in the set of states reached by the backward search so far (represented as the iterated application of preimages to the unsafe formula υ). The test at Line 3 is satisfiable when the states visited so far by the backward search includes a possible initial state (i.e., a state satisfying ι). If this is the case, then S is unsafe w.r.t. υ. Together with the unsafe outcome, the algorithm also returns an unsafe trace of the form (4.1), explicitly witnessing the sequence of transitions tr_i that, starting from the initial configurations, lead the system to a set of states satisfying the undesired conditions described by $\upsilon(\underline{x})$.

The procedure either does not terminate or returns a SAFE/UNSAFE result.

Given a SAS S and an unsafe formula υ, a SAFE (resp. UNSAFE) result is *correct* iff S is safe (resp. unsafe) w.r.t. υ.

We define some meta-properties for SASs.

Definition 4.1 Given a SAS S and an unsafe formula υ, a verification procedure for checking unsafety of S w.r.t. υ is: *(i) sound* if, when it terminates, it returns a correct result; *(ii) complete* if, whenever UNSAFE is the correct result, then UNSAFE is indeed returned.

Remark 4.1 The nomenclature used in the previous definition is non-standard in the verification literature, but we prefer to use it because, for the purpose of this work, it makes the presentation of the main results clearer and consistent.

In the following, *effectiveness* means that all subprocedures in the algorithm can be effectively executed.

We state now the main result of this section:

Theorem 4.1 *Let $\langle \Sigma, T \rangle$ be a DB schema. Then, for every SAS $S = \langle \Sigma, T, \underline{x}, \iota, \tau \rangle$, backward search BReach_{SAS} is effective and sound for checking unsafety of S wrt an unsafe formula υ.*

Proof First of all, we show that, instead of considering satisfiability of formulae of the form (4.1) in models of T, we can concentrate on T^*-satisfiability. We recall formula (4.1):

$$\iota(\underline{x}^0) \wedge \tau(\underline{x}^0, \underline{x}^1) \wedge \cdots \wedge \tau(\underline{x}^{k-1}, \underline{x}^k) \wedge \upsilon(\underline{x}^k) \ .$$

By definition, S is unsafe iff for some k, the formula (4.1) is satisfiable in a DB-instance of $\langle \Sigma, T \rangle$. Thanks to Assumption 4.1, T has the finite model property and consequently, as (4.1) is an existential Σ-formula, S is unsafe iff for some k, formula (4.1) is satisfiable in a model of T; furthermore, again by Assumption 4.1, T admits a model completion T^*. Hence, since the formulae of the form (4.1) are existential Σ-formulae, and by using the property that every model of a theory T embeds into a model of its model completion T^*, we conclude that S is unsafe iff for some k, formula (4.1) is satisfiable in a model of T^*. Thus, for establishing (un)safety of S, we can concentrate on satisfiability of formulae of the form (4.1) in models of T^*.

Now, we want to show the correctness of the results returned by Algorithm 1, i.e. that backward search is *sound*.

First, we preliminarily give some useful remarks on the algorithm. Let us call B_n (resp. ϕ_n), with $n \geq 0$, the status of the variable B (resp. ϕ) after n executions in Line 4 (resp. Line 6) of Algorithm 1 ($n = 0$ corresponds to the status of the variables in Line 1). We have that

$$T^* \models \phi_{j+1} \leftrightarrow Pre(\tau, \phi_j) \tag{4.2}$$

for all j and that

$$T \models B_n \leftrightarrow \bigvee_{0 \leq j < n} \phi_j \tag{4.3}$$

is an invariant of the algorithm.

We now show that if the procedure returns an UNSAFE outcome, this outcome is correct, i.e., S is really unsafe. Since we are considering satisfiability in models of T^*, we can apply quantifier elimination of T^*: it can be easily seen that the satisfiability of the quantifier-free formula we get in this way is equivalent to the satisfiability of $\iota \wedge \phi_n$: clearly, this is again a quantifier-free formula (because of Line 6 of Algorithm 1). Since T-satisfiability and T^*-satisfiability are equivalent (by definition of model completion) when dealing with existential (and in particular, quantifier-free) formulae, the T-satisfiability of $\iota \wedge \phi_n$ is decidable thanks to Assumption 4.1. Hence, if Algorithm 1 terminates with an UNSAFE outcome, then there exists a formula of the form (4.1) that is T^*-satisfiable. This exactly means that S is unsafe, as wanted.

We now show that if the algorithm returns a SAFE outcome, this outcome is correct, i.e., S is really safe.

Now consider the satisfiability test in Line 2. This is again a satisfiability test for a quantifier-free formula, thus it is decidable. In case of a SAFE outcome, we have that $T \models \phi_n \to B_n$; we claim that, if we continued executing the loop of Algorithm 1, we would nevertheless get that:

$$T^* \models B_m \leftrightarrow B_n \tag{4.4}$$

for all $m \geq n$. We justify Claim (4.4) below.

From $T \models \phi_n \to B_n$, taking into consideration that $T^* \supseteq T$ and that Formula (4.2) holds, we get $T^* \models \phi_{n+1} \to Pre(\tau, B_n)$. Since Pre commutes with disjunctions (i.e., $Pre(\tau, \bigvee_j \phi_j)$ is logically equivalent to $\bigvee_j Pre(\tau, \phi_j)$), we also have $T^* \models Pre(\tau, B_n) \leftrightarrow \bigvee_{1 \leq j \leq n} \phi_j$ by the Invariant (4.3) and by Formula (4.2) again. By using the entailment $T \models \phi_n \to B_n$ once more, we get $T^* \models \phi_{n+1} \to B_n$ and also that $T^* \models B_{n+1} \leftrightarrow B_n$, thus we finally obtain that $T^* \models \phi_{n+1} \to B_{n+1}$. Since $\phi_{n+1} \to B_{n+1}$ is quantifier-free, $T^* \models \phi_{n+1} \to B_{n+1}$ implies $T \models \phi_{n+1} \to B_{n+1}$. This argument can be repeated for all $m \geq n$, obtaining that $T^* \models B_m \leftrightarrow B_n$ for all $m \geq n$, i.e. Claim (4.4).

This would entail that $\iota \wedge \phi_m$ is always unsatisfiable (because of (4.3) and because $\iota \wedge \phi_j$ was unsatisfiable for all $j < n$), which is the same (as remarked above) as saying that all formulae (4.1) are unsatisfiable. Thus S is safe.

Remark 4.2 The main idea behind the proof of the previous theorem is that existential formulae are satisfiable in a model of T iff so are they in a model of T^* (which is *existentially closed*): in T^*, quantifier elimination is available. Thus, if an unsafe trace exists, it can be lifted to a model of T^*, so that the subprocedure $\mathsf{QE}_{SAS}(T^*, \phi)$ in Line 6 does not introduce over-approximations and consequently no spurious trace can be produced during the search performed by the procedure.

Backward search for SASs is not guaranteed to terminate. Indeed, the proof of Theorem 4.1 does not provide a termination argument in general. This is typical of generic array-based systems: in general, backward search is not guaranteed to terminate [146]. However, in case S is *unsafe* w.r.t. $\upsilon(\underline{x})$, an unsafe trace—which is finite—is found after finitely many iterations of the while loop: hence, in the unsafe case, backward search must terminate. Together with the theorem above, this means that the backward reachability procedure is at least a semi-decision procedure for detecting unsafety of SASs. In fact, we have the following corollary:

Corollary 4.1 BReach$_{SAS}$ *(Algorithm 1) is effective, sound and complete for checking unsafety of the SAS S w.r.t. $\upsilon(\underline{x})$.*

This corollary shows that backward search is a semi-decision procedure: if the system is unsafe, backward search always terminates and discovers it; if the system is safe, the procedure can diverge (but it is still correct). We will see in the next chapter that when an additional condition on the DB signature Σ is imposed (i.e., acyclicity), backward search is guaranteed to terminate and becomes a full decision procedure, for which we will also provide a complexity upper bound.

Remark 4.3 We remark that Theorem 4.1 holds also for DB extended-schemas (for example, adding "free relations" to the DB signatures). Moreover, notice that it can be shown that every existential formula $\varphi(\underline{x}, \underline{x}')$ can be turned into the form of Formula (3.4). We underline that the proof of Theorem 4.1 requires that the considered background theory T: *(i)* admits a model completion; *(ii)* is universal; and *(iii)* enjoys decidability of constraint satisfiability. Conditions *(ii)* and *(iii)* imply that one can decide whether a finite structure is a model of T. If *(ii)* holds, it is well-known that *(i)* implies amalgamation [66]. Notice also that *(ii)* is equivalent to the fact that T is closed under substructures (this is a standard preservation theorem in model theory [66]).

In our first-order setting, we can perform verification in a *purely symbolic* way, by using (semi-)decision procedures provided by SMT solvers, even when local finiteness fails. As mentioned before, local finiteness is guaranteed in the relational context, but it does not hold anymore when *arithmetic operations* are introduced. Note that the theory of a single uninterpreted binary relation (i.e., the theory of directed graphs) has a model completion, whereas it can be easily seen that the theory of one binary relation which is a partial function *does not* (since it is *not* amalgamable). If primary key dependencies are formalized using partial functions, model completability is compromized. So, the second distinctive feature of our setting naturally follows from this observation: thanks to our *many-sorted functional representation* of DB schemas (with keys), the amalgamation property, required by Theorem 4.1, holds, witnessing that our framework remains well-behaved even in the presence of key dependencies.

4.3 Parameterized Safety via Backward Reachability for U-RASs and RASs

As for SAS, an *unsafe* formula for a U-RAS S is a state formula $\upsilon(\underline{x}, \underline{a})$. We say that S is *safe with respect to* υ if there is no DB-instance M of $\langle \Sigma_{ext}, T \rangle$, no $k \geq 0$, and no assignment in M to the variables $\underline{x}^0, \underline{a}^0 \dots, \underline{x}^k, \underline{a}^k$ such that the formula

$$\iota(\underline{x}^0, \underline{a}^0) \wedge \tau(\underline{x}^0, \underline{a}^0, \underline{x}^1, \underline{a}^1)$$
$$\wedge \cdots \wedge \tau(\underline{x}^{k-1}, \underline{a}^{k-1}, \underline{x}^k, \underline{a}^k) \wedge \upsilon(\underline{x}^k, \underline{a}^k) \tag{4.5}$$

is true in M (here $\underline{x}^i, \underline{a}^i$ are renamed copies of $\underline{x}, \underline{a}$). Formula (4.5) is sometimes called *symbolic unsafe trace*. The safety problem is defined as for SAS.

Example 4.4 We consider an undesired configuration for the RAS from Example 3.6 that checks whether, after having received the evaluation notification, there are no applicants left without winner or loser status being assigned. Formally, this is encoded by the following unsafe formula:

$$\exists i\text{:appIndex}$$
$$\begin{pmatrix} pState = \texttt{notified} \wedge applicant[i] \neq \textsf{undef} \\ \wedge appResult[i] \neq \texttt{winner} \wedge appResult[i] \neq \texttt{loser} \end{pmatrix}$$

The job hiring RAS S_{hr} turns out to be safe with respect to this property (cf. Section 9.5).

Example 4.5 The following formula describes an undesired property for the U-RAS from Example 3.7, checking whether the evaluation notification goes to an applicant who was rejected:

$$\exists i\text{:appIndex}$$
$$\begin{pmatrix} applicant[i] \neq \textsf{undef} \wedge toNotify = applicant[i] \\ \wedge visaStat = \texttt{rejected} \wedge pState = \texttt{notified} \end{pmatrix}$$

We now discuss how to automatically verify (un)safety of U-RASs and RASs. We will use again a suitable SMT-based version of backward search. Unfortunately, we will discuss that this version can be proved to be fully sound only for RASs: for U-RASs we will need either to preprocess them by transforming them into plain RASs, or to suitably modify the procedure by introducing an approximation module. The consequence in both cases is that backward search can be still used to verify (un)safety of U-RASs, but only the SAFE outcome is guaranteed to be always correct.

Algorithm 2: BReach$_{RAS}$

Function BReach(v)

1      $\phi \longleftarrow v; B \longleftarrow \bot$;

2   **while** $\phi \wedge \neg B$ *is T-satisfiable* **do**

3   **if** $\iota \wedge \phi$ *is T-satisfiable* **then**
            $\llcorner$ **return** (UNSAFE, *unsafe trace* witness)

4          $B \longleftarrow \phi \vee B$;

5          $\phi \longleftarrow Pre(\tau, \phi)$;

6          $\phi \longleftarrow$ QE$_{RAS}(T^*, \phi)$;

     $\llcorner$ **return** SAFE;

Since for both RASs and U-RASs we employ backward search, we now present the procedure.

The interesting point is that, as already remarked, we can still run a modified version of the SMT-based backward search for handling safety problems in RASs, and for partially handling safety problems in U-RASs as well. We call this version for RASs BReach$_{RAS}$ (Algorithm 2). In fact, Algorithm 2 presents the same structure as Algorithm 1. Notice that in this case the definition of $Pre(\tau, \phi)$ gives us $\exists \underline{x}' \exists \underline{a}' (\tau(\underline{x}, \underline{a}, \underline{x}', \underline{a}') \wedge \phi(\underline{x}', \underline{a}'))$. The subprocedure QE$_{RAS}(T^*, \phi)$ mentioned in Line 6 is extended so as to convert the preimage $Pre(\tau, \phi)$ of a state formula ϕ into a state formula (equivalent to it modulo the axioms of T^*), witnessing its *regressability*: this is possible since T^* eliminates from primitive formulae the existentially quantified variables over the basic sorts, whereas elimination of quantified variables over artifact sorts is not possible, because these variables occur as arguments of artifact components (see Lemma 4.1 and Lemma 4.2 below for details). In addition, the satisfiability tests from Lines 2–3 can still be discharged (in fact, we prove in Lemma 4.3 below that the entailment between state formulae can be decided via instantiation techniques).

Similarly to the case of BReach$_{SAS}$, the procedure BReach$_{RAS}$ either does not terminate or returns a SAFE/UNSAFE result.

Given a U-RAS S and an unsafe formula v, a SAFE (resp. UNSAFE) result is *correct* iff S is safe (resp. unsafe) w.r.t. v. We define some meta-properties for U-RASs, similarly to what done for SASs.

Definition 4.2 Given a U-RAS S and an unsafe formula v, a verification procedure for checking unsafety of S w.r.t. v is: *(i) sound* if, when it terminates, it returns a correct result; *(ii) partially sound* if a SAFE result is always correct; *(iii) complete* if, whenever UNSAFE is the correct result, then UNSAFE is indeed returned.

Again, *effectiveness* means that all subprocedures in the algorithm can be effectively executed.

The following theorem is about the most general model of U-RASs, and states that BReach$_{RAS}$ can be used only partially to check unsafety of U-RASs.

Theorem 4.2 BReach$_{RAS}$ *is partially sound for checking unsafety of an Universal RAS S w.r.t. an unsafe formula v.*

The previous theorem implies that:

- When BReach$_{RAS}$ returns a SAFE outcome, then Universal RAS S is safe w.r.t. the unsafe formula υ.
- When BReach$_{RAS}$ returns a UNSAFE, nothing can be deduced since it could be the case that the found unsafe trace is *spurious*, so it is still possible that S is safe w.r.t. υ. If the outcome is UNSAFE, it is in principle possible to test whether the unsafe trace returned by the procedure as a formula is spurious or not: we will comment on this in Subsection 4.4.2.

In analogy to Theorem 4.1, we obtain for plain RASs the following theorem:

Theorem 4.3 *Let $\langle \Sigma, T \rangle$ be a DB schema. Then, for every RAS $S = \langle \Sigma, T, \Sigma_{ext}, \underline{x}, \underline{a}, \iota, \tau \rangle$, backward search BReach$_{RAS}$ (cf. Algorithm 2) is effective and sound for checking unsafety of S wrt an unsafe formula υ.*

The proof of Theorem 4.3 is the content of Section 4.5.

In the following, we sketch the main ideas for proving Theorem 4.2: full details can be found in Chapter 4 of [154]. The proof of the theorem consists of two parts:

1. first, one can show a syntactic transformation from U-RASs to RASs and prove that if the transformed RAS is safe wrt an unsafe formula υ, then the original U-RAS is safe wrt υ as well (in the transformed RAS there can be *more unsafe traces* than in the original U-RAS, but not less).
2. second, we conclude by using soundness of BReach$_{RAS}$ for checking safety of RASs (Theorem 4.3).

The first part of the proof will be discussed in Subsection 4.4.1.

There is an alternative method to attack verification of U-RASs, which consists of suitably modifying backward search so as to handle the universal quantifiers in universal guards. This modification is achieved by adding an approximate module that *dynamically* instantiates the universally quantified variables. This second method is briefly discussed in Subsection 4.4.2.

Similarly to SASs, backward search for RASs is not guaranteed to terminate. Indeed, the proof of Theorem 4.3 does not provide a termination argument in general. However, in case the RAS S is *unsafe* w.r.t. υ, an unsafe trace—which is finite—is found after finitely many iterations of the while loop: hence, in the unsafe case, backward search must terminate. Since in the transformation from U-RASs to RASs unsafe traces are preserved, the previous arguments holds also for U-RASs. Together with Theorem 4.3, this means that the backward reachability procedure is at least a semi-decision procedure for detecting unsafety of RASs. We will provide some termination results for BReach$_{RAS}$ in the next chapter.

We summarize all the results of this section in the following corollary:

Corollary 4.2 BReach$_{RAS}$ *(Algorithm 2) is effective, sound and complete for checking unsafety of any RAS S w.r.t. any unsafe formula υ, and is effective, partially sound and complete for checking unsafety of any U-RAS S' w.r.t. any unsafe formula υ'.*

4.4 Handling U-RASs via SMT-based Backward Reachability

In this section, we discuss two alternative ways for (partially) verifying safety of U-RASs. In order to do so, we provide two different procedures that can be shown to be partially sound and complete for the safety verification of U-RASs.

The first procedure relies on the elimination of the universal quantifiers in advance, by preprocessing the given U-RASs: this is obtained by introducing a syntactic transformation from U-RASs to plain RASs. This transformation is an approximation in the sense that the obtained systems admit *more* runs than the original one. After this step, one can apply BReach_{RAS} to the obtained system.

The second procedure consists of enriching the SMT-based version of backward search for RASs with *dynamic* forms of instantiation to handle the universal quantifiers. However, the instantiation module needs to be suitably combined with T^*-quantifier elimination module: indeed, when trying to prove the correctness of the procedure, one can note that these two modules may appear to interfere with each other. Nevertheless, it is possible to show that they interact harmlessly [141, 140]. The integration of these two modules results in an over-approximation of the symbolic computation of unsafe states, which could cause the resulting procedure, also in this case, to detect unsafety spuriously.

4.4.1 Eliminating Universal Quantifiers from U-RASs

In general, it is difficult to automate BReach for proper Universal RASs, i.e., when the transition formulae tr contain a universal guard γ_u (cf. Formula (3.7)). The main problem is that, in order to symbolically execute Formula (3.7), we need to check whether the the universal guards γ_u in τ holds for all the entries of an artifact relation (i.e. a finite but unknown number of tuples) rather than on a bounded number as it is the case for the (plain) guard γ. To solve this problem, the key idea is to design a syntactic transformation of the Universal RAS so as to obtain a sufficiently precise *abstraction* that preserves the safety properties. The abstraction is inspired by an analogous transformation introduced in [17], where this transformation is interpreted in a semantic way. In fact, in the context of [17], indexes $\underline{e}$ are not interpreted as entries of artifact relations as we do here, but as (identifiers of) processes. When dealing with real processes that should follow a protocol, it is usually legitimate to adopt the following *(stopping) failure model*: *processes can crash and crashed processes are not permitted to take an active role in the protocol*. In [17] it is proved that, when this model is adopted, (modulo bisimulation) universally guarded transitions can be replaced by transitions not containing universal quantifiers. Intuitively, this is possible since in the abstracted system the processes not satisfying the universal guards are interpreted as crashed: from the moment they crash, they stop being considered in the current run.

In order to verify Universal RASs, we take inspiration from the results proved in [17]. Although it is not clear how to import the semantical interpretation of crashing processes into our framework, it is still useful to introduce an analogous syntactic transformation for Universal RASs into (plain) RASs. This allows us to perform the safety verification on universal RASs via the backward reachability procedure bypassing the formal issues due to universal guards. We point out that the RAS obtained by this transformation is a more liberal array-based system, i.e., it has more runs than the original system. As a consequence, if a set of bad states represented by the unsafe formula v is shown to be unreachable for the abstracted system, then it will also be unreachable for the original system.

Let S be a Universal RAS as in Section 3.2.2, and v an unsafe formula describing a set of unsafe states.

The syntactic transformation is split into two different maps, namely $(\tilde{\cdot})$ and $(\hat{\cdot})$, defined on safety problems, i.e., pairs of a system and an unsafe formula.

The first map $(\tilde{\cdot})$ *introduces "failures" for some indexes* and transforms a Universal RAS (S, v) into what we call an *intermediate Universal RAS* $(\tilde{S}, \tilde{v})$. The last model is an instance of Universal RASs, since it still contains universal guards. The second map $(\hat{\cdot})$ *removes the universal guards by instantiating in a finite way the universal quantified variables*, and transforms $(\tilde{S}, \tilde{v})$ to a (plain) RAS $(\widehat{S}, \widehat{v})$. The last is a plain RAS since it does not contain universally quantified guards anymore.

The two maps are formally shown and explained in detail in Chapter 4 of [154], where all the proofs of the propositions below are also provided.

We recall that when the answer to a safety problem (S, v) is safe (unsafe), we say that *S is safe (unsafe, respectively) with respect to v*.

The first proposition states that if $\tilde{S}$ is safe w.r.t. $\tilde{v}$, then also S is safe w.r.t. v.

Proposition 4.1 *If $\tilde{S}$ is safe with respect to $\tilde{v}$, then S is safe with respect to v.*

This is a consequence of the fact that $\tilde{S}$ is an abstraction of S and contains more unsafe traces. Traces in intermediate Universal RASs $\tilde{S}$ that lead to bad states and that cannot be interpreted as legitimate runs in S are called *spurious traces*. Safety of the intermediate RAS $\tilde{S}$ implies safety of the original Universal RAS S. The contrary is false for arbitrary Universal RASs, because of the presence of spurious unsafe traces in intermediate Universal RASs.

The following proposition states that the safety problems for $\tilde{S}$ and $\widehat{S}$ are equivalent, i.e., that the safety problems $(\tilde{S}, \tilde{v})$ and $(\widehat{S}, \widehat{v})$ have the same answer.

Proposition 4.2 *Let $S = \langle \Sigma, T, \Sigma_{ext}, \underline{x}, \underline{a}, \iota, \tau \rangle$ be a Universal RAS and (S, v) be a safety problem for it. Then, $\tilde{S}$ is safe with respect to $\tilde{v}$ iff $\widehat{S}$ is safe with respect to $\widehat{v}$.*

Thus, traces in the RAS $\widehat{S}$ that lead to bad states that cannot be interpreted as legitimate runs in the original Universal RAS S are also called *spurious traces*.

We are now ready to state the main result about the transformation from Universal RASs to RASs, which is a consequence of Proposition 4.2 and Proposition 4.1:

Proposition 4.3 *Let $S = \langle \Sigma, T, \Sigma_{ext}, \underline{x}, \underline{a}, \iota, \tau \rangle$ be a Universal RAS and v be an unsafe formula. Then, if the (plain) RAS $\widehat{S}$ is safe with respect to $\widehat{v}$, then S is safe with respect to v.*

Algorithm 3: ApproxBReach$_{U-RAS}$

Input U-RAS $\langle\langle\Sigma, T\rangle, \Sigma_{ext}, \underline{x}, \underline{a}, \iota(\underline{x}, \underline{a}), \tau(\underline{x}, \underline{a}, \underline{x}', \underline{a}')\rangle$
(Unsafe) state formula $\upsilon(\underline{x}, \underline{a})$ **Function** BReach(υ)

1   $\quad P \longleftarrow \upsilon; \tilde{B} \longleftarrow \perp;$

2   $\quad$ **while** $P \wedge \neg\tilde{B}$ *is* T-*satisfiable* **do**

3   $\quad\quad$ **if** $\iota \wedge P$ *is* T-*satisfiable* **then**
    $\quad\quad\quad \lfloor$ **return** (UNSAFE, *unsafe trace* witness)

4   $\quad\quad \tilde{B} \longleftarrow P \vee \tilde{B};$

5   $\quad\quad P \longleftarrow InstPre(\tau, P);$

6   $\quad\quad P \longleftarrow$ QE$_{\mathsf{RAS}}(T^*, \phi);$

$\quad \lfloor$ **return** (SAFE, $\tilde{B}$);

The previous proposition is significant because it partially reduces the problem of assessing safety for Universal RASs to the one of assessing safety for plain RASs. Unfortunately, this reduction is partial because when the plain RAS $\widehat{S}$ is unsafe w.r.t. $\widehat{\upsilon}$, nothing can be established for the original Universal RAS S. If we are able to show that BReach$_{RAS}$ is sound for checking unsafety of RASs, then we conclude, thanks to the previous observations, that we can still run BReach$_{RAS}$ over $(\widehat{S}, \widehat{\upsilon})$, with S Universal RAS: in case we find out that the output is SAFE, we can conclude safety of S w.r.t. υ as well.

4.4.2 Modified SMT-based Backward Search for U-RASs

We now briefly discuss the alternative method for (partially) attacking safety verification of U-RASs. This method builds on top of the analogous algorithmic approximation techniques introduced in [141] for the verification of RABs, a restricted version of U-RASs that significantly extend RASs.

Algorithm 3 introduces the ApproxBReach$_{U-RAS}$ procedure for safety verification of U-RASs, which extends BReach$_{U-RAS}$ to handle the advanced features of U-RASs. ApproxBReach$_{U-RAS}$ takes as input a U-RAS S and an unsafe formula υ. Analogously to BReach$_{U-RAS}$, the main loop starts from the undesired states of the system (represented by υ), and explores *backwards* the state space by iteratively computing, symbolically, the set of states that can reach the undesired ones. Due to the presence of universal guards, however, τ can be reversed only in an approximated way. The computation of symbolic, approximated preimages is handled in Lines 5 and 6.

Let $\psi(\underline{x}, \underline{a})$ be a state formula describing the state of variables $\underline{x}, \underline{a}$. The *exact preimage* of the set of states captured by $\psi(\underline{x}, \underline{a})$ is the set of states captured by $Pre(\tau, \psi)$ This is the exact set of states that, by executing τ once, reaches the set of states described by ψ. The main issue we get in doing so is that a state formula is an existentially quantified Σ-formula over artifact sorts only. While ψ is a state formula, Pre is not, making it impossible to reiterate the preimage computation. This is due to universally quantified variable k of artifact sort and existentially quantified 'data' variables (of basic sort) $\underline{d}$ in τ. To attack this problem, we introduce in Lines 5 and 6 of $\mathsf{ApproxBReach}_{U-RAS}$ two modules guaranteeing that the preimage is a proper state formula and that we use preimage computation to *regress* undesired states arbitrarily many times.

The first approximation module (Line 5) compiles away the universal quantifier ranging over the index k through *instantiation*, by invoking $InstPre(\tau, \psi)$. Given $\tau := \bigvee_{r=1}^{p} \mathrm{tr}_r$, let $\forall k \; \gamma_u^r(k, \underline{e}, \underline{d}, \underline{x}, \underline{a})$ be the universal guard of tr_r for all $r = 1, \ldots, p$. $InstPre(\tau, \psi)$ approximates Pre by instantiating the universally quantified 'index' variable k with the existential 'index' variables appearing in $Pre(\mathrm{tr}_r, \psi)$, for all $r = 1, \ldots, p$. Formally, given $\psi := \exists \underline{e}_1 \varphi_1(\underline{e}_1, \underline{x}, \underline{a})$, $InstPre(\mathrm{tr}_r, \psi)$ is the formula obtained from

$$\exists \underline{x}', \underline{a}', \underline{e}, \underline{e}_1, \underline{d} \left(\begin{pmatrix} \gamma(\underline{e}, \underline{d}, \underline{x}, \underline{a}) \\ \wedge \bigwedge_{k \in \underline{e} \cup \underline{e}_1} \gamma_u^r(k, \underline{e}, \underline{d}, \underline{x}, \underline{a}) \\ \wedge \bigwedge_i x_i' = F_i(\underline{e}, \underline{d}, \underline{x}, \underline{a}) \\ \wedge \bigwedge_j a_j' = \lambda y. G_j(y, \underline{e}, \underline{d}, \underline{x}, \underline{a}) \end{pmatrix} \wedge \varphi_1(\underline{e}_1, \underline{x}', \underline{a}') \right)$$

by making the appropriate substitutions (followed by beta-reduction) in order to eliminate the existentially quantified variables $\underline{x}'$ and $\underline{a}'$ (see, e.g., [55] for details). The second module (Line 6) takes the so-computed result $InstPre(\tau, \psi) \equiv \exists \underline{e}_2, \underline{d} \; \varphi_2$, and compiles away the existentially quantified data variables $\underline{d}$ by invoking the QE algorithm in the model completion T^* given by $\mathsf{QE}_{RAS}(T^*, \phi)$, in complete analogy to what done in BReach_{U-RAS} to handle existentially quantified variables of basic sorts.

Both modules return formulae that are T-implied by the formula returned by the exact preimage operator, which means that two modules perform an *over-approximation* of the exact preimage.

Together, Lines 5 and 6 produce proper state formula ψ' that can be fed into another approximate preimage computation step. In fact, $\mathsf{ApproxBReach}_{U-RAS}$ iteratively computes such preimages starting from the unsafe formula υ, until one of two possible termination conditions holds: either a *fixpoint* is obtained, i.e., the set of current unsafe states is included in the set of states reached so far by the search and S is *safe* w.r.t. υ, or the initial states are intersected. In the last case, $\mathsf{ApproxBReach}_{U-RAS}$ stops returning that S is *unsafe* w.r.t. υ, together with a symbolic unsafe trace of the form (4.5). Such a trace provides a sequence of transitions tr_i that, starting from the initial configurations, witness how S can evolve from an initial state in ι, under some instance of its DB, to a state satisfying υ.

Being preimages computed in an over-approximated way, unsafety may be spuriously returned, together with an unsafe spurious trace that cannot be produced by a given U-RAS. Hence, also applying this second method we get the same conclusion as the one that we got in Subsection 4.4.1.

Analogously to what shown in [141], the following theorem holds:

Theorem 4.4 ApproxBReach$_{U-RAS}$ *is* effective, partially sound *and* complete *when verifying unsafety of U-RASs.*

Notice that, in case the U-RAS S does not contain any universal guards, ApproxBReach$_{U-RAS}$ coincides exactly with BReach$_{RAS}$.

If the outcome is unsafe, we already commented that the procedure returns a witness that reconstructs the unsafe trace as a formula, and with this formula one can test whether the trace is spurious or not. This feature can be tested via SMT solvers off-the-shelf [141]. In particular, trace formulae belong to the $\exists^*\forall^*$ (EPR) fragment of FOL, for which the Z3 solver [96] has a dedicated decision procedure. The complexity is the one of satisfiability checking in the EPR fragment, which is NEXPTIME-complete.

As a side remark, we notice (but it is out of scope of this book) that in [141] it is proved that when a *universal invariant* for S w.r.t. the unsafe formula υ exists, backward search cannot terminate with an UNSAFE outcome, so in this case no spurious trace can be found. This key result requires to prove, using model theory, that the subroutine QE$_{RAS}(T^*, \phi)$ and the approximation technique given by instantiation do not interfere with each other, but combine well. Notably, this invariance result is analogous, in spirit, to that in [175], but substantially differs from the technical point of view: it holds for a different verification procedure and covers the whole expressiveness of RABs, out of reach so far.

The following section is devoted to attack the problem of verifying safety of plain RASs via BReach$_{RAS}$ and showing that this procedure is sound for checking safety of BReach$_{RAS}$.

4.5 Effectiveness and Soundness for BReach$_{RAS}$

In this section, we prove effectiveness and soundness of BReach$_{RAS}$. Before doing that, we recall some notations.

When introducing our transition formulae in (3.4), (3.7) we made use of definable extensions and also of some function definitions via λ-abstraction. We already observed that such uses are due to notational convenience and do not really go beyond first-order logic. We are clarifying one more point now, before going into formal proofs. The lambda-abstraction definitions in (3.7) will make the proof of Lemma 4.1 below smooth. Recall that an expression like

$$b = \lambda y.F(y, \underline{z})$$

can be seen as a mere abbreviation of $\forall y\; b(y) = F(y, \underline{z})$. However, the use of such abbreviation makes clear that e.g. a formula like

$$\exists b\; (b = \lambda y.F(y, \underline{z}) \wedge \phi(\underline{z}, b))$$

is equivalent to

$$\phi(\underline{z}, \lambda y.F(y, \underline{z})/b) \ . \tag{4.6}$$

Since our $\phi(\underline{z}, b)$ is in fact a first-order formula, our b can occur in it only in terms like $b(t)$, so that in (4.6) all occurrences of λ can be eliminated by the so-called β-conversion: replace $\lambda y F(y, \underline{z})(t)$ by $F(t, \underline{z})$. Thus, in the end, whether we use definable extensions or definitions via lambda abstractions, *the formulae we manipulate can always be converted into plain first-order Σ- or Σ_{ext}-formulae.*

Let us call *extended state formulae* the formulae of the kind $\exists \underline{e} \ \phi(\underline{e}, \underline{x}, \underline{a})$, where ϕ is quantifier-free and the $\underline{e}$ are individual variables of both artifact and basic sorts.

Lemma 4.1 *The preimage of an extended state formula is logically equivalent to an extended state formula.*

Proof We manipulate the formula

$$\exists \underline{x}' \ \exists \underline{a}' \ (\tau(\underline{x}, \underline{a}, \underline{x}', \underline{a}') \wedge \exists \underline{e} \ \phi(\underline{e}, \underline{x}', \underline{a}')) \tag{4.7}$$

up to logical equivalence, where τ is given by[1]

$$\exists \underline{e}_0 \ (\gamma(\underline{e}_0, \underline{x}, \underline{a}) \wedge \underline{x}' = \underline{F}(\underline{e}_0, \underline{x}, \underline{a}) \wedge \underline{a}' = \lambda y.\underline{G}(y, \underline{e}_0, \underline{x}, \underline{a})) \tag{4.8}$$

(here we used plain equality for conjunctions of equalities, e.g. $\underline{x}' = \underline{F}(\underline{e}_0, \underline{x}, \underline{a})$ stands for $\bigwedge_i x_i' = F_i(\underline{e}, \underline{x}, \underline{a})$). Repeated substitutions show that (4.7) is equivalent to

$$\exists \underline{e} \ \exists \underline{e}_0 \ (\gamma(\underline{e}_0, \underline{x}, \underline{a}) \wedge \phi(\underline{e}, \underline{F}(\underline{e}_0, \underline{x}, \underline{a})/\underline{x}', \lambda y.\underline{G}(y, \underline{e}_0, \underline{x}, \underline{a})/\underline{a}')) \tag{4.9}$$

which is an extended state formula. $\qquad \square$

Lemma 4.2 *For every extended state formula there is a state formula equivalent to it in all Σ_{ext}-models of T^*.*

Proof Let $\exists \underline{e} \ \exists \underline{y} \ \phi(\underline{e}, \underline{y}, \underline{x}, \underline{a})$, be an extended state formula, where ϕ is quantifier-free, the $\underline{e}$ are variables whose sort is an artifact sort and the $\underline{y}$ are variables whose sort is a basic sort.

Now observe that, according to our definitions, the artifact components have an artifact sort as source sort and a basic sort as target sort; since equality is the only predicate, the literals in ϕ can be divided into equalities/inequalities between variables from $\underline{e}$ and literals where the $\underline{e}$ can only occur as arguments of an artifact component. Let $\underline{a}[\underline{e}]$ be the tuple of the terms among the terms of the kind $a_j[e_s]$ which are well-typed; using disjunctive normal forms, our extended state formula can be written as a disjunction of formulae of the kind

$$\exists \underline{e} \ \exists \underline{y} \ (\phi_1(\underline{e}) \wedge \phi_2(\underline{y}, \underline{x}, \underline{a}[\underline{e}]/\underline{z})) \tag{4.10}$$

where ϕ_1 is a conjunction of equalities/inequalities, $\phi_2(\underline{y}, \underline{x}, \underline{z})$ is a quantifier-free Σ-formula and $\phi_2(\underline{y}, \underline{x}, \underline{a}[\underline{e}]/\underline{z})$ is obtained from ϕ_2 by replacing the variables $\underline{z}$ by

---

[1] Actually, τ is a disjunction of such formulae, but it easily seen that disjunction can be accommodated by moving existential quantifiers back-and-forth through them.

the terms $\underline{a}[\underline{e}]$. Moving inside the existential quantifiers $\underline{y}$, we can rewrite (4.10) to

$$\exists \underline{e} \, (\phi_1(\underline{e}) \wedge \exists \underline{y} \, \phi_2(\underline{y}, \underline{x}, \underline{a}[\underline{e}]/\underline{z})) \qquad (4.11)$$

Since T^* has quantifier elimination, we have that there is $\psi(\underline{x}, \underline{z})$ which is equivalent to $\exists \underline{y} \, \phi_2(\underline{y}, \underline{x}, \underline{z}))$ in all models of T^*; thus in all Σ_{ext}-models of T^*, the formula (4.11) is equivalent to

$$\exists \underline{e} \, (\phi_1(\underline{e}) \wedge \psi(\underline{x}, \underline{a}[\underline{e}]/\underline{z}))$$

which is a state formula.   □

We underline that the proofs of Lemmas 4.1 and 4.2 both give an explicit effective procedure for computing equivalent (extended) state formulae. Used one after the other, such procedures extends the procedure $QE(T^*, \phi)$ in Line 6 of Algorithm 1 to (not simple) artifact systems. Thanks to such procedure, the only formulae we need to test for satisfiability in lines 2 and 3 of the backward reachability algorithm are the ∃∀-formulae introduced below.

Let us call ∃∀-formulae the formulae of the kind

$$\exists \underline{e} \, \forall \underline{i} \, \phi(\underline{e}, \underline{i}, \underline{x}, \underline{a}) \qquad (4.12)$$

where the variables $\underline{e}, \underline{i}$ are variables whose sort is an artifact sort and ϕ is quantifier-free. We remark that the only allowed *universally* quantified variables in ∃∀-formulae are all of artifact sorts.

The crucial point for the following lemma to hold is that the *universally* quantified variables in ∃∀-formulae are all of artifact sorts:

Lemma 4.3 *The satisfiability of a ∃∀-formula in a Σ_{ext}-model of T is decidable. Moreover, given a ∃∀-formula χ, the following three statements are equivalent:*
- *χ is satisfiable in a Σ_{ext}-model of T*
- *χ is satisfiable in a DB-instance of $\langle \Sigma_{ext}, T \rangle$*
- *χ is satisfiable in a Σ_{ext}-model of T^*.*

Proof First of all, notice that a ∃∀-formula (4.12) is equivalent to a disjunction of formulae of the kind

$$\exists \underline{e} \, (\text{AllDiff}(\underline{e}) \wedge \forall \underline{i} \, \phi(\underline{e}, \underline{i}, \underline{x}, \underline{a})) \qquad (4.13)$$

where $\text{AllDiff}(\underline{e})$ says that any two variables of the same sort from the $\underline{e}$ are distinct (to this aim, it is sufficient to guess a partition and to keep, via a substitution, only one element for each equivalence class).[2] So we can freely assume that ∃∀-formulae are all of the kind (4.13).

Let us consider now the set of all (sort-matching) substitutions σ mapping the $\underline{i}$ to the $\underline{e}$. The formula (4.13) is satisfiable (respectively: in a Σ_{ext}-model of T, in a DB-instance of $\langle \Sigma_{ext}, T \rangle$, in a Σ_{ext}-model of T^*) iff so it is the formula

---

[2] In the MCMT implementation, state formulae are always maintained so that all existential variables occurring in them are differentiated and there is no need of this expensive computation step.

$$\exists \underline{e}\, (\mathrm{AllDiff}(\underline{e}) \wedge \bigwedge_{\sigma} \phi(\underline{e}, \underline{i}\sigma, \underline{x}, \underline{a})) \tag{4.14}$$

(here $\underline{i}\sigma$ means the componentwise application of σ to the $\underline{i}$): this is because, if (4.14) is satisfiable in $\mathcal{M}$, then we can take as $\mathcal{M}'$ the same Σ_{ext}-structure as $\mathcal{M}$, but with the interpretation of the artifact sorts restricted only to the elements named by the $\underline{e}$ and get in this way a Σ_{ext}-structure $\mathcal{M}'$ satisfying (4.13) ($\mathcal{M}'$ is still a DB-instance of $\langle \Sigma_{ext}, T \rangle$ or a Σ_{ext}-model of T^*, if so was $\mathcal{M}$). Thus, we can freely concentrate on the satisfiability problem of formulae of the kind (4.14) only.

Now, by the way Σ_{ext} is built, the only atoms occurring in the subformula $\phi(\underline{e}, \underline{i}\sigma, \underline{x}, \underline{a})$ of (4.14) whose argument terms are terms of artifact sorts are of the kind $e_s = e_j$, so all such atoms can be replaced either by $\top$ or by $\bot$ (depending on whether we have $s = j$ or not). So we can assume that there are no such atoms in $\phi(\underline{e}, \underline{i}\sigma, \underline{x}, \underline{a})$ and as a result, the variables $\underline{e}$ can only occur there as arguments of the $\underline{a}$.

Let now $\underline{a}[\underline{e}]$ be the tuple of the terms among the terms of the kind $a_j[e_s]$ which are well-typed. Since in (4.14) the $\underline{e}$ can only occur as arguments of the artifact components, as observed above, the formula (4.14) is in fact of the kind

$$\exists \underline{e}\, (\mathrm{AllDiff}(\underline{e}) \wedge \psi(\underline{x}, \underline{a}[\underline{e}]/\underline{z})) \tag{4.15}$$

where $\psi(\underline{x}, \underline{z})$ is a quantifier-free Σ-formula and $\psi(\underline{x}, \underline{a}[\underline{e}]/\underline{z})$ is obtained from ψ by replacing the variables $\underline{z}$ with the terms $\underline{a}[\underline{e}]$ (the $\underline{z}$ are of basic sorts because the target sorts of the artifact components are basic sorts).

It is now evident that (4.15) is satisfiable (respectively: in a Σ_{ext}-model of T, in a DB-instance of $\langle \Sigma_{ext}, T \rangle$, in a Σ_{ext}-model of T^*) iff the formula

$$\psi(\underline{x}, \underline{z}) \tag{4.16}$$

is satisfiable (respectively: in a Σ-model of T, in a DB-instance of $\langle \Sigma, T \rangle$, in a Σ-model of T^*). In fact, if we are given a Σ-structure $\mathcal{M}$ and an assignment satisfying (4.16), we can easily expand $\mathcal{M}$ to a Σ_{ext}-structure by taking the e's themselves as the elements of the interpretation of the artifact sorts; in the so-expanded Σ_{ext}-structure, we can interpret the artifact components $\underline{a}$ by taking the $\underline{a}[\underline{e}]$ to be the elements assigned to the $\underline{z}$ in the satisfying assignment for (4.16).

Thanks to Assumption 4.1, the satisfiability of (4.16) in a Σ-model of T, in a DB-instance of $\langle \Sigma, T \rangle$, or in a Σ-model of T^* are all equivalent and decidable. □

The instantiation algorithm of Lemma 4.3 can be used to discharge the satisfiability tests in lines 2 and 3 of Algorithm 1 because the conjunction of a state formula and of the negation of a state formula is a $\exists\forall$-formula (ι is itself the negation of a state formula, according to (3.5)).

Theorem 4.3. Let $\langle \Sigma, T \rangle$ be a DB schema. Then, for every RAS $S = \langle \Sigma, T, \Sigma_{ext}, \underline{x}, \underline{a}, \iota, \tau \rangle$, backward search BReach$_{RAS}$ (cf. Algorithm 2) is effective and sound for checking unsafety of S wrt an unsafe formula υ.

Proof Recall that $\mathcal{S}$ is safe iff there is no DB-instance $\mathcal{M}$ of $\langle \Sigma_{ext}, T \rangle$, no $k \geq 0$ and no assignment in $\mathcal{M}$ to the variables $\underline{x}^0, \underline{a}^0 \ldots, \underline{x}^k, \underline{a}^k$ such that the formula (4.5)

$$\iota(\underline{x}^0, \underline{a}^0) \wedge \tau(\underline{x}^0, \underline{a}^0, \underline{x}^1, \underline{a}^1) \wedge \cdots \wedge \tau(\underline{x}^{k-1}, \underline{a}^{k-1}, \underline{x}^k, \underline{a}^k) \wedge \upsilon(\underline{x}^k, \underline{a}^k)$$

is true in $\mathcal{M}$. It is sufficient to show that this is equivalent to saying that there is no Σ_{ext}-model $\mathcal{M}$ of T^*, no $k \geq 0$ and no assignment in $\mathcal{M}$ to the variables $\underline{x}^0, \underline{a}^0 \ldots, \underline{x}^k, \underline{a}^k$ such that (4.5) is true in $\mathcal{M}$ (once this is shown, the proof goes in the same way as the proof of Theorem 4.1).

Now, the formula (4.5) is satisfiable in a Σ_{ext}-structure $\mathcal{M}$ under a suitable assignment iff the formula

$$\iota(\underline{x}^0, \underline{a}^0) \wedge \exists \underline{a}^1 \exists \underline{x}^1 (\tau(\underline{x}^0, \underline{a}^0, \underline{x}^1, \underline{a}^1) \wedge \cdots$$
$$\cdots \wedge \exists \underline{a}^k \exists \underline{x}^k (\tau(\underline{x}^{k-1}, \underline{a}^{k-1}, \underline{x}^k, \underline{a}^k) \wedge \upsilon(\underline{x}^k, \underline{a}^k)) \cdots)$$

is satisfiable in $\mathcal{M}$ under a suitable assignment; by Lemma 4.1, the latter is equivalent to a formula of the kind

$$\iota(\underline{x}, \underline{a}) \wedge \exists \underline{e} \, \exists \underline{y} \, \phi(\underline{e}, \underline{y}, \underline{x}, \underline{a}) \tag{4.17}$$

where $\exists \underline{e} \, \exists \underline{y} \, \phi(\underline{e}, \underline{y}, \underline{x}, \underline{a})$ is an extended state formula (thus ϕ is quantifier-free, the $\underline{e}$ are variables of artifact sorts and the $\underline{y}$ are variables of basic sorts - we renamed $\underline{x}^0, \underline{a}^0$ as $\underline{x}, \underline{a}$). However the satisfiability of (4.17) is the same as the satisfiability of $\exists \underline{e} \, (\iota(\underline{x}, \underline{a}) \wedge \phi(\underline{e}, \underline{y}, \underline{x}, \underline{a}))$; the latter, in view of (3.5), is a $\exists \forall$-formula and so Lemma 4.3 applies and shows that its satisfiability in a DB-instance of $\langle \Sigma_{ext}, T \rangle$ is the same as its satisfiability in a Σ_{ext}-model of T^*.   □

To sum up, in this section we remarked that for Algorithm 2, to be effective, we need decision procedures for discharging the satisfiability tests in Lines 2-3. Thanks to the subprocedure $\mathsf{QE}_{RAS}(T^*, \phi)$, the only formulae we need to test in these lines have a specific form (i.e. they are $\exists \forall$-formulae). In fact, by our hypotheses in Assumption 4.1, we can freely assume that all the runs we are interested in take place inside models of T^* (where we can eliminate quantifiers binding variables of basic sorts). Then, in two first technical lemmas (Lemmas 4.1 and 4.2) we show that the preimage of a state formula is an extended state formula and that such an extended state formula can be converted back (modulo T^*) into a state formula; finally, in a third technical lemma (Lemma 4.3), we show that entailments between state formulae (more generally, satisfiability of formulae of the kind $\exists \forall$) can be decided via finite instantiation techniques. These observations make both safety and fixpoint tests effective and constitute the skeleton of the proof of Theorem 4.3.

Remark 4.4 The role of quantifier elimination (Line 6 of Algorithm 1) is twofold: *(i)* It allows us to discharge the fixpoint test of Line 2 (see Lemma 4.3). *(ii)* It ensures termination in significant cases, namely those where *(strongly) local formulae*, introduced in the next chapter, are involved.

We end the section by showing also the main theorem about U-RASs, which is now a straightforward consequence of Proposition 4.3 and Thereom 4.3.

Theorem 4.2. BReach$_{RAS}$ is *partially sound* for checking unsafety of an Universal RAS S w.r.t. an unsafe formula v.

4.6 Examples of DB Schemas Satisfying the Assumption

We already stated the model-theoretic requirements that the DB theory T from Definition 3.1 must satisfy for our approach to work. In this section, we show some examples of theories that satisfy them, in particular the case of an acyclic signature Σ and with key dependencies (i.e., the setting presented in [186]).

4.6.1 Examples of DB Theories with the Finite Model Property

Observe that if Σ is acyclic, there are only finitely many terms involving a single variable x: in fact, there are as many terms as paths in $G(\Sigma)$ starting from the sort of x. If k_Σ is the maximum number of terms involving a single variable, then (since all function symbols are unary) there are at most $k_\Sigma \cdot n$ terms involving n variables.

Proposition 4.4 *Let* (Σ, T) *be a DB (extended-)schema;* T *has the finite model property in case* Σ *is acyclic.*

Proof If $T := \emptyset$, then congruence closure ensures that the finite model property holds and decides constraint satisfiability in polynomial time [41].

Otherwise, we reduce the argument to the Herbrand Theorem (recall that T is universal according to Definition 3.1). Indeed, suppose to have a finite set Φ of universal formulae and let $\phi(\underline{x})$ be the constraint we want to test for satisfiability. Replace the variables $\underline{x}$ with free constants $\underline{a}$. Herbrand Theorem states that $\Phi \cup \{\phi(\underline{a})\}$ has a model iff the set of ground $\Sigma^{\underline{a}}$-instances of $\Phi \cup \{\phi(\underline{a})\}$ has a model. These ground instances are finitely many by acyclicity, so we can apply congruence closure (as done in the case of the empty theory) to these ground instances.

Remark 4.5 If T is finitely axiomatized, Proposition 4.4 ensures decidability of constraint satisfiability. In order to obtain a decision procedure, it is sufficient to instantiate the axioms of T and the axioms of equality (reflexivity, transitivity, symmetry, congruence) and to use a SAT solver to decide constraint satisfiability. Alternatively, one can decide constraint satisfiability via congruence closure [41] and avoid instantiating the equality axioms.

Remark 4.6 Acyclity is a strong condition, often too strong. However, some condition must be imposed (otherwise we have undecidability, and then failure of finite model property, by reduction to word problem for finite presentations of monoids). In fact, the empty theory and the theory axiomatized by Axioms (3.1) both have the finite model property even without acyclicity assumptions.

4.6.2 Examples of Model Completions of DB Theories

We study some interesting cases where the model completion of T exists. The following Lemma gives a useful folklore technique for finding model completions:

Lemma 4.4 *Suppose that for every primitive Σ-formula $\exists x \, \phi(x, \underline{y})$ it is possible to find a quantifier-free formula $\psi(\underline{y})$ such that*

(i) $T \models \forall x \, \forall \underline{y} \, (\phi(x, \underline{y}) \to \psi(\underline{y}))$;

(ii)   *for every model M of T, for every tuple of elements $\underline{a}$ from the support of M such that $M \models \psi(\underline{a})$ it is possible to find another model N of T such that M embeds into N and $N \models \exists x \phi(x, \underline{a})$.*

Then T has a model completion T^* axiomatized by the infinitely many sentences

$$\forall \underline{y} \, (\psi(\underline{y}) \to \exists x \, \phi(x, \underline{y})) \,. \tag{4.18}$$

Proof From (i) and (4.18) we clearly get that $T^\star$ admits quantifier elimination: in fact, in order to prove that a theory enjoys quantifier elimination, it is sufficient to eliminate quantifiers from *primitive* formulae (then the quantifier elimination for all formulae can be easily shown by an induction over their complexity). This is exactly what is guaranteed by (i) and (4.18).

Let M be a model of T. We show (by using a chain argument) that there exists a model M' of $T^\star$ such that M embeds into M'. For every primitive formula $\exists x \phi(x, \underline{y})$, consider the pair $(\underline{a}, \exists x \phi(x, \underline{a}))$ such that $M \models \psi(\underline{a})$ (where ψ is related to ϕ as in (i)). By Zermelo's Theorem, the set of all pairs $\{(\underline{a}, \exists x \phi(x, \underline{a}))\}$ can be well-ordered: let $\{(\underline{a}_i, \exists x \phi_i(x, \underline{a}_i))\}_{i \in I}$ be such a well-ordered set (where I is an ordinal). By transfinite induction on this well-order, we define $M_0 := M$ and, for each $i \in I$, M_i as an extension of $\bigcup_{j < i} M_j$ such that $M_i \models \exists x \phi_i(x, \underline{a}_i)$, which exists for (ii) since $\bigcup_{j < i} M_j \models \psi(\underline{a}_i)$ (remember that validity of ground formulae is preserved passing through substructures and superstructures, and $M_0 \models \psi(\underline{a}_i)$).

Now we take the chain union $M^1 := \bigcup_{i \in I} M_i$: since T is universal, M^1 is again a model of T, and it is possible to construct an analogous chain M^2 as done above, starting from M^1 instead of M. Clearly, we get $M_0 := M \subseteq M^1 \subseteq M^2$ by construction. At this point, we iterate the same argument countably many times, so as to define a new chain of models of T:

$$M_0 := M \subseteq M^1 \subseteq \dots \subseteq M^n \subseteq \dots$$

Defining $M' := \bigcup_n M^n$, we trivially get that M' is a model of T such that $M \subseteq M'$ and satisfies all the sentences of type (4.18). The last fact can be shown using the following finiteness argument.

Fix ϕ, ψ as in (4.18). For every tuple $\underline{a}' \in \mathcal{M}'$ such that $\mathcal{M}' \models \psi(\underline{a}')$, by definition of $\mathcal{M}'$ there exists a natural number k such that $\underline{a}' \in \mathcal{M}^k$: since $\psi(a')$ is a ground formula, we get that also $\mathcal{M}^k \models \psi(\underline{a}')$. Therefore, we consider the step k of the countable chain: there, we have that the pair $(\underline{a}', \exists x \phi(x, \underline{a}'))))$ appears in the enumeration given by the well-ordered set of pairs $\{(\underline{a}_i, \exists x \phi_i(x, \underline{a}_i))\}_{i \in I}$ such that $\mathcal{M}^k \models \psi_i(\underline{a}_i)$. Hence, by construction, we have that $\mathcal{M}_i^k \models \exists x \phi(x, \underline{a}')$ for some i. In conclusion, since the existential formulae are preserved passing to extensions, we obtain $\mathcal{M}' \models \exists x \phi(x, \underline{a}')$, as wanted. □

Proposition 4.5 *T has a model completion in case it is axiomatized by universal one-variable formulae and Σ is acyclic.*

Proof We freely take inspiration from an analogous result in [252]. We preliminarily show that T is amalgamable. Then, for a suitable choice of ψ suggested by the acyclicity assumption, the amalgamation property will be used to prove the validity of the condition (ii) of Lemma 4.4: this fact (together with condition (i)) yields that T has a model completion which is axiomatized by the infinitely many sentences (4.18).

Let $\mathcal{M}_1$ and $\mathcal{M}_2$ two models of T with a submodel $\mathcal{M}_0$ of T in common (we suppose for simplicity that $|\mathcal{M}_1| \cap |\mathcal{M}_2| = |\mathcal{M}_0|$). We define a T-amalgam $\mathcal{M}$ of $\mathcal{M}_1, \mathcal{M}_2$ over $\mathcal{M}_0$ as follows (we use in an essential way the fact that Σ contains only *unary* function symbols). Let the support of $\mathcal{M}$ be the set-theoretic union of the supports of $\mathcal{M}_1$ and $\mathcal{M}_2$, i.e. $|\mathcal{M}| := |\mathcal{M}_1| \cup |\mathcal{M}_2|$. $\mathcal{M}$ has a natural Σ-structure inherited by the Σ-structures $\mathcal{M}_1$ and $\mathcal{M}_2$: for every function symbol f in Σ, we define, for each $m_i \in |\mathcal{M}_i|(i = 1, 2)$, $f^{\mathcal{M}}(m_i) := f^{\mathcal{M}_i}(m_i)$, i.e. the interpretation of f in $\mathcal{M}$ is the interpretation of f in $\mathcal{M}_i$ for every element $m_i \in |\mathcal{M}_i|$. This is well-defined since, for every $a \in |\mathcal{M}_1| \cap |\mathcal{M}_2| = |\mathcal{M}_0|$, we have that $f^{\mathcal{M}}(a) := f^{\mathcal{M}_1}(a) = f^{\mathcal{M}_0}(a) = f^{\mathcal{M}_2}(a)$. It is clear that $\mathcal{M}_1$ and $\mathcal{M}_2$ are substructures of $\mathcal{M}$, and their inclusions agree on $\mathcal{M}_0$.

We show that the Σ-structure $\mathcal{M}$, as defined above, is a model of T. By hypothesis, T is axiomatized by universal one-variable formulae: so, we can consider T as a theory formed by axioms ϕ which are universal closures of clauses with just one variable, i.e. $\phi := \forall x(A_1(x) \wedge \ldots \wedge A_n(x) \rightarrow B_1(x) \vee \ldots \vee B_m(x))$, where A_j and B_k $(j = 1, \ldots, n$ and $k = 1, \ldots, m)$ are atoms.

We show that $\mathcal{M}$ satisfies all such formulae ϕ. In order to do that, suppose that, for every $a \in |\mathcal{M}|$, $\mathcal{M} \models A_j(a)$ for all $j = 1, \ldots, n$. If $a \in |\mathcal{M}_i|$, then $\mathcal{M} \models A_j(a)$ implies $\mathcal{M}_i \models A_j(a)$, since $A_j(a)$ is a ground formula. Since $\mathcal{M}_i$ is model of T and so $\mathcal{M}_i \models \phi$, we get that $\mathcal{M}_i \models B_k(a)$ for some $k = 1, \ldots, m$, which means that $\mathcal{M} \models B_k(a)$, since $B_k(a)$ is a ground formula. Thus, $\mathcal{M} \models \phi$ for every axiom ϕ of T, i.e. $\mathcal{M} \models T$ and, hence, $\mathcal{M}$ is a T-amalgam of $\mathcal{M}_1, \mathcal{M}_2$ over $\mathcal{M}_0$, as wanted

Now, given a primitive formula $\exists x \phi(x, y)$, we find a suitable ψ such that the hypothesis of Lemma 4.4 holds. We define $\bar{\psi}(y)$ as the conjunction of the set of all quantifier-free $\chi(\underline{y})$-formulae such that $\phi(x, \underline{y})^- \rightarrow \chi(\underline{y})$ is a logical consequence of T (they are finitely many - up to T-equivalence - because Σ is acyclic). By definition, clearly we have that (i) of Lemma 4.4 holds.

We show that also condition (ii) is satisfied. Let $\mathcal{M}$ be a model of T such that $\mathcal{M} \models \psi(\underline{a})$ for some tuple of elements $\underline{a}$ from the support of $\mathcal{M}$. Then, consider the Σ-substructure $\mathcal{M}[\underline{a}]$ of $\mathcal{M}$ generated by the elements $\underline{a}$: this substructure is finite (since Σ is acyclic), it is a model of T and we trivially have that $\mathcal{M}[\underline{a}] \models \psi(\underline{a})$, since $\psi(\underline{a})$ is a ground formula. In order to prove that there exists an extension $\mathcal{N}'$ of $\mathcal{M}[\underline{a}]$ such that $\mathcal{N} \models \exists x \phi(x, \underline{a})$, it is sufficient to prove (by the Robinson Diagram Lemma) that the $\Sigma^{|\mathcal{M}[\underline{a}]| \cup \{e\}}$-theory $\Delta(\mathcal{M}[\underline{a}]) \cup \{\phi(e, \underline{a})\}$ is T-consistent. For reduction to absurdity, suppose that the last theory is T-inconsistent. Then, there are finitely many literals $l_1(\underline{a}), ..., l_m(\underline{a})$ from $\Delta(\mathcal{M}[\underline{a}])$ (remember that $\Delta(\mathcal{M}[\underline{a}])$ is a finite set of literals since $\mathcal{M}[\underline{a}]$ is a finite structure) such that $\phi(e, \underline{a}) \models_T \neg(l_1(\underline{a}) \wedge ... \wedge l_m(\underline{a}))$. Therefore, defining $A(\underline{a}) := l_1(\underline{a}) \wedge ... \wedge l_m(\underline{a})$, we get that $\phi(e, \underline{a}) \models_T \neg A(\underline{a})$, which implies that $\neg A(\underline{a})$ is one of the $\chi(y)$-formulae appearing in $\psi(\underline{a})$. Since $\mathcal{M}[\underline{a}] \models \psi(\underline{a})$, we also have that $\mathcal{M}[\underline{a}] \models \neg A(\underline{a})$, which is a contradiction: in fact, by definition of diagram, $\mathcal{M}[\underline{a}] \models A(\underline{a})$ must hold. Hence, there exists an extension $\mathcal{N}'$ of $\mathcal{M}[\underline{a}]$ such that $\mathcal{N}' \models \exists x \phi(x, \underline{a})$. Now, by amalgamation property, there exists a T-amalgam $\mathcal{N}$ of $\mathcal{M}$ and $\mathcal{N}'$ over $\mathcal{M}[\underline{a}]$: clearly, $\mathcal{N}$ is an extension of $\mathcal{M}$ and, since $\mathcal{N}' \hookrightarrow \mathcal{N}$ and $\mathcal{N}' \models \exists x \phi(x, \underline{a})$, also $\mathcal{N} \models \exists x \phi(x, \underline{a})$ holds, as required.   □

Remark 4.7 The proof of Proposition 4.5 gives an algorithm for quantifier elimination in the model completion. The algorithm works as follows (see the formula (4.18)): to eliminate the quantifier $\exists x$ from $\exists x \, \phi(x, y)$ take the conjunction of the clauses $\chi(y)$ implied by $\phi(x, y)$. This algorithm is highly impractical because it requires one to enumerate all such $\chi(y)$. However, contrary to what happens in linear arithmetics, the quantifier elimination needed to prove Proposition 4.5 has a much better behavior (from the complexity point of view) if obtained via a suitable version of the Knuth-Bendix procedure [24] or of the Superposition Calculus [213]: this will be the core of Chapter 7, where we will see that quantifier elimination becomes a *practical* problem. Specifically, we will see that, using a constrained version of Superposition, in the case of free unary functions and free relations the complexity has a *quadratic bound* even without assuming acyclicity.

A second limitation of the algorithm presented in Proposition 4.5 is that it uses the acyclicity assumption, whereas such assumption, as just noticed, is in general not needed for Proposition 4.5 to hold: for instance, when $T := \emptyset$ or when T contains only Axiom (3.1), a model completion can be proved to exist, even if Σ is not acyclic, again by using the constrained version of Superposition presented in Chapter 7.

Remark 4.8 Proposition 4.5 holds also for specific DB extended-schemas, i.e. DB schemas extended with n-ary relations and s.t. the universal one-variable formulae do not involve the relation symbols (so, the relations are "free"): as explained in Section 7.6, the implementation of the quantifier elimination algorithm takes into account also this case. More generally, the model completion exists whenever we consider an acyclic DB extended-schema with a DB extended-theory T that enjoys the amalgamation property.

We conclude this section by summarizing what we have proved so far. Indeed, as a corollary, we get that Assumption 4.1 is matched in the following three cases: *(i)* when

T is empty; *(ii)* when T is axiomatized by Axioms (3.1); *(iii)* when Σ is acyclic and T is axiomatized by universal one-variable formulae (such as Axioms (3.1)).

Hence, this proves in particular that artifact-centric model in the style of [102, 186] that we intended to capture (case *(ii)*) matches Assumption 4.1.

Remark 4.9 The arguments and the remarks above show that the DB extended-schemas obtained by adding "free" relations to the DB schemas of *(i)*, *(ii)*, *(iii)* above match Assumption 4.1. In addition, Assumption 4.1 is also satisfied in case the previous DB schemas are combined (always in the spirit of DB extended-schemas, cf. Subsection 3.1.2) with an arithmetic theory T' admitting quantifier elimination (e.g., linear real arithmetic): indeed, in this case, we clearly have that a model completion exists, i.e. $T' = T'^*$.

Notice that all the DB (extended)-schemas presented in Chapter 3 as examples satisfy Assumption 4.1.

4.7 Discussion

4.7.1 Model Checking via Quantifier Elimination in Model Completions

In Section 4.2, we argued that the presence of existentially quantified 'data' variables ranging over the DB instance creates serious issues when one tries to apply the SMT-based backward reachability procedure defined in [146] to DAP verification. Indeed, in order to guarantee the regressability of the backward search, one needs to 'eliminate' in some sense the existentially quantified 'data variables' that are introduced at each step of the main loop when computing preimages. The dramatic growth in the number of quantified variables would also affect the performance of the procedure. For these reasons, the 'elimination' of quantified variables is not only essential for guaranteeing the correctness of the procedure, but also for improving the overall performance of the implementation in MCMT. We also underline that the 'elimination' of existentially quantified variables is exactly the right ingredient that is needed to guarantee termination of backward search for two notable classes that will be discussed in detail in the next chapter, namely the one for acyclic SASs and the one for 'Local RASs' (see Chapter 5 for the definitions).

To summarize, a sort of 'elimination' of existentially quantified variables is essential for the purposes of this book. However, we already remarked that quantifier elimination is usually not available in the DB theories we study. This is the main reason we exploited the notion of model completions so as to retain quantifier elimination. Hence, the 'elimination of quantifiers' that we perform in the backward reachability procedure is not performed in the original DB theory T, but in its model completion T (that is unique, when it exists). Intuitively, given a DB theory T, the model completion of T is the 'minimal theory' T^* (in the same signature of T) that extends T so as to get quantifier elimination. As a side remark, we recall that when T admits quantifier elimination, then the model completion of T coincides with T itself, so in this corner case the meaning of 'minimal richer theory than T' is clear: it is the theory T itself. One can give to the term 'minimal' here many interpretations (all follow from the definition): one of these is that T and T^* have the same universal consequences (i.e., they entail the same universal sentences). Another way for interpreting the model completion T^* as the 'minimal enrichment' of T is given by the property that all models of T can be 'enlarged' to (more formally, embedded into) model of T^*. This implies that satisfiability of existential formulae in T and in T^* are equivalent problems.

The last facts are particularly interesting from the perspective of the model-checking technique introduced in this chapter. The main idea emerging from the proof of Theorem 4.1 is that detecting unsafe traces in models of T, which are overall existential formulae, is the same problem as detecting unsafe traces in the models of T^*. Intuitively, this can be done by 'lifting' unsafe traces in a $\mathcal{M}$ model of T a corresponding (extended) model $\mathcal{M}'$ of T^* into which $\mathcal{M}$ embeds (by definition of model completion): an unsafe trace in T is still an unsafe trace in T^*. Since all models of T^* are also models of T by definition (because $T \subseteq T^*$), then it is clear that an unsafe trace in a model $\mathcal{M}'$ of T^* is in particular an unsafe trace in a model $\mathcal{M}$ of T (i.e., $\mathcal{M}$ is exactly $\mathcal{M}'$). Thus, detecting unsafety in T is equivalent to detecting unsafety in T^*: this is exactly the main intuition behind the proof of Theorem 4.1, and we remark once again that this is true because unsafe traces are existential formulae.

A direct consequence of the discussion above is that whenever there exists an unsafe trace in T, there also exists an unsafe trace in T^*, and vice versa. Hence, when we 'eliminate quantifies' via the subroutine $\mathsf{QE}_{SAS}(T^*, \phi)$ we are *not* performing *any* approximation: the computed set of reachable states is *not* an over-approximation as it happens when (ordinary) interpolation-based methods are employed, but is *exact*, since it is the exact set of reachable states computed for a model trace that lives in a model of T^* (instead of living in a model of T).

In Part II we will see that eliminating quantifiers in model completions is equivalent to computing *uniform interpolants*, or (using an equivalent nomenclature) *covers*. We reveal this fact in advance in order to state the important moral conclusion of this paragraph: when computing ordinary interpolants, it is well-known that preimages are not exact and the set of reachable states is over-approximated. In contrast, when computing uniform interpolants, preimages are *exact* and no approximation of the set of reachable states is performed.

4.7.2 Freshness and Related Approaches

It is important to stress that the Array-Based Artifact Systems we introduced in this chapter are radically different from other formal models integrating dynamics with data, such as Data Petri Nets [185], ν-PNs [228] and multiset rewriting systems with data and constraints [97]. Let us consider Data Petri Nets as a representative example of this class of approaches.

In Data Petri Nets, one can generate tokens that carry fresh values not already present in the current marking. The requirement that a value is fresh can be encoded in the model [228]. Such values can only be mutually related using the comparison predicates over the underlying domain. In the context of artifact systems, there are different types of freshness that can be studied: a 'global' version and a 'local' version. The former concerns both the read-only database and the working memory, while the latter only considers the working memory. Only local freshness can be reasonably compared with the notion of freshness in Data Petri Nets: indeed, Data Petri Nets and related approaches do not contemplate any persistent storage (i.e., read-only databases) in their models; in contrast, the 'current marking' of a Petri net-based formalism can be related to the 'current state' of the U-RAS working memory, as we will see in Chapter 13.

We briefly argue why freshness is in general problematic in Array-based Artifact Systems. In this setting, the working memory may contain data elements arbitrarily taken from value sorts, or extracted from the (active domain of the) read-only database. When loading a data element from a value sort, this may or not be present in the active domain, and it may be *possibly* fresh in the global sense, i.e., different from all the values present in the active domain and in the current configuration of the working memory: notice that *proper* global freshness cannot be expressed in U-RASs, since this feature would require to use some sort of universal quantification ranging over the active domain of the read-only DB instance. In contrast, local freshness requires injecting some element taken from the values sorts or the (active domain of the) read-only database that is different from *all* the other elements currently present in the working memory. In the case of SASs, this can be trivially done, since the working memory only consists of a fixed number of artifact variables. In the case of RASs, this is not possible anymore: checking local freshness would require employing guards that inspect the content of *all* the tuples in each artifact relation (which are in principle finite but unbounded), and this check cannot be performed if only existential quantifiers over indexes are allowed. However, this check becomes possible in U-RASs, thanks to the presence of *universal* guards: it is sufficient to pick up an element that is different from *all* the elements contained in *any* location of the artifact components. To sum up, local freshness can be enforced in U-RASs: we will see in Chapter 13 that U-RASs can be employed to successfully model and verify interesting extensions of Data Petri Nets. As one can expect, U-RASs are significantly more expressive than RASs, but when we use them we pay the price of losing the soundness of our verification machinery, because of the possible presence of spurious unsafe traces.

We conclude the section by pointing out why the notion of model completion we used in this chapter is radically different from the one of 'enlarging models with fresh values'. When loading data elements from the read-only DB, it is crucial to consider that they are mutually related via constraints present therein. These constraints are primary keys, foreign keys, and additional axioms present in the DB theory. The read-only DB is fixed within a run, but model checking of safety properties is studied *parametrically* with respect to all possible read-only DBs over a given schema. During model checking, we are examining sets of reachable states described by logical formulae, whose validity depends on properties that might happen to be true in the read-only DB, depending on the constraints present therein. To handle data elements coming from the read-only DB and their corresponding constraints, we therefore need a specialized machinery that is different from the one typically used to tame the infinity brought by freshness. In fact, it is not enough to embed the read-only DB in a larger model that admits fresh values to obtain quantifier elimination, which is essential in our model checking algorithm. Quantifier elimination becomes available only when such a "larger model" possesses suitable model-theoretic properties, which we have studied in Section 4.1. In particular, we have argued that such properties are captured by the well-known model-theoretic notion of existentially closed structure and its intimately related notion of model completion. Notably, resorting to model completion can be seen as the "most natural" way to obtain quantifier elimination, as it is the "closest" theory to the original one that at once admits quantifier elimination and preserves satisfiability of existential formulae. This is precisely what we intensively exploit in our verification algorithm.

Chapter 5
Decidability Results via Termination of the Verification Machinery

In this chapter, we study how to guarantee termination of the backward reachability procedures defined in the previous chapter. Since both BReach$_{SAS}$ and BReach$_{RAS}$ have been proved to be semi-decision procedures for detecting safety of SASs and (plain) RASs respectively, termination would also ensure, in turn, that they are full decision procedures. However, termination is in general difficult to achieve, since array-based systems are not always well-structured transition systems [6], and in the most general cases the safety problem for them is *undecidable*: see, for instance, the undecidable case of Universal RASs discussed in Section 13.3.6, or the general case of [146].

In Section 5.1, we prove that the backward reachability procedure is guaranteed to terminate when applied to a safety problem involving a SAS with an *acyclic* DB signature (see Section 3.1 for the formal definition of acyclicity). This is achieved by strongly exploiting the quantifier elimination algorithm executed at each step of the main loop of the backward search. The idea behind this is that, thanks to this quantifier elimination algorithm, the number of variables of the involved formulae remains fixed: this implies that, since the DB signature is acyclic, the number of possible formulae (over a fixed number of variables) to consider during the backward search is *bounded*, hence this search is forced to terminate. This shows the decidability of the safety problem when acyclic SASs are concerned.

In Section 5.2, we exploit an argument based on *well-quasi-orders (wqos)* in order to prove the termination of backward search for safety problems involving two specific classes of plain RASs. These two classes of RASs present orthogonal features: the first one, called "RASs with Local Updates" (or, simply, "Local RASs"), restricts the syntax of transition formulae but only imposes that the DB signature is acyclic (as in the case of SASs); the second one, called "RASs with Tree-like Signatures" (or, simply, "Tree-like RASs"), does not pose restrictions on the syntactic format of the logical formulae of the system, but dictates that the (artifact setting over the) DB signature has a more restrictive shape, i.e., it is a *tree*. Both cases are sufficiently expressive to capture interesting and concrete data-aware process models: specifically, the first one is powerful enough to incorporate the model of [186]. The main results of this chapter, that is termination for RASs with Local Updates and

A. Gianola: *Verification of Data-Aware Processes via Satisfiability Modulo Theories*, LNBIP 470, pp. 97–120, 2023.
https://doi.org/10.1007/978-3-031-42746-6_5

for RASs with Tree-like Signatures, are respectively stated in Subsections 5.2.1 and 5.2.3, and proved in the respective subsequent subsections. We also provide in Subsections 5.2.2 and 5.2.4 two detailed examples of business processes that are respectively expressed as a RAS with Local Updates and a RAS with Tree-like Signature. Moreover, in Section 5.3 we analyze several types of updates and their corresponding encoding into transition formulae, discussing also in which cases termination is guaranteed. We conclude the chapter by comparing the main features of RASs with the related approaches (Section 5.4).

The technical content of this chapter was partially presented for the first time in [55].

5.1 Termination Result for SASs

In this section, we prove that in case of a SAS $S := \langle \Sigma, T, \underline{x}, \iota, \tau \rangle$, where $\langle \Sigma, T \rangle$ is a (standard) DB schema and Σ is acyclic, backward search BReach_{SAS} is guaranteed to terminate, and hence it is a full *decision procedure* for the safety problems of acyclic SASs.

Theorem 5.1 *if Σ is acyclic, BReach_{SAS} terminates and decides the safety problems for S in PSPACE in the combined size of $\underline{x}$, ι, and τ.*

Proof In case Σ is acyclic, there are only finitely many quantifier-free formulae (in which the finite set of variables $\underline{x}$ occur), so it is evident that the algorithm must terminate: because of (4.3), the unsatisfiability test of Line 2 must eventually succeed, if the unsatisfiability test of Line 3 never does so.

Concerning complexity, we need to modify Algorithm 1 (we make it nondeterministic and use Savitch's Theorem saying that PSPACE = NPSPACE).

Since Σ is acyclic, there are only finitely many terms involving a single variable, let this number be k_{Σ} (we consider T, Σ and hence k_{Σ} constant for our problems). Then, since all function symbols are unary, it is clear that we have at most $2^{O(n^2)}$ conjunctions of sets of literals involving at most n variables and that if the system is unsafe, unsafety can be detected with a run whose length is at most $2^{O(n^2)}$. Thus we introduce a counter to be incremented during the main loop (lines 2-6) of Algorithm 1. The fixpoint test in line 2 is removed and loop is executed only until the maximum length of an unsafe run is not exceeded (we remark that an exponential counter requires polynomial space).

Inside the loop, line 4 is removed (we do not need anymore the variable B) and line 6 is modified as follows. We replace line 6 of the algorithm by

$$6'. \quad \phi \longleftarrow \alpha(\underline{x});$$

where α is a non-deterministically chosen conjunction of literals implying $\mathsf{QE}(T^*, \phi)$. Notice that to check the latter, there is no need to compute $\mathsf{QE}(T^*, \phi)$: recalling the proof of Proposition 4.5 and Remark 4.7 it is sufficient to check that $T \models \alpha \rightarrow C$ holds for every clause $C(\underline{x})$ such that $T \models \phi \rightarrow C$.

The algorithm is now in PSPACE, because all the satisfiability tests we need are, as a consequence of the proof of Proposition 4.4, in NP: all such tests are reducible to T-satisfiability tests for quantifier-free Σ-formulae involving the variables $\underline{x}$ and the additional (skolemized) quantified variables occurring in the transitions [1]. In fact, all these satisfiability tests are applied to formulae whose length is polynomial in the size of $\underline{x}$, of ι and of τ.   □

Remark 5.1 We highlight that the proof of the decidability result of Theorem 5.1 requires that the considered background theory T: *(i)* admits a model completion; *(ii)* is *locally finite*, i.e., up to T-equivalence, there are only finitely many atoms involving a fixed finite number of variables (this condition is implied by acyclicity); *(iii)* is universal; and *(iv)* enjoys decidability of constraint satisfiability. Conditions *(iii)* and *(iv)* imply that one can decide whether a finite structure is a model of T. If *(ii)* and *(iii)* hold, it is well-known that *(i)* is equivalent to amalgamation [252],[188]. Moreover, *(ii)* alone always holds for relational signatures and *(iii)* is equivalent to T being closed under substructures (this is a standard preservation theorem in model theory [66]). It follows that *arbitrary relational signatures* (or *locally finite theories* in general, even allowing n-ary relation and n-ary function symbols) require only amalgamability and closure under substructures. We also recall that every existential formula $\phi(\underline{x},\underline{x}')$ can be turned into the form of Formula (3.4). Finally, we notice that thanks to all the previous observations Theorem 5.1 is reminiscent of an analogous result in [37], i.e., Theorem 5, the crucial hypotheses of which are exactly amalgamability and closure under substructures, although the setting in that paper is different (there, key dependencies are not discussed, whereas we are interested only in DB (extended-)theories). We will come back to this remark in case of *symbolic transition systems* in Section 7.2, when we will state Theorem 7.2.

5.2 Termination Results for RASs

Theorem 4.3 gives a semi-decision procedure for unsafety: if the system is unsafe, the procedure discovers it, but if the system is safe, the procedure (still correct) may not terminate. Termination is much more difficult to achieve for RASs, since acyclicity of Σ seems not to be sufficient to guarantee it. We present two termination results for RASs, both obtained via the use of well quasi-orders. The strategy for proving termination consists of isolating sufficient conditions that imply that the embeddability relation between DB instances is a well-quasi-ordering. Since there is no guarantee that this fact holds in general, RASs are *not* well-structured transition systems.

---

[1] For the test in line 3, we just need replace in ϕ the $\underline{x}$ by their values given by ι, conjoin the result with all the ground instances of the axioms of T and finally decide satisfiability with congruence closure algorithm of a polynomial size ground conjunction of literals.

5.2.1 Termination with Local Updates

Consider an acyclic signature Σ, a theory T (satisfying our Assumption 4.1), and an artifact setting $(\underline{x}, \underline{a})$ over an artifact extension Σ_{ext} of Σ. We call a state formula *local* if it is a disjunction of the formulae

$$\exists e_1 \cdots \exists e_k \, (\delta(e_1, \ldots, e_k) \wedge \textstyle\bigwedge_{i=1}^{k} \phi_i(e_i, \underline{x}, \underline{a})), \qquad (5.1)$$

and *strongly local* if it is a disjunction of the formulae

$$\exists e_1 \cdots \exists e_k \, (\delta(e_1, \ldots, e_k) \wedge \psi(\underline{x}) \wedge \textstyle\bigwedge_{i=1}^{k} \phi_i(e_i, \underline{a})). \qquad (5.2)$$

In (5.1) and (5.2), δ is a conjunction of variable equalities and disequalities, ϕ_i, ψ are quantifier-free, and $e_1, \ldots, e_k$ are individual variables varying over artifact sorts. The key expressivity limitation of local state formulae is that they cannot compare entries belonging to different tuples of artifact relations: in fact, each ϕ_i in (5.1) and (5.2) can contain only the existentially quantified variable e_i.

A transition formula tr is *local* (resp., *strongly local*) if whenever a formula ϕ is local (resp., strongly local), so is $Pre(\mathrm{tr}, \phi)$ (modulo the axioms of T^*).

We now state the first main result of this section, which will be proved in the following subsection:

Theorem 5.2 *If Σ is acyclic, backward search (cf. Algorithm 1) terminates when applied to solve the safety problem, with respect to a (strongly) local unsafe formula $\upsilon(\underline{x}, \underline{a})$, for a RAS $\langle \Sigma, T, \Sigma_{ext}, \underline{x}, \underline{a}, \iota(\underline{x}, \underline{a}), \tau(\underline{x}, \underline{a}, \underline{x}', \underline{a}') \rangle$, where τ is a disjunction of (strongly) local transition formulae.*

In Theorem 5.2 we show that (for acyclic Σ) Algorithm 1 terminates when applied to a local unsafe formula in a RAS whose τ is a disjunction of local transition formulae. Note that Theorem 5.2 can be used to reconstruct (restricted to safety problems) the essence of the decidability results of [186]. Specifically, it can be shown by a direct computation that transitions in [186] are strongly local which, in turn, can be shown using quantifier elimination (see Section 5.3) for all the details, where we also show how to represent transitions from [186] by the means of existentially quantified data variables). Interestingly, Theorem 5.2 can be applied to more cases not covered in [186]. For example, one can provide transitions enforcing *updates over unboundedly many* tuples (bulk updates) that are strongly local (cf. Section 5.3).

Theorem 5.2 covers also problems coming from a different source, like coverability problems for broadcast protocols [111, 98]: these problems can be encoded using local formulae over the trivial one-sorted signature containing just one basic sort, finitely many constants and one artifact sort with one artifact component. We remark that coverability for broadcast protocols can be decided with a non-primitive recursive lower bound [231]; this proves that our framework is quite expressive (the problems in [186] have for instance an EXPSPACE upper bound). Recalling that [186] handles verification of LTL-FO, thus going beyond safety problems, this shows that the two settings are incomparable. Finally, we highlight that Theorem 5.2 implies also the decidability of the safety problem for SASs, in case of Σ acyclic.

5.2.2 Proof of Theorem 5.2 and an Example of (Strongly) Local RAS

Before proving Theorem 5.2, we need to recall some basic facts about well-quasi-orders. Recall that a *well-quasi-order* (wqo) is a set W endowed with a reflexive-transitive relation $\leq$ having the following property: for every infinite succession

$$w_0, w_1, \ldots, w_i, \ldots$$

of elements from W there are i, j such that $i < j$ and $w_i \leq w_j$ The fundamental result about wqo's is the following theorem, which is a recursive version of Higman's lemma [162] and is a special case of the well-known Kruskal's Tree Theorem [182]:

Theorem 5.3 *If $(W, \leq)$ is a wqo, then so is the partial order of the finite lists over W, ordered by componentwise subword comparison (i.e. $w \leq w'$ iff there is a subword w_0 of w' of the same length as w, such that the i-th entry of w is less or equal to—in the sense of $(W, \leq)$—the i-th entry of w_0, for all $i = 0, \ldots |w|$).*

Various wqo's can be recognized by applying the above theorem; in particular, the theorem implies that the cartesian product of wqo's is a wqo. As an application, notice that $\mathbb{N}$ is a wqo, hence the following corollary (known as Dickson's Lemma) follows:

Corollary 5.1 *The cartesian product of k-copies of $\mathbb{N}$ (and also of $\mathbb{N} \cup \{\infty\}$), with componentwise ordering, is a wqo.*

Let $\tilde{\Sigma}$ be $\Sigma_{ext} \cup \{\underline{a}, \underline{x}\}$, that is, Σ_{ext} expanded with function symbols $\underline{a}$ and constants $\underline{x}$ (thus, a $\tilde{\Sigma}$-structure is a Σ_{ext}-structure endowed with an assignment to $\underline{x}$ and $\underline{a}$, which were variables and now are treated as symbols of $\tilde{\Sigma}$). For the following, we need the following definition:

Definition 5.1 A $\tilde{\Sigma}$-structure $\mathcal{M}$ is called *cyclic*[2] if it is generated by a *single* element $e \in E^{\mathcal{M}}$ (called *generator* of $\mathcal{M}$), where E is an artifact sort (i.e. e belongs to the interpretation of an artifact sort E).

The previous definition intuitively means that *all* the elements of the cyclic structures are obtained from the generator by applying the function symbols of $\tilde{\Sigma}$ to the generator.

Since Σ is acyclic, so is $\tilde{\Sigma}$, and then one can show that there are only finitely many cyclic $\tilde{\Sigma}$-structures $C_1, \ldots, C_N$ up to isomorphism. With a $\tilde{\Sigma}$-structure $\mathcal{M}$ we associate the tuple of numbers $k_1(\mathcal{M}), \ldots, k_N(\mathcal{M}) \in \mathbb{N} \cup \{\infty\}$ counting the

---

[2] This is unrelated to cyclicity of Σ defined in Section 3.1, and comes from universal algebra terminology.

numbers of elements generating (as singletons) cyclic substructures isomorphic to $C_1, \ldots, C_N$, respectively.

Now, we show that, if the tuple associated with M is component-wise bigger than the one associated with N, then M satisfies all the local formulae satisfied by N.

Lemma 5.1 *Let M, N be $\tilde{\Sigma}$-structures. If the inequalities*

$$k_1(M) \leq k_1(N), \ldots, k_N(M) \leq k_N(N)$$

hold, then all local formulae true in M are also true in N.

Proof Local formulae (viewed in $\tilde{\Sigma}$) are sentences, because they do not have free variable occurrences - the $\underline{a}, \underline{x}$ are now constant function symbols and individual constants, respectively. The proof of the lemma is fairly obvious: notice that, once we assigned some $\alpha(e_i)$ in M to the variable e_i, the truth of a formula like $\phi(e_i, \underline{x}, \underline{a})$ under such an assignment depends only on the $\tilde{\Sigma}$-substructure generated by $\alpha(e_i)$, because ϕ is quantifier-free and e_i is the only $\tilde{\Sigma}$-variable occurring in it. In fact, if a local state formula $\exists e_1 \cdots \exists e_k \left(\delta(e_1, \ldots, e_k) \wedge \bigwedge_{i=1}^{k} \phi_i(e_i, \underline{x}, \underline{a}) \right)$ is true in M, then there exist elements $\bar{e}_1, \cdots, \bar{e}_k$ (in the interpretation of some artifact sorts), each of which makes ϕ_i true. Hence, ϕ_i is also true in the corresponding cyclic structure generated by $\bar{e}_i$. Since $k_1(M) \leq k_1(N), \ldots, k_N(M) \leq k_N(N)$ hold, then also in N there are at least as many elements in the interpretation of artifact sorts as there are in M that validate all the ϕ_i. Thus, we get that the formula $\exists e_1 \cdots \exists e_k \left(\delta(e_1, \ldots, e_k) \wedge \bigwedge_{i=1}^{k} \phi_i(e_i, \underline{x}, \underline{a}) \right)$ is true also in N, as wanted.   □

Now we are ready to prove our first termination and decidability result.

Theorem 5.2. *If Σ is acyclic, backward search (cf. Algorithm 1) terminates when applied to solve the safety problem, with respect to a (strongly) local unsafe formula $\upsilon(\underline{x}, \underline{a})$, for a RAS $\langle \Sigma, T, \Sigma_{ext}, \underline{x}, \underline{a}, \iota(\underline{x}, \underline{a}), \tau(\underline{x}, \underline{a}, \underline{x}', \underline{a}') \rangle$, where τ is a disjunction of (strongly) local transition formulae.*

Proof Suppose the algorithm does not terminate. Then the fixpoint test of Line 2 fails infinitely often. Recalling that the T-equivalence of B_n and of $\bigvee_{0 \leq k < n} \phi_k$ is an invariant of the algorithm (here ϕ_n, B_n are the status of the variables ϕ, B after n execution of the main loop), this means that there are models

$$M_0, M_1, \ldots, M_j, \ldots$$

such that for all j, we have that $M_j \models \phi_j$ and $M_j \not\models \phi_i$ (all $i < j$). But the ϕ_j are all local formulae, so considering the tuple of cardinals $k_1(M_j), \ldots, k_N(M_j)$ and Lemma 5.1, we get a contradiction, in view of Dickson's Lemma. This is because, by Dickson's Lemma, $(\mathbb{N} \cup \{\infty\})^N$ is a wqo, so there exist i, j such that $i < j$ and $k_1(M_i) \leq k_1(M_j), \ldots, k_N(M_i) \leq k_N(M_j)$. Using Lemma 5.1, we get that ϕ_i, which is local and true in M_i, is also true in M_j, which is a contradiction.   □

Example 5.1 We now present a shorter version of Example 3.6, and we then notice that all the transitions of this version are strongly local.

We transform again the SAS of Example 3.4 into a RAS $\tilde{S}_{hr}$ containing a multi-instance artifact accounting for the evolution of *job applications*. Each job category may receive multiple applications from registered users. Such applications are then evaluated, finally deciding which are accepted and which are rejected.

As for the read-only DB, $\tilde{S}_{hr}$ works over the DB schema of Example 3.1, extended, as in Example 3.6, with a further value sort Score used to score job applications.

As for the working memory, $\tilde{S}_{hr}$ consists of two artifacts: the single-instance *job hiring* artifact tracking the three main phases of the overall process (and described in Example 3.4), and a multi-instance artifact accounting for the evolution of *user applications*. To model applications, we take the DB signature Σ_{hr} of the read-only database of human resources, and enrich it with an artifact extension containing an artifact sort appIndex used to *index* (i.e., *"internally" identify*) job applications. The management of job applications is then modeled by an artifact setting with: *(i)* artifact components with domain appIndex capturing the artifact relation that stores the different job applications; *(ii)* additional individual variables as a temporary memory to manipulate the artifact relation. Specifically, each application consists of a job category, the identifier of the applicant user and that of an HR employee responsible for the application, the application score, and the final result (indicating whether the application is among the winners or the losers for the job offer). These information slots are encapsulated into dedicated artifact components, i.e., function variables with domain appIndex that collectively realize the application artifact relation:

$$
\begin{aligned}
appJobCat &: \text{appIndex} \longrightarrow \text{JobCatId} \\
applicant &: \text{appIndex} \longrightarrow \text{UserId} \\
appResp &: \text{appIndex} \longrightarrow \text{EmpId} \\
appScore &: \text{appIndex} \longrightarrow \text{Score} \\
appResult &: \text{appIndex} \longrightarrow \text{String}
\end{aligned}
$$

We now discuss the relevant transitions for inserting and evaluating job applications. The insertion of an application into the system can be executed when the hiring process is enabled (cf. Example 3.4), and consists of two consecutive steps. To indicate when a step can be applied, also ensuring that the insertion of an application is not interrupted by the insertion of another one, we manipulate a string artifact variable *aState*. The first step is executable when *aState* is undef, and aims at loading the application data into dedicated artifact variables through the following simultaneous effects: *(i)* the identifier of the user who wants to submit the application, and that of the targeted job category, are selected and respectively stored into variables *uId* and *jId*; *(ii)* the identifier of an HR employee who becomes responsible for the application is selected and stored into variable *eId*, with the requirement that such an employee must be competent in the job category targeted by the application; *(iii)* *aState* evolves into state received. Formally:

$$\exists u\text{:UserId},\ j\text{:JobCatId},\ e\text{:EmpId},\ c\text{:CompInId}$$

$$\begin{pmatrix} pState = \texttt{enabled} \wedge aState = \texttt{undef} \\ \wedge\ u \neq \texttt{undef} \wedge j \neq \texttt{undef} \wedge e \neq \texttt{undef} \wedge c \neq \texttt{undef} \\ \wedge\ who(c) = e \wedge what(c) = j \\ \wedge\ pState' = \texttt{enabled} \wedge aState' = \texttt{received} \\ \wedge\ uId' = u \wedge jId' = j \wedge eId' = e \wedge cId' = c \end{pmatrix} \qquad (5.3)$$

The second step transfers the application data into the application artifact relation, using its corresponding function variables, at the same time resetting all application-related artifact variables to undef (including *aState*, so that new applications can be inserted). For the insertion, a "free" index (i.e., an index pointing to an undefined applicant) is picked. The newly inserted application gets a default score of -1 (thus initializing it to "not eligible"), while the final result is undef:

$$\exists i\text{:appIndex}$$

$$\begin{pmatrix} pState = \texttt{enabled} \wedge aState = \texttt{received} \\ \wedge\ applicant[i] = \texttt{undef} \\ \wedge\ pState' = \texttt{enabled} \wedge aState' = \texttt{undef} \wedge cId' = \texttt{undef} \\ \wedge\ appJobCat' = \lambda j.\ (\text{if } j = i \text{ then } jId \text{ else } appJobCat[j]) \\ \wedge\ applicant' = \lambda j.\ (\text{if } j = i \text{ then } uId \text{ else } applicant[j]) \\ \wedge\ appResp' = \lambda j.\ (\text{if } j = i \text{ then } eId \text{ else } appResp[j]) \\ \wedge\ appScore' = \lambda j.\ (\text{if } j = i \text{ then } -1 \text{ else } appScore[j]) \\ \wedge\ appResult' = \lambda j.\ (\text{if } j = i \text{ then undef else } appResult[j]) \\ \wedge\ jId' = \texttt{undef} \wedge uId' = \texttt{undef} \wedge eId' = \texttt{undef} \end{pmatrix}$$

Such a transition does not prevent the possibility of inserting exactly the same application twice, at different indexes. If this is not wanted, the transition can be suitably changed so as to guarantee that no two identical applications can coexist in the same artifact relation, as in Example 3.6.

Each application currently considered as not eligible can be made eligible by assigning a proper score to it:

$$\exists i\text{:appIndex},\ s\text{:Score}$$

$$\begin{pmatrix} pState = \texttt{enabled} \wedge appScore[i] = -1 \wedge s \geq 0 \\ \wedge\ pState' = \texttt{enabled} \wedge appScore'[i] = s \end{pmatrix}$$

Finally, application results are computed when the process moves to state `notified`. This is handled by the *bulk* transition:

$$pState = \texttt{enabled} \wedge pState' = \texttt{notified}$$

$$\wedge\ appResult' = \lambda j.\ \begin{pmatrix} \text{if } appScore[j] > 80 \text{ then } \texttt{winner} \\ \text{else } \texttt{loser} \end{pmatrix}$$

which declares applications with a score above 80 as winning, and the others as losing.

By inspecting the transitions of this example, one can see that all of them are strongly local. Consequently, it is decidable to check safety of local state formulae. For example, we show that the first transition is strongly local: the computations for all the other transitions are analogous, and all these computations and the details about the format of transitions that are (strongly) local can be found in Section 5.3.

The first transition represents the first step of the insertion of an application into the system. For simplicity, we can rewrite Formula 5.3 into the following equivalent but more succinct formula:

$$\exists \underline{d} \begin{pmatrix} \pi(\underline{x}_1, \underline{x}_2) \wedge \psi(\underline{d}) \wedge d_1 = \texttt{enabled} \wedge d_2 = \texttt{received} \\ \wedge (\underline{x}_1' := \underline{x}_1 \wedge \underline{x}_2' := \underline{d} \wedge \underline{a}' := \underline{a}) \end{pmatrix} \tag{5.4}$$

where $\underline{d} := \langle d_1, d_2, u, j, e, c \rangle$, $\underline{x}_1$ are the artifact variables of the system that are *not* updated, $\underline{x}_2$ are the artifact variables of the system that are updated, $\pi(\underline{x}_1, \underline{x}_2)$ and $\psi(\underline{d})$ are quantifier-free Σ-formulae and $\underline{a}$ are the artifact components of the systems.

We show that the preimage along (5.4) of a strongly local formula is strongly local.

Given a strongly local state formula ϕ, we can easily suppose that ϕ has the following format:

$$\phi := \psi'(\underline{x}) \wedge \exists \underline{i} \left(\text{AllDiff}(\underline{i}) \wedge \Theta(\underline{a}) \right)$$

where $\underline{x}$ are all the artifact variables of the system, $\underline{i}$ are variables of artifact sorts and Θ is a formula involving all the artifact components $\underline{a}$.

We compute the preimage $Pre(5.4, \phi)$:

$$\exists \underline{d} \begin{pmatrix} \pi(\underline{x}_1, \underline{x}_2) \wedge \psi(\underline{d}) \wedge d_1 = \texttt{enabled} \wedge d_2 = \texttt{received} \\ \wedge (\underline{x}_1' := \underline{x}_1 \wedge \underline{x}_2' := \underline{d} \wedge \underline{a}' := \underline{a}) \\ \wedge \psi'(\underline{x}') \wedge \exists \underline{i} \left(\text{AllDiff}(\underline{i}) \wedge \Theta(\underline{a}') \right) \end{pmatrix} \tag{5.5}$$

which can be rewritten as follows:

$$\exists \underline{d} \begin{pmatrix} \pi(\underline{x}_1, \underline{x}_2) \wedge \psi(\underline{d}) \wedge d_1 = \texttt{enabled} \wedge d_2 = \texttt{received} \\ \wedge \psi'(\underline{x}_1, \underline{d}) \wedge \exists \underline{i} \left(\text{AllDiff}(\underline{i}) \wedge \Theta(\underline{a}) \right) \end{pmatrix} \tag{5.6}$$

Now, we can move the existential quantifier $\exists \underline{d}$ in front of $\chi(\underline{d}, \underline{x}_1) := (\psi(\underline{d}) \wedge d_1 = \texttt{enabled} \wedge d_2 = \texttt{received} \wedge \psi'(\underline{x}_1, \underline{d}))$. We eliminate the quantifiers (applying the quantifier elimination procedure for T^*) from the subformula $\exists \underline{d}(\chi(\underline{d}, \underline{x}_1))$ obtaining a formula of the kind $\theta(\underline{x}_1)$.

The final result is

$$\pi(\underline{x}_1, \underline{x}_2) \wedge \theta(\underline{x}_1) \wedge \exists \underline{i} \left(\text{AllDiff}(\underline{i}) \wedge \Theta(\underline{a}) \right) \tag{5.7}$$

which is a strongly local formula.

Also the transitions of the hiring process from Example 3.6 are, in their current form, strongly local, with the exception of those operating over artifact relations in a way that ensures no repeated entries are inserted. Such transitions can be turned into strongly local ones if *repetitions in the artifact relations are allowed*. That is, multiple identical job offers and applications can be inserted in the corresponding relations, using different indexes. This approach realizes a sort of multiset semantics for artifact relations.

The interested reader can find additional details about applications of (strongly) local RASs to data-aware business processes in Section 5.3. Specifically, this section contains a running example (verified against several properties) that can be represented using a RAS that is strongly-local.

5.2.3 Termination with Tree-Like Signatures

Σ is *tree-like* if it is acyclic and all non-leaf nodes have outdegree 1. An artifact setting over Σ is tree-like if $\tilde{\Sigma} := \Sigma_{ext} \cup \{\underline{a}, \underline{x}\}$ is tree-like. In tree-like artifact settings, artifact relations have a single "data" component, and basic relations are unary or binary.

We first state the second main result of this section, that will be proved in the following subsection.

Theorem 5.4 *Backward search (cf. Algorithm 1) terminates when applied to a safety problem in a RAS with a tree-like artifact setting.*

5.2.4 Proof of Theorem 5.4 and an Example of Tree-Like RAS

Proving termination for RAS with a tree-like artifact setting is more complex, but follows a similar schema as in the case of local transition formulae.

If $(W, \leq)$ is a partial order, we consider the set $M(W)$ of finite multisets of W as a partial order in the following way:[3] say that $M \leq N$ holds iff there is an injection $p : M \longrightarrow N$ such that $m \leq p(m)$ holds for all $m \in M$ (in other words, p associates with every occurrence of an element m of M an occurrence $p(m)$ of an element of N such that $p(m) \geq m$ - this is moreover done injectively, i.e. in such a way that different occurrences are associated to different occurrences).

Corollary 5.2 *If $(W, \leq)$ is a wqo, then so is $(M(W), \leq)$ as defined above.*

Proof This is due to the fact that one can convert a multiset M to a list $L(M)$ so that if $L(M) \leq L(N)$ holds, then also $M \leq N$ holds (such a conversion L can be obtained by ordering the occurrences of elements in M in any arbitrarily chosen way). $\quad\square$

We assume that the graph $G(\tilde{\Sigma})$ associated to $\tilde{\Sigma}$ is a tree (the generalization to the case where such a graph is a forest is trivial). This means in particular that each sort is the domain of at most one function symbol and that there just one sort which is not the domain of any function symbol (let us call it the *root sort* of $\tilde{\Sigma}$ and let us denote it with S_r).

By induction on the height of a sort S (defined as the length of the longest path from S to a leaf) in the above graph, we define a wqo $w(S)$ (in the definition we use the fact the cartesian product of wqo's is a wqo and Corollary 5.2). Let $S_1, \ldots, S_n$ be the sons of S in the tree; put

$$w(S) := M(w(S_1)) \times \cdots \times M(w(S_n)) \tag{5.8}$$

(thus, if S is a leaf, $w(S)$ is the trivial one-element wqo - its only element is the empty tuple).

---

[3] This is not the canonical ordering used for multisets, as introduced, e.g., in [24].

Let now M be a finite $\tilde{\Sigma}$-structure; we indicate with S^M the interpretation in M of the sort S (it is a finite set). For $a \in S^M$, we define $M_M(a) \in w(S)$, again by induction on the height of S. Suppose that $S_1, \ldots, S_n$ are the sons of S and that the arc from S_i to S is labeled by the function symbol f_i; then we put

$$M_M(a) := \langle \{M_M(b_1) \mid b_1 \in S_1^M \text{ and } f_1^M(b_1) = a\}, \ldots$$
$$\ldots, \{M_M(b_n) \mid b_n \in S_n^M \text{ and } f_n^M(b_n) = a\}\rangle$$

where f_i^M $(i = 1, \ldots, n)$ is the interpretation of the symbol f_i in M.

Moreover, for every sort S, we let

$$M_M(S) := \{M_M(a) \mid a \in S^M\} \ . \tag{5.9}$$

Finally, we define

$$M(M) := M_M(S_r) \ . \tag{5.10}$$

For termination, the relevant lemma is the following:

Lemma 5.2 *Suppose that $\tilde{\Sigma}$ is tree-like and does not contain constant symbols; given two finite $\tilde{\Sigma}$-structures M and N, we have that if $M(M) \leq M(N)$, then M embeds into N. As a consequence, the finite $\tilde{\Sigma}$-structures are a wqo with respect to the embeddability quasi-order.*

Proof Again, we make an induction on the height of S, proving the claim for the subsignature of $\tilde{\Sigma}$ having S as a root (let us call this the S-subsignature).

Let M be a model over the S-subsignature. For every $a \in S^M$, and for every $f_i : S_i \longrightarrow S$, if we restrict M to the elements in the f_i-fibers of a, we get a model $M_{f_i,a}$ for the S_i-subsignature (an element $c \in \tilde{S}^M$ is in the f_i-fiber of a if, taking the term t corresponding to the composition of the functions symbols going from $\tilde{S}$ to S_i, we have that $f_i^M(t^M(c)) = a$). In addition, if $M_M(a) = (M_1, \ldots, M_n)$, then $M_i = M(M_{f_i,a})$ by definition. Finally, observe that the restriction of M to the S_i-subsignature is the disjoint union of the f_i-fibers models $M_{f_i,a}$, varying $a \in S^M$.

Suppose now that M, N are models over the S-subsignature such that $M(M) \leq M(N)$; this means that we can find an injective map μ mapping S^M into S^N so that $M_M(a) \leq M_N(\mu(a))$. If $M_M(a) = (M_1, \ldots, M_n)$ and $M_N(\mu(a)) = (N_1, \ldots, N_n)$, we then have that $M_i \leq N_i$ for every $i = 1, \ldots, n$. Considering that, as noticed above, $M_i = M_{f_i,a}$ and $N_i = N_{f_i,\mu(a)}$, by induction hypothesis, we have embeddings $\nu_{i,a}$ for the f_i-fibers models of a and $\mu(a)$ (for every $a \in S^M$ and $i = 1, \ldots, n$). Glueing these embeddings to the disjoint union (varying i, a) and adding them μ as S-component, we get the desired embedding of M into N. $\qquad\square$

Theorem 5.4. Backward search (cf. Algorithm 1) terminates when applied to a safety problem in a RAS with a tree-like artifact setting.

Proof For simplicity, we start giving the argument for the case where we do not have constants and artifact variables. Similarly to the proof of Theorem 5.2, suppose the algorithm does not terminate. Then the fixpoint test of Line 2 fails infinitely often. Recalling that the T-equivalence of B_n and of $\bigvee_{0 \leq k < n} \phi_k$ is an invariant of the algorithm (here ϕ_n, B_n are the status of the variables ϕ, B after n execution of the main loop), this means that there are models

$$\mathcal{M}_0, \mathcal{M}_1, \ldots, \mathcal{M}_j, \ldots$$

such that for all j, we have that $\mathcal{M}_j \models \phi_j$ and $\mathcal{M}_j \not\models \phi_i$ (all $i < j$). The models can be taken to be all finite, by Lemma 4.3. But the ϕ_j are all existential sentences in $\tilde{\Sigma}$, so this is incompatible to the fact that, by Lemma 5.2, there are $i < j$ with $\mathcal{M}_i$ embeddable into $\mathcal{M}_j$.

Concerning the general case, it is sufficient to consider the following observation that shows how to extend the proof to the case where we have constants and artifact variables. Recall that in $\tilde{\Sigma}$ the artifact variables are seen as constants, so we need to consider only the case of constants. Let $\tilde{\Sigma}^+$ be $\tilde{\Sigma}$ where each constant symbol c of sort S is replaced by a new sort S_c and a new function symbol $f_c : S_c \longrightarrow S$. Now every model $\mathcal{M}$ of $\tilde{\Sigma}$ can be transformed into a model $\mathcal{M}^+$ of $\tilde{\Sigma}^+$ by interpreting S_c as a singleton set $\{*\}$ and f_c as the map sending $*$ to $c^{\mathcal{M}}$. This transformation has the following property: $\tilde{\Sigma}$-embeddings of $\mathcal{M}$ into $\mathcal{N}$ are in bijective correspondence with $\tilde{\Sigma}^+$-embeddings of $\mathcal{M}^+$ into $\mathcal{N}^+$. Since $\tilde{\Sigma}^+$ is still tree-like and does not have constant symbols, this shows that Theorem 5.4 holds for $\tilde{\Sigma}$ too.   □

While tree-like RAS restrict artifact relations to be unary, their transitions are not subject to any locality restriction. This allows for expressing rich forms of updates, including general bulk updates (which allow us to capture non-primitive recursive verification problems[4]) and transitions comparing at once different tuples in artifact relations. The flight management process presented in the following example shows these advanced features, with a tree-like RAS whose safety verification is indeed decidable. Finally, notice that tree-like RASs are incomparable: *(i)* with the "tree" classes of [37], since the former use artifact relations, whereas the latter only individual variables; *(ii)* with the decidability class of [186], since tree-like RASs express transitions able to compare at once values stored in different tuples in artifact relations.

Example 5.2 We consider a simple RAS that falls in the scope of the tree-like decidability result. Specifically, this example has a tree-like artifact setting (see Figure 5.1), thus assuring that, when solving the safety problem for it, the backward search algorithm is guaranteed to terminate. Note, however, that the termination result adopted here is the one of Theorem 5.4 due to the non-locality of certain transitions, as explained in detail below.

The flight management process represents a simplified version of a flight management system adopted by an airline. To prepare a flight, the company picks a corresponding destination (that meets the aviation safety compliance indications) and consequently reports on a number of passengers that are going to attend the flight. Then, an airport dispatcher may pick a manned flight and put it in the airports

---

[4] The artifact setting described above to capture coverability problems for broadcast protocols is both local and tree-like.

flight plan. In case the flight destination becomes unsafe (e.g., it was struck by a hurricane or the hosting airport had been seized by terrorists), the dispatcher uses the system to inform the airline about this condition. In turn, the airline notifies all the passengers of the affected destination about the contingency, and temporary cancels their flights.

To formalize these different aspects, we make use of a DB signature Σ_{fm} that consists of: *(i)* two id sorts, used to identify flights and cities; *(ii)* one function symbol *destination* : FlightId $\longrightarrow$ CityId mapping flight identifiers to their corresponding destinations (i.e., city identifiers). Note that, in a classical relational model (cf. Section 3.1.1), our signature would contain two relations: one binary R_{FlightId} that defines flights and their destinations, and another unary R_{CityId} identifying cities, that are referenced by R_{FlightId} using *destination*.

We assume that the read-only flight management database contains data about at least one flight and one city. To start the process, one needs at least one city to meet the aviation safety compliances. It is assumed that, initially, all the cities are unsafe. An airport dispatcher, at once, may change the safety status only of one city.

We model this action by performing two consequent actions. First, we select the city identifier and store it in the designated artifact variable *safeCitytId*:

$$\exists c{:}\text{CityId}\ (c \neq \text{undef} \wedge safeCitytId = \text{undef} \wedge safeCitytId' = c)$$

Then, we place the extracted city identifier into a unary artifact relation *safeCity* : CityIndex $\longrightarrow$ CityId, that is used to represent safe cities and where CityIndex is its artifact sort.

$$\exists i{:}\text{CityIndex}$$
$$\begin{pmatrix} safeCity[i] = \text{undef} \wedge safeCitytId \neq \text{undef} \wedge safeCitytId' = \text{undef} \\ \wedge\ safeCity' = \lambda j. \begin{pmatrix} \text{if } j = i \text{ then } safeCitytId \\ \text{else if } safeCity[j] = safeCitytId \text{ then undef} \\ \text{else } safeCity[j] \end{pmatrix} \end{pmatrix}$$

Note that the two previous transitions can be rewritten as a unique one, hence showing a more compact way of specifying RAS transitions. This, in turn, can augment the performance of the verifier while working with large-scale cases. The unified transition actually looks as follows:

$$\exists c{:}\text{CityId},\ \exists i{:}\text{CityIndex}$$
$$\begin{pmatrix} c \neq \text{undef} \wedge safeCity[i] = \text{undef} \\ \wedge\ safeCity' = \lambda j. \begin{pmatrix} \text{if } j = i \text{ then } c \\ \text{else if } safeCity[j] = c \text{ then undef} \\ \text{else } safeCity[j] \end{pmatrix} \end{pmatrix}$$

Then, to register passengers with booked tickets on a flight, the airline needs to make sure that a corresponding flight destination is actually safe. To perform the passenger registration, the airline selects a flight identifier that is assigned to the route and uses it to populate entries in an unary artifact relation *regdPassenger* : PassengerIndex $\longrightarrow$ FlightId. Note that there may be more than one passenger taking the flight, and therefore, more than one entry in *regdPassenger* with the same flight identifier.

$$\exists i\text{:CityIndex}, f\text{:FlightId}, p\text{:PassengerIndex}$$

$$\left(\begin{array}{l} f \neq \text{undef} \wedge destination(f) = safeCity[i] \wedge regdPassenger[p] = \text{undef} \\ \wedge \, regdPassenger' = \lambda j. \left(\begin{array}{l} \text{if } j = p \text{ then } f \\ \text{else } regdPassenger[j] \end{array} \right) \end{array} \right)$$

We also assume that the airline owns aircraft of one type that can contain no more than k passengers. In case there were more than k passengers registered on the flight, the airline receives a notification about its overbooking and temporary suspends all passenger registrations associated to this flight. This is modeled by checking whether there are at least $k + 1$ entries in *regdPassenger*. If so, the flight identifier is added to a unary artifact relation *overbooked* : FligthIndex $\longrightarrow$ FlightId and all the passenger registrations in *regdPassenger* that reference this flight identifier are nullified by updating unboundedly many entries in the corresponding artifact relation:[5]

$$\exists p_1\text{:PassengerIndex}, \ldots p_{k+1}\text{:PassengerIndex}, m\text{:FligthIndex}$$

$$\left(\begin{array}{l} \bigwedge_{i,i' \in \{1,\ldots,k+1\}, i \neq i'} p_i \neq p_{i'} \wedge regdPassenger[p_i] \neq \text{undef} \\ \wedge \, regdPassenger[p_i] = regdPassenger[p_{i'}] \wedge overbooked[m] = \text{undef} \\ \wedge \, regdPassenger' = \lambda j. \left(\begin{array}{l} \text{if } regdPassenger[j] = regdPassenger[p_1] \text{ then undef} \\ \text{else } regdPassenger[j] \end{array} \right) \\ \wedge \, overbooked'[m] = regdPassenger[p_1] \end{array} \right)$$

This transition is not local, since its guard contains literals of the form $regdPassenger[p_i] = regdPassenger[p_{i'}]$ (with $p_i \neq p_{i'}$), which involve more than one element of one artifact sort.

In case of any contingency, the airport dispatcher may change the city status from *safe* to *unsafe*. To do it, we first select one of the safe cities, make it unsafe (i.e., remove it from *safeCity* relation) and store its identifier in the artifact variable *unsafeCityId*:

$$\exists i\text{:CityIndex} \left(\begin{array}{l} unsafeCityId = \text{undef} \wedge safeCity[i] \neq \text{undef} \wedge \\ \wedge \, unsafeCityId' = safeCity[i] \wedge safeCity'[i] = \text{undef} \end{array} \right)$$

Then, we use the remembered city identifier to cancel all the passenger registrations for flights that use this city as their destination:

$$\left(\begin{array}{l} unsafeCityId \neq \text{undef} \wedge unsafeCityId' = \text{undef} \wedge \\ \wedge \, regdPassenger' = \lambda j. \left(\begin{array}{l} \text{if } destination(regdPassenger[j]) = unsafeCityId \text{ then undef} \\ \text{else } regdPassenger[j] \end{array} \right) \end{array} \right)$$

Similarly to the previous case, this transition performs the intended action by updating unboundedly many entries in the artifact relation.

Also in this case, we can shrink the last two transitions into a single transition:

$$\exists i\text{:CityIndex} \left(\begin{array}{l} safeCity[i] \neq \text{undef} \wedge \\ \wedge \, regdPassenger' = \lambda j. \left(\begin{array}{l} \text{if } destination(regdPassenger[j]) = safeCity[i] \text{ then undef} \\ \text{else } regdPassenger[j] \end{array} \right) \end{array} \right)$$

---

[5] For simplicity of presentation, we simply remove such data from the artifact relation. In a real setting, this information would actually be transferred to a dedicated, historical table, so as to reconstruct the status of past, overbooked flights.

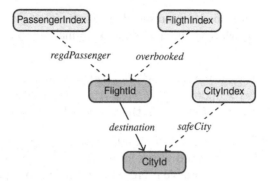

Fig. 5.1: A characteristic graph of the flight management process, where blue and yellow boxes respectively represent basic and artifact sorts.

However, as in the previous case, the transition turns out to be not local. Specifically, it is due to the literal $destination(regdPassenger[j]) = safeCity[i]$ that involves more than one element of (different) artifact sorts.

5.3 Operations Representable as Strongly Local Transitions

We now analyze in the current section how the transition formulae studied in [186][6] (deletion, insertion and propagation updates) can be lifted in the context of RASs. In addition, we discuss some modifications of the previous transitions and introduce new kinds of updates (like bulk updates). We prove that all these transitions are strongly local transitions, hence, in view of Thereom 5.2, the backward reachabilty procedure is guaranteed to terminate over a RAS employing them, when run against a strongly local unsafe formula. For the following, fix an acyclic signature Σ and an artifact setting $(\underline{x}, \underline{a})$ over it.

5.3.1 Deletion Updates

We want to remove a tuple $\underline{t} := (t_1, ..., t_m)$ from an m-ary artifact relation R and assign the values $t_1, ..., t_m$ to some of the artifact variables (let $\underline{x} := \underline{x}_1, \underline{x}_2$, where $\underline{x}_1 := (x_{i_1}, ..., x_{i_m})$ are the variables where we want to transfer the tuple $\underline{t}$). This operation has to be applied only if the current artifact variables $\underline{x}$ satisfy the precondition $\pi(\underline{x}_1, \underline{x}_2)$ and the updated artifact variables $\underline{x}' := \underline{x}'_1, \underline{x}'_2$ satisfy the post-condition $\psi(\underline{x}'_1, \underline{x}'_2)$ (π and ψ are quantifier-free formulae). The variables $\underline{x}_2$ are not

---

[6] For simplicity, since we are not considering hierarchical aspects, we assume that there is no input variable in the sense of [186]

propagated, i.e. they are nondeterministically reassigned. Let $\underline{r} := r_1, ..., r_m$ be the artifact components of R. Such an update can be formalized in a symbolic way as follows:

$$\exists \underline{d}\, \exists e \begin{pmatrix} \pi(\underline{x}_1, \underline{x}_2) \wedge \psi(\underline{x}'_1, \underline{x}'_2) \wedge r_1[e] \neq \text{undef} \wedge ... \\ \wedge\, r_n[e] \neq \text{undef} \wedge (\underline{x}'_1 := \underline{r}[e] \wedge \underline{x}'_2 := \underline{d} \wedge \underline{s}' := \underline{s} \wedge \\ \wedge\, \underline{r}' := \lambda j.(\text{if } j = e \text{ then undef else } \underline{r}[j])) \end{pmatrix} \quad (5.11)$$

where $\underline{s}$ are the artifact components of the artifact relations different from R. The $\underline{d}$ are nondeterministically produced values for the updated $\underline{x}'_2$. In the terminology of [186], notice that no artifact variable is propagated in a deletion update.

In place of the condition $r_1[e] \neq \text{undef} \wedge ... \wedge r_n[e] \neq \text{undef}$ one can consider the modified deletion update that is fired only if *some* (and not all) artifact components are not undef, or even the case when the transition is fired if *at least one* artifact component is not undef: the latter case can be expressed using a disjunction of transitions τ_i that, instead of $r_1[e] \neq \text{undef} \wedge ... \wedge r_n[e] \neq \text{undef}$, involve only the literal $r_i[e] \neq \text{undef}$ (for $i = 1, ..., n$). These modified deletion updates can be proved to be strongly local transitions by using trivial adaptations of the arguments shown below.

The formula (5.11) is not in the format (3.7) but can be easily converted into it as follows:

$$\exists \underline{d}\, \exists e \begin{pmatrix} \pi(\underline{x}_1, \underline{x}_2) \wedge \psi(\underline{r}[e], \underline{d}) \wedge r_1[e] \neq \text{undef} \wedge ... \\ \wedge\, r_n[e] \neq \text{undef} \wedge (\underline{x}'_1 := \underline{r}[e] \wedge \underline{x}'_2 := \underline{d} \wedge \underline{s}' := \underline{s} \wedge \\ \wedge\, \underline{r}' := \lambda j.(\text{if } j = e \text{ then undef else } \underline{r}[j])) \end{pmatrix} \quad (5.12)$$

We prove that the preimage along (5.12) of a strongly local formula is strongly local. Consider a strongly local formula

$$K := \psi'(\underline{x}) \wedge \exists \underline{e} \left(\text{Diff}(\underline{e}) \wedge \bigwedge_{e_r \in \underline{e}} \phi_{e_r}(\underline{r}[e_r]) \wedge \Theta \right)$$

where Θ is a formula involving the artifact components $\underline{s}$ (which are not updated) such that no e_r occurs in it.

Remark 5.2 Notice that equality is the only predicate, so a quantifier-free formula $\phi(e, \underline{a})$ involving a single variable e must be obtained from atoms of the kind $b[e] = b'[e]$ (for $b, b' \in \underline{a}$) by applying the Boolean connectives only: this is why we usually display such a formula as $\phi(\underline{a}[e])$. In addition, since the source sorts of the different artifact relations are different, we cannot employ the same variable as argument of artifact components of different artifact relations: in other words, we cannot employ the same variable e in terms like $r_i[e]$ and $s_j[e]$, in case r_i and s_j are components of two different artifact relation R and S (because e must have either type R or type S). Thus, the quantifier-free subformula $\phi_i(\underline{a}[e_i])$ in a local formula involving only the variable e_i must be of the kind $\phi_i(\underline{r}[e_i])$, for some artifact relation

R (here $\underline{r}$ are the artifact components of R). These observations will be often used in the sequel.

We compute the preimage $Pre(5.12, K)$

$$\exists \underline{d}\, \exists e, \underline{e}\, \exists \underline{x}_1', \underline{x}_2'\, \exists \underline{r}' \left(\begin{array}{c} \pi(\underline{x}_1, \underline{x}_2) \;\wedge\; \psi(\underline{r}[e], \underline{d}) \;\wedge\; \psi'(\underline{x}_1', \underline{x}_2') \;\wedge \\ \wedge\, \underline{x}_1' := \underline{r}[e] \;\wedge\; \underline{x}_2' := \underline{d} \;\wedge\; \text{Diff}(\underline{e}) \;\wedge\; \bigwedge_{e_r \in \underline{e}} \phi_{e_r}(\underline{r}'[e_r]) \;\wedge \\ \wedge\, \underline{r}' := \lambda j.(\text{if } j = e \text{ then undef else } \underline{r}[j]) \;\wedge\; \Theta \end{array} \right)$$

which can be rewritten as a disjunction of the following formulae:

1. $\exists \underline{d}\, \exists e, \underline{e} \left(\begin{array}{c} \text{Diff}(\underline{e}, e) \;\wedge\; \pi(\underline{x}_1, \underline{x}_2) \;\wedge\; \psi(\underline{r}[e], \underline{d}) \;\wedge \\ \wedge\, \psi'(\underline{r}[e], \underline{d}) \;\wedge\; \bigwedge_{e_r \in \underline{e}} \phi_{e_r}(\underline{r}[e_r]) \;\wedge\; \Theta \end{array} \right)$
   covering the case where e is different from all $e_j \in \underline{e}$

2. $\exists \underline{d}\, \exists e \left(\begin{array}{c} \text{Diff}(\underline{e}) \;\wedge\; \pi(\underline{x}_1, \underline{x}_2) \;\wedge\; \psi(\underline{r}[e_j], \underline{d}) \;\wedge\; \psi'(\underline{r}[e_j], \underline{d}) \;\wedge \\ \wedge\, \bigwedge_{e_r \in \underline{e}, e_r \neq e_j} \phi_{e_r}(\underline{r}[e_r]) \;\wedge\; \phi_{e_j}(\text{undef}) \;\wedge\; \Theta \end{array} \right)$
   covering the case where $e = e_j$, for some $e_j \in \underline{e}$

We can now move the existential quantifier $\exists \underline{d}$ in front of $\psi \wedge \psi'$. We eliminate the quantifiers (applying the quantifier elimination procedure for $T^\star$) from the subformula $\exists \underline{d}\, (\psi(\underline{r}[e], \underline{d}) \wedge \psi'(\underline{r}[e], \underline{d}))$ (or $\exists \underline{d}\, (\psi(\underline{r}[e], \underline{d}) \wedge \psi'(\underline{r}[e], \underline{d}))$, resp.) obtaining a formula of the kind $\theta(\underline{r}[e])$ (or $\theta(\underline{r}[e_j])$).

The final result is the disjunction of the formulae

1. $\exists e, \underline{e} \left(\text{Diff}(\underline{e}, e) \;\wedge\; \pi(\underline{x}_1, \underline{x}_2) \;\wedge\; \theta(\underline{r}[e]) \;\wedge\; \bigwedge_{e_r \in \underline{e}} \phi_{e_r}(\underline{r}[e_r]) \;\wedge\; \Theta \right)$

2. $\exists e \left(\begin{array}{c} \text{Diff}(\underline{e}) \;\wedge\; \pi(\underline{x}_1, \underline{x}_2) \;\wedge\; \theta(\underline{r}[e_j]) \;\wedge \\ \wedge\, \bigwedge_{e_r \in \underline{e}, e_r \neq e_j} \phi_{e_r}(\underline{r}[e_r]) \;\wedge\; \phi_{e_j}(\text{undef}) \;\wedge\; \Theta \end{array} \right)$

which is a strongly local formula.

Analogous arguments show that:

(i) transitions like Formula (5.11), where the literals $r_1[e] \neq$ undef $\wedge \ldots \wedge r_n[e] \neq$ undef are replaced with a generic constraint $\chi(\underline{r}[e])$;

(ii) transitions that remove a tuple from an artifact relation (without transferring its values to the corresponding artifact variables);

(iii) transitions that copy the the content of a tuple contained in an artifact relation to some artifact variables, non-deterministically reassigning the values of the other artifact variables;

(iv) transitions that combine (i) and (iii)

are also strongly local.

Remark 5.3 Deletion updates with the propagation of some artifact variables $\underline{x}_1$ (which are not allowed in [186] and in [102]) are *not* strongly local, since the preimage of a strongly local formula can produce formulae of the form $\psi(\underline{r}[e], \underline{x}_1)$. This preimage is *still* local: however, the preimage of a local state formula through a deletion update can generate formulae of the form $\psi(\underline{r}[e], \underline{r}[e'])$, with $e \neq e'$, destroying locality. Hence, the safety problem for a RAS containing deletion updates with propagation in its transitions, is not guaranteed to terminate.

5.3.2 Insertion Updates

We want to insert a tuple of values $\underline{t} := (t_1, ..., t_m)$ from the artifact variables
$\underline{x}_1 := (x_{i_1}, ..., x_{i_m})$ (let $\underline{x} := \underline{x}_1, \underline{x}_2$ as above) into an m-ary artifact relation R.
This operation has to be applied only if the current artifact variables $\underline{x}$ satisfy
the pre-condition $\pi(\underline{x}_1, \underline{x}_2)$ and the updated artifact variables $\underline{x}' := \underline{x}'_1, \underline{x}'_2$ satisfy
the post-condition $\psi(\underline{x}'_1, \underline{x}'_2)$. The variables $\underline{x}$ are all not propagated, i.e. they are
nondeterministically reassigned. Let $\underline{r} := r_1, ..., r_m$ be the artifact components of R.
Such an update can be formalized in a symbolic way as follows:

$$\exists \underline{d}_1, \underline{d}_2 \, \exists e \left(\begin{array}{l} \pi(\underline{x}_1, \underline{x}_2) \, \wedge \, \psi(\underline{x}'_1, \underline{x}'_2) \, \wedge \, \underline{r}[e] = \mathsf{undef} \\ \wedge \, (\underline{x}'_1 := \underline{d}_1 \, \wedge \, \underline{x}'_2 := \underline{d}_2 \, \wedge \, \underline{s}' := \underline{s} \, \wedge \\ \wedge \, \underline{r}' := \lambda j.(\mathtt{if} \, j = e \, \mathtt{then} \, \underline{x}_1 \, \mathtt{else} \, \underline{r}[j])) \end{array} \right) \tag{5.13}$$

where $\underline{s}$ are the artifact components of the artifact relations different from R. The
$\underline{d}_1, \underline{d}_2$ are nondeterministically produced values for the updated $\underline{x}'_1, \underline{x}'_2$. In the terminology of [186], no artifact variable is propagated in a insertion update. Notice that
the following arguments remain the same even if $\underline{r}[e] = \mathsf{undef}$ is replaced with a
conjunction of *some* literals of the form $r_j[e] = \mathsf{undef}$, for some $j = 1, ..., m$, or
even if $\underline{r}[e] = \mathsf{undef}$ is replaced with a generic constraint $\chi(\underline{r}[e])$.

In this transition, the insertion of the same content in correspondence to different
entries is allowed. If we want to avoid this kind of multiple insertions, the update r'
must be modified as follows:

$$\underline{r}' := \lambda j. \left(\begin{array}{l} \mathtt{if} \, j = e \, \mathtt{then} \, \underline{x}_1 \, \mathtt{else} \\ (\mathtt{if} \, \underline{r}[j] = \underline{x}_1 \, \mathtt{then} \, \mathsf{undef} \, \mathtt{else} \, \underline{r}[j]) \end{array} \right)$$

The formula (5.13) is not in the format (3.7) but can be easily converted into it as
follows:

$$\exists \underline{d}_1, \underline{d}_2 \, \exists e \left(\begin{array}{l} \pi(\underline{x}_1, \underline{x}_2) \, \wedge \, \psi(\underline{d}_1, \underline{d}_2) \, \wedge \, \underline{r}[e] = \mathsf{undef} \\ \wedge \, (\underline{x}'_1 := \underline{d}_1 \, \wedge \, \underline{x}'_2 := \underline{d}_2 \, \wedge \, \underline{s}' := \underline{s} \, \wedge \\ \wedge \, \underline{r}' := \lambda j.(\mathtt{if} \, j = e \, \mathtt{then} \, \underline{x}_1 \, \mathtt{else} \, \underline{r}[j])) \end{array} \right) \tag{5.14}$$

We prove that the preimage along (5.14) of a strongly local formula is strongly
local. Consider a strongly local formula

$$K := \psi'(\underline{x}) \wedge \exists \underline{e} \left(\mathrm{Diff}(\underline{e}) \wedge \bigwedge_{e_r \in \underline{e}} \phi_{e_r}(\underline{r}[e_r]) \wedge \Theta \right)$$

where Θ is a formula involving the artifact relations $\underline{s}$ (which are not updated) such
that no e_r occurs in it.

We compute the preimage $Pre(5.14, K)$

$$\exists \underline{d}_1, \underline{d}_2 \, \exists e, \underline{e} \, \exists \underline{x}_1', \underline{x}_2' \, \exists \underline{r}' \left(\begin{array}{c} \pi(\underline{x}_1, \underline{x}_2) \wedge \psi(\underline{d}_1, \underline{d}_2) \wedge \psi'(\underline{x}_1', \underline{x}_2') \wedge \underline{r}[e] = \text{undef} \\ \wedge \, \underline{x}_1' := \underline{d}_1 \wedge \underline{x}_2' := \underline{d}_2 \wedge \text{Diff}(\underline{e}) \wedge \bigwedge_{e_r \in \underline{e}} \phi_{e_r}(\underline{r}'[e_r]) \wedge \\ \wedge \, \underline{r}' := \lambda j.(\text{if } j = e_1 \text{ then } \underline{x}_1 \text{ else } \underline{r}[j]) \wedge \Theta \end{array} \right)$$

which can be rewritten as a disjunction of the following formulae:

1. $\exists \underline{d}_1, \underline{d}_2 \, \exists e, \underline{e} \left(\begin{array}{c} \text{Diff}(\underline{e}, e) \wedge \pi(\underline{x}_1, \underline{x}_2) \wedge \psi(\underline{d}_1, \underline{d}_2) \wedge \psi'(\underline{d}_1, \underline{d}_2) \\ \wedge \, \underline{r}[e] = \text{undef} \wedge \bigwedge_{e_r \in \underline{e}} \phi_{e_r}(\underline{r}[e_r]) \wedge \Theta \end{array} \right)$

   covering the case where e is different from all $e_j \in \underline{e}$

2. $\exists \underline{d}_1, \underline{d}_2 \, \exists \underline{e} \left(\begin{array}{c} \text{Diff}(\underline{e}) \wedge \pi(\underline{x}_1, \underline{x}_2) \wedge \psi(\underline{d}_1, \underline{d}_2) \wedge \psi'(\underline{d}_1, \underline{d}_2) \wedge \\ \wedge \, \underline{r}[e] = \text{undef} \wedge \bigwedge_{e_r \in \underline{e}, e_r \neq e_j} \phi_{e_r}(\underline{r}[e_r]) \wedge \phi_{e_j}(\underline{x}_1) \wedge \Theta \end{array} \right)$

   covering the case where $e = e_j$, for some $e_j \in \underline{e}$.

We can move the existential quantifiers $\exists \underline{d}_1, \underline{d}_2$ in front of $\psi \wedge \psi'$. We eliminate the quantifiers (applying the quantifier elimination procedure for $T^\star$) from the subformula $\exists \underline{d}_1 \underline{d}_2 \left(\psi(\underline{d}_1, \underline{d}_2) \wedge \psi'(\underline{d}_1, \underline{d}_2) \right)$ obtaining a ground formula θ.

The final result is a disjunction of formulae fo the kind

1. $\exists e, \underline{e} \left(\text{Diff}(\underline{e}, e) \wedge \pi(\underline{x}_1, \underline{x}_2) \wedge \underline{r}[e] = \text{undef} \wedge \theta \wedge \bigwedge_{e_r \in \underline{e}} \phi_{e_r}(\underline{r}[e_r]) \wedge \Theta \right)$

2. $\exists \underline{e} \left(\begin{array}{c} \text{Diff}(\underline{e}) \wedge \pi(\underline{x}_1, \underline{x}_2) \wedge \phi_{e_j}(\underline{x}_1) \wedge \underline{r}[e] = \text{undef} \wedge \\ \wedge \, \theta \wedge \bigwedge_{e_r \in \underline{e}, e_r \neq e_j} \phi_{e_r}(\underline{r}[e_r]) \wedge \Theta \end{array} \right)$

which is a strongly local formula.

Analogous arguments show that transitions that insert a tuple of values $\underline{t} := (t_1, ..., t_m)$ (where the values t_j are taken from the content of the artifact variables $\underline{x}_1 := (x_{i_1}, ..., x_{i_m})$ or are *constants*) into an m-ary artifact relation R are also strongly local; in addition, it is easy to see that "propagation" (in the sense of the following subsection) of variables from $\underline{x}$ is allowed in order to preserve strong locality of all those transitions. The transition introduced in Example 5.1:

$$\exists i : \text{appIndex}$$
$$\left(\begin{array}{l} pState = \texttt{enabled} \wedge aState = \texttt{received} \\ \wedge \, applicant[i] = \text{undef} \\ \wedge \, pState' = \texttt{enabled} \wedge aState' = \text{undef} \wedge cId' = \text{undef} \\ \wedge \, appJobCat' = \lambda j. (\text{if } j = i \text{ then } jId \text{ else } appJobCat[j]) \\ \wedge \, applicant' = \lambda j. (\text{if } j = i \text{ then } uId \text{ else } applicant[j]) \\ \wedge \, appResp' = \lambda j. (\text{if } j = i \text{ then } eId \text{ else } appResp[j]) \\ \wedge \, appScore' = \lambda j. (\text{if } j = i \text{ then } -1 \text{ else } appScore[j]) \\ \wedge \, appResult' = \lambda j. (\text{if } j = i \text{ then } \text{undef} \text{ else } appResult[j]) \\ \wedge \, jId' = \text{undef} \wedge uId' = \text{undef} \wedge eId' = \text{undef} \end{array} \right)$$

presents the described format.

We close this section with an important remark. When we forbid the insertion at different indexes of multiple identical tuples in an artifact relation, transitions break the strong locality requirement. A way to restore locality is to simply admit such repeated insertions. Notably, if one focuses on the fragment of strongly local RAS that coincides with the model in [102, 186], it can be shown, exactly reconstructing the same line of reasoning from [102], that the safety verification problems (in the restricted common fragment) for artifact systems working over sets (i.e., insertions are performed over working memory without possible repetitions) and those working over multisets, are indeed *equivalent*, in the sense that, in spite of the semantic differences on how the data component is interpreted (in particular regarding set vs multiset semantics), the verdict of safety verification (SAFE or UNSAFE) is unchanged.

5.3.3 Propagation Updates

We want to propagate a tuple $\underline{t} := (t_1, ..., t_m)$ of values contained in the artifact variables $\underline{x}_1 := (x_{i_1}, ..., x_{i_m})$ (let $\underline{x} := \underline{x}_1, \underline{x}_2$) to the corresponding updated artifact variables $\underline{x}'_1$. This operation has to be applied only if the current artifact variables $\underline{x}$ satisfy the pre-condition $\pi(\underline{x}_1, \underline{x}_2)$ and the updated artifact variables $\underline{x}' := \underline{x}'_1, \underline{x}'_2$ satisfy the post-condition $\psi(\underline{x}'_1, \underline{x}'_2)$. In this transition no update of artifact component is involved.

Such an update can be formalized in a symbolic way as follows:

$$\exists \underline{d} \left(\pi(\underline{x}_1, \underline{x}_2) \,\wedge\, \psi(\underline{x}'_1, \underline{x}'_2) \wedge (\underline{x}'_1 := \underline{x}_1 \,\wedge\, \underline{x}'_2 := \underline{d} \,\wedge\, \underline{s}' := \underline{s})\right) \qquad (5.15)$$

where $\underline{s}$ stands for all the artifact components. The $\underline{d}$ are nondeterministically produced values for the updated $\underline{x}'_2$. In the terminology of [186], the artifact variables $\underline{x}_1$ are propagated.

The formula (5.15) is not in the format (3.7) but can be easily converted into it as follows:

$$\exists \underline{d} \left(\pi(\underline{x}_1, \underline{x}_2) \,\wedge\, \psi(\underline{x}_1, \underline{d}) \wedge (\underline{x}'_1 := \underline{x}_1 \,\wedge\, \underline{x}'_2 := \underline{d} \,\wedge\, \underline{s}' := \underline{s})\right) \qquad (5.16)$$

We prove that the preimage along (5.16) of a strongly local formula is strongly local. Consider a strongly local formula

$$K := \psi'(\underline{x}) \wedge \exists \underline{e} \left(\mathrm{Diff}(\underline{e}) \wedge \Theta \right)$$

where Θ is a formula involving all the artifact relations $\underline{s}$ (which are not modified in a propagation update), such that K fits the format of (5.2).

We compute the preimage $Pre(5.15, K)$

$$\exists \underline{d} \, \exists \underline{x}'_1, \underline{x}'_2 \left(\begin{array}{l} \pi(\underline{x}_1, \underline{x}_2) \,\wedge\, \psi(\underline{x}_1, \underline{d}) \,\wedge\, \psi'(\underline{x}_1, \underline{x}'_2) \,\wedge \\ \wedge \, \underline{x}'_1 := \underline{x}_1 \,\wedge\, \underline{x}'_2 := \underline{d} \,\wedge\, \mathrm{Diff}(\underline{e}) \,\wedge\, \Theta \end{array} \right)$$

which can be rewritten as follows:

$$\exists \underline{d} \, \exists \underline{e} \left(\begin{array}{l} \mathrm{Diff}(\underline{e}) \wedge \pi(\underline{x}_1, \underline{x}_2) \wedge \psi(\underline{x}_1, \underline{d}) \,\wedge \\ \wedge \, \psi'(\underline{x}_1, \underline{d}) \,\wedge\, \Theta \end{array} \right)$$

We can move the existential quantifier $\exists \underline{d}$ in front of $\psi \wedge \psi'$. We eliminate the quantifiers (applying the quantifier elimination procedure for $T^\star$) from the subformula $\exists \underline{d}(\psi(\underline{x}_1, \underline{d}) \wedge \psi'(\underline{x}_1 \underline{d}))$ obtaining a formula of the kind $\theta(\underline{x}_1)$.

The final result is

$$\exists \underline{e} \left(\text{Diff}(\underline{e}) \ \wedge \ \pi(\underline{x}_1, \underline{x}_2) \ \wedge \ \theta(\underline{x}_1) \ \wedge \ \Theta \right)$$

which is a strongly local formula.

Consider a transition that inserts constants or a non-deterministically generated new value d' (or a tuple of new values $\underline{d}'$) into an artifact component r_i (or more than one) of an m-ary artifact relation $\underline{r}$, propagating all the other components and the artifact variables $\underline{x}_1$ (with $\underline{x} := \underline{x}_1, \underline{x}_2$). Formally, this transition can be written in the following way:

$$\exists \underline{d}, d' \, \exists e \left(\begin{array}{c} \pi(\underline{x}_1, \underline{x}_2) \ \wedge \ \psi(\underline{x}'_1, \underline{x}'_2) \ \wedge \ \chi_1(d') \ \wedge \ \chi_2(\underline{r}[e]) \ \wedge \\ \wedge \ (\underline{x}'_1 := \underline{x}_1 \ \wedge \ \underline{x}'_2 := \underline{d} \ \wedge \ r'_i = \lambda j.(\text{if } j = e \text{ then } d' \text{ else } r[j]) \ \wedge \ \underline{s}' := \underline{s}) \end{array} \right)$$
(5.17)

where $\underline{s}$ stands for all the artifact components different from r_i, and χ_1 and χ_2 are quantifier-free formulae. The $\underline{d}$ are nondeterministically produced values for the updated $\underline{x}'_2$. In the terminology of [186], the artifact variables $\underline{x}_1$ are propagated.

The formula (5.17) is not in the format (3.7) but can be easily converted into it as follows:

$$\exists \underline{d}, d' \, \exists e \left(\begin{array}{c} \pi(\underline{x}_1, \underline{x}_2) \ \wedge \ \psi(\underline{x}_1, \underline{d}) \ \wedge \ \chi_1(d') \ \wedge \ \chi_2(\underline{r}[e]) \ \wedge \\ \wedge \ (\underline{x}'_1 := \underline{x}_1 \ \wedge \ \underline{x}'_2 := \underline{d} \ \wedge \ r'_i = \lambda j.(\text{if } j = e \text{ then } d' \text{ else } r[j]) \ \wedge \ \underline{s}' := \underline{s}) \end{array} \right)$$
(5.18)

Since d' does not occur in literals involving artifact variables, arguments analogous to the previous ones show that this transition is strongly local.

The following transition (described in Example 5.1):

$$\exists i:\text{joIndex}, s:Score$$
$$\left(\begin{array}{l} pState = \texttt{enabled} \\ \wedge \ applicant[i] \neq \text{undef} \ \wedge \ appScore[i] = -1 \\ aState = \text{undef} \ \wedge \ aState' = \text{undef} \ \wedge \ s \geq 0 \\ \wedge \ pState' = \texttt{enabled} \ \wedge \ appScore'[i] = s \end{array} \right)$$

that assesses a Score to an applicant presents the structure of (5.18), so it is a strongly local transition. The same conclusion holds for the transition:

$$\exists u:\text{UserId}, j:\text{JobCatId}, e:\text{EmpId}, c:\text{CompInId}$$
$$\left(\begin{array}{l} pState = \texttt{enabled} \ \wedge \ aState = \text{undef} \\ \wedge \ u \neq \text{undef} \ \wedge \ j \neq \text{undef} \ \wedge \ e \neq \text{undef} \ \wedge \ c \neq \text{undef} \\ \wedge \ who(c) = e \ \wedge \ what(c) = j \\ \wedge \ pState' = \texttt{enabled} \ \wedge \ aState' = \texttt{received} \\ \wedge \ uId' = u \ \wedge \ jId' = j \ \wedge \ eId' = e \ \wedge \ cId' = c \end{array} \right)$$

presented in Example 5.1.

5.3.4 Bulk Updates

We want to unboundedly (bulk) update one (or more than one) artifact component(s) r_i of one (or more than one) artifact relation(s) $\underline{r}$: if some conditions over the artifacts are satisfied for some entries, a global update that involves all those entries (inserting some constant c_1) is fired. In our symbolic formalism, we write:

$$\exists \underline{d} \left(\begin{array}{c} \pi(\underline{x}_1, \underline{x}_2) \wedge \psi(\underline{x}'_1, \underline{x}'_2) \wedge (\underline{x}'_1 := \underline{x}_1 \wedge \underline{x}'_2 := \underline{d} \wedge \underline{s}' := \underline{s} \wedge \\ \wedge r'_1 := r_1 \wedge \dots \wedge r'_i := \lambda j.(\text{if } \kappa_1(\underline{r}[j]) \text{ then } c_1 \text{ else } r_i[j])) \wedge \dots \wedge r'_n := r_n) \end{array} \right)$$
(5.19)

where $\underline{x} := \underline{x}_1, \underline{x}_2$ are artifact variables and $\underline{x}_1$ are propagated, $\underline{r}$ are the artifact components of an artifact relation R, $\underline{s}$ are the remaining artifact components, κ_1 is a quantifier-free formula[7], c_1 is a constant. The artifact component r_i is updated in a global, unbounded way: we call this kind of update "bulk update".

The formula (5.19) is not in the format (3.7) but can be easily converted into it as follows:

$$\exists \underline{d} \left(\begin{array}{c} \pi(\underline{x}_1, \underline{x}_2) \wedge \psi(\underline{x}_1, \underline{d}) \wedge (\underline{x}'_1 := \underline{x}_1 \wedge \underline{x}'_2 := \underline{d} \wedge \underline{s}' := \underline{s} \wedge \\ \wedge r'_1 := r_1 \wedge \dots \wedge r'_i := \lambda j.(\text{if } \kappa_1(\underline{r}[j]) \text{ then } c_1 \text{ else } r_i[j])) \wedge \dots \wedge r'_n := r_n) \end{array} \right)$$
(5.20)

We prove that the preimage along (5.20) of a strongly local formula is strongly local. Consider a strongly local formula

$$K := \psi'(\underline{x}) \wedge \exists \underline{e} \left(\text{Diff}(\underline{e}) \wedge \bigwedge_{e_r \in \underline{e}} \phi_{e_r}(\underline{r}[e_r]) \wedge \Theta \right)$$

where Θ is a formula involving the artifact relations $\underline{s}$ (which are not updated) such that no e_r occurs in it.

We compute the preimage $Pre(5.20, K)$

$$\exists \underline{d}\, \exists \underline{e} \left(\begin{array}{c} \text{Diff}(\underline{e}) \wedge \pi(\underline{x}_1, \underline{x}_2) \wedge \psi(\underline{x}_1, \underline{d}) \wedge \psi'(\underline{x}_1, \underline{d}) \\ \wedge (\underline{x}'_1 := \underline{x}_1 \wedge \underline{x}'_2 := \underline{d} \wedge \underline{s}' := \underline{s} \wedge \bigwedge_{e_r \in \underline{e}} \phi_{e_r}(\underline{r}'[e_r]) \wedge \Theta \\ \wedge r'_1 := r_1 \wedge \dots \wedge r'_i := \lambda j.(\text{if } \kappa_1(\underline{r}[j]) \text{ then } c_1 \text{ else } r_i[j])) \wedge \dots \wedge r'_n := r_n) \end{array} \right)$$
(5.21)

which can be rewritten as a disjunction of the following formulae indexed by a function f that associates to every e_r a boolean value in $0, 1$:

$$\exists \underline{d},\, \exists \underline{e} \left(\begin{array}{c} \text{Diff}(\underline{e}) \wedge \pi(\underline{x}_1, \underline{x}_2) \wedge \psi(\underline{x}_1, \underline{d}) \wedge \psi'(\underline{x}_1, \underline{d}) \wedge \\ \bigwedge_{e_r \in \underline{e}}(\epsilon_f(e_r)\kappa_1(\underline{r}[e_r]) \wedge \phi(r_1[e_r], \dots \delta_f(e_r), \dots, r_n[e_r])) \wedge \Theta \end{array} \right)$$
(5.22)

---

[7] From the computations below, it is clear that strong locality holds also in case κ_1 depends also on the variables $\underline{x}$, on the condition that $\kappa_1(\underline{x}, \underline{r}[j])$ has the form $h_0(\underline{x}) \wedge h_1(\underline{r}[j])$, with h_0 and h_1 quantifier-free formulae

where $\epsilon_f(e_r) := \neg$ if $f(e_r) = 0$, otherwise $\epsilon_f(e_r) := \emptyset$, and $\delta_f(e_r) := c_1$ if $f(e_r) = 0$, otherwise $\delta_f(e_r) := r_i[e_r]$.

We can conclude as above (cf. propagation updates), by eliminating the existentially quantified variable $\underline{d}$, that this formula is strongly local.

The previous arguments remain the same if $r_i' :=$ $\lambda j.(\text{if } \kappa_1(\underline{r}[j]) \text{ then } c_1 \text{ else } r_i[j]))$ in Formula (5.19) is replaced by $r_i' := \lambda j.(\text{if } \kappa_1(\underline{r}[j]) \text{ then } c_1 \text{ else } c_2)$, with c_2 a constant. Even in this case, the modified bulk transition is strongly local.

Analogous arguments show that transitions involving more than one artifact relations which are updated like r_i are also strongly local.

The transition introduced in Example 5.1

$$pState = \texttt{enabled} \wedge pState' = \texttt{notified}$$
$$aState = \texttt{undef} \wedge aState' = \texttt{undef} \wedge appResult' = \lambda j. \begin{pmatrix} \text{if } appScore[j] > 80 \text{ then } \texttt{winner} \\ \text{else } \texttt{loser} \end{pmatrix}$$

is a bulk update transition in the format described in this subsection, so it is a strongly local transition.

5.4 A Summary of the Comparison with Related DAP Formalisms

We conclude the chapter by summarizing how our framework relates to the settings of [37] and of [186].

U-RASs and RASs are in general more expressive than the database-driven systems studied in [37], because the latter only employ individual variables (i.e., what we call artifact variables) in the working memory. For this reason, these systems can be compared only with the SAS model. As discussed in Remark 5.1, the database-driven systems from [37] admit a slightly more general query language for guards (i.e., they can use n-ary functions, with the proviso that the background theory is locally finite), but we can enrich our SASs with the same capabilities without breaking the decidability result stated in Theorem 5.1 (for this enrichment, see Chapter 7). Keeping these considerations in mind, we notice also that Theorem 5.1 essentially states the same decidability result of Theorem 5 in [37], when we restrict our attention to a first-order setting. We also remark that the decidability result obtained for Local RASs comprises the decidable case of SASs.

Concerning RASs, we highlighted several times that RASs with the (standard) DB schema comprising Axioms (3.1) are able to capture all the expressive features of the artifact systems (the HAS^* models) presented in [186]. Specifically, the restrictions imposed in [186] to guarantee decidability are analogous to the locality condition stated in Section 5.2.1: Theorem 5.2 faithfully reconstructs the decidability result for HAS^* models when we restrict their verification language to express only safety properties, and we know from Section 5.3 that all the operations supported by HAS^*

models fall into the spectrum of (strong) locality. In general, HAS^* models and RASs are incomparable: indeed, the former are verified against generic temporal properties and not only for safety, while the latter are strictly more expressive, since, for example, RASs support operations such as "bulk updates" that cannot be performed in HAS^* models.

Finally, we remark that our framework is the first in the DAP literature to make use of well-established and highly performing verification tools like SMT solvers.

Part II
Automated Reasoning Techniques for Data-Aware Process Verification

Chapter 6
Preliminaries for (Uniform) Interpolation

In this chapter, we provide preliminaries and basic notions on the logical notion of (uniform) interpolation. We also relate it to other well-known concepts in logic and automated reasoning, such as the equality interpolating condition and Beth Definability.

6.1 General Preliminaries

We recall some preliminaries from Chapter 2 that are useful also in this part of the book. Again, We adopt the usual first-order syntactic notions of signature, term, atom, (ground) formula, and so on; our signatures are always *finite* or *countable*, are multi-sorted and include equality for every sort. This implies that variables are sorted as well. To avoid considering limit cases, we assume that signatures always contain at least an individual constant per sort. For simplicity, most basic definitions in this section will be supplied for single-sorted languages only. However, the adaptation to multi-sorted languages is straightforward: for example, a multi-sorted signature Σ must contain not only constant, function and relation symbols, but also sorts. We compactly represent a tuple $\langle x_1, \ldots, x_n \rangle$ of variables as $\underline{x}$. The notation $t(\underline{x}), \phi(\underline{x})$ means that the term t, the formula ϕ has free variables included in the tuple $\underline{x}$. Our tuples are assumed to be formed by *distinct variables*, thus we underline that, writing e.g. $\phi(\underline{x}, \underline{y})$, we mean that the tuples $\underline{x}, \underline{y}$ are made of distinct variables that are also disjoint from each other.

We assume that a function arity can be deduced from the context. Whenever we build terms and formulae, we always assume that they are well-typed, in the sense that the sorts of variables, constants, and function sources/targets match. The definition of universal and existential forrmulae are as in Chapter 2.

From the semantic side, we use the standard notion of a Σ-structure $\mathcal{M}$ and of truth of a formula in a Σ-structure under a free variables assignment. The *support* of a structure $\mathcal{M}$ is the disjoint union of the interpretations of the Σ-sorts in $\mathcal{M}$ and is indicated with $|\mathcal{M}|$.

A. Gianola: *Verification of Data-Aware Processes via Satisfiability Modulo Theories*,
LNBIP 470, pp. 123–128, 2023.
https://doi.org/10.1007/978-3-031-42746-6_6

A Σ-*theory* T is a set of Σ-sentences; a *model* of T is a Σ-structure $\mathcal{M}$ where all sentences in T are true. The notation $T \models \phi$, the notion of T-*satisfiability*, of Σ-*constraint* and of *constraint satisfiability problem* for T are the same as in Chapter 2.

We recall that a theory T has *quantifier elimination* iff for every formula $\phi(\underline{x})$ in the signature of T there is a quantifier-free formula $\phi'(\underline{x})$ such that $T \models \phi(\underline{x}) \leftrightarrow \phi'(\underline{x})$. We also recall from Chapter 2 that quantifier elimination holds in case we can eliminate quantifiers from *primitive* formulae, i.e. from formulae of the kind $\exists \underline{y}\, \phi(\underline{x}, \underline{y})$, where ϕ is a constraint. We assume again that when we talk about quantifier elimination, an effective procedure for eliminating quantifiers is given.

We adopt here, given a Σ-structure $\mathcal{M}$, the same notation $\Sigma^{|\mathcal{M}|}$ for the expanded signature defined in Chapter 2. Moreover, the notions of Σ-embedding, substructure, extension, amalgamation and diagram are the same as in Chapter 2. We remind the reader that the typical use of the Robinson Diagram Lemma (cf. Chapter 2) is the following: suppose we want to show that some structure $\mathcal{M}$ can be embedded into a structure $\mathcal{N}$ in such a way that some set of sentences Θ are true. Then, by the Lemma, this turns out to be equivalent to the fact that the set of sentences $\Delta(\mathcal{M}) \cup \Theta$ is consistent: thus, the Diagram Lemma can be used to transform an *embeddability* problem into a *consistency* problem.

6.1.1 Preliminaries on Uniform Interpolants or Covers

We report the notion of *cover* taken from [157]. Covers turn out to be equivalent, in the context of first-order logic, to the well-known notion of uniform interpolant, originally studied in the context of non-classical logics starting from the pioneering work by Pitts [215].

We first give the general definition of ordinary interpolants, and then we define what uniform interpolants are in general. We fix a logic or a theory T and a suitable fragment L (propositional, first-order quantifier-free, etc.) of its language.

Definition 6.1 (Ordinary Interpolant) Given two L-formulae $\phi(\underline{x}, \underline{y})$ and $\psi(\underline{x}, \underline{z})$ (here $\underline{x}, \underline{y}$ are the variables occurring in ϕ and $\underline{x}, \underline{z}$ are the variables occurring in ψ) such that $\phi(\underline{x}, \underline{y}) \vdash_T \psi(\underline{x}, \underline{z})$, an *ordinary interpolant* for (ϕ, ψ) is an L-formula $\phi'(\underline{x})$ where only the $\underline{x}$ occur, and that satisfies the following two properties: *(i)* $\phi(\underline{x}, \underline{y}) \vdash_T \phi'(\underline{x})$; *(ii)* $\phi'(\underline{x}) \vdash_T \psi(\underline{x}, \underline{z})$.

We say that T has ordinary interpolation if for every pair of L-formulae $\phi(\underline{x}, \underline{y})$ and $\psi(\underline{x}, \underline{z})$ there exists an ordinary interpolant ϕ' for (ϕ, ψ). In case T is a first-order Σ-theory and L is the quantifier-free fragment (i.e., ϕ, ϕ' and ψ are quantifier-free Σ-formulae), we say that an ordinary interpolant as defined above is a (ordinary quantifier-free) T-interpolant.

We now give the general definition of uniform interpolants.

Definition 6.2 (Uniform Interpolant) Given an L-formula $\phi(\underline{x}, \underline{y})$ (here $\underline{x}, \underline{y}$ are the variables occurring in ϕ), a *uniform interpolant* of ϕ (w.r.t. $\underline{y}$) is an L-formula $\phi'(\underline{x})$

where only the x occur, and that satisfies the following two properties: *(i)* $\phi(\underline{x}, y) \vdash_T$ $\phi'(\underline{x})$; *(ii)* for any further L-formula $\psi(\underline{x}, \underline{z})$ such that $\phi(\underline{x}, y) \vdash_T \psi(\underline{x}, \underline{z})$, we have $\phi'(\underline{x}) \vdash_T \psi(\underline{x}, \underline{z})$.

We say that T has uniform interpolation if for every L-formula $\phi(\underline{x}, y)$, there exists an uniform interpolant ϕ' of ϕ w.r.t. y. In case T is a first-order Σ-theory and L is the quantifier-free fragment (i.e., ϕ, ϕ' and ψ are quantifier-free Σ-formulae), we say that a uniform interpolant as defined above is a uniform (quantifier-free) T-interpolant.

Whenever uniform interpolants exist, one can compute an interpolant for an entailment like $\phi(\underline{x}, y) \vdash_T \psi(\underline{x}, \underline{z})$ in a way that is *independent* of ψ. Notably, if T has uniform quantifier-free interpolation, then it has ordinary quantifier-free interpolation, in the sense that if we have $\phi(\underline{x}, y) \vdash_T \psi(\underline{x}, \underline{z})$ (for L-formulae ϕ, ϕ'), then there is an L-formula $\phi'(\underline{x})$ such that $\phi(\underline{x}, y) \vdash_T \phi'(\underline{x})$ and $\phi'(\underline{x}) \vdash_T \psi(\underline{x}, \underline{z})$. In fact, let us suppose that $\phi(\underline{x}, y) \vdash_T \psi(\underline{x}, \underline{z})$. If T has uniform quantifier-free interpolation, then there exists a uniform interpolant ϕ' (independent on ψ): the same $\phi'(\underline{x})$ can be used as *ordinary* interpolant for all entailments $\phi(\underline{x}, y) \vdash_T \psi(\underline{y}, \underline{z})$, varying ψ.

We now turn to define the notion of cover, in the context of a first-order logic theory T.

Definition 6.3 (Cover) Fix a theory T and an existential formula $\exists \underline{e}\, \phi(\underline{e}, y)$; call a *residue* of $\exists \underline{e}\, \phi(\underline{e}, y)$ any quantifier-free formula belonging to the set of quantifier-free formulae

$$Res(\exists \underline{e}\, \phi) = \{\theta(\underline{y}, \underline{z}) \mid T \models \exists \underline{e}\, \phi(\underline{e}, y) \rightarrow \theta(\underline{y}, \underline{z})\} = \{\theta(\underline{y}, \underline{z}) \mid T \models \phi(\underline{e}, y) \rightarrow \theta(\underline{y}, \underline{z})\}.$$

A quantifier-free formula $\psi(y)$ is said to be a T-*cover* (or, simply, a *cover*) of $\exists \underline{e}\, \phi(\underline{e}, y)$ iff $\psi(y) \in Res(\exists \underline{e}\, \bar{\phi})$ and $\psi(y)$ implies (modulo T) all the other formulae in $Res(\exists \underline{e}\, \phi)$.

It is immediately seen that covers are unique (modulo T-equivalence). The cover $\psi(y)$ does not depend anymore on the variables $\underline{e}$ appearing in the existential formula $\exists \underline{e}\, \phi(\underline{e}, y)$, hence these variables have been intuitively 'eliminated' in some sense. By definition, it is always true that $T \vdash \exists \underline{e}\, \phi(\underline{e}, y) \rightarrow \psi(y)$; however, in general $T \nvdash \psi(y) \rightarrow \exists \underline{e}\, \phi(\underline{e}, y)$. We remark that in case the theory T admits quantifier elimination, we get also that $T \vdash \psi(y) \rightarrow \exists \underline{e}\, \phi(\underline{e}, y)$ and the cover $\psi(y)$ is exactly the quantifier-free formula that eliminates the quantified variables $\underline{e}$ from $\exists \underline{e}\, \phi(\underline{e}, y)$.

It is straightforward to see that, in case of a first theory T, the notion of T-(quantifier-free) uniform interpolant and of T-cover are equivalent. In the following, we usually prefer to adopt the nomenclature of cover, because of its connection to the model checking literature (e.g., [157, 52, 56]).

We say that a theory T *admits covers* iff every existential formula $\exists \underline{e}\, \phi(\underline{e}, y)$ (equivalently, every primitive formula $\exists \underline{e}\, \phi(\underline{e}, y)$) has a T-cover. Given the equivalence between covers and uniform interpolants, T admits covers *iff* T has uniform quantifier-free interpolation.

Example 6.1 Consider the existential formula $\exists e\, (f(e, y_1) = y_2 \wedge f(e, y_3) = y_4)$: it can be shown that its uniform $\mathcal{EUF}$-interpolant is $y_1 = y_3 \rightarrow y_2 = y_4$.

Since it is easily seen that existential quantifiers commute with disjunctions, we notice that it is sufficient to compute covers for *primitive* formulae, i.e. for formulae of the kind $\exists \underline{e}\, \phi(\underline{e}, \underline{z})$, where ϕ is a constraint. A similar fact holds when performing quantifier elimination instead of computing covers.

6.2 Preliminaries on the Equality Interpolating Condition and Beth Definability

We report here some definitions and results we need concerning combined quantifier-free interpolation. Most definitions and result come from [45], but are simplified here because we restrict them to the case of universal convex theories.

A theory T is *stably infinite* iff every T-satisfiable constraint is satisfiable in an infinite model of T.

A theory T is *convex* iff for every constraint δ, if $T \vdash \delta \rightarrow \bigvee_{i=1}^{n} x_i = y_i$ then $T \vdash \delta \rightarrow x_i = y_i$ holds for some $i \in \{1, ..., n\}$. Strictly speaking, convexity applies to a set of literals ϕ and to a not empty disjunction of *variables* $\bigvee_{i=1}^{n} x_i = y_i$, guaranteeing that whenever we have $T \models \phi \rightarrow \bigvee_{i=1}^{n} x_i = y_i$, then we get also $T \models \phi \rightarrow x_i = y_i$ for some $i = 1, \ldots, n$. If, instead of variables, we have *terms*, the same property nevertheless applies: if we have $T \models \phi \rightarrow \bigvee_{i=1}^{n} t_i = u_i$, then for fresh variables x_i, y_i we get $T \models \phi \land \bigwedge_{i=1}^{n} (x_i = t_i \land y_i = u_i) \rightarrow \bigvee_{i=1}^{n} x_i = y_i$, which implies, by applying the definition of convexity, the same property for terms.

A convex theory T is 'almost' stably infinite in the sense that it can be shown that every constraint which is T-satisfiable in a T-model whose support has at least two elements is satisfiable also in an infinite T-model. The one-element model can be used to build counterexamples, though: e.g., the theory of Boolean algebras is convex (like any other universal Horn theory) but the constraint $x = 0 \land x = 1$ is only satisfiable in the degenerate one-element Boolean algebra. Since we take into account these limit cases, we do not assume that convexity implies stable infiniteness.

Definition 6.4 (Equality Interpolating Property) A convex universal theory T is *equality interpolating* iff for every pair y_1, y_2 of variables and for every pair of *constraints* $\delta_1(\underline{x}, \underline{z}_1, y_1), \delta_2(\underline{x}, \underline{z}_2, y_2)$ such that

$$T \vdash \delta_1(\underline{x}, \underline{z}_1, y_1) \land \delta_2(\underline{x}, \underline{z}_2, y_2) \rightarrow y_1 = y_2 \qquad (6.1)$$

there exists a term $t(\underline{x})$ such that

$$T \vdash \delta_1(\underline{x}, \underline{z}_1, y_1) \land \delta_2(\underline{x}, \underline{z}_2, y_2) \rightarrow y_1 = t(\underline{x}) \land y_2 = t(\underline{x}). \qquad (6.2)$$

The theorem below (taken from [45]) states that quantifier-free interpolation and the equality interpolation condition can be semantically characterized using the notion of *strong amalgamation*. We first define this algebraic notion. We recall from Chapter 2 that a universal theory T has the *amalgamation property* iff whenever we are given models $\mathcal{M}_1$ and $\mathcal{M}_2$ of T and a common substructure $\mathcal{M}_0$ of them, there exists a further model M of T endowed with embeddings $\mu_1 : M_1 \longrightarrow M$ and $\mu_2 : M_2 \longrightarrow M$ whose restrictions to $|M_0|$ coincide. We say that a universal theory T has the *strong amalgamation property* if the above embeddings μ_1, μ_2 and the above model M can be chosen so as to satisfy the following additional condition: if for some m_1, m_2 we have $\mu_1(m_1) = \mu_2(m_2)$, then there exists an element a in $|M_0|$ such that $m_1 = a = m_2$.

Theorem 6.1 *[45] The following two conditions are equivalent for a convex universal theory T: (i) T is equality interpolating and has quantifier-free interpolation; (ii) T has the strong amalgamation property.*

The proof of implication (i) $\Rightarrow$ (ii), which is the only fact used in Chapter 8, is reported in Chapter 6 of [154]

We underline that Theorem 6.1 extends also to the non-convex case provided the notion of an equality interpolating theory is suitably adjusted [45].

The equality interpolating property in a theory T can be equivalently characterized using *Beth definability* as follows.

Consider a primitive formula $\exists \underline{z} \phi(\underline{x}, \underline{z}, y)$ (here ϕ is a conjunction of literals); we say that $\exists \underline{z} \, \phi(\underline{x}, \underline{z}, y)$ *implicitly defines* y in T iff the formula

$$\forall y \, \forall y' \, (\exists \underline{z} \phi(\underline{x}, \underline{z}, y) \wedge \exists \underline{z} \phi(\underline{x}, \underline{z}, y') \rightarrow y = y') \tag{6.3}$$

is T-valid. We say that $\exists \underline{z} \phi(\underline{x}, \underline{z}, y)$ *explicitly defines* y in T iff there is a term $t(\underline{x})$ such that the formula

$$\forall y \, (\exists \underline{z} \phi(\underline{x}, \underline{z}, y) \rightarrow y = t(\underline{x})) \tag{6.4}$$

is T-valid.

For future use, we notice that, by trivial logical manipulations, the formulae (6.3) and (6.4) are logically equivalent to

$$\forall y \forall \underline{z} \forall y' \forall \underline{z}' (\phi(\underline{x}, \underline{z}, y) \wedge \phi(\underline{x}, \underline{z}', y') \rightarrow y = y') \quad . \tag{6.5}$$

and to

$$\forall y \forall \underline{z} (\phi(\underline{x}, \underline{z}, y) \rightarrow y = t(\underline{x})) \tag{6.6}$$

respectively (we shall use such equivalences without explicit mention).

We say that a theory T has the *Beth definability property for primitive formulae* iff whenever a primitive formula $\exists \underline{z} \, \phi(\underline{x}, \underline{z}, y)$ implicitly defines the variable y then it also explicitly defines it.

Theorem 6.2 *[45] A convex theory T having quantifier-free interpolation is equality interpolating iff it has the Beth definability property for primitive formulae.*

Proof We recall the easy proof of the left-to-right side (this is the only side we need). Suppose that T is equality interpolating and that

$$T \vdash \phi(\underline{x}, \underline{z}, y) \wedge \phi(\underline{x}, \underline{z}', y') \rightarrow y = y' \; ;$$

then there is a term $t(\underline{x})$ such that

$$T \vdash \phi(\underline{x}, \underline{z}, y) \wedge \phi(\underline{x}, \underline{z}', y') \rightarrow y = t(\underline{x}) \wedge y' = t(\underline{x}) \ .$$

Replacing $\underline{z}', y'$ by $\underline{z}, y$ via a substitution, we get precisely (6.6).   □

Chapter 7
Uniform Interpolation for Database Theories (and Beyond)

In the first part of this book, we introduced two categories of (Array-Based) Artifact Systems, called SASs and (Universal) RAS respectively, and we devised the theoretical machinery for verifying these systems based on a declarative version of the backward reachability procedure. We noticed in Chapter 4 that, in order to employ backward search in the context of Artifact Systems interacting with a read-only database, suitable quantifier elimination algorithms are needed. Specifically, given a DB theory T formalizing the read-only database, at each iteration of the main loop of the procedure, an algorithm performing quantifier elimination in an enriched theory of T (i.e., the model completion T^*) is executed and applied to the formulae representing preimages of states. Unfortunately, the quantifier elimination algorithms described in Chapter 4 are purely theoretical and are highly impractical, since they require enumerating all the quantifier-free formulae built up from a fixed tuple of variables in the signature of T.

This second part of the book is devoted to studying sophisticated automated reasoning techniques to solve efficiently the problem of eliminating quantifiers in model completions.

In order to do so, we first show in Section 7.1 that eliminating quantifiers in model completions T^* is equivalent to the problem of computing T-*covers*. The notion of cover has been studied in symbolic model checking in the context of program synthesis and verification; covers are well-known also in the tradition of non-classical logics, but under the name of *uniform interpolants*. Given this equivalence, we can lift our focus to *computing covers*: in Section 7.2, we argue how computing covers is not only essential for verifying Artifact Systems, but also for slightly more general systems (that we call *declarative transition systems*) comprising different frameworks from the literature.

We dedicate the main portion of this chapter to attacking the problem of finding *practical* and *efficient* algorithms for covers on two of the most useful (and minimal) theories for DB schemas. The first DB theory is expressive enough to represent relational databases with primary and foreign keys (cf. Section 3.1), whereas the second one captures the framework from [102, 186].

© The Author(s), under exclusive license to Springer Nature Switzerland AG 2023
A. Gianola: *Verification of Data-Aware Processes via Satisfiability Modulo Theories*,
LNBIP 470, pp. 129–153, 2023.
https://doi.org/10.1007/978-3-031-42746-6_7

We locate the problem of computing covers in a more general setting: instead of restricting our attention to (functional) DB signatures, we consider generic signatures comprising also n-ary functions and n-ary relations, and we prove that some conditions over DB schemas studied in Section 4.6 (e.g., acyclicity) can be removed. This is achieved by providing in Section 7.3 a general algorithm for computing covers based on a constrained version of the well-established Superposition Calculus, called SuperCover calculus: the Superposition Calculus is currently the state-of-the-art inference system used in saturation-based theorem proving for first-order logic with equality, and currently implemented in most efficient theorem provers. In Section 7.4, we specialize the SuperCover calculus to the fragment needed to formalize DB schemas extended with free n-ary relations (which is sufficient for our applications), and we show that in this fragment the calculus is computationally tractable: we provide a quadratic upper bound in time.

We finally report on the implementation of our algorithm for computing covers in the state-of-the-art MCMT model checker (http://users.mat.unimi.it/users/ghilardi/mcmt/). In fact, we built on top of this tool creating a specific module for supporting the verification of Artifact Systems like U-RASs: we call this module *database-driven mode* of MCMT, which will be presented in detail in Chapter 9.

The content of this chapter stems directly from [52, 56].

7.1 Uniform Interpolation, Covers and Model Completions

This main topic of this chapter is computing covers: this notion has been already defined formally in the preliminaries of this part (cf. Chapter 6). We will see how covers play a fundamental role for DAP verification, and in particular for the safety verification of (Universal) RASs and SASs. In order to do so, we first link covers to model completions.

In this section, we show that the problem of eliminating quantifiers in model completions is strictly related to the problem of computing uniform interpolants or, equivalently, covers. More formally, we prove that when covers exist in a a first-order universal theory T, the model completion T^* of T exists, and vice versa. Moreover, we show that computing covers in T is *equivalent* to eliminating quantifiers in its model completion T^*.

We first state and prove the following Lemma (to be widely used throughout Part II), which supplies a semantic counterpart to the notion of cover:

Lemma 7.1 (Cover-by-Extensions) *A formula $\psi(y)$ is a T-cover of $\exists \underline{e}\, \phi(\underline{e}, y)$ iff it satisfies the following two conditions: (i) $T \models \forall y\, (\exists \underline{e}\, \phi(\underline{e}, y) \rightarrow \psi(y))$; (ii) for every model M of T, for every tuple of elements $\underline{a}$ from the support of $\bar{M}$ such that $M \models \psi(\underline{a})$ it is possible to find another model N of T such that M embeds into N and $N \models \exists \underline{e}\, \phi(\underline{e}, \underline{a})$.*

Proof *Suppose that $\psi(y)$ satisfies conditions (i) and (ii) above.* Condition (i) says that $\psi(y) \in Res(\exists \underline{e}\, \phi)$, so ψ is a residue. In order to show that ψ is also a cover, we have to prove that $T \models \forall y, \underline{z}(\psi(y) \to \theta(y, \underline{z}))$, for every $\theta(y, \underline{z})$ that is a residue for $\exists \underline{e}\, \phi(\underline{e}, y)$. Given a model $\mathcal{M}$ of T, take a pair of tuples $\underline{a}, \underline{b}$ of elements from $|\mathcal{M}|$ and suppose that $\mathcal{M} \models \psi(\underline{a})$. By condition (ii), there is a model $\mathcal{N}$ of T such that $\mathcal{M}$ embeds into $\mathcal{N}$ and $\mathcal{N} \models \exists \underline{e}\, \phi(\underline{e}, \underline{a})$. Using the definition of $Res(\exists \underline{e}\, \phi)$, we have $\mathcal{N} \models \theta(\underline{a}, \underline{b})$, since $\theta(y, \underline{z}) \in Res(\exists \underline{x}\, \phi)$. Since $\mathcal{M}$ is a substructure of $\mathcal{N}$ and θ is quantifier-free, $\mathcal{M} \models \theta(\underline{a}, \underline{b})$ as well, as required.

Suppose that $\psi(y)$ is a cover. The definition of residue implies condition (i). To show condition (ii) we have to prove that, given a model $\mathcal{M}$ of T, for every tuple $\underline{a}$ of elements from $|\mathcal{M}|$, if $\mathcal{M} \models \psi(\underline{a})$, then there exists a model $\mathcal{N}$ of T such that $\mathcal{M}$ embeds into $\mathcal{N}$ and $\mathcal{N} \models \exists \underline{x}\, \phi(\underline{x}, \underline{a})$. Using Robinson Diagram Lemma, we can reformulate the latter embeddability statement into a consistency statement: so what we need to prove is that $\Delta(\mathcal{M}) \cup \{\exists \underline{x}\, \phi(\underline{x}, \underline{a})\}$ is a T-consistent $\Sigma^{|\mathcal{M}|}$-set of sentences (Σ is the signature of T). By reduction to absurdity, suppose that this is not the case: by compactness, there is a finite number of literals $\ell_1(\underline{a}, \underline{b}), ..., \ell_m(\underline{a}, \underline{b})$ (for some tuple $\underline{b}$ of elements from $|\mathcal{M}|$) such that $\mathcal{M} \models \ell_i(\underline{a}, \underline{b})$ (for all $i = 1, \ldots, m$) and

$$(*) \quad T \models \exists \underline{e}\, \phi(\underline{e}, \underline{a}) \to \neg(\ell_1(\underline{a}, \underline{b}) \wedge \cdots \wedge \ell_m(\underline{a}, \underline{b})) \ .$$

Now, the constants $\underline{a}, \underline{b}$ do not occur in the axioms of T and do not belong to Σ, hence we can replace them by variables $y, \underline{z}$ in the T-proof witnessing $(*)$: indeed, since they do not occur in the axioms of T, they are generic from the point of view of T. As a consequence, we then get

$$T \models \exists \underline{e}\, \phi(\underline{e}, y) \to (\neg\ell_1(y, \underline{z}) \vee \cdots \vee \neg\ell_m(y, \underline{z})).$$

By definition of residue, clearly $(\neg\ell_1(y, \underline{z}) \vee \cdots \vee \neg\ell_m(y, \underline{z})) \in Res(\exists \underline{x}\, \phi)$; then, since $\psi(y)$ is a cover, $T \models \psi(y) \to (\neg\ell_1(y, \underline{z}) \vee \cdots \vee \neg\ell_m(y, \underline{z}))$. Replacing back the variables $y, \underline{z}$ by the constants $\underline{a}, \underline{b}$ and recalling that $\mathcal{M} \models \psi(\underline{a})$, this implies that $\mathcal{M} \models \neg\ell_j(\underline{a}, \underline{b})$ for some $j = 1, \ldots, m$, which is a contradiction. Thus, $\psi(y)$ satisfies conditions (ii) too. □

We recall from Chapter 2 that, in view of Proposition 2.1, a *universal* theory T has a *model completion* iff there is a stronger theory $T^* \supseteq T$ (still within the same signature Σ of T) such that (i) every Σ-constraint that is satisfiable in a model of T is satisfiable in a model of T^*; (ii) T^* eliminates quantifiers.

A close relationship between model completion and uniform interpolation emerged in the area of propositional logic (see the book [150]) and can be formulated roughly as follows. It is well-known that most propositional calculi, via Lindenbaum constructions, can be algebraized: the algebraic analogue of classical logic are Boolean algebras, the algebraic analogue of intuitionistic logic are Heyting algebras, the algebraic analogue of modal calculi are suitable varieties of modal algebras, etc. Under suitable hypotheses, it turns out that a propositional logic has uniform interpolation (for the global consequence relation) iff the equational theory axiomatizing the corresponding variety of algebras has a model completion [150].

In the context of first-order theories, we can prove an even more direct connection, which will be crucial for our applications to data-aware processes verification:

Theorem 7.1 *Suppose that T is a universal theory. Then T has a model completion T^* iff T has uniform quantifier-free interpolation. If this happens, T^* is axiomatized by the infinitely many sentences*

$$\forall \underline{y} \, (\psi(\underline{y}) \rightarrow \exists \underline{e} \, \phi(\underline{e}, \underline{y})) \tag{7.1}$$

where $\exists \underline{e} \, \phi(\underline{e}, \underline{y})$ is a primitive formula and ψ is a cover of it.

Proof Suppose first that there is a model completion T^* of T and let $\exists \underline{e} \, \phi(\underline{e}, \underline{y})$ be a primitive formula. Since T^* eliminates quantifiers, we have $T^* \models \exists \underline{e} \, \phi(\underline{e}, \underline{y}) \leftrightarrow \psi(\underline{y})$ for some quantifier-free formula $\psi(\underline{y})$. Since T and T^* prove the same quantifier-free formulae, from the left-to-right side $T^* \models \phi(\underline{e}, \underline{y}) \rightarrow \psi(\underline{y})$ we have that $\psi(\underline{y}) \in Res(\exists \underline{e} \, \phi)$. If $\theta(\underline{y}, \underline{z}) \in Res(\exists \underline{e} \, \phi)$, then we have $T \models \phi(\underline{e}, \underline{y}) \rightarrow \theta(\underline{y}, \underline{z})$; the same entailment holds in T^* too, where we have $T^* \models \psi(\underline{y}) \rightarrow \theta(\underline{y}, \underline{z})$. Since $\psi(\underline{y}) \rightarrow \theta(\underline{y}, \underline{z})$ is quantifier-free, we have also $T \models \psi(\underline{y}) \rightarrow \theta(\underline{y}, \underline{z})$, showing that ψ is a cover of $\exists \underline{e} \, \phi(\underline{e}, \underline{y})$. Thus T has uniform interpolation, because we found a cover for every primitive formula.

Suppose vice versa that T has uniform interpolation. Let T^* be the theory axiomatized by all the formulae (7.1) above. From (i) of Lemma 7.1 and (7.1) above, we clearly get that T^* admits quantifier elimination: in fact, in order to prove that a theory enjoys quantifier elimination, it is sufficient to eliminate quantifiers from *primitive* formulae (then the quantifier elimination for all formulae can be easily shown by an induction over their complexity). This is exactly what is guaranteed by (i) of Lemma 7.1 and (7.1).

Let $\mathcal{M}$ be a model of T. By using a chain argument [55] (see [66], Lemma 3.5.7 for an almost identical construction), we show that there exists a model $\mathcal{M}'$ of T^* such that $\mathcal{M}$ embeds into $\mathcal{M}'$. Consider the set of all pairs $(\underline{a}, \exists \underline{e} \, \phi(\underline{e}, \underline{a}))$ where $\underline{a}$ is a tuple from $|\mathcal{M}|$, $\exists \underline{e} \, \phi(\underline{e}, \underline{y})$ is a primitive formula and $\mathcal{M} \models \psi(\underline{a})$ (here ψ is a cover of ϕ). By Zermelo's Theorem, the set of such pairs $(\underline{a}, \exists \underline{e} \, \phi(\underline{e}, \underline{a}))$ can be well-ordered: let $\{(\underline{a}_i, \exists \underline{e}_i \, \phi_i(\underline{e}_i, \underline{a}_i))\}_{i \in I}$ be such a well-ordered set of pairs, where I is some ordinal.[1] By transfinite induction on this well-order, we define $\mathcal{M}_0 := \mathcal{M}$ and, for each $i \in I$, $\mathcal{M}_i$ as an extension of $\bigcup_{j<i} \mathcal{M}_j$ such that $\mathcal{M}_i \models \exists \underline{e}_i \, \phi_i(\underline{e}_i, \underline{a}_i)$, which exists for (ii) of Lemma 7.1 since $\bigcup_{j<i} \mathcal{M}_j \models \psi_i(\underline{a}_i)$ (remember that validity of ground formulae is preserved passing through substructures and superstructures, and $\mathcal{M}_0 \models \psi_i(\underline{a}_i)$).

Now we take the chain union $\mathcal{M}^1 := \bigcup_{i \in I} \mathcal{M}_i$: since T is universal, $\mathcal{M}^1$ is again a model of T. Thanks to this construction, we added, for every pair $(\underline{a}_i, \exists \underline{e}_i \, \phi_i(\underline{e}_i, \underline{a}_i))$ (with $\underline{a}_i \in \mathcal{M}$ and $\mathcal{M} \models \psi_i(\underline{a}_i)$), a corresponding tuple $\underline{b}_i$ such that $\mathcal{M}^1 \models \phi_i(\underline{b}_i, \underline{a}_i)$; however, this only guarantees that such a tuple $\underline{b}_i$ exists for every pair $(\underline{a}_i, \exists \underline{e}_i \, \phi_i(\underline{e}_i, \underline{a}_i))$ such that the tuple $\underline{a}_i$ is from $|\mathcal{M}|$, whereas nothing is said for the pairs where the tuple $\underline{a}$ is in $|\mathcal{M}^1| \setminus |\mathcal{M}|$. Then, we iteratively repeat

---

[1] I is possibly different from ω (there can be uncountably many tuples $\underline{a}_i$).

the chain construction above for these new $\underline{a}$. Indeed, it is possible to construct, by an analogous chain argument, a model $\mathcal{M}^2$ as done above, starting from $\mathcal{M}^1$ instead of $\mathcal{M}$. Clearly, we get $\mathcal{M}_0 := \mathcal{M} \subseteq \mathcal{M}^1 \subseteq \mathcal{M}^2$ by construction.

At this point, we iterate the same argument countably many times, so as to define a new chain of models of T:

$$\mathcal{M}_0 := \mathcal{M} \subseteq \mathcal{M}^1 \subseteq \dots \subseteq \mathcal{M}^n \subseteq \dots$$

Defining $\mathcal{M}' := \bigcup_n \mathcal{M}^n$, we trivially get that $\mathcal{M}'$ is a model of T such that $\mathcal{M} \subseteq \mathcal{M}'$ and satisfies all the sentences of type (7.1): the last fact is immediate, recalling that truth of ground formulae (in expanded languages with names from support sets) is preserved by substructures and extensions. After ω steps we are done, because every tuple $\underline{a} \in |\mathcal{M}'|$ occurs after finitely many steps, and its corresponding $\underline{b}$ in the construction are added at the immediately subsequent step.   □

To sum up, Theorem 7.1 proves that a universal theory T admits a model completion iff T admits covers. Additionally, Theorem 7.1 states that, thanks to Formulae (7.1), the T-uniform interpolant (or T-cover) ψ of the formula $\exists \underline{e} \, \phi(\underline{e}, y)$ is exactly the T^*-equivalent quantifier-free formula that *eliminates* the quantified variables $\underline{e}$ from $\exists \underline{e} \, \phi(\underline{e}, y)$: this means that *computing covers in T is equivalent to eliminating quantifiers in its model completion T^**.

7.2 Model-Checking Applications

In this section we supply old and new motivations for investigating covers and model completions in view of model-checking applications. The notion of cover was introduced in [157] in the context of symbolic model checking for computing images of reachable states through transitions. The forward reachability procedure based on cover computation can be successfully employed for program analysis and verification, and it is the dual counterpart of the backward reachability procedure for the transition systems defined in this section.

We provide a generic definition of *declarative (quantifier-free) transition system* that comprises and generalizes both the framework from [157] and a "non-functional" version of SASs (cf. Section 3.2.1). In this version updates are not functional as in standard SASs because they do not use case-defined functions; instead, transitions are generic quantifier-free formulae in individual variables x, x'. This notion of declarative transition system is useful to give a slightly more general setting (i.e., without an explicit reference to DB schemas and/or specific formats of transition formulae) where computing covers is crucial. In fact, we recall from Chapter 4 that BReach_{SAS} (and BReach_{RAS} as well) requires the elimination of existential quantifiers in model completions of DB theories: in view of Theorem 7.1, we know that eliminating quantifiers in model completions T^* is equivalent to computing covers in T. This motivates for *SASs* the study of (efficient) cover algorithms. We will see in this section that cover computation is important for declarative transition systems in general.

For the sake of simplicity, it is sufficient to investigate symbolic model-checking via model completions (or, equivalently, via covers) in the basic case where system variables are represented as individual variables; for more advanced applications where system variables are both individual and higher order variables, e.g., in RASs, all the results in this chapter still hold. Indeed, we already commented in Section 4.3 how the quantifier elimination procedure in BReach_{SAS} can be easily extended to the one in BReach_{RAS}. In the rest of this chapter, we will then restrict our attention on declarative transition systems using only individual variables.

For completeness, we remark also that similar ideas, i.e., 'to use quantifier elimination in the model completion even if T does not allow quantifier elimination', were used in [239] for interpolation and symbol elimination.

Definition 7.1 (Declarative Transition System) A *declarative (quantifier-free) transition system* is a tuple

$$ S = \langle \Sigma, T, \underline{x}, \iota(\underline{x}), \tau(\underline{x}, \underline{x}') \rangle $$

where: *(i)* Σ is a signature and T is a Σ-theory; *(ii)* $\underline{x} = x_1, \ldots, x_n$ are individual variables; *(iii)* $\iota(\underline{x})$ is a quantifier-free formula; *(iv)* $\tau(\underline{x}, \underline{x}')$ is a quantifier-free formula (here the $\underline{x}'$ are renamed copies of the $\underline{x}$).

Notice that the theory T mentioned in the previous definition, contrary to DB theories, can contain n-ary function symbols. An *unsafe* formula for a transition system S is a further quantifier-free formula $\upsilon(\underline{x})$ describing undesired states of S. We say that S is *safe with respect to* υ if the system has no finite run leading from ι to υ, i.e. (formally) if there is no model $\mathcal{M}$ of T and no $k \geq 0$ such that the formula

$$ \iota(\underline{x}^0) \wedge \tau(\underline{x}^0, \underline{x}^1) \wedge \cdots \wedge \tau(\underline{x}^{k-1}, \underline{x}^k) \wedge \upsilon(\underline{x}^k) \tag{7.2} $$

is satisfiable in $\mathcal{M}$ (here $\underline{x}^i$'s are renamed copies of $\underline{x}$). The *safety problem* for S is the following: *given υ, decide whether S is safe with respect to υ.*

Suppose now that the theory T mentioned in Definition 7.1 (i) is universal, has decidable constraint satisfiability problem and admits covers. Notice that, apart from the finite model property (which is essential for database applications), the other conditions match Assumption 4.1 for DB schemas: indeed, admitting covers is equivalent to admitting model completions, thanks to Theorem 7.1. A variant of the backward reachability procedure (i.e., Algorithm 4), called BReach_{DTS}, can be used to assess safety of declarative transition systems as well. Algorithm 4 describes the *backward reachability algorithm* for handling the safety problem for S (the dual algorithm working via forward search is described in [157]).

An integral part of the algorithm is to compute preimages. As it happens for Array-Based Artifact Systems (cf. Chapter 4), for any $\varphi_1(\underline{x}, \underline{x}')$ and $\varphi_2(\underline{x})$ (where $\underline{x}'$ are renamed copies of $\underline{x}$),

$Pre(\varphi_1, \varphi_2)$ is the formula $\exists \underline{x}'(\varphi_1(\underline{x}, \underline{x}') \wedge \varphi_2(\underline{x}'))$. The *preimage* of the set of states described by a state formula $\phi(\underline{x})$ is the set of states described by $Pre(\tau, \phi)$.

Algorithm 4: Backward search for declarative transition systems

---

Function BReach(v)

  1     $\phi \longleftarrow v$; $B \longleftarrow \bot$;

  2   **while** $\phi \wedge \neg B$ *is T-satisfiable* **do**

  3   **if** $\iota \wedge \phi$ *is T-satisfiable.* **then**
           └ **return** unsafe

  4        $B \longleftarrow \phi \vee B$;

  5        $\phi \longleftarrow Pre(\tau, \phi)$;

  6        $\phi \longleftarrow \mathsf{Covers}_{\underline{x}}(T, \phi)$;

      └ **return** safe;

The subprocedure $\mathsf{Covers}_{\underline{x}}(T, \phi')$ in Line 6 computes a T-cover of the existential formula ϕ, maintaining the variables $\underline{x}$ and resulting in a sort of 'elimination' of the existential variables $\underline{x}'$ in $\phi' := Pre(\tau, \phi)$. Formally, the procedure $\mathsf{Covers}_{\underline{x}}(T, \alpha)$ takes as input an existential formula $\alpha := \exists \underline{x}' \varphi(\underline{x}, \underline{x}')$ and computes the T-cover $\psi(\underline{x})$, which does not depend on the existentially quantified variables $\underline{x}'$ anymore: this easily follows from the definition of cover. Without the application of this subprocedure, the existential prefix generated by the computation of preimages would grow in an unlimited way and some decidability results (see, e.g., the locally finite case mentioned below) would be compromised.

Algorithm 4 computes iterated preimages of v (storing their disjunction into the variable B) and applies to them quantifier elimination, until a fixpoint is reached or until a set intersecting the initial states (i.e., satisfying ι) is found. *Inclusion* (Line 2) and *disjointness* (Line 3) tests produce proof obligations that can be discharged because T has decidable constraint satisfiability problem. Notice that, in case of SASs, Theorem 7.1 implies $\mathsf{Covers}_{\underline{x}}(T, \phi) = \mathsf{QE}_{SAS}(T^*, \phi)$, and this algorithm exactly coincides with BReach_{SAS}.

We adopt for declarative transition systems the same nomenclature (i.e., *effectiveness*, *soundness* etc.) that we used for Array-Based Artifact Systems.

Theorem 7.2 is a slight variant of the Theorem 4.1 from SASs:

Theorem 7.2 *Suppose that the universal Σ-theory T has decidable constraint satisfiability problem and admits covers. For every declarative transition system $S = \langle \Sigma, T, \underline{x}, \iota, \tau \rangle$, the backward search algorithm (Algorithm 4) is effective and correct for solving safety problems for S.*

Its proof can be adapted from the proof of Theorems 4.1. Theorem 7.2 is a crucial fact: notice that it implies decidability of the safety problems in some interesting cases. For instance, we can get this result by adapting the proof of Theorem 5.1, when in T there are only finitely many quantifier-free formulae in which $\underline{x}$ occur, as in case T has a purely relational signature or, more generally, T is *locally finite*[2].

---

[2] We recall that T is locally finite iff for every finite tuple of variables $\underline{x}$ there are only finitely many T-equivalence classes of atoms $A(\underline{x})$.

Using the same arguments as in Remark 5.1, it follows that Theorem 7.2 can be used to cover the decidability result stated in Theorem 5 of [37] (once restricted to transition systems over a first-order definable class of Σ-structures).

7.2.1 Covers for Database Schemas

We already noticed that declarative transition systems slightly generalize SASs, and that Algorithm 4 coincides with BReach_{SAS} when applied to SASs: this implies that studying efficient ways for computing covers inherits all the interest that we devoted to quantifier elimination in model completions when verifying Array-Based Artifact Systems (cf. Part I). As deeply discussed in Part I, the application of these techniques relates to the verification of integrated models of (business) processes and data [47], referred to as artifact systems [250], where the behavior of the process is influenced by data stored in a relational database with constraints. We extensively studied several models of artifact systems, but, as argued, in this chapter it is sufficient to restrict our attention on SASs only. We remind the reader that the data contained therein are read-only: they can be queried by the process and stored in a working memory, which in the context of SASs is constituted by a set of system variables. In this context, safety amounts to checking whether the system never reaches an undesired property, irrespectively of what is contained in the read-only database.

As described in Section 3.1, in these systems the database is formalized through a DB schema $\langle \Sigma, T \rangle$ and is constrained by the axioms of the DB theory T. Notice that, given a DB signature Σ, using $T := \mathcal{EUF}$ over Σ as DB theory is sufficient to handle the sophisticated setting of artifact systems from Part I, because relational databases with key dependencies do not require additional axioms. The role of a non-empty DB theory is to encode background axioms to express additional constraints. We recall from Section 3.1 a typical background axiom (i.e., Axiom (3.1)), needed to tackle the possible presence of *undefined identifiers/values* in the different sorts. This, in turn, allows us to capture artifact systems whose working memory is initially undefined, so as to fulfil all the requirements of [102, 186]. To accommodate this, in Section 3.1 we added to every sort of Σ a constant undef, used to specify an undefined value. Then, for each function symbol f of Σ, we can impose the following additional constraint involving undef (adding it to $\mathcal{EUF}$):

$$\forall x \ (x = \mathsf{undef} \leftrightarrow f(x) = \mathsf{undef})$$

This axiom (namely, Axiom (3.1)) states that the application of f to the undefined value produces an undefined value, and it is the only situation for which f is undefined. A slightly different approach may handle *many* undefined values for each sort: this adaptation is trivial and is left to the reader. We just point out that in most cases the kind of axioms that we need for our DB theories T are just *one-variable universal axioms* (like Axioms 3.1), so that they fit the hypotheses of Proposition 4.5

from Chapter 4: for the sake of completeness, we summarize here the main results achieved for such a class of DB theories in Section 4.6.

Proposition 7.1 *A DB theory T has decidable constraint satisfiability problem and admits a model completion in case it is axiomatized by finitely many universal one-variable formulae and Σ is acyclic.*

We recall the algorithm for quantifier elimination in T^* (or, equivalently, for computing T-covers) suggested by the proof of the previous result: given a primitive formula $\exists \underline{e}\, \phi(\underline{e}, \underline{y})$, the output $\psi(\underline{y})$ of the algorithm is the conjunction of the set of all quantifier-free $\chi(\underline{y})$ formulae such that $\phi(\underline{e}, \underline{y}) \to \chi(\underline{y})$ is a logical consequences of T (they are finitely many - up to T-equivalence - because Σ is acyclic).

This algorithm is *highly impractical*, although it works in theory and in the proof. Indeed, even in case of $T := \mathcal{EUF}$, it requires to check whether $\phi(\underline{e}, \underline{y}) \to \chi(\underline{y})$ is logically true *for every quantifier-free formula* $\chi(\underline{y})$ (with the proviso of not choosing a formula χ from a T-equivalence class more than once). The number of all such formulae, although finite, quickly explodes exponentially in the size of $\underline{y}$. This is one of the reasons why in the next sections we study more efficient algorithms, based on a constrained version of the Superposition Calculus, for computing $\mathcal{EUF}$-covers and for the interesting DB theory containing Axioms (3.1). We show that in case the DB theory is $\mathcal{EUF}$ over a DB signature Σ, the algorithm has a quadratic bound. These algorithms are quite general, and comprise the case the signature is *not acyclic*.

7.3 Covers via Constrained Superposition

Of course, a model completion may not exist at all. Proposition 4.5 shows that it exists in case T is a DB theory axiomatized by universal one-variable formulae and Σ is acyclic. The second hypothesis is unnecessarily restrictive and the algorithm for quantifier elimination suggested by the proof of Proposition 4.5 is highly impractical: for this reason we are trying a different approach.

In this section, we study the problem of computing covers efficiently, and for that we devise a sophisticated procedure based on a constrained version of the Superposition Calculus, which we call SuperCover. We locate the contribution of this section in *the general setting provided by declarative transition systems*, since SuperCover can be used, e.g., as the subroutine Covers_x in Algorithm 4. Indeed, from now on, we drop the acyclicity hypothesis and examine the case where we have $\mathcal{EUF}$ as background theory and its signature Σ may contain *function and relation symbols of any arity*: hence, we analyze a case that is strictly more general than the one of DB schemas needed for DAP verification. Covers in this general context were claimed to exist already in [157], using an algorithm that, very roughly speaking, determines all the conditional equations that can be derived concerning the nodes of the congruence closure graph. However, this algorithm contains some bugs that need to be fixed: see below for a counterexample.

We follow a different plan and we want to produce covers (and show that they exist) using *saturation-based theorem proving*. The natural idea to proceed in this sense is to take the matrix $\phi(\underline{e}, y)$ of the primitive formula $\exists \underline{e}\, \phi(\underline{e}, y)$ we want to compute the cover of: this is a conjunction of literals, so we consider each variable as a free constant, we saturate the corresponding set of ground literals and finally we output the literals involving only the y. For saturation, one can use any version of the superposition calculus [213]. However, this procedure for our problem is not sufficient. As a trivial counterexample consider the primitive formula $\exists e\, (R(e, y_1) \land \neg R(e, y_2))$: the set of literals $\{R(e, y_1), \neg R(e, y_2)\}$ is saturated (recall that we view e, y_1, y_2 as constants), however the formula has a non-trivial cover $y_1 \neq y_2$ which is *not* produced by saturation. If we move to signatures with function symbols, the situation is even worse: the set of literals $\{f(e, y_1) = y_1', f(e, y_2) = y_2'\}$ is saturated but the formula $\exists e\, (f(e, y_1) = y_1' \land f(e, y_2) = y_2')$ has the *conditional equality* $y_1 = y_2 \rightarrow y_1' = y_2'$ as cover. *Disjunctions of disequations* might also arise: the cover of $\exists e\, h(e, y_1, y_2) \neq h(e, y_1', y_2')$ (as well as the cover of $\exists e\, f(f(e, y_1), y_2) \neq f(f(e, y_1'), y_2')$, see Example 7.1 below) is $y_1 \neq y_1' \lor y_2 \neq y_2'$. This example points out a problem that needs to be fixed in the algorithm presented in [157]: that algorithm in fact outputs only equalities, conditional equalities and single disequalities, so it cannot correctly handle this example.

Notice that our problem is different from the problem of producing ordinary quantifier-free interpolants via saturation based theorem proving [180]: for ordinary Craig interpolants, we have as input *two* quantifier-free formulae $\phi(\underline{e}, y), \phi'(y, \underline{z})$ such that $\phi(\underline{e}, y) \rightarrow \phi'(y, \underline{z})$ is valid; here we have a *single* formula $\phi(\underline{e}, y)$ as input and we are asked to find an interpolant which is good *for all possible* $\phi'(y, \underline{z})$ such that $\phi(\underline{e}, y) \rightarrow \phi'(y, \underline{z})$ is valid. Ordinary interpolants can be extracted from a refutation of $\phi(\underline{e}, y) \land \neg \phi'(y, \underline{z})$, whereas here we are not given any refutation at all (and we are not even supposed to find one).

What we are going to show is that, nevertheless, saturation via superposition can be used to produce covers, if suitably adjusted. In this section we consider signatures with n-ary function symbols (for all $n \geq 1$). For simplicity, we omit n-ary relation symbols (they can be easily handled by rewriting $R(t_1, \ldots, t_n)$ as $R(t_1, \ldots, t_n) = true$, as customary in the paramodulation literature [213]).

We are going to compute the cover of a primitive formula $\exists \underline{e}\, \phi(\underline{e}, y)$ to be fixed for the remainder of this section. We call variables $\underline{e}$ *existential* and variables y *parameters*. By applying abstraction steps, we can assume that ϕ is *primitive flat*, i.e. that it is a conjunction of $\underline{e}$-flat literals, defined below. [By an abstraction step we mean replacing $\exists \underline{e}\, \phi$ with $\exists \underline{e}\, \exists e'\, (e' = u \land \phi')$, where e' is a fresh variable and ϕ' is obtained from ϕ by replacing some occurrences of a term $u(\underline{e}, y)$ by e'].

A term or a formula are said to be $\underline{e}$-free iff the existential variables do not occur in it. An $\underline{e}$-flat term is an $\underline{e}$-free term $t(y)$ or a variable from $\underline{e}$ or again it is of the kind $f(u_1, \ldots, u_n)$, where f is a function symbol and $u_1, \ldots, u_n$ are $\underline{e}$-free terms or variables from $\underline{e}$. An $\underline{e}$-flat literal is a literal of the form

$$t = a, \quad a \neq b$$

where t is an $\underline{e}$-flat term and a, b are either $\underline{e}$-free terms or variables from $\underline{e}$.

We assume the reader is familiar with standard conventions used in rewriting and paramodulation literature: in particular $s_{|p}$ denotes the subterm of s in position p and $s[u]_p$ denotes the term obtained from s by replacing $s_{|p}$ with u. We use $\equiv$ to indicate coincidence of syntactic expressions (as strings) to avoid confusion with equality symbol; when we write equalities like $s = t$ below, we may mean both $s = t$ or $t = s$ (an equality is seen as a multiset of two terms). For information on reduction orderings, see for instance [24].

We first replace variables $\underline{e} = e_1, \ldots, e_n$ and $\underline{y} = y_1, \ldots, y_m$ by free constants - we keep the names $e_1, \ldots, e_n, y_1, \ldots, y_m$ for these constants. Let $>$ be a reduction ordering that is total for ground terms such that $\underline{e}$-flat literals $t = a$ are always oriented from left to right in the following two cases: (i) t is not $\underline{e}$-free and a is $\underline{e}$-free; (ii) t is not $\underline{e}$-free, it is not equal to any of the $\underline{e}$ and a is a variable from $\underline{e}$. To obtain such properties, one may for instance choose a suitable Knuth-Bendix ordering taking weights in some transfinite ordinal (see, e.g., [189]).

Given two $\underline{e}$-flat terms t, u, we indicate with $E(t, u)$ the following procedure, which intuitively is a unification algorithm for the terms t and u where the $\underline{e}$ variables are treated as constants; as shown by Lemma 7.2 below, $E(t, u)$ collects 'the equalities that are needed in order to force $t = u$', whenever the $\underline{e}$ are assumed to be free (i.e. not to satisfy any specific equational constraint):

- $E(t, u)$ fails if t is $\underline{e}$-free and u is not $\underline{e}$-free (or vice versa);
- $E(t, u)$ fails if $t \equiv e_i$ and (either $u \equiv f(t_1, \ldots, t_k)$ or $u \equiv e_j$ for $i \neq j$);
- $E(t, u) = \emptyset$ if $t \equiv u$;
- $E(t, u) = \{t = u\}$ if t and u are different but both $\underline{e}$-free;
- $E(t, u)$ fails if neither of t, u is $\underline{e}$-free, $t \equiv f(t_1, \ldots, t_k)$ and $u \equiv g(u_1, \ldots, u_l)$ for $f \not\equiv g$;
- $E(t, u) = E(t_1, u_1) \cup \cdots \cup E(t_k, u_k)$ if neither of t, u is $\underline{e}$-free, $t \equiv f(t_1, \ldots, t_k)$, $u \equiv f(u_1, \ldots, u_k)$ and none of the $E(t_i, u_i)$ fails.

Notice that, whenever $E(t, u)$ succeeds, the formula $\bigwedge E(t, u) \rightarrow t = u$ is universally valid. The definition of $E(t, u)$ is motivated by the next lemma.

Lemma 7.2 *Let R be a convergent (i.e. terminating and confluent) ground rewriting system, whose rules consist of $\underline{e}$-free terms. Suppose that t and u are $\underline{e}$-flat terms with the same R-normal form. Then $E(t, u)$ does not fail and all pairs from $E(t, u)$ have the same R-normal form as well.*

Proof This is due to the fact that if t is not $\underline{e}$-free, no R-rewriting is possible at root position because rules from R are $\underline{e}$-free. □

In the following, we handle *constrained* ground flat literals of the form $L \parallel C$ where L is a ground flat literal and C is a conjunction of ground equalities among $\underline{e}$-free terms. The logical meaning of $L \parallel C$ is the Horn clause $\bigwedge C \rightarrow L$.

In the literature, various calculi with constrained clauses were considered, starting, e.g., from the non-ground constrained versions of the Superposition Calculus of [26, 212]. The calculus we propose here is inspired by such versions and it has close similarities with a subcase of hierarchic superposition calculus [27], or rather to its "weak abstraction" variant from [33].

The rules of our *Constrained Superposition Calculus* (SuperCover) follow; each rule applies provided the E subprocedure called by it does not fail. The symbol $\perp$ indicates the empty clause. Further explanations and restrictions to the calculus are given in the Remarks below.

Superposition Right (Constrained)	$\dfrac{l = r \parallel C \qquad s = t \parallel D}{s[r]_p = t \parallel C \cup D \cup E(s_{\mid p}, l)}$	if $l > r$ and $s > t$
Superposition Left (Constrained)	$\dfrac{l = r \parallel C \qquad s \neq t \parallel D}{s[r]_p \neq t \parallel C \cup D \cup E(s_{\mid p}, l)}$	if $l > r$ and $s > t$
Reflection (Constrained)	$\dfrac{t \neq u \parallel C}{\perp \parallel C \cup E(t, u)}$	
Demodulation (Constrained)	$\dfrac{L \parallel C, \qquad l = r \parallel D}{L[r]_p \parallel C}$	if $\quad l > r,\ L_{\mid p} \equiv l$ and $C \supseteq D$

Remark 7.1 The first three rules are inference rules: they are non-deterministically selected for application, until no rule applies anymore. The selection strategy for the rule to be applied is not relevant for the correctness and completeness of the algorithm (some variant of a 'given clause algorithm' can be applied). An inference rule *is not applied in case one premise is $\underline{e}$-free* (we have no reason to apply inferences to $\underline{e}$-free premises, since we are not looking for a refutation).

Remark 7.2 The Demodulation rule is a simplification rule: its application not only adds the conclusion to the current set of constrained literals, but it also removes the first premise. It is easy to see (e.g., representing literals as multisets of terms and extending the total reduction ordering to multisets), that one cannot have an infinite sequence of consecutive applications of Demodulation rules.

Remark 7.3 The calculus takes $\{L \parallel \emptyset \mid L$ is a flat literal from the matrix of $\phi\}$ as the initial set of constrained literals. It terminates when a *saturated* set of constrained literals is reached. We say that S is saturated iff every constrained literal that can be produced by an inference rule, after being exhaustively simplified via Demodulation, is already in S (there are more sophisticated notions of 'saturation up to redundancy' in the literature, but we do not need them). When it reaches a saturated set S, the algorithm outputs the conjunction of the clauses $\bigwedge C \rightarrow L$, varying $L \parallel C$ among the $\underline{e}$-free constrained literals from S.

We need some rule application policy to ensure termination: without any such policy, a set like

$$\{e = y \parallel \emptyset, f(e) = e \parallel \emptyset\} \tag{7.3}$$

may produce by Right Superposition the infinitely many literals (all oriented from right to left) $f(y) = e \parallel \emptyset$, $f(f(y)) = e \parallel \emptyset$, $f(f(f(y))) = e \parallel \emptyset$, etc. The next remark explains the policy we follow.

Remark 7.4 **[Policy Remark]** We apply Demodulation *only in case the second premise is of the kind* $e_j = t(y) \| D$, *where t is* $\underline{e}$-*free*. Demodulation is applied with *higher priority* with respect to the inference rules.[3] Inside all possible applications of Demodulation, we give priority to the applications where *both premises have the form* $e_j = t(y) \| D$ (for the same e_j but with possibly different D's - the D from the second premise being included in the D of the first). In case we have two constrained literals of the kind $e_j = t_1(y) \| D$, $e_j = t_2(y) \| D$ inside our current set of constrained literals (notice that the e_j's and the D's here are the same), among the two possible applications of the Demodulation rule, we apply the rule that keeps the smallest t_i. Notice that in this way two different constrained literals cannot simplify each other.

We say that a constrained literal $L \| C$ belonging to a set of constrained literals S is *simplifiable in S* iff it is possible to apply (according to the above policy) a Demodulation rule removing it. A first effect of our policy is:

Lemma 7.3 *If a constrained literal $L \| C$ is simplifiable in S, then after applying to S any sequence of rules, it remains simplifiable until it gets removed. After being removed, if it is regenerated, it is still simplifiable and so it is eventually removed again.*

Proof Suppose that $L \| C$ can be simplified by $e = t \| D$ and suppose that a rule is applied to the current set of constrained literals. Since there are simplifiable constrained literals, that rule cannot be an inference rule by the priority stated in Remark 7.4. For simplification rules, keep in mind again Remark 7.4. If $L \| C$ is simplified, it is removed; if none of $L \| C$ and $e = t \| D$ get simplified, the situation does not change; if $e = t \| D$ gets simplified, this can be done by some $e = t' \| D'$, but then $L \| C$ is still simplifiable - although in a different way - using $e = t' \| D'$ (we have that D' is included in D, which is in turn included in C). Similar observations apply if $L \| C$ is removed and re-generated. □

Due to Lemma 7.3, if we show that a derivation (i.e., a sequence of applications of rules) can produce terms only from a finite set, it is clear that when no new constrained literal is produced, saturation is reached. First notice that:

Lemma 7.4 *Every constrained literal $L \| C$ produced during the run of the algorithm is $\underline{e}$-flat.*

Proof The constrained literals from initialization are $\underline{e}$-flat. The Demodulation rule, applied according to Remark 7.4, produces an $\underline{e}$-flat literal out of an $\underline{e}$-flat literal. The same happens for the Superposition rules: in fact, since both the terms s and l from these rules are $\underline{e}$-flat, a Superposition may take place at root position or may rewrite some $l \equiv e_j$ with $r \equiv e_i$ or with $r \equiv t(y)$.[4] □

---

[3] Thus we cannot apply Superposition to $\{e = y \| \emptyset, f(e) = e \| \emptyset\}$ until Demodulation is exhaustively applied (the latter causes the deletion of $f(e) = e \| \emptyset$ and its replacement with $f(y) = y \| \emptyset$, thus blocking the above generation of infinitely many clauses).

[4] Notice that Superposition Left is considerably restricted in our calculus: recall in fact that $\underline{e}$-flat *negative* literals must be of the kind $s \neq t$ where s, t are either variables from $\underline{e}$ or $\underline{e}$-free terms.

There are in principle infinitely many $\underline{e}$-flat terms that can be generated out of the $\underline{e}$-flat terms occurring in ϕ (see the above counterexample (7.3)). We show however that only finitely many $\underline{e}$-flat terms can in fact occur during saturation and that one can determine in advance the finite set they are taken from.

To formalize this idea, let us introduce a hierarchy of $\underline{e}$-flat terms (this hierarchy concerns terms, not clauses or constraints - although it will be used to delimit the kind of clauses or constraints that might occur in a saturation process). Let D_0 be the $\underline{e}$-flat terms occurring in ϕ and let D_{k+1} be the set of $\underline{e}$-flat terms obtained by simultaneous rewriting of an $\underline{e}$-flat term from $\bigcup_{i \leq k} D_i$ via rewriting rules of the kind $e_j \rightarrow t_j(y)$ where the t_j are $\underline{e}$-free terms from $\bigcup_{i \leq k} D_i$. The *degree* of an $\underline{e}$-flat term is the minimum k such that it belongs to set D_k (it is necessary to take the minimum because the same term can be obtained at different stages and via different rewritings).

Lemma 7.5 *Let the $\underline{e}$-flat term t' be obtained by a rewriting $e_j \rightarrow u(y)$ from the $\underline{e}$-flat term t; then, if t has degree $k > 1$ and u has degree at most $k - 1$, we have that t' has degree at most k.*

Proof This is clear, because at the k-stage one can directly produce t' instead of just t: in fact, all rewriting producing directly t' replace an occurrence of some e_i by an $\underline{e}$-free term, so they are all done in parallel positions. [We illustrate the phenomenon via an example: suppose that t is $f(e_1, g(g(c)))$ and that t' is obtained from t by rewriting e_1 to $g(c)$. Now it might well be that t has degree 2, being obtained from $f(e_1, e_2)$ via $e_2 \mapsto g(g(c))$ (the latter having been previously obtained from $g(e_3)$ via $e_3 \mapsto g(c)$). Now t' still has degree 2 because it can be directly obtained from $f(e_1, e_2)$ via the parallel rewritings $e_1 \mapsto g(c)$, $e_2 \mapsto g(g(c))$.] $\qquad \square$

Proposition 7.2 *The saturation of the initial set of $\underline{e}$-flat constrained literals always terminates after finitely many steps.*

Proof We show that all $\underline{e}$-flat terms that may occur during saturation have at most degree n (where n is the cardinality of $\underline{e}$). This shows that the saturation must terminate, because only finitely many terms may occur in a derivation (see the above observations). Let the algorithm during saturation reach the state S; we say that *a constraint C allows the explicit definition of e_j in S* iff S contains a constrained literal of the kind $e_j = t(y) \| D$ with $D \subseteq C$. Now we show by mutual induction two facts concerning a constrained literal $L \| C \in S$:

(1) if an $\underline{e}$-flat term u of degree k occurs in L, then C allows the explicit definition of k different e_j in S;

Since rules do not apply to $\underline{e}$-free literals, the only possibility is that the term s from the literal $s \neq t$ of the right premise of Superposition Left is a variable from $\underline{e}$ and that the term l from the left premise concides with it. Thus Superposition Left looks like a Demodulation, however it is *not* a Demodulation because the constraint of its left premise may not be included into the constraint of its right premise. It would be harmless to allow a more liberal version of Superposition Left, but we do not need it.

(2) if L is of the kind $e_i = t(\underline{y})$, for an $\underline{e}$-free term t of degree k, then either $e_i = t \parallel C$ can be simplified in S or C allows the explicit definition of $k + 1$ different e_j in S (e_i itself is of course included among these e_j).

Notice that (1) is sufficient to exclude that any $\underline{e}$-flat term of degree bigger than n can occur in a constrained literal arising during the saturation process.

We prove (1) and (2) by induction on the length of the derivation leading to $L \parallel C \in S$. Notice that it is sufficient to check that (1) and (2) hold for the first time where $L \parallel C \in S$ because if C allows the explicit definition of a certain variable in S, it will continue to do so in any S' obtained from S by continuing the derivation (the definition may be changed by the Demodulation rule, but the fact that e_i is explicitly defined is forever). Also, by Lemma 7.3, a literal cannot become not simplifiable if it is simplifiable.

(1) and (2) are evident if S is the initial status. To show (1), suppose that u occurs for the first time in $L \parallel C$ as the effect of the application of a certain rule: we can freely assume that u does not occur in the literals from the premises of the rule (otherwise induction trivially applies) and that u of degree k is obtained by rewriting *in a non-root position* some u' occurring in a constrained literal $L' \parallel D'$ via some $e_j \to t \parallel D$. This might be the effect of a Demodulation or Superposition in a non-root position (Superpositions in root position do not produce new terms). If u' has degree k, then by induction D' contains the required k explicit definitions, and we are done because D' is included in C. If u' has lower degree, then t must have degree at least $k - 1$ (otherwise u does not reach degree k by Lemma 7.5). Then by induction on (2), the constraint D (also included in C) has $(k - 1) + 1 = k$ explicit definitions (when a constraint $e_j \to t \parallel D$ is selected for Superposition or for making Demodulations in a non-root position, it is itself not simplifiable according to the procedure explained in Remark 7.4).

To show (2), we analyze the reasons why the nonsimplifiable constrained literal $e_i = t(y) \parallel C$ is produced (let k be the degree of t). Suppose it is produced from $e_i = u' \parallel C$ via Demodulation with $e_j = u(y) \parallel D$ (with $D \subseteq C$) in a non-root position; if u' has degree at least k, we apply induction for (1) to $e_i = u' \parallel C$: by such induction hypotheses, we get k explicit definitions in C and we can add to them the further explicit definition $e_i = t(y)$ (the explicit definitions from C cannot concern e_i because $e_i = t(y) \parallel C$ is not simplifiable). Otherwise, u' has degree less than k and u has degree at least $k - 1$ by Lemma 7.5 (recall that t has degree k): by induction, $e_j = u \parallel D$ is not simplifiable (it is used as the active part of a Demodulation in a non-root position, see Remark 7.4) and supplies k explicit definitions, inherited by $C \supseteq D$. Note that e_i cannot have a definition in D, otherwise $e_i = t(y) \parallel C$ would be simplifiable, so with $e_i = t(y) \parallel C$ we get the required $k + 1$ definitions.

The remaining case is when $e_i = t(y) \parallel C$ is produced via Superposition Right. Such a Superposition might be at root or at a non-root position. We first analyze the case of a root position. This might be via $e_j = e_i \parallel C_1$ and $e_j = t(y) \parallel C_2$ (with $e_j > e_i$ and $C = C_1 \cup C_2$ because $E(e_j, e_j) = \emptyset$), but in such a case one can easily apply induction. Otherwise, we have a different kind of Superposition at root position: $e_i = t(y) \parallel C$ is obtained from $s = e_i \parallel C_1$ and $s' = t(y) \parallel C_2$, with $C = C_1 \cup C_2 \cup E(s, s')$. In this case, by induction for (1), C_2 supplies k explicit definitions, to be inherited by C. Among such definitions, there cannot be an explicit definition of e_i otherwise $e_i = t(\underline{y}) \parallel C$ would be simplifiable, so again we get the required $k + 1$ definitions.

In case of a Superposition at a non-root-position, we have that $e_i = t(\underline{y}) \parallel C$ is obtained from $u' = e_i \parallel C_1$ and $e_j = u(\underline{y}) \parallel C_2$, with $C = C_1 \cup C_2$; here t is obtained from u' by rewriting e_j to u. This case is handled similarly to the case where $e_i = t(\underline{y}) \parallel C$ is obtained via Demodulation rule.   □

Having established termination, we now prove that our calculus computes covers. To this aim, we rely on refutational completeness of unconstrained Superposition Calculus: thus, our technique resembles the technique used [27, 33] in order to prove refutational completeness of hierarchic superposition, although it is not clear whether Theorem 7.3 below can be derived from the results concerning hierarchic superposition[5]. We state the following theorem:

Theorem 7.3 *Let T be the theory $\mathcal{E}\mathcal{U}\mathcal{F}$. Suppose that the above algorithm, taking as input the primitive $\underline{e}$-flat formula $\exists \underline{e}\, \phi(\underline{e}, y)$, gives as output the quantifier-free formula $\psi(y)$. Then the latter is a T-cover of $\exists \underline{e}\, \phi(\underline{e}, y)$.*

Proof Let S be the saturated set of constrained literals produced upon termination of the algorithm; let $S = S_1 \cup S_2$, where S_1 contains the constrained literals in which the $\underline{e}$ do not occur and S_2 is its complement. Clearly $\exists \underline{e}\, \phi(\underline{e}, y)$ turns out to be logically equivalent to

$$\bigwedge_{L \parallel C \in S_1} (\bigwedge C \to L) \wedge \exists \underline{e} \bigwedge_{L \parallel C \in S_2} (\bigwedge C \to L)$$

so, as a consequence, in view of Lemma 7.1 it is sufficient to show that every model $\mathcal{M}$ satisfying $\bigwedge_{L \parallel C \in S_1} (\bigwedge C \to L)$ via an assignment $\mathcal{I}$ to the variables y can be embedded into a model $\mathcal{M}'$ such that for a suitable extension $\mathcal{I}'$ of $\mathcal{I}$ to the variables $\underline{e}$ we have that $(\mathcal{M}', \mathcal{I}')$ satisfies also $\bigwedge_{L \parallel C \in S_2} (\bigwedge C \to L)$.

Fix $\mathcal{M}, \mathcal{I}$ as above. The diagram $\Delta(\mathcal{M})$ of $\mathcal{M}$ is obtained as follows. We take one free constant for each element of the support of $\mathcal{M}$ (by Löwenheim-Skolem theorem one can keep $\mathcal{M}$ at most countable, if one likes) and we put in $\Delta(\mathcal{M})$ all the literals of the kind $f(c_1, \ldots, c_k) = c_{k+1}$ and $c_1 \neq c_2$ which are true in $\mathcal{M}$ (here the c_i are names for the elements of the support of $\mathcal{M}$). Let R be the set of ground equalities of the form $y_i = c_i$, where c_i is the name of $\mathcal{I}(y_i)$. Extend our reduction ordering in the natural way (so that $y_i = c_i$ and $f(c_1, \ldots, c_k) = c_{k+1}$ are oriented from left to right). Consider now the set of clauses

$$\Delta(\mathcal{M}) \cup R \cup \{\bigwedge C \to L \mid (L \parallel C) \in S\} \qquad (7.4)$$

(below, we distinguish the positive and the negative literals of $\Delta(\mathcal{M})$ so that $\Delta(\mathcal{M}) = \Delta^+(\mathcal{M}) \cup \Delta^-(\mathcal{M})$). We want to saturate the above set in the standard Superposition

---

[5] An important difference between our proof and the proof of completeness for hierarchic superposition is that we must build an expansion *of a superstructure* of the model $\mathcal{M}$ below (expanding $\mathcal{M}$ to a larger signature without enlarging its domain might not be possible in principle).

Calculus. Clearly the rewriting rules in R, used as reduction rules, replace everywhere y_i by c_i inside the clauses of the kind $\bigwedge C \rightarrow L$. At this point, the negative literals from the equality constraints all disappear: if they are true in M, they $\Delta^+(M)$-normalize to trivial equalities $c_i = c_i$ (to be eliminated by standard reduction rules) and if they are false in M they become part of clauses subsumed by true inequalities from $\Delta^-(M)$. Similarly all the $\underline{e}$-free literals not coming from $\Delta(M) \cup R$ get removed. Let $\tilde{S}$ be the set of survived literals involving the $\underline{e}$ (they are not constrained anymore and they are $\Delta^+(M) \cup R$-normalized): we show that they cannot produce new clauses. Let in fact (π) be an inference from the Superposition Calculus [213] applying to them. Since no superposition with $\Delta(M) \cup R$ is possible, this inference must involve only literals from $\tilde{S}$; suppose it produces a literal $\tilde{L}$ from the literals $\tilde{L}_1, \tilde{L}_2$ (coming via $\Delta^+(M) \cup R$-normalization from $L_1 \| C_1 \in S$ and $L_2 \| C_2 \in S$) as parent clauses. Then, by Lemma 7.2, our constrained inferences produce a constrained literal $L \| C$ such that the clause $\bigwedge C \rightarrow L$ normalizes to $\tilde{L}$ via $\Delta^+(M) \cup R$. Since S is saturated, the constrained literal $L \| C$, after simplification, belongs to S. Now simplifications via our Constrained Demodulation and $\Delta(M)^+ \cup R$-normalization commute (they work at parallel positions, see Remark 7.4), so the inference (π) is redundant because $\tilde{L}$ simplifies to a literal already in $\tilde{S} \cup \Delta(M)$.

Thus the set of clauses (7.4) saturates without producing the empty clause. By the completeness theorem of the Superposition Calculus [166, 25, 213] it has a model M'. This M' by construction fits our requests by Robinson Diagram Lemma. □

Theorem 7.3, thanks to the relationship between model completions and covers stated in Theorem 7.1, proves also the existence of the model completion of $\mathcal{EUF}$.

Example 7.1 We compute the cover of the primitive formula $\exists e\, f(f(e, y_1), y_2) \neq f(f(e, y'_1), y'_2)$. Flattening gives the set of literals

$$\{ f(e, y_1) = e_1,\ f(e_1, y_2) = e'_1,\ f(e, y'_1) = e_2,\ f(e_2, y'_2) = e'_2,\ e'_1 \neq e'_2 \} .$$

Superposition Right produces the constrained literal $e_1 = e_2 \| \{y_1 = y'_1\}$; supposing that we have $e_1 > e_2$, Superposition Right gives first $f(e_2, y_2) = e'_1 \| \{y_1 = y'_1\}$ and then also $e'_1 = e'_2 \| \{y_1 = y'_1, y_2 = y'_2\}$. Superposition Left and Reflection now produce $\bot \| \{y_1 = y'_1, y_2 = y'_2\}$. Thus the clause $y_1 = y'_1 \wedge y_2 = y'_2 \rightarrow \bot$ will be part of the output (actually, this will be the only clause in the output).

We apply our algorithm to an additional example, taken from [157].

Example 7.2 We compute the cover of the primitive formula $\exists e\, (s_1 = f(y_3, e) \wedge s_2 = f(y_4, e) \wedge t = f(f(y_1, e), f(y_2, e)))$, where s_1, s_2, t are terms in $\underline{y}$. Flattening gives the set of literals

$$\{ f(y_3, e) = s_1,\ f(y_4, e) = s_2,\ f(y_1, e) = e_1,\ f(y_2, e) = e_2,\ f(e_1, e_2) = t \} .$$

Suppose that we have $e > e_1 > e_2 > t > s_1 > s_2 > y_1 > y_2 > y_3 > y_4$. Superposition Right between the 3rd and the 4th clauses produces the constrained 6th clause $e_1 = e_2 \| \{y_1 = y_2\}$. From now on, we denote the application of a

Superposition Right to the ith and jth clauses with $R(i, j)$. We list a derivation performed by our calculus:

$$R(3,4) \implies e_1 = e_2 \,\|\, \{y_1 = y_2\} \quad \text{(6th clause)}$$
$$R(1,2) \implies s_1 = s_2 \,\|\, \{y_3 = y_4\} \quad \text{(7th clause)}$$
$$R(5,6) \implies f(e_2, e_2) = t \,\|\, \{y_1 = y_2\} \quad \text{(8th clause)}$$
$$R(1,3) \implies e_1 = s_1 \,\|\, \{y_1 = y_3\} \quad \text{(9th clause)}$$
$$R(1,4) \implies e_2 = s_1 \,\|\, \{y_2 = y_3\} \quad \text{(10th clause)}$$
$$R(2,3) \implies e_1 = s_2 \,\|\, \{y_1 = y_4\} \quad \text{(11th clause)}$$
$$R(2,4) \implies e_2 = s_2 \,\|\, \{y_2 = y_4\} \quad \text{(12th clause)}$$
$$R(5,9) \implies f(s_1, e_2) = t \,\|\, \{y_1 = y_3\} \quad \text{(13th clause)}$$
$$R(5,11) \implies f(s_2, e_2) = t \,\|\, \{y_1 = y_4\} \quad \text{(14th clause)}$$
$$R(6,9) \implies e_2 = s_1 \,\|\, \{y_1 = y_3, y_1 = y_2\} \quad \text{(15th clause)}$$
$$R(6,11) \implies e_2 = s_2 \,\|\, \{y_1 = y_2, y_1 = y_4\} \quad \text{(16th clause)}$$
$$R(8,10) \implies f(s_1, s_1) = t \,\|\, \{y_1 = y_3, y_2 = y_3\} \quad \text{(17th clause)}$$
$$R(8,12) \implies f(s_2, s_2) = t \,\|\, \{y_1 = y_4, y_2 = y_4\} \quad \text{(18th clause)}$$
$$R(13,12) \implies f(s_1, s_2) = t \,\|\, \{y_1 = y_3, y_2 = y_4\} \quad \text{(19th clause)}$$
$$R(14,10) \implies f(s_2, s_1) = t \,\|\, \{y_1 = y_4, y_2 = y_3\} \quad \text{(20th clause)}$$
$$R(9,11) \implies s_1 = s_2 \,\|\, \{y_1 = y_3, y_1 = y_4\} \quad \text{(21th clause)}$$

The set of clauses above is saturated. The 7th, 17th, 18th, 19th and 20th clauses are exactly the output clauses of [157]. The non-simplified clauses that do not appear as output in [157] are redundant and they could be simplified by introducing a Subsumption rule as an additional simplification rule of our calculus.

7.4 Complexity Analysis of the Fragment for Database-Driven Applications

The saturation procedure of Theorem 7.3 can in principle produce double exponentially many clauses, because there are exponentially many terms of degree n (if n is the cardinality of the variables to be eliminated); it is not clear whether we can improve this bound to a simple exponential one, by limiting the kind of terms that can be produced. An estimation of the complexity costs of computing uniform interpolants in $\mathcal{EUF}$ is better performed within approaches making use of compressed DAG-representations of terms [131]. In this work, however, we are especially interested (for our applications to DAP verification) in the special case where the signature Σ contains only unary function symbols and relations of arbitrary arity: in fact, this is exactly the kind of symbols appearing in DB schemas (cf. Section 3.1 and Subsection 7.2.1). In this special case, important remarks apply. In fact, we shall see below that if the signature Σ contains only unary function symbols, only empty constraints can be generated; in case Σ contains also relation symbols of arity $n > 1$, the only constrained clauses that can be generated have the form $\perp \| \{t_1 = t'_1, \ldots, t_{n-1} = t'_{n-1}\}$. Also, it is not difficult to see that in a derivation at most one explicit definition $e_i = t(y) \| \emptyset$ can occur for every e_i: as soon as this definition is produced, all occurrences of e_i are rewritten to t. This implies that Constrained Superposition computes covers in polynomial time for the empty theory, whenever the signature Σ matches the restrictions of Definition 3.1 for DB schemas. We give here a finer complexity analysis, in order to obtain a quadratic bound.

In this section, *we assume that our signature Σ contains only unary function and m-ary relation symbols.* In order to attain the optimized quadratic complexity bound, we need to follow a *different strategy in applying the rules of our constrained superposition calculus* (this different strategy would not be correct for the general case). Thanks to this different strategy, we can make our procedure close to the algorithm of [157]: in fact, such algorithm is correct for the case of unary functions and requires only a minor adjustment for the case of unary functions and m-ary relations. Since relations play a special role in the present restricted context, we prefer to treat them as such, i.e. not to rewrite $R(t_1, \ldots, t_n)$ as $R(t_1, \ldots, t_n) = true$; the consequence is that we need an additional Constrained Resolution Rule[6]. We preliminarily notice that when function symbols are all unary, the constraints remain all *empty* during the run of the saturation procedure, except for the case of the newly introduced Resolution Rule below. This fact follows from the observation that given two terms u_1 and u_2, procedure $E(u_1, u_2)$ does not fail iff:

(1) either u_1 and u_2 are both terms containing only variables from y, or

(2) u_1 and u_2 are terms that syntactically coincide.

In case (1), $E(u_1, u_2)$ is $\{u_1 = u_2\}$ and in case (2), $E(u_1, u_2)$ is $\emptyset$. In case (1), Superposition Rules are not applicable. To show this, suppose that $u_1 \equiv s_{|p}$ and $u_2 \equiv l$; then, terms l and r use only variables from y, and consequently cannot be fed into Superposition Rules, since Superposition Rules are only applied when variables from $\underline{e}$ occur in both premises. Reflection Rule does not apply too in case (1), because this rule (like any other rule) cannot be applied to an $\underline{e}$-free literal.

Thus, in the particular case of m-ary relations and unary functions, the rules of the calculus are the following:

We still restrict the use of our rules to the case where all premises are not $\underline{e}$-free literals; again Demodulation is applied only in the case where $l = r$ is of the kind $e_i = t(y)$. For the order of applications of the Rules, Lemma 7.6 below show that we can apply (restricted) Superpositions, Demodulations, Reflections and Resolutions in this order and then stop.

---

[6] We extend the definition of an $\underline{e}$-flat literal so as to include also the literals of the kind $R(t_1, .., t_n)$ and $\neg R(t_1, .., t_n)$ where the terms t_i are either $\underline{e}$-free terms or variables from $\underline{e}$.

Superposition
$$\frac{l = r \qquad L}{L[r]_p}$$
if   (i) $l > r$;
(ii) if $L \equiv s = t$ or
$L \equiv s \neq t$, then
$s > t$ and $p \in Pos(s)$;
(iii) $E(s_{|p}, l)$ does not fail.

Resolution
$$\frac{R(t_1, \ldots, t_n)\ \neg R(s_1, \ldots, s_n)}{\perp \parallel \bigcup_i E(s_i, t_i)}$$
if $E(s_i, t_i)$ does not fail
for all $i = 1, \ldots, n$

Reflection
$$\frac{t \neq u}{\perp}$$
if $E(t, u)$ does not fail

Demodulation
$$\frac{L \qquad l = r}{L[r]_p}$$
if $l > r$ and $L_{|p} \equiv l$

An important preliminary observation to obtain such a result is that *we do not need to apply Superposition Rules whose left premise $l = r$ is of the kind $e_i = t(y)$*: this is because constraints are always empty (unless the constrained clause is the empty clause), so that a Superposition Rule with the left premise $e_i = t(y)$ can be replaced by a Demodulation Rule. [7] If the left premise of Superposition is not of the kind $e_i = t(y)$, then since our literals are e-flat, it can be either of the kind $e_i = e_j$ (with $e_i > e_j$) or of the kind $f(e_i) = t$. In the latter case t is either $e_k \in e$ or it is an e-free term; for Superposition Left (i.e. for Superposition applied to a negative literal), the left premise can only be $e_i = e_j$, because our literals are e-flat and so negative literals L cannot have a position p such that $L_{|p} \equiv f(e_i)$.

Let S be a set of e-flat literals with empty constraints; we say that S is *RS-closed* iff it is closed under *Restricted Superposition Rules*, i.e under Superposition Rules whose left premise is not of the kind $e_i = t(y)$. In equivalent terms, as a consequence of the above discussion, S is RS-closed iff it satisfies the following two conditions:

- if $\{f(e_i) = t, f(e_i) = v\} \subseteq S$, then $t = v \in S$;
- if $\{e_i = e_j, L\} \subseteq S$ and $e_i > e_j$ and $L_{|p} \equiv e_i$, then $L[e_j]_p \in S$.

Since Restricted Superpositions do not introduce essentially new terms (newly introduced terms are just rewritings of variables with variables), it is clear that we can make a finite set S of e-free literals RS-closed in finitely many steps. This can be naively done in time quadratic in the size of the formula. As an alternative, we can apply a *congruence closure algorithm* to S and produce a set of e-free constraints S' which is RS-closed and logically equivalent to S: the latter can be done in $O(n \cdot log(n))$-time, as it is well-known from the literature [208, 211, 173].

---

[7] This is not true in the general case where constraints are not empty, because the Demodulation Rule does not merge incomparable constraints.

Lemma 7.6 *Let S be a RS-closed set of empty-constrained $\underline{e}$-flat literals. Then, to saturate S it is sufficient to first exhaustively apply the Demodulation Rule, and then Reflection and Resolution Rules.*

Proof Let $\tilde{S}$ be the set obtained from S after having exhaustively applied Demodulation. Notice that the final effect of the reiterated application of Demodulation can be synthetically described by saying that literals in S are rewritten by using some explicit definitions

$$e_{i_1} = t_1(\underline{y}), \ldots, e_{i_k} = t_k(\underline{y}) \ . \tag{7.5}$$

These definitions are either in S, or are generated through the Demodulations themselves (we can freely assume that Demodulations are done in appropriate order: first all occurrences of e_{i_1} are rewritten to t_1, then all occurrences of e_{i_2} are rewritten to t_2, etc.).[8]

Suppose now that a pair $L, l = r \in \tilde{S}$ can generate a new literal $L[r]_p$ by Superposition. We know from above that we can limit ourselves to Restricted Superposition, so l is either of the form e_j or of the form $f(e_j)$, where moreover e_j is not among the set $\{e_{i_1}, \ldots, e_{i_k}\}$ from (7.5). The literals L and $l = r \in \tilde{S}$ happen to have been obtained from literals L' and $l = r'$ belonging to S by applying the rewriting rules (7.5) (notice that l cannot have been rewritten). Since such rewritings must have occurred in positions parallel to p and since S was closed under Restricted Superposition, we must have that S contained the literal $L'[r']_p$ that rewrites to $L[r]_p$ by the rewriting rules (7.5). This shows that $L[r]_p$ is already in $\tilde{S}$ (thus, in particular, Demodulation does not destroy RS-closedness) and proves the lemma, because Reflection and Resolution can only produce the empty clause and no rule applies to the empty clause. $\qquad\square$

Thus the strategy of applying (in this order)

> Restricted Superposition+Demodulation+Reflection+Resolution

always saturates.

To produce an output in optimized format, it is convenient to get it in a DAG-like form. This can be simulated via explicit acyclic definitions as follows. When we write $Def(\underline{e}, \underline{y})$ (where $\underline{e}, \underline{y}$ are tuples of distinct variables), we mean any flat formula of the kind (let $\underline{e} := e_1 \ldots, e_n$) $\bigwedge_{i=1}^{n} e_i = t_i$, where in the term t_i only the variables $e_1, \ldots, e_{i-1}, \underline{y}$ can occur. We shall supply the output in the form

$$\exists \underline{e}' \ (Def(\underline{e}', \underline{y}) \wedge \psi(\underline{e}', \underline{y})) \tag{7.6}$$

where the $\underline{e}'$ is a subset of the $\underline{e}$ and ψ is quantifier-free. The *DAG-format* (7.6) is not quantifier-free but can be converted to a quantifier-free formula by unravelling the acyclic definitions of the $\underline{e}'$.

Thus our procedure for computing a cover in DAG-format of a primitive formula $\exists \underline{e}\, \phi(\underline{e}, \underline{y})$ (in case the function symbols of the signature Σ are all unary) runs by

---

[8] In addition, if we happen to have, say, two different explicit definitions of e_{i_1} as $e_{i_1} = t_1, e_{i_1} = t_1'$, we decide to use just one of them (and always the same one, until the other one is eventually removed by Demodulation).

performing the following steps, one after the other. Let OUT be a quantifier-free formula (initially OUT is $\top$).

(1) We preprocess ϕ in order to produce a RS-closed set S of empty-constrained $\underline{e}$-flat literals.

(2) We *mark* the variables $\underline{e}$ in the following way (initially, all variables are un-marked): we scan S and, as soon as we find an equality of the kind $e_i = t$ where all variables from $\underline{e}$ occurring in t are marked, we mark e_i. This loop is repeated until no more variable gets marked.

(3) If Reflection is applicable, we output $\bot$ and exit.

(4) We conjoin OUT with all literals where, besides the $\underline{y}$, only marked variables occur.

(5) For every literal $R(t_1, \ldots, e, \ldots, t_m)$ that contains at least an unmarked e, we scan S until a literal of the type $\neg R(t_1, \ldots, e, \ldots, t_m)$ is found: then, we try to apply Resolution and if we succeed getting $\bot \parallel \{u_1 = u'_1, \ldots, u_m = u'_m\}$, we conjoin $\bigvee_j u_j \neq u'_j$ to OUT.

(6) We prefix to OUT a string of existential quantifiers binding all marked variables and output the result.

One remark is in order: when running the subprocedures $E(s_i, t_i)$ required by the Resolution Rule in (5) above, *all marked variables must be considered as part of the $\underline{y}$* (thus, e.g. $R(e, t), \neg R(e, v)$ produces $\bot \parallel \{t = u\}$ if both t and u contain, besides the $\underline{y}$, only marked variables).

Proposition 7.3 *Let T be the theory $\mathcal{EUF}$ in a signature with unary functions and m-ary relation symbols. Consider a primitive formula $\exists \underline{e} \, \phi(\underline{e}, \underline{y})$; then, the above algorithm returns a T-cover of $\exists \underline{e} \, \phi(\underline{e}, \underline{y})$ in DAG-format in time $O(n^2)$, where n is the size of $\exists \underline{e} \, \phi(\underline{e}, \underline{y})$.*

Proof The preprocessing step (1) requires an abstraction phase for producing $\underline{e}$-flat literals and a second phase in order to get a RS-closed set: the first phase requires linear time, whereas the second one requires $O(n \cdot log(n))$ time (via congruence closure). All the remaining steps require linear time, except steps (2) and (5) that requires quadratic time. This is the dominating cost, thus the entire procedure requires $O(n^2)$ time. $\square$

Although we do not deeply investigate the problem here, we conjecture that it might be possible to further lower down the above complexity to $O(n \cdot log(n))$.

7.5 An Extension of the Constrained Superposition Calculus

We consider an extension of our Constrained Superposition Calculus SuperCover that is useful for our applications to verification of data-aware processes. Let us assume that we have a theory whose axioms are (3.1), namely, for every function symbol f:

$$\forall x \, (x = \mathsf{undef} \leftrightarrow f(x) = \mathsf{undef}) \ .$$

One direction of the above equivalence is equivalent to the ground literal $f(\text{undef}) = \text{undef}$ and as such it does not interfere with the completion process (we just add it to our constraints from the very beginning).

To handle the other direction, we need to modify our Calculus. First, we add to the Constrained Superposition Calculus of Section 7.3 the following extra Rule

Inference Rule $Ext(\text{undef})$ $$\frac{f(e_j) = u(\underline{y}) \,\|\, D}{e_j = \text{undef} \,\|\, D \cup \{u(\underline{y}) = \text{undef}\}}$$
(Constrained)

The Rule is sound because $u(\underline{y}) = \text{undef} \wedge f(e_j) = u(\underline{y}) \rightarrow e_j = \text{undef}$ follows from the axioms (3.1). For cover computation with our new axioms, we need a restricted version of Paramodulation Rule:

Paramodulation $$\frac{e_j = r \,\|\, C \qquad L \,\|\, D}{L[r]_p \,\|\, C \cup D}$$ (if $e_j > r$ & $L_{|p} \equiv e_j$)
(Constrained)

Notice that we can have $e_j > r$ only in case r is either some existential variable e_i or it is an $\underline{e}$-free term $u(\underline{y})$. Paramodulation Rule (if it is not a Superposition) can only apply to a right member of an equality and such a right member must be e_j itself (because our literals are flat). Thus, the rule cannot introduce new terms and consequently it does not compromize the termination argument of Proposition 7.2.

Theorem 7.4 *Let T be the theory $\bigcup_{f \in \Sigma} \{\forall x \, (x = \text{undef} \leftrightarrow f(x) = \text{undef})\}$. Suppose that the algorithm from Section 7.3, taking as input the primitive $\underline{e}$-flat formula $\exists \underline{e} \, \phi(\underline{e}, \underline{y})$, gives as output the quantifier-free formula $\psi(\underline{y})$. Then the latter is a T-cover of $\exists \underline{e} \, \phi(\underline{e}, \underline{y})$.*

Proof The proof of Theorem 7.3 can be easily adjusted as follows. We proceed as in the proof of Theorem 7.3, so as to obtain the set $\Delta(M) \cup R \cup \tilde{S}$ which is saturated in the standard (unconstrained) Superposition Calculus. Below, we refer to the general refutational completeness proof of the Superposition Calculus given in [213]. Since we only have unit literals here, in order to produce a model of $\Delta(M) \cup R \cup \tilde{S}$, we can just consider the convergent ground rewriting system $\rightarrow$ consisting of the oriented equalities in $\Delta^+(M) \cup R \cup \tilde{S}$: the support of such model is formed by the $\rightarrow$-normal forms of our ground terms with the obvious interpretation for the function and constant symbols. For simplicity, we assume that undef is in normal form. [9] We need to check that whenever we have [10] $f(t) \rightarrow^* \text{undef}$ then we have also $t \rightarrow^* \text{undef}$: we prove this by induction on the reduction ordering for our ground

---

[9] To be pedantic, according to the definition of $\Delta^+(M)$, there should be an equality $\text{undef} = c_0$ in $\Delta^+(M)$ so that c_0 is the normal form of undef.

[10] We use $\rightarrow^*$ for the reflexive-transitive closure of $\rightarrow$ and $\rightarrow^+$ for the transitive closure of $\rightarrow$.

terms. Let t be a term such that $f(t) \to^*$ undef: if t is $\underline{e}$-free then the claim is trivial (because the axioms (3.1) are supposed to hold in $\mathcal{M}$). Suppose also that induction hypothesis applies to all terms smaller than t. If t is not in normal form, then let $\tilde{t}$ be its normal form; then we have $f(t) \to^+ f(\tilde{t}) \to^*$ undef, by the fact that $\to$ is convergent. By induction hypothesis, $\tilde{t} \to$ undef, hence $t \to^+ \tilde{t} \to^*$ undef, as desired. Finally, let us consider the case in which t is in normal form; since $f(t)$ is reducible in root position by some rule $l \to r$, our rules $l \to r$ are $\underline{e}$-flat and t is not $\underline{e}$-free, we have that $t \equiv e_j$ for some existential variable e_j. Then, we must have that S contains an equality of the kind $f(e_j) = u(\underline{y}) \parallel D$ or of the kind $f(e_j) = e_i \parallel D$ (the constraint D being true in $\mathcal{M}$ under the given assignment to the $\underline{y}$). The latter case is reduced to the former, since $e_i \to^*$ undef (by the convergence of $\to^*$) and since S is closed under Paramodulation. In the former case, by the rule Ext(undef), we must have that S contains $e_j =$ undef $\parallel D \cup \{u(\underline{y}) = $ undef$\}$. Now, since $f(e_j) = u(\underline{y}) \parallel D$ belongs to S and D is true in $\mathcal{M}$, we have that the normal forms of $f(e_j)$ and of $u(\underline{y})$ are the same; since the normal form of $f(e_j)$ is undef, the normal form of $u(\underline{y})$ is undef too, which means that $u(\underline{y}) = $ undef is true in $\mathcal{M}$. But $e_j = $ undef $\parallel D \cup \{u(\underline{y}) = $ undef$\}$ belongs to S, hence $e_j = $ undef belongs to $\tilde{S}$, which implies $e_j \to^*$ undef, as desired. $\square$

7.6 Remarks on MCMT Implementation

As evident from Subsection 7.2.1, our main motivation for investigating covers originated from the verification of DAPs (Data-Aware Processes). Such applications require database (DB) signatures to contain only unary function symbols (besides relations of every arity). We observed that computing covers of primitive formulae in such signatures requires only polynomial time. In addition, if relation symbols are at most binary, *the cover of a primitive formula is a conjunction of literals* (this is due to the fact that the constrained literals produced during saturation either have empty constraints or are of the kind $\bot \parallel t_1 = t_2$): this is crucial in applications, because model checkers like MCMT [147] and CUBICLE [80] represent sets of reachable states as primitive formulae, i.e., existentially quantified 'cubes' (which means conjunctions of literals). Indeed, these model checkers do not need any DNF conversion (which would cause an exponential blow-up) after computing covers in the above-mentioned restricted case: in contrast, a DNF conversion would have been needed if the output of the cover algorithm had been a generic formula. This makes cover computations a quite attractive technique in DAP verification.

Our cover algorithm for DB signatures has been implemented in the model checker MCMT. The implementation is however still partial, nevertheless the tool is able to compute covers for the $\mathcal{EUF}$-fragment with unary function symbols, unary relations and binary relations. The optimized procedure of Section 7.4 has not yet been implemented, instead MCMT uses a customary Knuth-Bendix completion (in fact, for the above mentioned fragments the constraints are always trivial and our constrained Superposition Calculus essentially boils down to Knuth-Bendix completion for ground literals in $\mathcal{EUF}$).

Axioms (3.1) are also covered in the following way. We assume that constraints of which we want to compute the cover always contain either the literal $e_j = $ undef or the literal $e_j \neq $ undef for every existential variable e_j. Whenever a constraint contains the literal $e_j \neq $ undef, the completion procedure adds the literal $u(y_i) \neq $ undef whenever it had produced a literal of the kind $f(e_j) = u(y_i)$.[11]

We wonder whether we are justified in assuming that all constraints of which we want to compute the cover always contain either the literal $e_j = $ undef or the literal $e_j \neq $ undef for every existential variable e_j. The answer is affirmative: according to the backward search algorithm implemented in array-based systems tools, the variable e_j to be eliminated always comes from the guard of a transition and we can assume that such a guard contains the literal $e_j \neq $ undef (if we need a transition with $e_j = $ undef - for an existentially quantified variable e_j - it is possible to write trivially this condition without using a quantified variable). The MCMT User Manual (available from the distribution) contains precise instructions on how to write specifications following the above prescriptions: for the sake of completeness, we will report a summary of the User Manual in Chapter 9.

A first experimental evaluation (based on the existing benchmark provided in [186]) will be described in Chapter 9, where we will extensively use the implemented cover algorithms when backward search needs to eliminate quantified data variables (see Chapter 4 for details on this). The first experiments are very encouraging: MCMT is able to solve in few seconds almost all the examples from the benchmark and the cover computations generated automatically during the model-checking search were discharged instantaneously.

---

[11] This is sound because $e \neq $ undef implies $f(e) \neq $ undef according to (3.1), so $u(y_i) \neq $ undef follows from $f(e_j) = u(y_i)$ and $e \neq $ undef.

Chapter 8
Combination of Uniform Interpolants for DAPs Verification

In this chapter, we attack the problem of computing covers in theory combinations. Theory combination is an important topic in automated reasoning: it deals with the problem of transferring properties and methods to the *union* (i.e., *the combination*) of theories, so as to modularly exploit the properties and the methods of the component theories. The possibility of the transfer to combination is usually one of the *desiderata* of every automated reasoning methodology, because it avoids developing *ad hoc* techniques for every theory that can be seen as a combination of theories for which these techniques already exist. Indeed, it allows to operationally exploit the techniques working for the component theories in a modular way (i.e., using these techniques *as black boxes*) and to lift them to more general machinery that works for the combination. The goal of this chapter is to develop a combined cover algorithm that computes covers for the combination of two theories by employing the cover algorithms of the component theories.

Computing combined covers is particularly interesting in view of DAP verification. In fact, we showed in the previous chapter how to (efficiently) compute covers for minimal (but still sufficiently expressive) DB schemas (e.g., $\mathcal{EUF}$). We would like to investigate a general method that works for combination of DB schemas for which cover (or quantifier elimination) algorithms exist: in this way, whenever we get such algorithms for the component theories, we can easily combine them so as to get a combined cover algorithm for the combined DB schema. This would be especially useful for DB extended-schemas (cf. Section 3.1.2): in fact, if T' is a theory admitting covers, or, even better, quantifier elimination like linear real arithmetic ($\mathcal{LRA}$), we would immediately get a combined cover algorithm that would allow us to verify U-RASs containing, e.g., arithmetic guards. Fortunately, in case of combinations of DB schemas (like $\mathcal{EUF}$) admitting model completion and arithmetic theories like $\mathcal{LRA}$, it is possible to develop such a combined cover algorithm: we will prove in Section 8.5 that this is possible in the general case of what we call *tame combinations* (cf. Section 2). However, given generic first-order theories admitting covers, their combination does not necessarily admit covers: we show a counterexample in Section 8.4, in the case one of the component theories is not convex.

© The Author(s), under exclusive license to Springer Nature Switzerland AG 2023
A. Gianola: *Verification of Data-Aware Processes via Satisfiability Modulo Theories*,
LNBIP 470, pp. 155–176, 2023.
https://doi.org/10.1007/978-3-031-42746-6_8

In this chapter, we study the problem of combined covers from a general perspective: in Section 8.3 we prove that, for generic first-order theories that are convex and have disjoint signatures, cover algorithms can be transferred to theory combinations under the same hypothesis needed to transfer quantifier-free interpolation (i.e., the equality interpolating property). We do so by exhibiting a concrete combined algorithm (called ConvexCombCover) that modularly exploits the cover algorithms for the component theories. The key feature of this algorithm relies on the extensive usage of the Beth definability property (defined in Section 6). As shown in Subsection 8.3.1, the hypotheses devised for the combined algorithm are *minimal*, in the sense that they are necessary for obtaining combined covers of *minimal* (and extremely important in practice) theory combinations. ConvexCombCover can be, e.g., used to compute covers of a mono-sorted combined *value theory* T' (from a suitable DB extended-schema $\langle \Sigma \cup \Sigma', T \cup T' \rangle$, cf. Subsection 3.1.2) satisfying the requirements for combination from Section 8.3: an example of such a T' is the theory $\mathcal{LRA} \cup \mathcal{EUF}$ combining linear real arithmetic with uninterpreted symbols.

Finally, in Section 8.5, we conclude the chapter by giving a combined cover algorithm (called TameCombCover) for possibly non-convex theories, in case the combination is tame. TameCombCover can be successfully applied, e.g., to DB extended-schemas that are the tame combination of a DB schema and of a suitable (possibly combined) value theory T', such as $\mathcal{LIA}$ or the theory $\mathcal{LRA} \cup \mathcal{EUF}$. We will see a concrete example of such a DB extended-theory in Example 8.2.

The content of this chapter stems directly from [54, 57].

8.1 Interpolation, Equality Interpolating Condition and Beth Definability

We report here some definitions and results we need concerning combined quantifier-free interpolation. Some of them are also in the preliminaries of this part of the book (Chapter 6), but we recall them here since they will be extensively used in the course of the current chapter. Most definitions and result are proved in [45]: however, they are simplified here because we restrict them to the case of universal convex theories.

As defined in Chapter 6, theory T is *stably infinite* iff every T-satisfiable constraint is satisfiable in an infinite model of T. The following lemma comes from a compactness argument:

Lemma 8.1 *If T is stably infinite, then every finite or countable model $\mathcal{M}$ of T can be embedded in a model $\mathcal{N}$ of T such that $|\mathcal{N}| \setminus |\mathcal{M}|$ is countable.*

Proof Consider $T \cup \Delta(\mathcal{M}) \cup \{c_i \neq a \mid a \in |\mathcal{M}|\}_i \cup \{c_i \neq c_j\}_{i \neq j}$, where $\{c_i\}_i$ is a countable set of fresh constants: by the Diagram Lemma and the downward Löwenheim-Skolem theorem [66], it is sufficient to show that this set is consistent. Suppose not; then by compactness $T \cup \Delta_0 \cup \Delta_1 \cup \Delta_2$ is not satisfiable, for a finite subset Δ_0 of $\Delta(\mathcal{M})$, a finite subset Δ_1 of $\{c_i \neq a \mid a \in |\mathcal{M}|\}_i$ and a finite subset Δ_2

of $\cup\{c_i \neq c_j\}_{i\neq j}$. However, this is a contradiction because by stable infiniteness Δ_0 (being satisfiable in $\mathcal{M}$) is satisfiable in an infinite model of T.   □

We recall that a theory T is *convex* iff for every constraint δ, if $T \vdash \delta \rightarrow \bigvee_{i=1}^{n} x_i = y_i$ then $T \vdash \delta \rightarrow x_i = y_i$ holds for some $i \in \{1, ..., n\}$. We also recall that a convex universal theory T is *equality interpolating* iff for every pair y_1, y_2 of variables and for every pair of *constraints* $\delta_1(\underline{x}, \underline{z}_1, y_1), \delta_2(\underline{x}, \underline{z}_2, y_2)$ such that

$$T \vdash \delta_1(\underline{x}, \underline{z}_1, y_1) \wedge \delta_2(\underline{x}, \underline{z}_2, y_2) \rightarrow y_1 = y_2$$

there exists a term $t(\underline{x})$ such that

$$T \vdash \delta_1(\underline{x}, \underline{z}_1, y_1) \wedge \delta_2(\underline{x}, \underline{z}_2, y_2) \rightarrow y_1 = t(\underline{x}) \wedge y_2 = t(\underline{x}).$$

Next two results (supplied without proof) will be used only in Subsection 8.3.1 to show that, in some sense, the sufficient conditions of our main combination Theorem 7.3 are also necessary.

Theorem 8.1 *[253, 45] Let T_1 and T_2 be two universal, convex, stably infinite theories over disjoint signatures Σ_1 and Σ_2. If both T_1 and T_2 are equality interpolating and have the quantifier-free interpolation property, then so does $T_1 \cup T_2$.*

There is a converse of the previous result; for a signature Σ, let us call $\mathcal{EUF}(\Sigma)$ the pure equality theory over the signature Σ (this theory is equality interpolating and has the quantifier-free interpolation property).

Theorem 8.2 *[45] Let T be a stably infinite, universal, convex theory admitting quantifier-free interpolation and let Σ be a signature disjoint from the signature of T containing at least a unary predicate symbol. Then, $T \cup \mathcal{EUF}(\Sigma)$ has quantifier-free interpolation iff T is equality interpolating.*

In [45] the above definitions and results are extended to the non-convex case and a long list of universal quantifier-free interpolating and equality interpolating theories is given. The list includes $\mathcal{EUF}(\Sigma)$, recursive data theories, as well as linear arithmetics. For linear arithmetics (and fragments thereof), it is essential to make a very careful choice of the signature, see again [45] (especially Subsection 4.1) for details. All the above theories admit a model completion (which coincides with the theory itself in case the theory admits quantifier elimination).

The equality interpolating property in a theory T can be equivalently characterized using Beth definability. We first recall the notion of Beth definability (from Chapter 6). Consider a primitive formula $\exists \underline{z}\phi(\underline{x}, \underline{z}, y)$; we say that $\exists \underline{z}\,\phi(\underline{x}, \underline{z}, y)$ *implicitly defines* y in T iff the formula $\forall y \forall y'\ (\exists \underline{z}\phi(\underline{x}, \underline{z}, y) \wedge \exists \underline{z}\phi(\underline{x}, \underline{z}, y')) \rightarrow y = y')$ is T-valid. We say that $\exists \underline{z}\phi(\underline{x}, \underline{z}, y)$ *explicitly defines* y in T iff there is a term $t(\underline{x})$ such that the formula $\forall y\ (\exists \underline{z}\phi(\underline{x}, \underline{z}, y) \rightarrow y = t(\underline{x}))$ is T-valid. A theory T has the *Beth definability property for primitive formulae* iff whenever a primitive formula $\exists \underline{z}\,\phi(\underline{x}, \underline{z}, y)$ implicitly defines the variable y then it also explicitly defines it.

Theorem 6.2([45]) A convex theory T having quantifier-free interpolation is equality interpolating iff it has the Beth definability property for primitive formulae.

In the following, we need only the left-to-right implication of the previous theorem, which is proved in Chapter 6.

8.2 Convex Theories

We now collect some useful facts concerning convex theories. We fix for this section a *convex, stably infinite, equality interpolating universal theory T admitting a model completion T^**. We let Σ be the signature of T.

We fix also a *Σ-constraint* $\phi(\underline{x}, \underline{y})$, where we assume that $\underline{y} = y_1, \ldots, y_n$ (recall that the tuple $\underline{x}$ is disjoint from the tuple $\underline{y}$ according to our conventions from Section 6).

For $i = 1, \ldots, n$, we let the formula $\mathtt{ImplDef}^T_{\phi, y_i}(\underline{x})$ be the *quantifier-free* formula equivalent in T^* to the formula

$$\forall \underline{y} \, \forall \underline{y}' (\phi(\underline{x}, \underline{y}) \wedge \phi(\underline{x}, \underline{y}') \rightarrow y_i = y'_i) \tag{8.1}$$

where the $\underline{y}'$ are renamed copies of the $\underline{y}$. Notice that the variables occurring free in ϕ are $\underline{x}, \underline{y}$, whereas only the $\underline{x}$ occur free in $\mathtt{ImplDef}^T_{\phi, y_i}(\underline{x})$ (the variable y_i is among the $\underline{y}$ and does not occur free in $\mathtt{ImplDef}^T_{\phi, y_i}(\underline{x})$): these facts coming from our notational conventions are crucial and should be kept in mind when reading this and next section. We need a first semantic technical lemma.

Lemma 8.2 *Suppose that we are given a model $\mathcal{M}$ of T and elements $\underline{a}$ from the support of $\mathcal{M}$ such that $\mathcal{M} \not\models \mathtt{ImplDef}^T_{\phi, y_i}(\underline{a})$ for all $i = 1, \ldots, n$. Then there exists an extension $\mathcal{N}$ of $\mathcal{M}$ such that for some $\underline{b} \in |\mathcal{N}| \setminus |\mathcal{M}|$ we have $\mathcal{N} \models \phi(\underline{a}, \underline{b})$.*

Proof Since T has a model completion, it has uniform quantifier-free interpolants by Theorem 7.1, hence it has also (ordinary) quantifier-free interpolants. By Theorem 6.1 it is strongly amalgamable because it is equality interpolating. In conclusion, *we are allowed to use strong amalgamation in our proof.* By strong amalgamability, we can freely assume that $\mathcal{M}$ is generated, as a Σ-structure, by the $\underline{a}$: in fact, if we prove the statement for the substructure generated by the $\underline{a}$, then strong amalgamability will provide the model we want.

By using the Robinson Diagram Lemma, what we need is to prove the consistency of $T \cup \Delta(\mathcal{M})$ with the set of ground sentences

$$\{\phi(\underline{a}, \underline{b})\} \cup \{b_i \neq t(\underline{a})\}_{t, b_i}$$

where $t(\underline{x})$ varies over $\Sigma(\underline{x})$-terms, the $\underline{b} = b_1, \ldots, b_n$ are fresh constants and i vary over $1, \ldots, n$. By convexity,[1] this set is inconsistent iff there exist a term $t(\underline{x})$ and $i = 1, \ldots, n$ such that

---

[1] As noticed in Chapter 6, convexity implies that if, for a set of literals ϕ and for a not empty disjunction of *terms* $\bigvee_{i=1}^n t_i = u_i$, we have $T \models \phi \rightarrow \bigvee_{i=1}^n t_i = u_i$, then we have also $T \models \phi \rightarrow t_i = u_i$ for some $i = 1, \ldots, n$.

$$T \cup \Delta(\mathcal{M}) \vdash \phi(\underline{a}, y) \rightarrow y_i = t(\underline{a}) \ .$$

This however implies that $T \cup \Delta(\mathcal{M})$ has the formula

$$\forall \underline{y} \, \forall \underline{y}' (\phi(\underline{a}, \underline{y}) \wedge \phi(\underline{a}, \underline{y}') \rightarrow y_i = y_i')$$

as a logical consequence. If we now embed $\mathcal{M}$ into a model $\mathcal{N}$ of T^*, we have that $\mathcal{N} \models \mathtt{ImplDef}^T_{\phi, y_i}(\underline{a})$, which is in contrast to $\mathcal{M} \not\models \mathtt{ImplDef}^T_{\phi, y_i}(\underline{a})$ (because $\mathcal{M}$ is a substructure of $\mathcal{N}$ and $\mathtt{ImplDef}^T_{\phi, y_i}(\underline{a})$ is quantifier-free). $\qquad\square$

The following lemma supplies terms which will be used as ingredients in our combined covers algorithm:

Lemma 8.3 *Let* $L_{i1}(\underline{x}) \vee \cdots \vee L_{ik_i}(\underline{x})$ *be the disjunctive normal form (DNF) of* $\mathtt{ImplDef}^T_{\phi, y_i}(\underline{x})$. *Then, for every* $j = 1, \ldots, k_i$, *there is a* $\Sigma(\underline{x})$-*term* $t_{ij}(\underline{x})$ *such that*

$$T \vdash L_{ij}(\underline{x}) \wedge \phi(\underline{x}, \underline{y}) \rightarrow y_i = t_{ij} \ . \tag{8.2}$$

As a consequence, a formula of the kind $\mathtt{ImplDef}^T_{\phi, y_i}(\underline{x}) \wedge \exists \underline{y} \, (\phi(\underline{x}, \underline{y}) \wedge \psi)$ *is equivalent (modulo T) to the formula*

$$\bigvee_{j=1}^{k_i} \exists \underline{y} \, (y_i = t_{ij} \wedge L_{ij}(\underline{x}) \wedge \phi(\underline{x}, \underline{y}) \wedge \psi) \ . \tag{8.3}$$

Proof We have that $(\bigvee_j L_{ij}) \leftrightarrow \mathtt{ImplDef}^T_{\phi, y_i}(\underline{x})$ is a tautology, hence from the definition of $\mathtt{ImplDef}^T_{\phi, y_i}(\underline{x})$, we have that

$$T^* \vdash L_{ij}(\underline{x}) \rightarrow \forall \underline{y} \, \forall \underline{y}' (\phi(\underline{x}, \underline{y}) \wedge \phi(\underline{x}, \underline{y}') \rightarrow y_i = y_i') \ ;$$

however this formula is trivially equivalent to a universal formula (L_{ij} does not depend on $\underline{y}, \underline{y}'$), hence since T and T^* prove the same universal formulae, we get

$$T \vdash L_{ij}(\underline{x}) \wedge \phi(\underline{x}, \underline{y}) \wedge \phi(\underline{x}, \underline{y}') \rightarrow y_i = y_i' \ .$$

Using Beth definability property (Theorem 6.2), we get (8.2), as required, for some terms $t_{ij}(\underline{x})$. Finally, the second claim of the lemma follows from (8.2) by trivial logical manipulations. $\qquad\square$

In all our concrete examples, the theory T has its quantifier-free fragment decidable (namely it is decidable whether a quantifier-free formula is a logical consequence of T or not), thus the terms t_{ij} mentioned in Lemma 8.3 can be computed just by enumerating all possible $\Sigma(\underline{x})$-terms: the computation terminates, because the above proof shows that the appropriate terms always exist. However, this is terribly inefficient and, from a practical point of view, one needs to have at disposal dedicated algorithms to find the required equality interpolating terms. For some common theories ($\mathcal{EUF}$, Lisp-structures, linear real arithmetic), such algorithms are designed in [253]; in [45] [Lemma 4.3 and Theorem 4.4], the algorithms for computing equality interpolating terms are connected to quantifier elimination algorithms in the case of universal theories admitting quantifier elimination.

The following lemma will be useful in the next section:

Lemma 8.4 *Let T have a model completion T^* and let the constraint $\phi(\underline{x}, \underline{y})$ be of the kind $\alpha(\underline{x}) \wedge \phi'(\underline{x}, \underline{y})$, where $\underline{y} = y_1, \ldots, y_n$. Then for every $i = 1, \ldots, n$, the formula $\mathrm{ImplDef}^T_{\phi, y_i}(\underline{x})$ is T-equivalent to $\alpha(\underline{x}) \rightarrow \mathrm{ImplDef}^T_{\phi', y_i}(\underline{x})$.*

Proof According to (8.1), the formula $\mathrm{ImplDef}^T_{\phi, y_i}(\underline{x})$ is obtained by eliminating quantifiers in T^* from

$$\forall \underline{y} \, \forall \underline{y}' (\alpha(\underline{x}) \wedge \phi'(\underline{x}, \underline{y}) \wedge \alpha(\underline{x}) \wedge \phi'(\underline{x}, \underline{y}') \rightarrow y_i = y_i') \tag{8.4}$$

The latter is equivalent, modulo logical manipulations, to

$$\alpha(\underline{x}) \rightarrow \forall \underline{y} \, \forall \underline{y}' (\phi'(\underline{x}, \underline{y}) \wedge \phi'(\underline{x}, \underline{y}') \rightarrow y_i = y_i') \tag{8.5}$$

hence the claim (eliminating quantifiers in T^* from (8.4) and (8.5) gives quantifier-free T^*-equivalent formulae, hence also T-equivalent formulae because T and T^* prove the same quantifier-free formulae).   □

8.3 The Convex Combined Cover Algorithm

Let us now fix two theories T_1, T_2 over disjoint signatures Σ_1, Σ_2. We assume that both of them satisfy the assumptions from the previous section, meaning that they are convex, stably infinite, equality interpolating, universal and admit model completions T_1^*, T_2^* respectively. We will prove in this section (Theorem 8.3) that $T_1 \cup T_2$ admits a model completion too. We achieve this by supplying a combined algorithm, called ConvexCombCover, for computing $T_1 \cup T_2$-covers: in order to construct the $T_1 \cup T_2$-cover, this combined algorithm exploits the cover algorithms of the component theories T_i ($i = 1, 2$).

We need to compute a cover for $\exists \underline{e} \, \phi(\underline{x}, \underline{e})$, where ϕ is a conjunction of $\Sigma_1 \cup \Sigma_2$-literals. By applying rewriting purification steps like

$$\phi \implies \exists d \, (d = t \wedge \phi(d/t))$$

(where d is a fresh variable and t is a pure term, i.e. it is either a Σ_1- or a Σ_2-term), we can assume that our formula ϕ is of the kind $\phi_1 \wedge \phi_2$, where ϕ_1 is a Σ_1-formula and ϕ_2 is a Σ_2-formula. Thus we need to compute a cover for a formula of the kind

$$\exists \underline{e} \, (\phi_1(\underline{x}, \underline{e}) \wedge \phi_2(\underline{x}, \underline{e})), \tag{8.6}$$

where ϕ_i is a conjunction of Σ_i-literals ($i = 1, 2$). We also assume that both ϕ_1 and ϕ_2 contain the literals $e_i \neq e_j$ (for $i \neq j$) as a conjunct: this can be achieved by guessing a partition of the $\underline{e}$ and by replacing each e_i with the representative element of its equivalence class.

Remark 8.1 It is not clear whether this preliminary guessing step can be avoided. In fact, Nelson-Oppen [207] combined satisfiability for *convex* theories does not need it; however, combining covers algorithms is a more complicated problem than combining mere satisfiability algorithms and for technical reasons related to the correctness and completeness proofs below, we were forced to introduce guessing at this step.

To manipulate formulae, our algorithm employs acyclic explicit definitions as follows. When we write $\mathtt{ExplDef}(\underline{z},\underline{x})$ (where $\underline{z},\underline{x}$ are tuples of distinct variables), we mean any formula of the kind (let $\underline{z} := z_1 \ldots, z_m$)

$$\bigwedge_{i=1}^{m} z_i = t_i(z_1, \ldots, z_{i-1}, \underline{x})$$

where the term t_i is pure (i.e. it is a Σ_i-term) and only the variables $z_1, \ldots, z_{i-1}, \underline{x}$ can occur in it. When we assert a formula like $\exists \underline{z} \, (\mathtt{ExplDef}(\underline{z},\underline{x}) \wedge \psi(\underline{z},\underline{x}))$, we are in fact in the condition of recursively eliminating the variables $\underline{z}$ from it via terms containing only the parameters $\underline{x}$ (the 'explicit definitions' $z_i = t_i$ are in fact arranged acyclically).

A *working formula* is a formula of the kind

$$\exists \underline{z} \, (\mathtt{ExplDef}(\underline{z},\underline{x}) \wedge \exists \underline{e} \, (\psi_1(\underline{x}, \underline{z}, \underline{e}) \wedge \psi_2(\underline{x}, \underline{z}, \underline{e}))) \, , \tag{8.7}$$

where ψ_1 is a conjunction of Σ_1-literals and ψ_2 is a conjunction of Σ_2-literals. The variables $\underline{x}$ are called *parameters*, the variables $\underline{z}$ are called *defined variables* and the variables $\underline{e}$ *(truly) existential variables*. The parameters do not change during the execution of the algorithm. We assume that ψ_1, ψ_2 in a working formula (8.7) always contain the literals $e_i \neq e_j$ (for distinct e_i, e_j from $\underline{e}$) as a conjunct.

In our starting formula (8.6), there are no defined variables. However, if via some syntactic check it happens that some of the existential variables can be recognized as defined, then it is useful to display them as such (this observation may avoid redundant cases - leading to inconsistent disjuncts - in the computations below).

A working formula like (8.7) is said to be *terminal* iff for every existential variable $e_i \in \underline{e}$ we have that

$$T_1 \vdash \psi_1 \rightarrow \neg \mathtt{ImplDef}^{T_1}_{\psi_1, e_i}(\underline{x}, \underline{z}) \quad \text{and} \quad T_2 \vdash \psi_2 \rightarrow \neg \mathtt{ImplDef}^{T_2}_{\psi_2, e_i}(\underline{x}, \underline{z}) \, . \tag{8.8}$$

Roughly speaking, we can say that in a terminal working formula, all variables which are not parameters are either explicitly definable or recognized as not implicitly definable by both theories; of course, a working formula with no existential variables is terminal.

Lemma 8.5 *Every working formula is equivalent (modulo $T_1 \cup T_2$) to a disjunction of terminal working formulae.*

Proof To compute the required terminal working formulae, it is sufficient to apply the following non-deterministic procedure (the output is the disjunction of all possible outcomes). The non-deterministic procedure applies one of the following alternatives.

(1) Update ψ_1 by adding to it a disjunct from the DNF of $\bigwedge_{e_i \in \underline{e}} \neg \texttt{ImplDef}^{T_1}_{\psi_1, e_i}(\underline{x}, \underline{z})$ and ψ_2 by adding to it a disjunct from the DNF of $\bigwedge_{e_i \in \underline{e}} \neg \texttt{ImplDef}^{T_2}_{\psi_2, e_i}(\underline{x}, \underline{z})$;

(2.i) Select $e_i \in \underline{e}$ and $h \in \{1, 2\}$; then update ψ_h by adding to it a disjunct L_{ij} from the DNF of $\texttt{ImplDef}^{T_h}_{\psi_h, e_i}(\underline{x}, \underline{z})$; the equality $e_i = t_{ij}$ (where t_{ij} is the term mentioned in Lemma 8.3)[2] is added to $\texttt{ExplDef}(\underline{z}, \underline{x})$; the variable e_i becomes in this way part of the defined variables.

If alternative (1) is chosen, the procedure stops, otherwise it is recursively applied again and again: we have one truly existential variable less after applying alternative (2.i), so the procedure terminates, since eventually either no truly existential variable remains or alternative (1) is applied. The correctness of the procedure is due to the fact that the following formula is trivially a tautology:

$$\left(\bigwedge_{e_i \in \underline{e}} \neg \texttt{ImplDef}^{T_1}_{\psi_1, e_i}(\underline{x}, \underline{z}) \wedge \bigwedge_{e_i \in \underline{e}} \neg \texttt{ImplDef}^{T_2}_{\psi_2, e_i}(\underline{x}, \underline{z}) \right) \vee$$
$$\vee \bigvee_{e_i \in \underline{e}} \texttt{ImplDef}^{T_1}_{\psi_1, e_i}(\underline{x}, \underline{z}) \vee \bigvee_{e_i \in \underline{e}} \texttt{ImplDef}^{T_2}_{\psi_2, e_i}(\underline{x}, \underline{z})$$

The first disjunct is used in alternative (1), the other disjuncts in alternative (2.i). At the end of the procedure, we get a terminal working formula. Indeed, if no truly existential variable remains, then the working formula is trivially terminal. It remains to prove that the working formula obtained after applying alternative (1) is indeed terminal. Let ψ'_k (for $k = 1, 2$) be the formula obtained from ψ_k after applying alternative (1). We have that ψ'_k is $\alpha(\underline{x}, \underline{z}) \wedge \psi_k(\underline{x}, \underline{z}, \underline{e})$, where α is a disjunct of the DNF of $\bigwedge_{e_i \in \underline{e}} \neg \texttt{ImplDef}^{T_k}_{\psi_k, e_i}(\underline{x}, \underline{z})$. We need to show that $T_k \vdash \psi'_k \rightarrow \neg \texttt{ImplDef}^{T_k}_{\psi'_k, e_j}(\underline{x}, \underline{z})$ for every j. Fix such a j; according to Lemma 8.4, we must show that

$$T_k \vdash \alpha(\underline{x}, \underline{z}) \wedge \psi_k(\underline{x}, \underline{z}, \underline{e}) \rightarrow \neg(\alpha(\underline{x}, \underline{z}) \rightarrow \texttt{ImplDef}^{T_k}_{\psi_k, e_j}(\underline{x}, \underline{z}))$$

which is indeed the case because $\alpha(\underline{x}, \underline{z})$ logically implies $\neg \texttt{ImplDef}^{T_k}_{\psi'_k, e_j}(\underline{x}, \underline{z})$, since $\alpha(\underline{x}, \underline{z})$ is a disjunct of the DNF of $\bigwedge_{e_i \in \underline{e}} \neg \texttt{ImplDef}^{T_k}_{\psi_k, e_i}(\underline{x}, \underline{z})$. □

Thus we are left to the problem of computing a cover of a terminal working formula; this problem is solved in the following proposition:

Proposition 8.1 *A cover of a terminal working formula (8.7) can be obtained just by unravelling the explicit definitions of the variables $\underline{z}$ from the formula*

---

[2] Lemma 8.3 is used taking as $\underline{y}$ the tuple $\underline{e}$, as $\underline{x}$ the tuple $\underline{x}, \underline{z}$, as $\phi(\underline{x}, \underline{y})$ the formula $\psi_h(\underline{x}, \underline{z}, \underline{e})$ and as ψ the formula ψ_{3-h}.

$$\exists \underline{z}\, (\texttt{ExplDef}(\underline{z}, \underline{x}) \wedge \theta_1(\underline{x}, \underline{z}) \wedge \theta_2(\underline{x}, \underline{z})) \tag{8.9}$$

where $\theta_1(\underline{x}, \underline{z})$ is the T_1-cover of $\exists \underline{e} \psi_1(\underline{x}, \underline{z}, \underline{e})$ and $\theta_2(\underline{x}, \underline{z})$ is the T_2-cover of $\exists \underline{e} \psi_2(\underline{x}, \underline{z}, \underline{e})$.

Proof In order to show that Formula (8.9) is the $T_1 \cup T_2$-cover of a terminal working formula (8.7), we apply Lemma 7.1. The first condition of that lemma is easily fulfilled. Concerning the second condition, we prove that, for every $T_1 \cup T_2$-model $\mathcal{M}$, for every tuple $\underline{a}, \underline{c}$ from $|\mathcal{M}|$ such that $\mathcal{M} \models \theta_1(\underline{a}, \underline{c}) \wedge \theta_2(\underline{a}, \underline{c})$ there is an extension $\mathcal{N}$ of $\mathcal{M}$ such that $\mathcal{N}$ is still a model of $T_1 \cup T_2$ and $\mathcal{N} \models \exists \underline{e}(\psi_1(\underline{a}, \underline{c}, \underline{e}) \wedge \psi_2(\underline{a}, \underline{c}, \underline{e}))$. By a Löwenheim-Skolem argument, since our languages are countable, we can suppose that $\mathcal{M}$ is at most countable and actually that it is countable by stable infiniteness of our theories, see Lemma 8.1 (the fact that $T_1 \cup T_2$ is stably infinite in case both T_1, T_2 are such, comes from the proof of Nelson-Oppen combination result, see [207],[243], [128]).

According to the conditions (8.8) and the definition of a cover (notice that the formulae $\neg\texttt{ImplDef}_{\psi_h,e_i}^{T_h}(\underline{x}, \underline{z})$ do not contain the $\underline{e}$ and are quantifier-free) we have that

$$T_1 \vdash \theta_1 \rightarrow \neg\texttt{ImplDef}_{\psi_1,e_i}^{T_1}(\underline{x}, \underline{z}) \quad \text{and} \quad T_2 \vdash \theta_2 \rightarrow \neg\texttt{ImplDef}_{\psi_2,e_i}^{T_2}(\underline{x}, \underline{z})$$

(for every $e_i \in \underline{e}$). Thus, since $\mathcal{M} \not\models \texttt{ImplDef}_{\psi_1,e_i}^{T_1}(\underline{a}, \underline{c})$ and $\mathcal{M} \not\models \texttt{ImplDef}_{\psi_2,e_i}^{T_2}(\underline{a}, \underline{c})$ hold for every $e_i \in \underline{e}$, we can apply Lemma 8.2 and conclude that there exist a T_1-model $\mathcal{N}_1$ and a T_2-model $\mathcal{N}_2$ such that $\mathcal{N}_1 \models \psi_1(\underline{a}, \underline{c}, \underline{b}_1)$ and $\mathcal{N}_2 \models \psi_2(\underline{a}, \underline{c}, \underline{b}_2)$ for tuples $\underline{b}_1 \in |\mathcal{N}_1|$ and $\underline{b}_2 \in |\mathcal{N}_2|$, both disjoint from $|\mathcal{M}|$. By a Löwenheim-Skolem argument, we can suppose that $\mathcal{N}_1, \mathcal{N}_2$ are countable and by Lemma 8.1 even that they are both countable extensions of $\mathcal{M}$.

The tuples $\underline{b}_1$ and $\underline{b}_2$ have equal length because the ψ_1, ψ_2 from our working formulae entail $e_i \neq e_j$, where e_i, e_j are different existential variables. Thus there is a bijection $\iota : |\mathcal{N}_1| \rightarrow |\mathcal{N}_2|$ fixing all elements in $\mathcal{M}$ and mapping component-wise the $\underline{b}_1$ onto the $\underline{b}_2$. But this means that, exactly as it happens in the proof of the completeness of the Nelson-Oppen combination procedure, the Σ_2-structure on $\mathcal{N}_2$ can be moved back via ι^{-1} to $|\mathcal{N}_1|$ in such a way that the Σ_2-substructure from $\mathcal{M}$ is fixed and in such a way that the tuple $\underline{b}_2$ is mapped to the tuple $\underline{b}_1$. In this way, $\mathcal{N}_1$ becomes a $\Sigma_1 \cup \Sigma_2$-structure which is a model of $T_1 \cup T_2$ and which is such that $\mathcal{N}_1 \models \psi_1(\underline{a}, \underline{c}, \underline{b}_1) \wedge \psi_2(\underline{a}, \underline{c}, \underline{b}_1)$, as required. □

From Lemma 8.5, Proposition 8.1 and Theorem 7.1, we immediately get

Theorem 8.3 *Let T_1, T_2 be convex, stably infinite, equality interpolating, universal theories over disjoint signatures admitting a model completion. Then $T_1 \cup T_2$ admits a model completion too. Covers in $T_1 \cup T_2$ can be effectively computed as shown above.*

We recall from Theorem 8.1 that the equality interpolating property transfers to combination of theories too, when it holds in the component theories.

We now summarize the steps of the combined cover algorithm ConvexCombCover that takes as input the primitive formula $\exists \underline{e}\, \phi(\underline{x}, \underline{e})$, where ϕ is a conjunction of $\Sigma_1 \cup \Sigma_2$-literals:

1: Apply rewriting purification steps, like $\phi \implies \exists d\, (d = t \wedge \phi(d/t))$ (where d is a fresh variable and t is a pure term), until $\phi = \phi_1 \wedge \phi_2$, where ϕ_i is a Σ_i-formula ($i = 1, 2$).

2: Guess a partition of the $\underline{e}$ and replace each e_k with the representative element of its equivalence class.

3: Apply the non-deterministic procedure of Lemma 8.5 to ϕ so as to get a disjunction of terminal working formulae TW_j, where each disjunct TW_j is $\exists \underline{z}\, (\texttt{ExplDef}_j(\underline{z}, \underline{x}) \wedge \exists \underline{e}\, (\psi_{j,1}(\underline{x}, \underline{z}, \underline{e}) \wedge \psi_{j,2}(\underline{x}, \underline{z}, \underline{e})))$

4: For every disjunct TW_j, compute the T_1-cover of $\exists \underline{e}\psi_{j,1}(\underline{x}, \underline{z}, \underline{e})$, say $\theta_{j,1}(\underline{x}, \underline{z})$, and the T_2-cover of $\exists \underline{e}\psi_{j,2}(\underline{x}, \underline{z}, \underline{e})$, say $\theta_{j,2}(\underline{x}, \underline{z})$.

5: Return as output the disjunction $\bigvee_j \exists \underline{z}\, (\texttt{ExplDef}_j(\underline{z}, \underline{x}) \wedge \theta_{j,1}(\underline{x}, \underline{z}) \wedge \theta_{j,2}(\underline{x}, \underline{z}))$.

Notice that the input cover algorithms in the above combined cover computation algorithm are used not only in the final step described in Proposition 8.1, but also every time we need to compute a formula $\texttt{ImplDef}^{T_h}_{\psi_h, e_i}(\underline{x}, \underline{z})$: according to its definition, this formula is obtained by eliminating quantifiers in T_i^* from (8.1) (this is done via a cover computation, reading $\forall$ as $\neg \exists \neg$). In practice, implicit definability is not very frequent, so that in many concrete cases $\texttt{ImplDef}^{T_h}_{\psi_h, e_i}(\underline{x}, \underline{z})$ is trivially equivalent to $\bot$ (in such cases, Step (2.i) above can obviously be disregarded).

Example 8.1 Let $T' := \mathcal{EUF} \cup \mathcal{LRA}$, where $\mathcal{LRA}$ is linear real arithmetic. Since both $\mathcal{EUF}$ and $\mathcal{LRA}$ are convex, stably infinite, equality interpolating, universal theories over disjoint signatures, $\mathcal{EUF}$ admits a model completion (cf. Section 7.3) and $\mathcal{LRA}$ admits quantifier elimination, Theorem 8.3 applies and we can apply ConvexCombCover to compute T'-covers. This example will be continued in Section 8.5, where T' will be the (combined) value theory of a suitable DB extended-schema.

8.3.1 The Necessity of the Equality Interpolating Condition.

The following result shows that equality interpolating is a necessary condition for a transfer result, in the sense that it is already required for minimal combinations with signatures adding uninterpreted symbols:

Theorem 8.4 *Let T be a convex, stably infinite, universal theory admitting a model completion and let Σ be a signature disjoint from the signature of T containing at least a unary predicate symbol. Then $T \cup \mathcal{EUF}(\Sigma)$ admits a model completion iff T is equality interpolating.*

Proof The necessity can be shown by using the following argument. By Theorem 7.1, $T \cup \mathcal{EUF}(\Sigma)$ has uniform quantifier-free interpolation, hence also ordinary quantifier-free interpolation. We can now apply Theorem 8.2 and get that T must be equality interpolating. Conversely, the sufficiency comes from Theorem 8.3 together with the fact that $\mathcal{EUF}(\Sigma)$ is trivially universal, convex, stably infinite, has a model completion (see Chapter 7) and is equality interpolating [253],[45].   □

8.3.2 An Example of Cover Computation

We now analyze an example in detail. Our results apply for instance to the case where T_1 is $\mathcal{EUF}(\Sigma)$ and T_2 is linear real arithmetic $\mathcal{LRA}$. We recall that covers are computed in real arithmetic by quantifier elimination (using, e.g., the Fourier-Motzkin procedure, that we call FM-QE), whereas for $\mathcal{EUF}(\Sigma)$ one can apply the superposition-based algorithm from Chapter 7. Let us show that the cover of

$$\exists e_1 \cdots \exists e_4 \begin{pmatrix} e_1 = f(x_1) \ \wedge \ e_2 = f(x_2) \ \wedge \\ \wedge \ f(e_3) = e_3 \ \wedge \ f(e_4) = x_1 \ \wedge \\ \wedge \ x_1 + e_1 \leq e_3 \ \wedge \ e_3 \leq x_2 + e_2 \ \wedge \ e_4 = x_2 + e_3 \end{pmatrix} \tag{8.10}$$

is the following formula

$$\begin{array}{l} [x_2 = 0 \ \wedge \ f(x_1) = x_1 \ \wedge \ x_1 \leq 0 \ \wedge \ x_1 \leq f(0)] \ \vee \\ \vee \ [x_1 + f(x_1) < x_2 + f(x_2) \ \wedge \ x_2 \neq 0] \ \vee \\ \vee \ \begin{bmatrix} x_2 \neq 0 \ \wedge \ x_1 + f(x_1) = x_2 + f(x_2) \ \wedge \ f(2x_2 + f(x_2)) = x_1 \ \wedge \\ \wedge \ f(x_1 + f(x_1)) = x_1 + f(x_1) \end{bmatrix} \end{array} \tag{8.11}$$

Formula (8.10) is already purified. Notice also that the variables e_1, e_2 are in fact already explicitly defined (only e_3, e_4 are truly existential variables).

We first make the partition guessing. There is no need to involve defined variables into the partition guessing, hence we need to consider only two partitions; they are described by the following formulae:

$$P_1(e_3, e_4) \equiv e_3 \neq e_4$$
$$P_2(e_3, e_4) \equiv e_3 = e_4$$

We first analyze **the case of** P_1. The formulae ψ_1 and ψ_2 to which we need to apply exhaustively Step (1) and Step (2.i) of our algorithm are:

$$\psi_1 \equiv f(e_3) = e_3 \ \wedge \ f(e_4) = x_1 \ \wedge \ e_3 \neq e_4$$
$$\psi_2 \equiv x_1 + e_1 \leq e_3 \ \wedge \ e_3 \leq x_2 + e_2 \ \wedge \ e_4 = x_2 + e_3 \ \wedge \ e_3 \neq e_4$$

We first compute the implicit definability formulae for the truly existential variables with respect to both T_1 and T_2.

-   We first consider $\texttt{ImplDef}^{T_1}_{\psi_1, e_3}(\underline{x}, z)$. Here we show that the cover of the negation of formula (8.1) is equivalent to $\top$ (so that $\texttt{ImplDef}^{T_1}_{\psi_1, e_3}(\underline{x}, z)$ is equivalent to

$\bot$). We must quantify over truly existential variables and their duplications, thus we need to compute the cover of

$$f(e_3') = e_3' \wedge f(e_3) = e_3 \wedge f(e_4') = x_1 \wedge f(e_4) = x_1 \wedge e_3 \neq e_4 \wedge e_3' \neq e_4' \wedge e_3' \neq e_3$$

This is a saturated set according to the superposition based procedure SuperCover from Chapter 7, hence the result is $\top$, as claimed.

- The formula $\mathtt{ImplDef}_{\psi_1,e_4}^{T_1}(\underline{x},\underline{z})$ is also equivalent to $\bot$, by the same argument as above.
- To compute $\mathtt{ImplDef}_{\psi_2,e_3}^{T_2}(\underline{x},\underline{z})$ we use Fourier-Motzkin quantifier elimination (FM-QE). We need to eliminate the variables e_3, e_3', e_4, e_4' (intended as existentially quantified variables) from

$$x_1 + e_1 \le e_3' \le x_2 + e_2 \wedge x_1 + e_1 \le e_3 \le x_2 + e_2 \wedge e_4' = x_2 + e_3' \wedge$$
$$\wedge\, e_4 = x_2 + e_3 \wedge e_3 \neq e_4 \wedge e_3' \neq e_4' \wedge e_3' \neq e_3 \ .$$

This gives $x_1 + e_1 \neq x_2 + e_2 \wedge x_2 \neq 0$, so that $\mathtt{ImplDef}_{\psi_2,e_3}^{T_2}(\underline{x},\underline{z})$ is $x_1 + e_1 = x_2 + e_2 \wedge x_2 \neq 0$. The corresponding equality interpolating term for e_3 is $x_1 + e_1$.
- The formula $\mathtt{ImplDef}_{\psi_2,e_4}^{T_2}(\underline{x},\underline{z})$ is also equivalent to $x_1 + e_1 = x_2 + e_2 \wedge x_2 \neq 0$ and the equality interpolating term for e_4 is $x_1 + e_1 + x_2$.

So, if we apply Step 1 we get

$$\exists e_1 \cdots \exists e_4 \begin{pmatrix} e_1 = f(x_1) \ \wedge\ e_2 = f(x_2) \ \wedge \\ \wedge\ f(e_3) = e_3 \ \wedge\ f(e_4) = x_1 \ \wedge\ e_3 \neq e_4 \ \wedge \\ \wedge\ x_1 + e_1 \le e_3 \ \wedge\ e_3 \le x_2 + e_2 \ \wedge\ e_4 = x_2 + e_3 \ \wedge\ x_1 + e_1 \neq x_2 + e_2 \end{pmatrix}$$
$$(8.12)$$

(notice that the literal $x_2 \neq 0$ is entailed by ψ_2, so we can simplify it to $\top$ in $\mathtt{ImplDef}_{\psi_2,e_3}^{T_2}(\underline{x},\underline{z})$ and $\mathtt{ImplDef}_{\psi_2,e_4}^{T_2}(\underline{x},\underline{z})$). If we apply Step (2.i) (for i=3), we get (after removing implied equalities)

$$\exists e_1 \cdots \exists e_4 \begin{pmatrix} e_1 = f(x_1) \ \wedge\ e_2 = f(x_2) \ \wedge\ e_3 = x_1 + e_1 \ \wedge \\ \wedge\ f(e_3) = e_3 \ \wedge\ f(e_4) = x_1 \ \wedge\ e_3 \neq e_4 \ \wedge \\ \wedge\ e_4 = x_2 + e_3 \ \wedge\ x_1 + e_1 = x_2 + e_2 \end{pmatrix} \qquad (8.13)$$

Step (2.i) (for i=4) gives a formula logically equivalent to (8.13). Notice that (8.13) is terminal too, because all existential variables are now explicitly defined (this is a lucky side-effect of the fact that e_3 has been moved to the defined variables). Thus the exhaustive application of Steps (1) and (2.i) is concluded.

Applying the final step of Proposition 8.1 to (8.13) is quite easy: it is sufficient to unravel the acyclic definitions. The result, after little simplification, is

$$x_2 \neq 0 \wedge x_1 + f(x_1) = x_2 + f(x_2) \wedge$$
$$\wedge\ f(x_2 + f(x_1 + f(x_1))) = x_1 \wedge f(x_1 + f(x_1)) = x_1 + f(x_1);$$

this can be further simplified to

$$x_2 \neq 0 \wedge x_1 + f(x_1) = x_2 + f(x_2) \wedge$$
$$\wedge f(2x_2 + f(x_2)) = x_1 \wedge f(x_1 + f(x_1)) = x_1 + f(x_1); \tag{8.14}$$

As to formula (8.12), we need to apply the final cover computations mentioned in Proposition 8.1. The formulae ψ_1 and ψ_2 are now

$$\psi_1' \equiv \qquad f(e_3) = e_3 \wedge f(e_4) = x_1 \wedge e_3 \neq e_4$$
$$\psi_2' \equiv x_1 + e_1 \leq e_3 \leq x_2 + e_2 \wedge e_4 = x_2 + e_3 \wedge x_1 + e_1 \neq x_2 + e_2 \wedge e_3 \neq e_4$$

The T_1-cover of ψ_1' is $\top$. For the T_2-cover of ψ_2', eliminating with FM-QE the variables e_4 and e_3, we get

$$x_1 + e_1 < x_2 + e_2 \wedge x_2 \neq 0$$

which becomes

$$x_1 + f(x_1) < x_2 + f(x_2) \wedge x_2 \neq 0 \tag{8.15}$$

after unravelling the explicit definitions of e_1, e_2. Thus, *the analysis of the case of the partition P_1 gives, as a result, the disjunction of* (8.14) *and* (8.15).

We now analyze **the case of P_2**. Before proceeding, we replace e_4 with e_3 (since P_2 precisely asserts that these two variables coincide); our formulae ψ_1 and ψ_2 become

$$\psi_1'' \equiv f(e_3) = e_3 \wedge f(e_3) = x_1$$
$$\psi_2'' \equiv x_1 + e_1 \leq e_3 \wedge e_3 \leq x_2 + e_2 \wedge 0 = x_2$$

From ψ_1'' we deduce $e_3 = x_1$, thus we can move e_3 to the explicitly defined variables (this avoids useless calculations: the implicit definability condition for variables having an entailed explicit definition is obviously $\top$, so making case split on it produces either tautological consequences or inconsistencies). In this way we get the terminal working formula

$$\exists e_1 \cdots \exists e_3 \begin{pmatrix} e_1 = f(x_1) \wedge e_2 = f(x_2) \wedge e_3 = x_1 \\ \wedge f(e_3) = e_3 \wedge f(e_3) = x_1 \wedge \\ \wedge x_1 + e_1 \leq e_3 \wedge e_3 \leq x_2 + e_2 \wedge 0 = x_2 \end{pmatrix} \tag{8.16}$$

Unravelling the explicit definitions, we get (after exhaustive simplifications)

$$x_2 = 0 \wedge f(x_1) = x_1 \wedge x_1 \leq 0 \wedge x_1 \leq f(0) \tag{8.17}$$

Now, the disjunction of (8.14),(8.15) and (8.17) is precisely the final result (8.11) claimed above. This concludes our detailed analysis of our example.

Notice that the example shows that combined cover computations may introduce terms with arbitrary alternations of symbols from both theories (like $f(x_2 + f(x_1 + f(x_1)))$ above). The point is that when a variable becomes explicitly definable via a term in one of the theories, then using such additional variable may in turn cause some other variables to become explicitly definable via terms from the other theory, and so on and so forth; when ultimately the explicit definitions are unraveled, highly nested terms arise with many symbol alternations from both theories.

8.4 The Non-Convex Case: a Counterexample

In this section, we show by giving a suitable counterexample that the convexity hypothesis cannot be dropped from Theorems 8.3, 8.4. We make use of basic facts about ultrapowers (see [66] for the essential information we need). We take as T_1 integer difference logic $\mathcal{IDL}$, i.e. the theory of integer numbers under the unary operations of successor and predecessor, the constant 0 and the strict order relation $<$. This is stably infinite, universal and has quantifier elimination (thus it coincides with its own model completion). It is not convex, but it satisfies the equality interpolating condition, once the latter is suitably adjusted to non-convex theories, see [45] for the related definition and all the above mentioned facts.

As T_2, we take $\mathcal{EUF}(\Sigma_f)$, where Σ_f has just one unary free function symbol f (this f is supposed not to belong to the signature of T_1).

Proposition 8.2 *Let T_1, T_2 be as above; the formula*

$$\exists e \ (0 < e \wedge e < x \wedge f(e) = 0) \tag{8.18}$$

does not have a cover in $T_1 \cup T_2$.

Proof Suppose that (8.18) has a cover $\phi(x)$. This means (according to Cover-by-Extensions Lemma 7.1) that for every model $\mathcal{M}$ of $T_1 \cup T_2$ and for every element $a \in |\mathcal{M}|$ such that $\mathcal{M} \models \phi(a)$, there is an extension $\mathcal{N}$ of $\mathcal{M}$ such that $\mathcal{N} \models \exists e \ (0 < e \wedge e < a \wedge f(e) = 0)$.

Consider the model $\mathcal{M}$, so specified: the support of $\mathcal{M}$ is the set of the integers, the symbols from the signature of T_1 are interpreted in the standard way and the symbol f is interpreted so that 0 is not in the image of f. Let a_k be the number $k > 0$ (it is an element from the support of $\mathcal{M}$). Clearly it is not possible to extend $\mathcal{M}$ so that $\exists e \ (0 < e \wedge e < a_k \wedge f(e) = 0)$ becomes true: indeed, we know that all the elements in the interval $(0, k)$ are definable as iterated successors of 0 and, by using the axioms of $\mathcal{IDL}$, no element can be added between a number and its successor, hence this interval cannot be enlarged in a superstructure. We conclude that $\mathcal{M} \models \neg\phi(a_k)$ for every k.

Consider now an ultrapower $\prod_D \mathcal{M}$ of $\mathcal{M}$ modulo a non-principal ultrafilter D and let a be the equivalence class of the tuple $\langle a_k \rangle_{k \in \mathbb{N}}$; by the fundamental Los theorem [66], $\prod_D \mathcal{M} \models \neg\phi(a)$. We claim that it is possible to extend $\prod_D \mathcal{M}$ to a superstructure $\mathcal{N}$ such that $\mathcal{N} \models \exists e \ (0 < e \wedge e < a \wedge f(e) = 0)$: this would entail, by definition of cover, that $\prod_D \mathcal{M} \models \phi(a)$, contradiction. We now show why the claim is true. Indeed, since $\langle a_k \rangle_{k \in \mathbb{N}}$ has arbitrarily big numbers as its components, we have that, in $\prod_D \mathcal{M}$, a is bigger than all standard numbers. Thus, if we take a further non-principal ultrapower $\mathcal{N}$ of $\prod_D \mathcal{M}$, it becomes possible to change in it the evaluation of $f(b)$ for some $b < a$ and set it to 0 (in fact, as it can be easily seen, there are elements $b \in |\mathcal{N}|$ less than a but not in the support of $\prod_D \mathcal{M}$). □

The counterexample still applies when replacing integer difference logic with linear integer arithmetic.

8.5 Tame Combinations

So far, we only analyzed the mono-sorted case. However, many interesting examples arising in model-checking verification are multi-sorted: this is the case of array-based systems [146] and in particular of the array-based system used in DAP verification studied in Part I. The above examples suggest restrictions on the theories to be combined other than convexity, in particular they suggest restrictions that make sense in a multi-sorted context. In this section we present a combined cover algorithm, called TameCombCover, for multi-sorted theories that could be possibly non-convex and for which requirements different from disjointness are imposed for the signatures.

Most definitions we gave in Chapter 6 have straightforward natural extensions to the multi-sorted case (we leave the reader to formulate them). A little care is needed however for the disjoint signatures requirement. Let T_1, T_2 be multisorted theories in the signatures Σ_1, Σ_2; we say that the combination $\Sigma_1 \cup \Sigma_2$ is 'almost disjoint' if the only function or relation symbols in $\Sigma_1 \cap \Sigma_2$ are the equality predicates over the sorts in $\Sigma_1 \cap \Sigma_2$ (if there is any sort in $\Sigma_1 \cap \Sigma_2$). We want to strengthen this requirement: we say that an almost disjoint combination $T_1 \cup T_2$ is *tame* iff the sorts in $\Sigma_1 \cap \Sigma_2$ *can only be the codomain sort* (and not a domain sort) of a symbol from Σ_1 other than an equality predicate. In other words, if a relation or a function symbol has as among its domain sorts a sort from $\Sigma_1 \cap \Sigma_2$, then this symbol is from Σ_2 (and not from Σ_1, unless it is the equality predicate). Notice that the notion of a tame combination is not symmetric in T_1 and T_2: to see this, notice that if the sorts of Σ_1 are included in the sorts of Σ_2, then T_1 must be a pure equality theory (but this is not the case if we swap T_1 with T_2).

Tame combinations arise in infinite-state model-checking (in fact, the definition is suggested by this application domain), where signatures can be split into a signature Σ_2 used to represent 'datatypes' like integers and a signature Σ_1 for representing elements contained in a database: this is customary in DAP verification as shown in Part I.

The combination of $\mathcal{IDL}$ and $\mathcal{EUF}(\Sigma)$ used in the counterexample of Section 8.4 is not tame: even if we formulate $\mathcal{EUF}(\Sigma)$ as a two-sorted theory, the unique sort of $\mathcal{IDL}$ must be a sort of $\mathcal{EUF}(\Sigma)$ too, as witnessed by the impure atom $f(e) = 0$ in the formula (8.18). Because of this, for the combination to be tame, $\mathcal{IDL}$ should play the role of T_2 (the arithmetic operation symbols are defined on a shared sort); however, the unary function symbol $f \in \Sigma$ has a shared sort as domain sort, so the combination is not tame anyway.

In a tame combination, an atomic formula A can only be of two kinds: (1) we say that A is of the *first kind* iff the sorts of its root predicate are from $\Sigma_1 \setminus \Sigma_2$; (2) we say that A is of the *second kind* iff the sorts of its root predicate are from Σ_2. We use the roman letters $e, x, \ldots$ for variables ranging over sorts in $\Sigma_1 \setminus \Sigma_2$ and the greek letters $\eta, \xi, \ldots$ for variables ranging over sorts in Σ_2. Thus, if we want to display free variables, atoms of the first kind can be represented as $A(e, x, \ldots)$, whereas atoms of the second kind can be represented as $A(\eta, \xi, \ldots, t(e, x, \ldots), \ldots)$, where the t are Σ_1-terms.

Suppose that $T_1 \cup T_2$ is a tame combination and that T_1, T_2 are universal theories admitting model completions T_1^*, T_2^*. We propose the following algorithm to compute the cover of a primitive formula; this formula must be of the kind

$$\exists \underline{e}\ \exists \underline{\eta}(\phi(\underline{e}, \underline{x}) \wedge \psi(\underline{\eta}, \underline{\xi}, \underline{t}(\underline{e}, \underline{x}))) \tag{8.19}$$

where ϕ is a Σ_1-conjunction of literals, ψ is a conjunction of Σ_2-literals and the $\underline{t}$ are Σ_1-terms. The algorithm TameCombCover has three steps.

(i)   We flatten (8.19) and get

$$\exists \underline{e}\ \exists \underline{\eta}\ \exists \underline{\eta}'\ (\phi(\underline{e}, \underline{x}) \wedge \underline{\eta}' = \underline{t}(\underline{e}, \underline{x}) \wedge \psi(\underline{\eta}, \underline{\xi}, \underline{\eta}'))) \tag{8.20}$$

where the $\underline{\eta}'$ are fresh variables abstracting out the $\underline{t}$ and $\underline{\eta}' = \underline{t}(\underline{e}, \underline{x})$ is a component-wise conjunction of equalities.

(ii)   We apply the cover algorithm of T_1 to the formula

$$\exists \underline{e}\ (\phi(\underline{e}, \underline{x}) \wedge \underline{\eta}' = \underline{t}(\underline{e}, \underline{x}))\ ; \tag{8.21}$$

this gives as a result a formula $\tilde{\phi}(\underline{x}, \underline{\eta}')$ that we put in DNF. A disjunct of ϕ will have the form $\phi_1(\underline{x}) \wedge \phi_2(\underline{\eta}', \underline{t}'(\underline{x}))$ after separation of the literals of the first and of the second kind. We pick such a disjunct $\phi_1(\underline{x}) \wedge \phi_2(\underline{\eta}', \underline{t}'(\underline{x}))$ of the DNF of $\tilde{\phi}(\underline{x}, \underline{\eta}')$ and update our current primitive formula to

$$\exists \underline{\xi}'\ (\underline{\xi}' = \underline{t}'(\underline{x}) \wedge (\exists \underline{\eta}\ \exists \underline{\eta}'\ (\phi_1(\underline{x}) \wedge \phi_2(\underline{\eta}', \underline{\xi}') \wedge \psi(\underline{\eta}, \underline{\xi}, \underline{\eta}')))) \tag{8.22}$$

(this step is nondeterministic: in the end we shall output the disjunction of all possible outcomes). Here again the $\underline{\xi}'$ are fresh variables abstracting out the terms $\underline{t}'$. Notice that, according to the definition of a tame combination, $\phi_2(\underline{\eta}', \underline{\xi}')$ must be a conjunction of equalities and disequalities between variable terms, because it is a Σ_1-formula (it comes from a T_1-cover computation) and $\underline{\eta}', \underline{\xi}'$ are variables of Σ_2-sorts.

(iii)   We apply the cover algorithm of T_2 to the formula

$$\exists \underline{\eta}\ \exists \underline{\eta}'\ (\phi_2(\underline{\eta}', \underline{\xi}') \wedge \psi(\underline{\eta}, \underline{\xi}, \underline{\eta}')) \tag{8.23}$$

this gives as a result a formula $\psi_1(\underline{\xi}, \underline{\xi}')$. We update our current formula to

$$\exists \underline{\xi}'\ (\underline{\xi}' = \underline{t}'(\underline{x}) \wedge \phi_1(\underline{x}) \wedge \psi_1(\underline{\xi}, \underline{\xi}'))$$

and finally to the equivalent quantifier-free formula

$$\phi_1(\underline{x}) \wedge \psi_1(\underline{\xi}, \underline{t}'(\underline{x})) \ . \tag{8.24}$$

We now show that the above algorithm is correct under very mild hypotheses. We need some technical facts about stably infinite theories in a multi-sorted context. We say that a multi-sorted theory T is *stably infinite with respect to a set of sorts $\mathcal{S}$ from its signature* iff every T-satisfiable constraint is satisfiable in a model $\mathcal{M}$ where, for every $S \in \mathcal{S}$, the set $S^{\mathcal{M}}$ (namely the interpretation of the sort S in $\mathcal{M}$) is infinite. The next Lemma is a light generalization of Lemma 8.1 and is proved in the same way:

Lemma 8.6 *Let T be stably infinite with respect to a subset $\mathcal{S}$ of the set of sorts of the signature of T. Let $\mathcal{M}$ be a model of T and let, for every $S \in \mathcal{S}$, X_S be an at most countable superset of $S^{\mathcal{M}}$. Then there is an extension $\mathcal{N}$ of $\mathcal{M}$ such that for all $S \in \mathcal{S}$ we have $S^{\mathcal{N}} \supseteq X_S$.*

Proof Let us expand the signature of T with the set C of fresh constants (we take one constant for every $c \in X_S \setminus S^{\mathcal{M}}$). We need to prove the T-consistency of $\Delta(\mathcal{M})$ with a the set D of disequalities asserting that all $c \in C$ are different from each other and from the names of the elements of the support of $\mathcal{M}$. By compactness, it is sufficient to ensure the T-consistency of $\Delta_0 \cup D_0$, where Δ_0 and D_0 are finite subsets of $\Delta(\mathcal{M})$ and D, respectively. Since $\mathcal{M} \models \Delta_0$, this set is T-consistent and hence it is satisfied in a T-model $\mathcal{M}'$ where all the sorts in $\mathcal{S}$ are interpreted as infinite sets; in such $\mathcal{M}'$, it is trivially seen that we can interpret also the constants occurring in D_0 so as to make D_0 true too. □

Lemma 8.7 *Let T_1, T_2 be universal signature disjoint theories which are stably infinite with respect to the set of shared sorts (we let Σ_1 be the signature of T_1 and Σ_2 be the signature of T_2). Let $\mathcal{M}_0$ be model of $T_1 \cup T_2$ and let $\mathcal{M}_1$ be a model of T_i extending the Σ_i-reduct of $\mathcal{M}_0$ ($i = 1, 2$). Then there exists a model $\mathcal{N}$ of $T_1 \cup T_2$, extending $\mathcal{M}_0$ as a $\Sigma_1 \cup \Sigma_2$-structure and whose Σ_i-reduct extends $\mathcal{M}_1$.*

Proof Using the previous lemma, we build infinitely many models $\mathcal{M}_0, \mathcal{M}_1, \mathcal{M}_2, \ldots$ such that: (i) $\mathcal{M}_{2j}$ is a Σ_{3-i}-structure which is a model of T_{3-i}; (ii) $\mathcal{M}_{2j+1}$ is a Σ_i-structure which is a model of T_i; (iii) $\mathcal{M}_{2j+2}$ is a Σ_{3-i}-extension of $\mathcal{M}_{2j}$; (iv) $\mathcal{M}_{2j+3}$ is a Σ_i-extension of $\mathcal{M}_{2j+1}$; (v) the supports of the $\mathcal{M}_k$, once restricted to the $\Sigma_1 \cap \Sigma_2$-sorts (call $|\mathcal{M}_k|$ such restrictions), form an increasing chain $|\mathcal{M}_0| \subseteq |\mathcal{M}_1| \subseteq |\mathcal{M}_2| \subseteq \cdots$. The union over this chain of models will be the desired $\mathcal{N}$. □

We are now ready for the main result of this section:

Theorem 8.5 *Let $T_1 \cup T_2$ be a tame combination of two universal theories admitting a model completion. If T_1, T_2 are also stably infinite with repect to their shared sorts, then $T_1 \cup T_2$ has a model completion. Covers in $T_1 \cup T_2$ can be computed as shown in the above three-steps algorithm.*

Proof Since condition (i) of Lemma 7.1 is trivially true, we need only to check condition (ii), namely that given a $T_1 \cup T_2$-model $\mathcal{M}$ and elements $\underline{a}, \underline{b}$ from its support such that $\mathcal{M} \models \phi_1(\underline{a}) \wedge \psi_1(\underline{b}, t'(\underline{a}))$ as in (8.24), then there is an extension $\mathcal{N}$ of $\mathcal{M}$ such that (8.19) is true in $\mathcal{N}$ when evaluating $\underline{x}$ over $\underline{a}$ and $\underline{\xi}$ over $\underline{b}$.

If we let $\underline{b}'$ be the tuple such that $\mathcal{M} \models \underline{b}' = t'(\underline{a})$, then we have $\mathcal{M} \models \underline{b}' = t'(\underline{a}) \wedge \phi_1(\underline{a}) \wedge \psi_1(\underline{b}, \underline{b}')$. Since $\psi_1(\underline{\xi}, \underline{\xi}')$ is the T_2-cover of (8.23), the Σ_2-reduct of $\mathcal{M}$ embeds into a T_2-model where (8.23) is true under the evaluation of the $\underline{\xi}$ as the $\underline{b}$. By Lemma 8.7, this model can be embedded into a $T_1 \cup T_2$-model $\mathcal{M}'$ in such a way that $\mathcal{M}'$ is an extension of $\mathcal{M}$ and that $\mathcal{M}' \models \underline{b}' = t'(\underline{a}) \wedge \phi_1(\underline{a}) \wedge \phi_2(\underline{c}', \underline{b}') \wedge \psi(\underline{c}, \underline{b}, \underline{c}')$ for some $\underline{c}, \underline{c}'$. Since $\phi_1(\underline{x}) \wedge \phi_2(\eta', t'(\underline{x}))$ implies the T_1-cover of (8.21) and $\mathcal{M}' \models \phi_1(\underline{a}) \wedge \phi_2(\underline{c}', t(\underline{a}))$, then the Σ_1-reduct of $\mathcal{M}'$ can be expanded to a T_1-model where (8.21) is true when evaluating the $\underline{x}, \eta'$ to the $\underline{a}, \underline{c}'$. Again by Lemma 8.7, this model can be expanded to a $T_1 \cup T_2$-model $\mathcal{N}$ such that $\mathcal{N}$ is an extension of $\mathcal{M}'$ (hence also of $\mathcal{M}$) and $\mathcal{N} \models \phi(\underline{a}', \underline{a}) \wedge \underline{c}' = t(\underline{a}', \underline{a}) \wedge \psi(\underline{c}, \underline{b}, \underline{c}')$, that is $\mathcal{N} \models \phi(\underline{a}', \underline{a}) \wedge \psi(\underline{c}, \underline{b}, t(\underline{a}', \underline{a}))$. This means that $\mathcal{N} \models \exists \underline{e} \, \exists \eta (\phi(\underline{e}, \underline{a}) \wedge \psi(\eta, \underline{b}, t(\underline{e}, \underline{a})))$, as desired. $\square$

In the context of DAP verification, where data representation and manipulation capabilities can be extended with arithmetic, the following minimal type of tame combinations becomes extremely interesting: consider the combination $T_{DB} \cup T_{int}$, where T_{DB} is a multi-sorted version of $\mathcal{EUF}(\Sigma)$ in a signature Σ containing only unary function symbols and relation symbols of any arity, and where T_{int} is typically some fragment of linear arithmetics, where T_{int}-sorts are considered as *value sorts*. We elaborate on this intuition in more detail in the Example 8.2, where, by employing the nomenclature of Chapter 3, we generalize the discussion to DB extended-schemas.

We recall from Chapter 7 that T_{DB} -cover computation for primitive formulae is quadratic in complexity. Model-checkers like MCMT represent sets of reachable states by using conjunctions of literals and during preimage computations quantifier elimination needs to be applied to primitive formulae. Now, if all relation symbols are at most binary, T_{DB} -cover computation produces conjunctions of literals out of primitive formulae. Thus, step (ii) in the algorithm from Section 8.5 becomes deterministic and the only reason such an algorithm may become expensive (i.e., nonpolynomial) lies in the final quantifier elimination step for T_{int}^*. This step might be extremely expensive if substantial arithmetic is involved, but it might still be efficiently handled in practical cases where only very limited arithmetic is used (e.g., difference bound constraints like $x - y \leq n$ or $x \leq n$, where n is a constant). Our algorithm for covers in tame combinations has been implemented in version 3.0 of MCMT.

Example 8.2 Let $\langle \Sigma \cup \Sigma', T \cup T' \rangle$ be a DB extended-schema that is a tame combination of a (plain) DB schema $\langle \Sigma, T \rangle$ admitting covers, and $T' := \mathcal{EUF} \cup \mathcal{LRA}$ as in Example 8.1. A concrete example of plain DB schema is the following: $\mathcal{EUF}$ over a signature Σ comprising three sorts $\mathcal{S}_1, \mathcal{S}_2, \mathcal{S}_3$, and two function symbols $f_{R,1} : \mathcal{S}_1 \to \mathcal{S}_2$ and $f_{R,2} : \mathcal{S}_1 \to \mathcal{S}_3$. We know by Chapter 7 that $\mathcal{EUF}$ admits covers, and we can use SuperCover to compute them. Moreover, from Chapter 3, we can interpret this DB schema as a classical database schema containing a ternary relational schema $R(id : S_1, a_1 : S_2, a_2 : S_3)$, where the attribute id is the primary key and S_3 is a value sort.

We suppose that the unique sort of T' coincides with S_3. It can be trivially seen that this combination is tame. We already know from Example 8.1 that T'-covers exist and we can use ConvexCombCover to compute them: this procedure modularly uses the cover algorithms for the component theories, which are SuperCover for $\mathcal{EUF}$ and Fourier-Motzkin quantifier elimination (FM-QE) for $\mathcal{LRA}$.

Since $T \cup T'$ is a tame combination, we can then employ TameCombCover to compute $T \cup T'$-covers. To summarize, for the DB extended-schema $\langle \Sigma \cup \Sigma', T \cup T' \rangle$ covers exist and can be computed by exploiting the algorithms TameCombCover, ConvexCombCover, SuperCover and FM-QE. We recall from Section 4.1 that existence of covers (or, equivalently, the existence of model completions) is exactly one of the requirements (together with finite model property and the decidability of constraint satisfiability) to make our machinery work for verifying U-RASs.

8.5.1 An Example of Combined Covers for the Tame Combination

Let T_1 be $\mathcal{EUF}(\Sigma_1)$, where Σ_1 is a multisorted signature with three sorts S_1, S_2 and S_3 and with a function symbol $f : S_1 \times S_2 \to S_3$. Let T_2 be $\mathcal{LIA}$ (which is *not* convex), where its (unique) sort is S_3, which is in common with Σ_1. We notice that $T_1 \cup T_2$ is a tame combination, since the common sort S_3 is the codomain sort (and not the domain sort) of the unique symbol f from Σ_1 different from equality. We show a simple example on how to compute a $T_1 \cup T_2$-cover using the algorithm above.

Let

$$\exists e \begin{pmatrix} f(e,x_1) \leq f(e,x_2) \wedge 2\xi_2 \leq f(e,x_1) + \xi_1 \\ \wedge\, f(e,x_2) + \xi_3 < 4\xi_4 \wedge \xi_3 \leq \xi_1 \end{pmatrix} \tag{8.25}$$

be the formula for which we would like to compute a $T_1 \cup T_2$-cover: the only truly existentially quantified variable here is e.

We first apply Step (i), and we abstract out $f(e,x_1)$ and $f(e,x_2)$ by introducing two fresh variables η_1' and η_2':

$$\exists e, \eta_1', \eta_2' \begin{pmatrix} \eta_1' = f(e,x_1) \wedge \eta_2' = f(e,x_2) \wedge 2\xi_2 \leq \eta_1' + \xi_1 \\ \wedge\, \eta_2' + \xi_3 < 4\xi_4 \wedge \xi_3 \leq \xi_1 \wedge \eta_1' \leq \eta_2' \end{pmatrix} \tag{8.26}$$

Then, in order to apply Step (ii), we need to compute the T_1-cover of the following formula:

$$\exists e\, (\eta_1' = f(e,x_1) \wedge \eta_2' = f(e,x_2)) \tag{8.27}$$

and we obtain:

$$x_1 = x_2 \to \eta_1' = \eta_2'$$

which, in turn, is equivalent to the following formula in DNF form:

$$x_1 \neq x_2 \vee \eta_1' = \eta_2'$$

Now, we analyze the two different cases create by each disjunct in the previous formula.

First Case. If we pick up the disjunct $x_1 \neq x_2$, after updating Formula (8.26), we get the following equivalent formula:

$$\exists \eta_1', \eta_2' \begin{pmatrix} x_1 \neq x_2 \wedge 2\xi_2 \leq \eta_1' + \xi_1 \wedge \eta_2' + \xi_3 \leq 1 + 4\xi_4 \\ \wedge \ \xi_3 \leq \xi_1 \wedge \eta_1' \leq \eta_2' \end{pmatrix} \tag{8.28}$$

We now apply Step (iii), by computing the T_2-cover of the formula:

$$\exists \eta_1', \eta_2' \begin{pmatrix} 2\xi_2 \leq \eta_1' + \xi_1 \wedge \eta_2' + \xi_3 \leq 1 + 4\xi_4 \\ \wedge \ \xi_3 \leq \xi_1 \wedge \eta_1' \leq \eta_2'. \end{pmatrix} \tag{8.29}$$

This is in general achieved by applying the Cooper's algorithm [82]. In this case, it is sufficient to notice that Formula (8.29) implies:

$$2\xi_2 - \xi_1 \leq \eta_1' \wedge \eta_1' \leq \eta_2' \wedge \eta_2' \leq 1 + 4\xi_4 - \xi_3$$

which provide lower and upper bounds for both η_1' and η_2', as wanted. Hence, the T_2-cover of Formula (8.29) is:

$$2\xi_2 - \xi_1 \leq 1 + 4\xi_4 - \xi_3 \wedge \xi_3 \leq \xi_1 \tag{8.30}$$

We then update our Formula (8.28) and we get the first disjunct of our $T_1 \cup T_2$-cover:

$$x_1 \neq x_2 \wedge 2\xi_2 - \xi_1 \leq 1 + 4\xi_4 - \xi_3 \wedge \xi_3 \leq \xi_1 \tag{8.31}$$

Second Case. If we pick up the disjunct $\eta_1' = \eta_2'$, after updating Formula (8.26), we get the following equivalent formula:

$$\exists \eta_1', \eta_2' \begin{pmatrix} \eta_1' = \eta_2' \wedge 2\xi_2 \leq \eta_1' + \xi_1 \wedge \eta_2' + \xi_3 \leq 1 + 4\xi_4 \\ \wedge \ \xi_3 \leq \xi_1 \wedge \eta_1' \leq \eta_2' \end{pmatrix} \tag{8.32}$$

We now apply Step (iii), by computing the T_2-cover of the previous formula. In this case, it is sufficient to notice that Formula (8.32) implies:

$$2\xi_2 - \xi_1 \leq \eta_1' \wedge \eta_1' = \eta_2' \wedge \eta_2' \leq 1 + 4\xi_4 - \xi_3$$

which provide lower and upper bounds for both η_1' and η_2', as wanted. Hence, the T_2-cover of Formula (8.32) is:

$$2\xi_2 - \xi_1 \leq 1 + 4\xi_4 - \xi_3 \wedge \xi_3 \leq \xi_1 \tag{8.33}$$

We then update our Formula (8.32) and we get the second disjunct of our $T_1 \cup T_2$-cover:

$$2\xi_2 - \xi_1 \leq 1 + 4\xi_4 - \xi_3 \; \wedge \; \xi_3 \leq \xi_1 \qquad (8.34)$$

Hence, by taking the disjunction of Formula (8.31) and of Formula (8.34) it is straightforward to see that the $T_1 \cup T_2$-cover of Formula (8.25) is equivalent to:

$$2\xi_2 - \xi_1 \leq 1 + 4\xi_4 - \xi_3 \; \wedge \; \xi_3 \leq \xi_1 \qquad (8.35)$$

8.6 Discussion on Related Works on Covers

We conclude the chapter by discussing the related work on covers.

We noticed in Section 7.3 that our problem is different from the problem of computing *ordinary* quantifier-free interpolants via saturation based theorem proving [180]: for ordinary interpolants, we have as input *two* quantifier-free formulae $\phi(\underline{e}, \underline{y}), \phi'(\underline{y}, \underline{z})$ such that $\phi(\underline{e}, \underline{y}) \rightarrow \phi'(\underline{y}, \underline{z})$ holds; in the context of covers, we have a *single* formula $\phi(\underline{e}, \underline{y})$ as input and we need to find an interpolant which is good *for all possible* $\phi'(\underline{y}, \underline{z})$ such that $\phi(\underline{e}, \underline{y}) \rightarrow \phi'(\underline{y}, \underline{z})$ holds. Ordinary interpolants can be extracted from a refutation of $\phi(\underline{e}, \underline{y}) \wedge \neg\phi'(\underline{y}, \underline{z})$, whereas in our case no refutation is given at all (and we are not even supposed to find one).

The algorithm for computing $\mathcal{EUF}$-covers shown in [157] is quite different from ours: very roughly speaking, determines all the conditional equations that can be derived concerning the nodes of the congruence closure graph. However, that algorithm presents some issues/bugs that need to be fixed: indeed, the example exhibited in Section 7.3 points out that, in some cases, covers must contain *disjunctions of disequations*, whereas the algorithm from [157] outputs only equalities, conditional equalities and single disequalities, so it cannot correctly handle this example. In addition, the correctness proof has never been published (the technical report mentioned in [157] is not available).

We mention here a subsequent work (i.e., [132, 134]) that we carried out *after* the introduction of SuperCover (and, specifically, after the publication of their corresponding papers [52, 56]): in this work, we studied additional algorithms for computing covers in $\mathcal{EUF}$ (their correctness proof still relies on Lemma 7.1). These algorithms are quite different in their shapes from SuperCover: they are not based, as SuperCover, on well-established automated reasoning techniques such as Superposition Calculus, but they exploit efficient dedicated Directed Acyclic Graph (DAG)-based representations of terms for computing covers in a compact form.

Turning to combined covers, it is worth mentioning that Gulwani and Musuvathi in [157] also have a combined cover algorithm for some convex, signature disjoint theories. However, a full correctness and completeness proof for such an algorithm is missing, since, as remarked above, the technical report mentioned in [157] has never been published. Moreover, their algorithm looks quite different from ours, and we underline that our combined algorithm is rooted on different hypotheses. In fact, we only need the equality interpolating condition and we show that this hypothesis is not only sufficient, but also necessary for cover transfer in convex theories; consequently, our result is formally stronger. The equality interpolating condition was known to the authors of [157] (but not even mentioned in their paper [157]): in fact, it was introduced by one of them some years before [253]. The equality interpolating condition was then extended to the nonconvex case in [45], where it was also semantically characterized via the strong amalgamation property.

Chapter 9
MCMT: a Concrete Model Checker for DAPs

We implemented a prototype of our backward reachability algorithm for artifact systems on top of the MCMT model checker, extending it with the features required to formalize and verify (Universal) RASs. As mentioned before, Model Checker Modulo Theories (MCMT)[1] is a model checker for checking safety of infinite-state systems: the tool is based on the integration of SMT solving and the backward reachability procedure. Roughly speaking, as explained in Section 4.3, backward search requires to perform an *inclusion test* and a *disjointness test*: these tests are satisfiability checks that are discharged to a backend SMT solver via proof obligations. MCMT manages safety verification by exploiting as its model-theoretic framework the declarative formalism of array-based systems. In this chapter, after a very brief overview of MCMT and its working, we describe in Section 9.2 the basic syntax of its language. Then, we focus on the general format of the MCMT specification files. Specifically, in Section 9.3 we present how to use the "database-driven" mode and how to declare in the input file the DB schema, the initialization, the unsafe formula, the existentially quantified variables to eliminate and the transitions of our U-RAS model; in Section 9.4 we comment on how to run the tool and we give a useful explanation on the displayed information after its execution. Finally, in Section 9.5 we describe the experiments on running MCMT over an interesting and significant benchmark of data-aware processes encoded into RASs.

9.1 MCMT: a Brief Overview

Since their first introduction in [143, 146], array-based systems have been provided with various implementations of the standard backward reachability algorithms (including more sophisticated variants and heuristics). Starting from its first version [147], MCMT was successfully applied to cache coherence and mutual exclusions protocols [146], timed [61] and fault-tolerant [17, 16] distributed systems, and

---

[1] http://users.mat.unimi.it/users/ghilardi/mcmt/

© The Author(s), under exclusive license to Springer Nature Switzerland AG 2023   177
A. Gianola: *Verification of Data-Aware Processes via Satisfiability Modulo Theories*,
LNBIP 470, pp. 177–196, 2023.
https://doi.org/10.1007/978-3-031-42746-6_9

then to imperative programs [18, 20]; interesting case studies concerned waiting time bounds synthesis in parameterized timed networks [44] and internet protocols [43]. Further related tools include SAFARI [14] and ASASP [13]; finally, [80, 81, 78, 79] implement the array-based setting on a parallel architecture with further powerful extensions.

The work principle of MCMT is rather simple: the tool generates the proof obligations arising from the safety and fixpoint tests in backward search (Lines 2-3 of Algorithm 2) and passes them to the background SMT solver (currently it is Yices [107]). In practice, the situation is more complicated because SMT solvers are quite efficient in handling satisfiability problems in combined theories at quantifier-free level, but may encounter difficulties with quantifiers. For this reason, MCMT implements modules for *quantifier elimination* and *quantifier instantiation*. A *specific module* for the quantifier elimination problems mentioned in Line 6 of Algorithm 2 has been added to Version 2.8 of MCMT.

The following three sections should be considered as a relevant summary of the information contained in the User Manual of MCMT (http://users.mat. unimi.it/users/ghilardi/mcmt/) that are needed for the database-driven setting we propose: most of the material is taken, summarized and adapted from there. We report this summary here for the sake of completeness and to make the interested reader familiar with the use of MCMT.

9.2 Basic Syntax of MCMT

The basic MCMT syntax is based on types, index variables and array variables. Types that can be recognized by MCMT include int, real, bool, i.e., integer, real numbers and booleans, and also the additional types coming from 'db-sorts' of the 'db_driven' mode. New types can also be declared by the user: to declare a free sort (say S), one need to use

```
:smt (define-type S)
```

An MCMT specification file defines an *array based system*: thus, it is possible to employ a set of indices index and arrays defined on this set. Since it is reasonable and customary to associate to each element of index a natural number (which is its identifier / its address), MCMT *interprets* index *with a subset of the natural numbers* (typically index is finite, however index can be the whole set of natural numbers).

MCMT uses the names

```
z1, z2, z3,...
```

for index variables; in addition, there are three *special* index variables

```
x, y, j
```

whose use will be explained in the next section.

Arrays are the most important ingredient in array based systems. MCMT syntax distinguishes between two kinds of array variables, i.e., *local* and *global* array variables. *Local* array variables are introduced by the declaration

```
:local <arrayvar-id>  <type-id>
```

This is the way for declaring an array variable with identifier `<arrayvar-id>` whose elements are of type `<type-id>` (the domain of the array variable is the implicitly declared type `index`).

When an array is declared as a local array variable, for different index values (i.e., for different locations corresponding to these index values) the corresponding elements of the array may be different. On the contrary, *global* array variables represent constant arrays and are introduced by the declaration

```
:global <arrayvar-id>  <type-id>
```

Contrary to local arrays, for different index values the corresponding elements of global array are forced to be identical. Hence, global arrays do not really denote arrays, but single values (that MCMT internally treats as constant arrays).

The functional application of an array to an index (i.e., the 'read' operation) is represented by using the notation `[-]`; more precisely, if `zi` is an index variable and `a` is an array variable identifier, `a[zi]` is a valid term in the MCMT syntax, whose type is the one of the codomain of `a`. Similarly, `a[x]`, `a[y]`, `a[j]` are valid terms too.

The previously defined terms can be combined to build more complex terms and literals, using the operations and relations available for each type, and following a format that takes inspiration from SMT-LIB2. For example, using the above declarations, one can write the following literals:

```
(> s[z2] 3),    (= (and w[z1] v) true),    (not (= a[z1] 2)),
(= s[z1]  z2).
```

Other valid terms (of types `int` and `bool`, respectively) are for instance `(+ s[x] 2)` and `(or v, w[j])`.

The input language of MCMT is *dereference flat* [19]: this means that subterms like `a[t]` are allowed only in case `t` is a variable. Thus, expressions like `s[1]`, `s[2]`, ... are *not* valid: instead of the atom `(< s[9] 0)`, one must write the conjunction of

```
(= z1  9)   (< s[z1]  0)
```

which is syntactically correct (the variables `zi` are always implicitly existentially quantified, as it will be explained later).

It is possible to declare free constant and function symbols: as customary in many automated reasoning and SMT contexts, *n*-ary relation symbols are represented as *n*-ary function symbols returning a boolean value. For instance, the expression

```
:smt (define c::int))
```

defines a constant of type `int`, whereas

```
:smt (define S::(-> int int bool))
```

declares a binary predicate `S` on integer numbers. In principle, it is also possible to declare macros like

```
:smt (define (MC p::bool n1::int n2::int )::bool (=> p
(= n1 n2) ))
```

(meaning that from now on expressions like `(MC b k l)` have to be interpreted as the expression `(=> b (= k l) ))`.

9.3 MCMT Specifications: Database-Driven Mode

Each line in an input specification file for MCMT needs to begin with a keyword preceded by a colon.

We have already discussed the syntax of commands like

```
:smt    <string>
```

to define types, symbols and macros.

We now focus our attention on the database driven mode of MCMT, which allows us to write array-based specification files formalizing U-RAS in the format of the MCMT syntax.

9.3.1 DB Schema Declaration

As already known from the theory of U-RAS, a Universal RAS supports two kinds of relations: the *static relations* belonging to a *read-only* database DB (the last-mentioned relations are not updated during a run of the system) and the *artifact relations*: artifact relations can be evolved during a run of the system, for instance by using insertion or deletion updated.

In the MCMT encoding, the read-only database relations are declared via SMT assertions (see below), whereas the artifact relations are encoded via *entries* and *local array variables*, as specified in the following. Indeed, an n-ary artifact relation $R(a_1, \ldots, a_n)$ can be seen as an n-tuple of local arrays

```
:local r1
      ...
:local rn
```

The index sort is now interpreted as the sort of the *entries* of the artifact relations (this will be a subtype of int, and MCMT has a special unary predicate to identify it for internal use, see below). Artifact *variables* are representeed as global arrays.

To exploit the specificity of U-RASs, MCMT needs to be executed in a dedicated mode, available since version 2.8. To activate this mode, the specification file needs to contain (before any other relevant declaration) the line

```
:db_driven  < id >
```

where <id> is a string naming the 'entries predicate' (if <id> is left empty, then ENTRY is used as a default name).

Whereas artifact components and artifact variables are specified via local and global arrays, the read-only database, i.e., the DB schema of the U-RAS, needs to be declared following specific instructions. Sorts, unary functions (i.e., attributes of DB relations equipped with key dependencies) and 'plain' relations (for relations not possessing a key in DB extended-schemas) must be declared to the SMT solver

following the syntax explained in Section 9.2. To define, e.g., the id-sort S from the
DB signature Σ, use

```
:smt (define-type S)
```

To declare a constant c of sort S, use

```
:smt (define c ::S)
```

In the db-driven mode, DB constants are assumed to be distinct ('unique name
assumption') and to be distinct from the null-entry constants (see below).

For example, the sorts from the DB schema of the running example of Chapter 3
are declared as follows:

```
:smt (define-type CompInId)
:smt (define-type JobCatId)
:smt (define-type EmpId)
:smt (define-type UserId)
:smt (define-type Num)
:smt (define-type String)
```

To declare a unary function f from Σ_{fun} of domain sort S and codomain sort T
(supposing S and T have already been declared), the user needs to use

```
:smt (define f :: (-> S T))
```

For example, the unary functions from the DB schema of the running example
are declared as follows:

```
:smt (define what :: (-> CompInId JobCatId))
:smt (define who :: (-> CompInId EmpId))
:smt (define jobCatDescr :: (-> JobCatId String))
:smt (define empName :: (-> EmpId String))
:smt (define userName :: (-> UserId String))
```

To define a binary relation R of domain sorts S and T, the user must use

```
:smt (define R :: (-> S T bool))
```

Unary relations follow the natural corresponding syntax as well as ternary, quater-
nary, etc. relations. However, we remark that the cover algorithm for the DB theory
$T := \mathcal{EUF}(\Sigma) \cup \{\text{Axiom} (3.1)\}$ (or, equivalently, quantifier elimination algorithms
in T^*) has been implemented only for unary and binary relations so far, but this is
enough for all the examples and the benchmark we consider.

MCMT checks whether the signature Σ of the read-only database is *acyclic*; if it
is not, the reader is warned that there might be (in principle, but unlikely) spurious
unsafety answers due to insufficient instantiations in satisfiability checks.

After having declared the above data, the user needs also to provide a summary of
the declarations (the summary is necessary, because in principle one might not want
all the declared data to be part of the read-only database). The summary is formed
by lines of the kind

$$: \text{db\_sorts} \quad < \text{id1} > \cdots < \text{idn} >$$
$$: \text{db\_functions} \quad < \text{id1} > \cdots < \text{idn} >$$
$$: \text{db\_relations} \quad < \text{id1} > \cdots < \text{idn} >$$

listing all the declared sorts, functions and relations that should be part of the read-only database. The sorts `int` and `real` should not be included in the above list of DB sorts, although it may be the case that a DB function has `int` or `real` as codomain sort.

MCMT adds by itself a further constant NULL_S for all the above listed sorts S, formalizing the undef-entry for each of these sorts. undef-entries NULL_int and NULL_real of sort `int` and of sort `real`, respectively, are also added. These undef-entries can occur in the specification file at any place, and they must not be declared by the user. The constants NULL_S correspond to the constants called `undef` (cf. Section 3.1).

When the DB schema has been declared, we then need to initialize the system, to declare the unsafe formula and the existentially quantified variables the system needs to eliminate, and finally to define the transitions. This is exactly what is described in the next subsections.

9.3.2 Initialization

A Universal RAS must be initialized: in particular, its local array variables (e.g., the artifact relations) and its global variables (i.e., the artifact variables). In our specification files, initialization is constrained by a universally quantified formula. The following is the format used for declaring the initialization:

```
: initial
 : var     <indexvar-id>
 : cnj     <list-of-quantifier-free-formulae>
```

There may be one or two occurrences of the keyword `:var`; `<indexvar-id>` needs to be the special index variable x or the special index variable y.
The string `<list-of-quantifier-free-formulae>` is a finite list of quantifier-free formulae (intended conjunctively, cf. the keyword `:cnj`), where only the variables declared by `:var` can occur. Such variables are implicitly *universally* quantified, so, for example, the expression

```
: initial
 : var     x
 : cnj     (= a[x] 1)  (= s[x] false)  (= w[x] false)
```

is interpreted as the formula (in Yices format)

```
(forall ((x::index))
(and (= a[x] 1) (= s[x] false) (= w[x] false)))
```

In the specific case of U-RASs, usually they are initialized by setting the global array variables and all the locations of local array variables to NULL_S (where S is the suitable sort of the array variable), i.e., to the undefined value undef.

For example, the initial formula of the (extended version of the) running example (Example 3.6) is the following:

```
:initial
:var x
:cnj (= T1_uid NULL_UserId) (= T1_eid NULL_EmpId) (= T1_jid
    NULL_JobCatId) (= T1_jtype NULL_String) (= T1_timeout
    NULL_Num) (= T1_score -1) (= T1_pos_status NULL_String) (=
    T1_date NULL_String) (= T2_uid NULL_UserId) (= T2_eid
    NULL_EmpId) (= T2_jid NULL_JobCatId) (= T2_jtype
    NULL_String) (= T2_app_status NULL_String) (= T3_uid
    NULL_UserId) (= T3_eid NULL_EmpId) (= T3_jid NULL_JobCatId) (=
    T3_withdraw_status NULL_String) (= SelectedJob false) (=
    SelectedApplication false) (= actT2 false) (= actT3 false) (=
    Init true) (= JobOffers1[x] NULL_JobCatId) (= JobOffers2[x]
    NULL_String) (= JobOffers3[x] NULL_String) (= JobOffers4[x]
    NULL_String) (= Application1[x] NULL_UserId) (=
    Application2[x] NULL_JobCatId) (= Application3[x]
    NULL_EmpId) (= Application4[x] -1) (= Application5[x]
    NULL_String)
```

9.3.3 Unsafe States

State formulae for U-RASs are obtained by prefixing a string $\exists z_1 \cdots \exists z_n$ of index existential quantifiers to a quantifier-free matrix ϕ (in ϕ only the variables $z_1, \ldots, z_n$ can occur free). A state formula is primitive (or a *cube*) iff its matrix is a conjunction of literals and is *primitive differentiated* [145] iff it is primitive and the matrix contains all disequations $z_i \neq z_j$ for $i, j = 1, \ldots, n$ and $i \neq j$. MCMT uses primitive differentiated formulae to represent (backward) reachable sets of states. In such formulae, the disequations $z_i \neq z_j$ are left implicit, in the sense that the user does not need to write them since they are always automatically added by the tool. The external existential quantifiers are left implicit as well.

The first state formula that the user needs to write in the specification file is the unsafe formula, i.e., the formula describing the set of unsafe states (the states we desire the system not to be able to reach). Such a formula is declared as follows:

```
: unsafe
: var    <indexvar-id>
: cnj    <list-of-literals>
```

Here `<list-of-literals>` is a list of literals that should be written by following the same rules as for the case of the `:initial` command. However, here the user must declare and eemploy the standard index variables `z1`, `z2`, `z3`, `z4` instead of the special ones.

So, for example, the specification

```
: unsafe
: var    z1
: var    z2
: cnj    (= a[z1] 7) (= a[z2] 5)
```

should be interpreted as the formula (in Yices format)

```
(exists (z1::index z2::index)
    (and (not (= z1 z2)) (= a[z1] 7) (= a[z2] 5)))
```

For example, the unsafe formula for the running example (Example 4.3) is the following:

```
:u_cnj (= T1_pos_status Notified)(not (= Application1[z1]
    NULL_UserId))(not (= Winner Application5[z1]))(not (= Loser
    Application5[z1]))
```

If the set of unsafe states is described by a state formula which is *not* primitive differentiated, it is always possible to convert such a formula to a disjunction of primitive differentiated ones. In such a case, there is a special syntax for the second, third, etc. disjuncts: these can all be introduced by the following single commands

```
:u_cnj    <list-of-literals>
```

For these formulae, there is no need to use `:var` declarations for the index variables `z1`, `z2`, `z3`, etc. In case the user uses only `:u_cnj` declarations and omit the unsafe formula (i.e., if one omits the `:unsafe` declaration), MCMT works correctly: it just automatically adds `false` as a first unsafe formula.

Remark 9.1 Notice that for unsafe formulae only lists of *literals* can be employed after a `:cnj` or a `:u_cnj` declaration; for initial formulae on the contrary, lists of arbitrary quantifier-free formulae can be used after the `:cnj` declaration.

In conclusion: *MCMT behaves correctly if the above instructions for writing specification files are **strictly** followed.* Deviations from the above instructions produce displayed warnings and may cause MCMT to pass to the underlying SMT solver not well-typed proof obligations. Deviations include user-defined macros and cyclic signatures; more serious and possibly harmful deviations (e.g., the use of `real` and/or `int` as non-value sorts) produce stronger warnings and possibly also spurious outcomes.

9.3.4 Elimination of Existentially Quantified Variables

To model real-time systems in the timed automata style, existentially quantified (real, integer) variables for data values may be used in guards. These variables are not allowed in state formulae, hence they must be eliminated. These variables were already supported in the versions of MCMT older than 2.8. Since version 2.8, the algorithm for computing covers in the standard DB (extended-)theory (or, equivalently, for quantifier elimination in its model completions T^*) has been implemented in MCMT so as to correctly eliminate existentially quantified data variables ranging over the read-only database of U-RASs.

The main novelty introduced since version 2.9 is that `int` and `real` can be now used as *value sorts* in DB extended-schemas (cf. Section 3.1.2). Being value sorts, there can be DB functions having `int` or `real` *as codomain sorts*; however, `int` and `real` should not be domain sorts of DB functions nor arguments of DB relations: there are serious theoretical limitations for this restriction (model completions may not exist, see Section 8.4) and the tool may not behave properly if such restriction is violated (the user is informed about the problem - when it arises - via a displayed message and is asked to confirm that she is aware of the consequences).

Existential variables to be eliminated are introduced in MCMT as follows. First, before writing any transition, the user needs to declare such variables using the instruction

```
:eevar <char> <type-id>
```

where `<char>` is a single character (the name of the existentially quantified variable) and `<type-id>` can be `real` or `int` or S (for some sort S from the DB schema).

Whereas MCMT knows that variables $x, y, j, z1, z2, \ldots$ must range over entries for artifact relations, the situation is different for existentially quantified variables declared as `:eevar`. As clear from the declaration, these variables can only range over reals, integers or over sorts of the read-only database and are subject to *quantifier elimination*.

Once the preimage of the formula representing a set of states is computed, the real variable is eliminated by using Fourier Motzkin quantifier elimination [232]. As to the integer variable, the situation is more complex because MCMT does not support yet full integer quantifier elimination. The procedure applied instead is the following. First, integer literals like (< t u) are replaced by (<= (+ t 1) u). After that, Fourier Motzkin is used: the user is informed that the set of backward reachable states obtained in this way is over-approximated and, in case an unsafe trace is found, he is warned once again about the fact the trace could be spurious because of over-approximation. However, in some trivial cases, Fourier Motzkin and integer quantifier elimination coincide: in such cases, there is no over-approximation at all and no over-approximation warning is displayed. To sum up, the current implementation quantifier elimination in linear real/integer arithmetic is *in principle incomplete*, but still sufficient to handle all the examples and benchmark contained in this book.

In addition to the quantifier elimination for linear integer and real arithmetic, we have a specific quantifier elimination procedure for the data variables from the sorts of the DB schema. This procedure refers to results on cover computation (or, equivalently, quantifier elimination in model completions) and in their combinations. Currently, MCMT provides cover computations only for relational signatures with *free unary or binary predicates* and *free unary functions* and their combinations with linear (both integer and real) arithmetic, following the procedures explained above in the previous chapter.

Cover computations for data variables *should not fail in principle*, unless the user uses some deviating constructs (e.g. in case she introduced some macros via smt assertions). In such cases, the tool does not abort: it converts the non-eliminated variable into a genuine existentially quantified variable interpreted in the complement of the entry predicate (which is ENTRY by default, see above).

The user should take care of the following limitations of MCMT:

1. one can declare at most one existentially quantified variable of type int, at most one existentially quantified variable of type real and up to 10 existentially quantified variables ranging over the other sorts of the read only database;
2. inside the same transition, one cannot use variables of different sorts, unless such sorts are all non-numerical sorts of the read only database (i.e., id sorts);
3. the identifier of an existentially quantified variable must be a single character;
4. an existentially quantified variable of sort S is assumed to to range over elements which are distinct from NULL_S (this assumption simplifies cover computations).

9.3.5 Transitions

Transitions represent how the system evolves: at each step of the evolution of the system, one transition is nondeterministically chosen and executed, if possible.

In a U-RAS, transition are composed by a guard and an update function. The guard is an existentially quantified (both over artifact sorts and basic sorts) primitive differentiated formula: MCMT accepts guards with at most two existentially quantified variables, which can be either x or y. The update function is a case-defined function which is given in lambda-abstraction notation (the lambda-abstracted variable must be j).

The allowed format for a transition declaration is the following:

```
: transition
  : var       x
  : var       y
  : var       j
  : guard     <list-of-literals>
  : uguard    <list-of-literals>
     ...
  : uguard    <list-of-literals>
  : numcases  <pos-int>
  : case      (= x j)
  : val       <term1-1>
  : val       <term1-2>
     ...
  : case      <list-of-literals>
  : val       <term2-1>
  : val       <term2-2>
     ...
     ...
```

where
1. :var j is mandatory, :var x is needed for one and two-variables transitions and :var y is needed only for two-variables transitions;
2. the <list-of-literals> following :guard is the lists of literals that forms the body of the guard of the transition;
3. the lines starting with :uguard are optional and will be discussed in Subsection 9.3.6;
4. <pos-int> is a positive integer giving the number of cases of the case-definable function specifying the update of the transition;
5. the :cases specify, through suitable conjunctions of literals, the case-partition used in the definition of the update function;
6. each keyword :val is followed by a well-formed term of appropriate type:[2] this term gives the updated value of corresponding array in the given case; the number of :val keywords must be equal to the number of array declarations

If the transition has one or two variables (i.e., if :var x has been declared), the first occurrence of the :case keyword must be followed by the single literal (= x j); in case (= x j) is omitted in the first :case declaration, the system automatically makes the correction. Similarly, in the second, third, etc. :case, the

---

[2] In the term, only the declared variables can occur (i.e. we can have occurrences of x, j and also of y, in case the transition has two existentially quantified index variables).

system always automatically adds the literal (not (= x j)) to the list of literals following the :case keyword.

If the variables x, y *have been declared both*, the system assumes that (not (= x y)) in the guard (the guard is primitive differentiated by default).

We give an example of a transition from the extended version of our running example. This transition formalizes a non-deterministic event that can happen during the period while it is possible to submit applications for a job position: the precondition of this even is that the status of the job position is still open and the "timeout" has not reached "Zero" yet. When this transition is non-deterministically fired, the time allowed for the position to remain open passes and the expiration date is reached, causing the effect of updating the "timeout" to "Zero". This implies that new applications are not possible anymore, and the call for job position has been closed.

```
:comment T_1 Waiting
:comment T4
:transition
:var j
:guard   (= actT2 false)(= actT3 false)(= Init false)(=
    SelectedJob false)(= SelectedApplication false)(not (=
    T1_pos_status Open))(not (= T1_timeout Zero))
:numcases 1
:case
:val JobOffers1[j]
:val JobOffers2[j]
:val JobOffers3[j]
:val JobOffers4[j]
:val Application1[j]
:val Application2[j]
:val Application3[j]
:val Application4[j]
:val Application5[j]


:val T1_uid
:val T1_eid
:val T1_jid
:val T1_jtype
:val Zero
:val T1_score
:val T1_pos_status
:val T1_date
:val T2_uid
:val T2_eid
:val T2_jid
:val T2_jtype
:val T2_app_status
:val T3_uid
:val T3_eid
:val T3_jid
:val T3_score
:val T3_withdraw_status
```

```
:val actT2
:val actT3
:val Init
:val SelectedJob
:val SelectedApplication
```

9.3.6 Universal Quantifiers in Guards

U-RAS have a limited form of universal quantification in the guards. The kind of universal quantification we are considering leads to guards of the kind

$$\exists x, eevar\, (\phi(x, eevar) \wedge \forall j\, \psi(j, x, eevar)) \qquad (9.1)$$

where ϕ, ψ are quantifier-free formulae: in ϕ only x (of artifact sort) and *eevar* (of basic sort) occur and in ψ j (of artifact sort), x and *eevar* can occur. These guards make the task of employing the backward reachability procedure challenging, but this problem can be solved by adopting the strategy described in Section 4.4.1: this is achieved by transforming the original U-RAS into a plain RAS that has eliminated the universal guard.

Notice that *a safety proof for the transformed RAS implies a safety certification for the original U-RAS too*, because the latter has fewer runs. In case an unsafe trace is discovered, however, the trace might be spurious (and MCMT displays a further warning in this sense).

Now, we exhibit how to insert universal quantifiers in the guards of the transitions of the specification file. The formula $\psi(j, x, eevar)$ in (9.1) can be converted to DNF, i.e., a disjunction of conjunctions of literals: these conjunctions of literals can be introduced one after the other by using the keyword :uguard.

In order to declare a universal guard, the user needs to add, just right after the :guard statement, the following lines:

```
:uguard    <list-of-literals>

...

:uguard    <list-of-literals>
```

where the <list-of-literals> following :uguard is the lists of literals that forms the body of one disjunct of the universal guard.

9.4 Running MCMT

The distribution of MCMT v.3.0 contains an executable file called mcmt; to execute an MCMT specification file, the user needs to type (from command line)

```
./bin/mcmt [options] <filename>
```
The arguments [options] are not necessary (see the User Manual for details about the options that can be used). One useful option for parsing/debugging is −y, which produces an executable file for z3/yices named .smt−log; if the user has z3/yices in her path, she can run

```
z3 −smt2 .smt−log
```

or respectively
```
yices .smt−log
```

to detect syntax errors from the input file.

9.4.1 Displayed Information

If not executed in silent mode (see the user manual for this), MCMT displays some information about heuristics, reachable states formulae, trace invariants found, and statistics. We provide here a short description of the node representation. The interpretation of the displayed line

$$\text{node19} = [\text{t5\_2\_3}][\text{t6\_2}][\text{t7\_2}][\text{t6\_1}][\text{t7\_1}][0] \tag{9.2}$$

is that MCMT is considering a formula representing a set of states that can reach an unsafe state by executing transitions t5, t6, t7, t6, t7 in this order. It is also possible to obtain additional information from this line. Formula (9.2) is primitive differentiated and has three quantified variables of artifact sort, that is it is of the kind $\exists z_1 \exists z_2 \exists z_3 \psi$ (it is possible to see this formula by inspecting, e.g., the SMT-LIB2 file produce by the option −y). One can also deduce that the formula has three quantified variables by the fact that 3 is the maximum number following an underscore occurring in (9.2). More precisely, to get an unsafe state from a state satisfying the formula $\exists z_1 \exists z_2 \exists z_3 \, \psi$ one first applies transition 5 to z_2, z_3, then transition 6 to z_2, etc. (when we say that transition 5 is applied to z_2, z_3, we mean that transition 5 has two existentially quantified variables x, y in its guard and that x is mapped to z_2 whereas y is mapped to z_3). Notation (9.2) is quite informative, but it is slightly incomplete because it does not mention which case in the case-defined update functions applies to each variable: displaying this information would cause a quite complicated outcome, hence, in case of ambiguity, it is necessary to consult the full information supplied by files produced by running the options −y, −r.

The other messages displayed by MCMT should be clear enough. We only remark that MCMT provides warnings for the only two cases where un unsafe outcome might be spurious:

1. because of universal quantifiers in transition guards, hence the unsafety trace can in principle not good for the intended model (in this case, consistently with the results of [17], MCMT warns that the 'stopping failure model' has been adopted);

2. due to incomplete implementation, quantifier elimination of integer data variables occurring in the guards have been done imprecisely by over-approximating the set of backward reachable states.

In particular, if neither universally quantified index variables (see Subsection 9.3.6) nor existentially quantified data variables (see Subsection 9.3.4) occur in the guards, *unsafety traces are not spurious.*

In case an unsafe trace is found, this implies that the last displayed formula (9.2) is consistent with the initial formula. To get an assignment describing a state that can reach an unsafe configuration, the user may try to exploit the model building facilities of z3/yices when running the SMT-LIB2 file `.smt-log` produced by the option `-y`. In case a risk of spuriousness has been detected, it is in principle still possible to check spuriousness of the trace, but currently this can be performed only manually by the user.

9.5 Experiments on Concrete Data-Aware Processes

We base our experimental evaluation on the already existing benchmark provided in [186], that samples 33 (32 plus one variant) real-world BPMN processes published in the official BPM website (`http://www.bpmn.org/`). Specifically, we provide a faithful encoding of *all* these 33 models into the array-based specifications of U-RASs, by exploiting the syntax of the database-driven mode of MCMT (from Version 2.8). Moreover, we enrich our experimental set with an extended version of the running example of this book from Chapter 3. Each example from the benchmark has been checked against 12 conditions, where at least one is safe and one is unsafe; our running example has been checked against 33 conditions. Overall, we ran MCMT over 429 specification files.

Experiments were performed on a machine with macOS High Sierra 10.13.3, 2.3 GHz Intel Core i5 and 8 GB RAM. The full benchmark set is available on the following website: `https://github.com/AlessandroGianola/SMT-based-Data-Aware-Processes-Verification/tree/RAS-benchmark-in-MCMT`. A selected subset of this benchmark is also available, as part of the last distribution 2.8 of MCMT: `http://users.mat.unimi.it/users/ghilardi/mcmt/` (see the subdirectory `/examples/dbdriven` of the distribution). For the information on how to use the capabilities of the new version of MCMT (by activating the "db_driven" mode), how to encode RASs in MCMT specifications and how to produce user-defined examples in the database driven framework, see the previous sections of this chapter; for more details on MCMT in general, its use and heuristics also in different contexts, see the user manual, also included in the distribution.

We provide two tables describing the benchmark run in MCMT: Table 9.1 lists the name of tested examples and gives relevant information on the size of the input specification files, whereas Table 9.2 summarizes the experimental results obtained running MCMT over those files.

	Example	Ar	#AC	#AV	#T	#Q	#In
E1	Acquisition-following-RFQ	n	6	13	28	14	7
E2	Airline-Check-In	y	1	33	48	3	5
E3	Amazon-Fulfillment	n	2	28	38	17	11
E4	BPI-Web-Registration-with-Moderator	n	5	25	22	9	4
E5	BPI-Web-Registration-without-Moderator	n	5	25	20	9	4
E6	Bank-Account-Opening	y	7	25	16	6	4
E7	Book-Writing-and-Publishing	n	4	14	14	10	4
E8	Commercial-Financing	n	7	14	34	4	9
E9	Credit-Review-and-Approval	n	12	24	23	3	13
E10	Customer-Quotation-Request	n	9	11	21	11	8
E11	Employee-Expense-Reimbursement-Alternative-1	y	3	17	21	8	1
E12	Employee-Expense-Reimbursement-Alternative-2	y	3	17	21	8	1
E13	Incident-Management-as-Collaboration	n	3	20	20	10	3
E14	Incident-Management-as-Detailed-Collaboration	n	3	20	20	10	3
E15	Insurance-Claim-Processing	y	4	22	22	13	3
E16	Journal-Review-Process	n	6	25	47	19	9
E17	LaserTec-Production-Process	y	0	18	13	8	0
E18	Mortgage-Approval	n	3	18	21	9	3
E19	New-Car-Sales	y	0	23	31	10	0
E20	Order-Fulfillment-and-Procurement	n	3	11	24	7	2
E21	Order-Fulfillment	y	7	17	27	7	4
E22	Order-Processing-with-Credit-Card-Authorization	y	9	18	20	2	7
E23	Order-Processing	y	9	14	17	2	7
E24	OrderFulfillment_new	y	1	17	15	7	4
E25	Patient-Treatment-Abstract-Process	n	6	17	34	14	20
E26	Patient-Treatment-Collaboration-Choreography	n	6	17	34	15	20
E27	Patient-Treatment-Collaboration	n	6	17	34	15	20
E28	Pizza-Co.-Delivery-Process	y	2	32	32	10	2
E29	Property-and-Casualty-Insurance-Claim-Processing	n	2	7	15	3	3
E30	Ship-Process-of-a-Hardware-Retailer	y	0	28	26	9	0
E31	The-Pizza-Collaboration	y	2	32	37	12	2
E32	Travel-Booking-with-Event-Sub-processes	y	14	32	51	9	14
E33	Travel-Booking	y	14	32	43	8	10
E+	JobHiring	y	9	18	15	7	6

Table 9.1: Summary of the tested examples

Ex	#U	#S	MeanT	MaxT	StDvT	Avg#(N)	AvgD	Avg#(calls)
E01	9	3	0.82	1.28 (U)	0.36	60.1	8.25	3398.2
E02	6	6	0.31	0.37 (S)	0.04	6.7	4.33	4011.4
E03	6	6	0.74	2.49 (S)	0.69	24.4	6.75	4301.8
E04	5	7	0.32	0.64 (U)	0.18	15.0	7.67	1899.7
E05	5	7	0.23	0.51 (U)	0.14	10.9	6.17	1656.8
E06	5	7	0.17	0.34 (U)	0.08	14.6	6.58	1496.4
E07	10	2	0.18	0.62 (U)	0.16	21.8	3.75	1126.1
E08	6	6	0.65	2.50 (S)	0.67	34.2	8.75	3036.4
E09	9	3	19.76	171.63 (S)	48.42	175.8	12.00	20302.4
E10	9	3	0.22	0.46 (S)	0.14	15.1	4.75	1550.3
E11	7	5	0.14	0.37 (S)	0.10	17.3	7.25	1305.7
E12	7	5	0.15	0.37 (S)	0.10	16.4	6.92	1292.6
E13	8	4	0.65	2.39 (U)	0.80	47.4	7.67	2764.8
E14	8	4	0.62	2.24 (U)	0.77	46.5	7.67	2724.0
E15	7	5	0.37	0.76 (U)	0.21	32.3	9.5	2283.4
E16	8	4	0.96	5.47 (U)	1.43	38.3	11.0	5151.8
E17	7	5	0.08	0.13 (U)	0.02	11.3	8.67	768.5
E18	6	6	0.11	0.19 (U)	0.04	9.0	5.33	1212.6
E19	6	6	0.37	0.74 (U)	0.15	31.3	8.17	2416.2
E20	6	6	0.11	0.17 (U)	0.03	10.9	5.5	1026.5
E21	7	5	0.37	1.22 (S)	0.29	30.8	13.25	2352.8
E22	9	3	6.71	43.76 (U)	14.10	134.3	8.16	8355.4
E23	8	4	0.99	3.73 (S)	1.48	35.3	7.09	2995.9
E24	7	5	0.08	0.11 (S)	0.02	9.5	5.42	942.2
E25	6	6	4.52	24.74 (S)	9.43	27.1	4.83	7486.7
E26	6	6	4.97	17.79 (S)	7.55	28.2	4.92	4811.1
E27	7	5	4.59	20.81 (S)	7.42	26.9	4.91	4633.7
E28	7	5	0.22	0.45 (U)	0.08	9.1	6.17	2699.0
E29	6	6	0.08	0.42 (S)	0.11	11.3	5.42	648.8
E30	6	6	0.31	0.79 (U)	0.20	26.4	5.42	2316.2
E31	8	4	0.35	0.68 (U)	0.18	17.9	8.58	3325.0
E32	9	3	2.48	8.49 (U)	2.41	97.3	17.75	9231.3
E33	9	3	1.27	4.24 (S)	1.16	66.7	16.83	6637.8
E+	22	11	7.39	98.27 (S)	23.55	75.7	9.15	5612.5

Table 9.2: Experimental results for safety properties

In Table 9.1:

- the column **#AC** represents, for each example, the number of artifact components;
- the column **#AV** represents, for each example, the number of artifact variables;
- the column **#T** represents, for each example, the number of transitions;
- the column **#Q** represents, for each example, the number of transitions containing quantified data variables;
- the column **#In** represents, for each example, the number of transitions manipulating at least one index;

- finally, in column **#(Ar)** we write "y" if the corresponding example contains arithmetic operations, and "n" otherwise.

All the verified examples include transitions with quantified "data" variables (as one can see from column **#Q**), and rely on and the algebraic framework of DB theories introduced in the Section 3.1.

To stress test our encoding, we manually created a few formulae to be verified that have a clear semantic interpretation in terms of the described configurations. We chose not to generate them automatically from syntactic templates as done in [186]: we preferred to check meaningful properties so that one can check that the outcome returned by the tool corresponds to our expectation. Each example is then endowed with one of these formulae, which is declared as unsafe property in a MCMT specification file: in the provided benchmark set at the link above, file EXPY.txt corresponds to the example EX (with $X := 1, ..., 33$ or $X := +$) verified against property PY (with $Y := \{01, 02, ..., 11, 12\}$ if $X := \{01, 02, ..., 32, 33\}$, or $Y := \{01, 02, ..., 32, 33\}$ if $X := +$); at the same link, the time-log.txt file containing the list of the execution times of all the previous files EXPY.txt is also available. The verification outcome that MCMT can have is of the two following types: SAFE and UNSAFE. The MCMT tool returns SAFE, if the undesirable property it was asked to verify represents a configuration that the system cannot reach. The result is UNSAFE if there exists a path of the system execution that reaches "bad" states.

In Table 9.2, we report several measures for each example: when we say that a measure is "an average for that example" we mean that it is obtained by computing the arithmetic mean of that measure over the properties tested for the same example. We now explain the content of Table 9.2.

- The column **#U** shows the number of UNSAFE outcomes among the tested properties for each example.
- Analogously, the column **#S** shows the number of SAFE outcomes.
- The column **MeanT** is the arithmetic mean over the MCMT execution times (in seconds) of the tested properties for each example.
- Column **MaxT** reports the maximum execution time (in seconds) for the tested properties per example (in brackets it is also reported if the maximum corresponds to a SAFE or UNSAFE outcome).
- Column **StDvT** shows the standard deviation of the execution times (in seconds) over the sample of the tested properties for each example.
- The last three measures shown in Table 9.2 are **Avg#(N)**, **AvgD** and **Avg#(calls)** that respectively define the average number of nodes, the average depth of the tree used for the backward reachability procedure adopted by MCMT, and the average number of the SMT solver calls performed by MCMT for that example.

Indeed, MCMT computes the iterated preimages of the formula describing the unsafe states along the various transitions. Such a computation produces a tree, whose nodes are labeled by formulae describing sets of states that can reach an unsafe state and whose arcs are labeled by a transition. In other words, an arc $t : \phi \rightarrow \psi$ means that ϕ is equal to $Pre(t, \psi)$.

We notice from Table 9.2 that the means of the execution times are relatively small: more than 76% of the examples has a timing mean that is less than one second, and more than 52% of the example have maximum execution time less than one second. As one can see from the `time-log.txt` file, overall MCMT terminates in less than one second for 85.5% of the tested files (367 out of 429). We also remark that in most cases the standard deviation is very low (in more than 58% of the times it is less than 0.5, and in more than 70% of the times it is less than 1), which means that the mean is a good indicator of the behavior of the tested files for each example. Moreover, notice that the maximum execution time per file in the benchmark is for testing file `E09P06.txt`, which took MCMT 171.63 seconds (less than 3 minutes). As shown in `time-log.txt`, there are some other outliers: for example, 28.42 seconds for file `E09P04.txt`, 43.76 and 28.23 seconds for files `E22P10.txt` and `E22P12.txt` resp., 24.74 and 24.63 for files `E25P05.txt` and `E25P10.txt` resp., 41.55, 90.36 and 98.27 seconds for files `E+P14.txt`, `E+P15.txt` and `E+P17.txt` resp.

One can see, for example, that the job hiring RAS has been proved by MCMT to be SAFE w.r.t. the property defined in Example 4.4. The details about the successfully completed verification task are the following: the tool constructed a tree with 3 nodes and a depth of 3 with 1238 calls to the SMT solver, and returned SAFE in 0.16 seconds. For the same job hiring RAS, if we slightly modify the safe condition discussed in Example 4.4 by removing, for instance, the check that a selected applicant is not a winning one, we obtain a description (see below) of a configuration in which it is still the case that an applicant could win:

$$\exists i : \mathsf{applIndex} \begin{pmatrix} pState = \mathtt{notified} \wedge applicant[i] \neq \mathsf{undef} \\ \wedge\ appResult[i] \neq \mathtt{loser} \end{pmatrix}$$

In this case, the job hiring process analyzed against the devised property is evaluated as UNSAFE by the tool in 0.87 seconds (this property corresponds to file `E+P03.txt`). When checking safety properties, MCMT also prints the sequence of transitions of an unsafe path of a given example in case the verification result is UNSAFE.

Since MCMT performs safety verification parameterized on the read-only DB, the result is *independent* on the size of specific DB instances. Moreover, MCMT can in principle handle unbounded DB schemas and unboundedly many DB constants: we decided not to explicitly report in Table 9.1 the size of DB schemas since we noticed it does not affect the performances as much as the number of artifact components, of transitions and of transitions containing quantified index variables. We leave for future work a systematic experimental evaluation of those preliminary observations.

To conclude, we would like to point out that contrasting the high number of SMT solver calls in #(**SMT-calls**) against relatively low execution time demonstrates that MCMT could be considered as a promising tool supporting the presented line of research. This is due to the following two reasons. On the one hand, the SMT technology underlying solvers like Yices [107] is quite mature and impressively well-performing. On the other hand, the backward reachability algorithm generates proof obligations which are relatively easy to be analyzed as (un)satisfiable by the solver.

A thorough comparison with VERIFAS [186] is at the moment rather problematic, for various reasons, due for instance to the different specification languages and to the different types of theoretical frameworks adopted by two tools. In fact, the two systems tackle incomparable verification problems: on the one hand, we deal with safety problems, whereas VERIFAS handles properties expressed in a variant of LTL-FO. On the other hand, we tackle features not available in VERIFAS, like bulk updates and comparisons between artifact tuples. The reason why we chose to manually encode the same BPMN benchmark attacked by VERIFAS was to demonstrate the feasibility of our approach on concrete, real-world-inspired examples. Although the encoding of the examples is faithfully in line with the semantics of the systems verified by VERIFAS, the different kind of involved logics for expressing the properties prevented us from checking these systems against the same properties. Nevertheless, while the properties verified by VERIFAS are synthetically generated (and, hence, in many cases they are meaningless), every safety condition that we checked in MCMT was manually created after a careful analysis of the semantical behavior of every example. We leave this comparison for future, more experimentally-oriented, work. The comparison might be interesting because the two tools apply quite different technologies (VERIFAS is based on Vector Addition System with States (VASS) encoding, whereas MCMT follows a purely declarative paradigm).

Part III
Applications

Chapter 10
Business Process Management and Petri Nets: Preliminaries

In this chapter we provide a brief overview of the fundamental notions from the BPM literature and from Colored Petri nets that are useful for the following chapters.

10.1 Business Process Management

We recall that BPM can be seen as the research field that investigates methods and techniques for describing, managing and improving business processes within companies and organizations, from both the theoretical and the practical points of view, so as to ensure that the activities are performed in the best way possible and the desired objectives are achieved. Hence, the first concept that is worth clarifying is the one of *business process*.

Business processes can be seen as "chains of events, activities and decisions" [105], i.e., a collection of instantaneous events that can have a concrete effect on the work in an organization, of activities performed by some actors within a business entity (e.g., a company), and of decision points involving these actors and possible objects/artifacts that these actors deal with during their work. These decision points usually generate several branches in the evolution of the process and lead to different outcomes: the outcomes are not always the same, since some of them fulfil the intended requirements of the process and reach the desired goals, whereas some of them may result in an unwanted behavior that violates (some of) the predetermined objectives defined by the company.

The concept of business process is at the same time formally studied by BPM researchers and concretely employed by BPM practitioners in the industry: this is possible thanks to the existence of standard modeling languages for business processes, such as in particular BPMN (Business Process Model and Notation) [1]. This language gives the possibility to experts from different fields (managers, IT specialists, stakeholders etc.) to share their knowledge and comprehension about processes using a common, non-ambiguous formalism. Providing such a common interface for reasoning about business processes helps the different involved specialists to

© The Author(s), under exclusive license to Springer Nature Switzerland AG 2023   199
A. Gianola: *Verification of Data-Aware Processes via Satisfiability Modulo Theories*,
LNBIP 470, pp. 199–211, 2023.
https://doi.org/10.1007/978-3-031-42746-6_10

understand better the complexity of the process and to discover in time and possibly prevent critical issues that could affect the performance of the organization.

We now review the main ingredients for modeling business processes via the BPMN language. We consider here the latest version of BPMN, which is BPMN 2.0. This version was released as a standard by the Object Management Group (OMG) in 2011.

10.1.1 BPMN Basic Blocks and Concepts

The basic components of a business process are *activities* and *events*. Activities should be thought as units of work that have a duration and are performed by human individuals or automated actors in the organization (e.g., "candidate evaluation" in a job hiring process): in case the activity can be considered as atomic (i.e., it is not decomposed into multiple sub-activities), it is called *task*. In contrast, events should be thought as circumstances occurring instantaneously that affect the evolution of the process (e.g., an incoming message/order from a different department of a company).

Activities (and, in particular tasks) are depicted with rounded rectangles (Figure 10.1a), whereas events with circles (Figure 10.1b).

(a) Task block.   (b) Intermediate event block.

Fig. 10.1: Tasks and events

Usually, activities have a duration and during their evolution they pass though different *states* that determine their *lifecycle*: when the activity is not currently executed but can be potentially started, we say that it is in the *idle* state; when the execution activity is triggered by some other block in the process flow, we say that it is in the *enabled* state; during its execution, we say it is in the *active* state; finally, when the execution of the activity terminates, it ends in the *completed* state. This is a simplified version of what is called the "activity lifecycle". Since events do not have a duration but occur instantaneously, their lifecycle can be in the same state as activities, apart from the active state.

In the following, we restrict our attention to *block-structured* BPMN. As it will be discussed later, in this book we only focus on this fragment of BPMN since it allows us to define a direct execution semantics also for advanced constructs and to exploit this upon verifying the obtained models: in particular, this choice makes possible to implement a parser of the resulting BPMN diagram that can be automatically translated in the specification language of MCMT (see Chapter 9). We will comment in more detail the reasons behind this choice in Chapters 11 and 12.

Events and activities do not usually happen alone, and usually are not completely disconnected. In contrast, events and activities within the same business process are usually strictly interconnected and causally related and/or temporally ordered: that is why the notion of "sequence flow" of events/activities is needed in order to faithfully represent a concrete process. A *sequence* of two activities B_1 and B_2 is simply a more complex process where B_1 is executed first and then, when B_1 is completed, the activity B_2 is enabled and finally performed. To connect the blocks B_1 and B_2 so as to create a sequence, BPMN supports a third basic concept, i.e. *arcs*. Arcs are depicted with arrows with a full arrow-head that connect the two blocks B_1 and B_2.

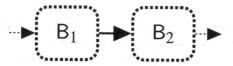

In BPMN, every process is assumed to be triggered by some event (e.g., by the opening of a job position) and to be ended by some other (e.g., by the fulfillment of the job hiring process): the former is called "start event" and the latter "end event". Start and end events play a crucial role in modeling processes: the start event indicates when *instances* of the process start whereas the end event indicates when instances complete. Start (resp., end) events and the blocks that follow (resp., precede) them are interconnected by arcs. These two events are depicted with two slightly different symbols: as it can be seen in the following picture, which shows a *process block*, start events are represented by circles with a thin border, while end events are represented by circles with a thick border.

Process blocks can be used to formalize a (sub-)process that is part of a bigger (super-)process: in this case, the sub-process as a whole can be thought as a single macro-activity of its parent process. Sometimes, for the sake of simplicity, BPMN users prefer avoiding the representation of the explicit content of sub-processes, e.g., in case the information about their internal structure is not relevant for performing the tasks of the parent process. Subprocesses that hide their internal steps are called "collapsed subprocesses", and are depicted as follows:

In BPMN, it is customary to give names to activities and events: the reader that is interested in the nomenclature conventions should see Chapter 3 of [105]. Events

that may occur during the evolution of the process that are neither start or end events are called "'intermediate" events.

10.1.2 Process Cases and Execution Semantics: an Informal View

As already noticed, start events trigger the creation of instances of the process: for example, in the case of a job hiring process, a new instance is generated whenever a new job is posted and becomes open for applications. For every business process of interest, contemporary organizations execute in parallel a variety of different instances, usually called *cases*, which are all independent of each other.

Concerning the execution semantics, BPMN models are similar in spirit to Petri nets (see Section 10.2 for more details on this). The creation of every case of the process is associated with the generation of a new *token* which should be intended as an implicit identifier of the running case in consideration: this identifier is useful to represent the state of each case in every moment of the execution, and to track its progression along the workflow of the process. As it happens for Petri nets, tokens are generated in correspondence of the start event, and flow through the process until they reach an end event, where they are consumed in order to terminate the corresponding case. The nature of tokens' flow is determined by the characteristics of the process, which, in turn, depends on the specific features of its building blocks. For example, if the token identifying the current case reaches a sequence block connecting two sub-blocks B_1 and B_2, its behavior can be easily described. It first enters into block B_1 as soon as this block is enabled, it passes through it during B_1 execution and exits it when B_1 becomes completed. At this point, the token flows through the arc connecting B_1 and B_2 and, as soon as B_2 is enabled, it is taken by the second block. The token remains in B_2 for all the duration of its execution, until B_2 completes its activity. Finally, the token exits the sequence block. In general, tokens follow the flow induced by the arcs in the BPMN diagram. We will see in the next paragraph that BPMN diagram can contain blocks that are more complex than basic ones, and we will informally describe the behavior of tokens when flowing through them.

10.1.3 Complex BPMN blocks

Sequence block is not the only way for composing activities and events: indeed, activities are not forced to be always executed sequentially, i.e., one after the other. For example, one may want to represent the case where two activities are performed in parallel. To model patterns that are different from the sequential composition of blocks, it is necessary to introduce *gateways*. Gateways are used to manage and guide the flow of tokens through the process: indeed, they formalize both the case when the token incoming to the gate is split into more than one tokens that are sent to different branches of the process executed in parallel, and the case when tokens are merged together because different parallel executions converge. In the first case, they are called *split gateways*, which describe a point where the the process flow (with a single incoming arc) is split into branches (i.e., into more than one outgoing arcs); in the second case, they are called *join gateways*, describing a point in the diagram where the process flow converges and different branches of the process (i.e., more than one incoming arc) are merged into a single branch (i.e., into a single outgoing arc). In BPMN, split and join gateways are both represented using diamonds.

We now describe some of the most important blocks that involve gateways and briefly present their token semantics.

In some concrete cases there are activities that are *independent* of each other and can be run in parallel, i.e. they can be executed at the same time. In these cases, we employ the following *parallel block*: an *AND-split* is used to model the creation of of two (or more) branches that are run in parallel (with sub-blocks B_1 and B_2), and an *AND-join* is used to synchronize again these created branches into a single one when their executions is completed.

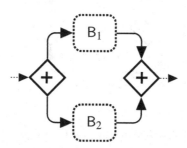

We notice that an AND-split receiving in input one token returns as output as many tokens as the number of branches created, and each of these token flows in parallel through the corresponding branch; similarly, an AND-join receives in input a bunch of tokens coming from the different branches and merges them into a unique token that is then released to the arc departing from the AND-join.

In other cases, there are activities that are *alternative* to each other and, hence, are mutually exclusive, i.e. only one of the them can be executed. For formalizing such cases, BPMN gives us the possibility of using the *exclusive (XOR) block*: this block consists of a *XOR-split* to branch the execution into two (or more) different mutually exclusive alternatives, of two (or more) sub-blocks B_1, B_2 etc. that are alternatively run in the corresponding branches, and of a *XOR-join* that merge the alternative branches. The exclusive block is depicted as follows:

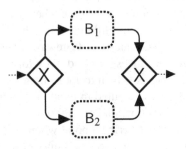

Notice that the token that passes through a XOR-split is then sent to one (and only one) alternative branch, because only one branch is executed. When the token reaches the XOR-join, the block is completed and the token is passed though an outgoing arc to the subsequent block.

If the choice on which of the alternative branches to execute is determined by a condition φ, the exclusive block is called *exclusive choice (XOR) block* (see the following picture): in this case, if the condition φ on the first outgoing arc is satisfied, then the first branch is taken, otherwise the second branch is taken.

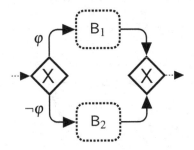

Notice that the token semantics for this block is the same as the one of the exclusive-block to the previous one: the only difference is that the choice of the branch is guided by the satisfaction of the condition φ.

In yet other cases, there is an alternative choice of activities to perform, but this choice is not exclusive and different alternatives are possible at the same time: sometimes only one activity in the alternative is executed, sometimes more than one are chosen and executed. This situation is formalized using the following block, called *inclusive choice (OR) block*: similarly to the exclusive choice block, we use an *OR-split* to branch the execution in different branches containing the sub-blocks B_i $(i = 1, 2, ...)$, each of which is chosen upon the satisfaction of a condition φ_i; we use a *OR-join* to merge all the branches.

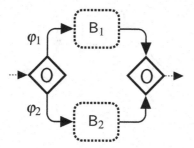

The reader should be careful when considering the token semantics of this case. Indeed, as in the exclusive choice case, when a token reaches the OR-split, one token is returned as output in correspondence of the branch satisfying its condition φ: however, for the inclusive choice block there could be more than one φ_i that are satisfied, so more than one branch that are executable. If this is the case, the OR-split generates as many tokens as the number of branches whose conditions are satisfied. These tokens flow in parallel through the enabled branches. The inclusive choice block is completed when *all* the enabled branches terminate their execution, i.e., when all the created tokens reach the OR-join gateway.

If the decision to take on which branch to follow in an exclusive choice block is determined not by an activity, but by the first among different potentially incoming events, the XOR-split gateway is represented in a different way:

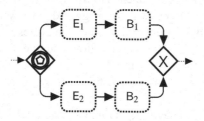

We call this block *event-driven block*. Here, E_1 and E_2 must be intermediate events.

Another essential block is given by the *loop block*: it is used to formalize the repetition of some activities (the block B_1), called *repetition pattern*. The main characteristic of this block is that the last of its activities needs to be a decision activity, i.e., an activity where a decision is made: in fact, based on this decision, either the repetition pattern is run again (after the execution of block B_2) or the loop block becomes completed. In the latter case the execution continues following the subsequent blocks in the rest of the process flow. Usually, the decision depends upon the satisfaction of a condition φ. The following picture represents a common way for formalizing a loop block in BPMN:

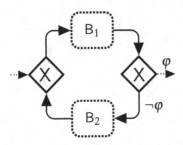

The token semantics in this case should be clear enough: the token first enters the loop and flows through the repetition pattern B_1, and when B_1 is completed it enters the XOR-split gateway. This gateway splits the execution into two branches. In fact, each branch is chosen depending on the outcome of the decision made in B_1, and the possible outcomes are two: if φ is satisfied, then the token exits the loop block, otherwise it remains in the loop, flows through the downward branch (and B_2 is executed) and finally reaches the XOR-join gateway on the left. In this way, the token is ready to move again through the repetition pattern for a new iteration of the loop.

Sometimes, during the execution of an activity, some exception/error may occur, making the process diverge from the expected behavior: in this case, we would like to model a (possible) interruption of the "regular" execution of the process when such an exception happens, and to indicate that the process should instead follow an alternative branch for handling the occurred exception. In this respect, we notice that intermediate events can also been attached to BPMN activities. Their meaning in that case is to indicate an exception flow that is triggered whenever the event is delivered to the process instance during the execution of the corresponding activities. There are in general two modes for the exception flow: the one interrupting the activities and the one non-interrupting the activities, as discussed below. In BPMN, this is done with the following three blocks (the first two are interrupting, the third one is non-interrupting).

The first one models *backward exception*, i.e. a situation when, during the execution of a sub-block A, and error e occurs and then the downward branch is activated, inducing the execution of the "exception handler" sub-block B. After the exception has been handled, the sub-block A is executed again. This block is represented as follows:

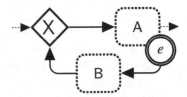

The token semantics in this case is particularly interesting: while the tokens identifying the current case are taken by A (because A is active), an error event may happen, which causes *all* the tokens at the moment present in A to be "destroyed" (because all the sub-activities of A must be immediately interrupted). At the same, a new token identifying the current case is created in the exception handler block and moved through the sub-block B. When b terminates its activity, the token is moved to the left XOR-join gateway, ready to repeat the activity A. The fact that the token is fed back to initial activity A explains why this block is called "backward exception".

The second exception block is called *forward-exception* (see the following picture).

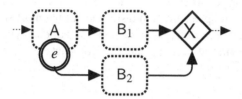

It models a situation that is symmetric to the previous one, since instead of formalizing a "backward" exception, it formalizes a "forward" exception: when the exception happens in an activity A, it is handled without going back to A. More precisely, the only difference with the previous block is that, after handling the exception via sub-block B_2, the execution of the process continues without repeating A. If the exception does not occur, the sub-block B_1, which corresponds to the expected behavior of the system, is executed instead of B_2. The token semantics of this block is analogous the one of the previous block. Again, we need to immediately terminate all the sub-blocks of A when the exception/error occurs.

We conclude with the last exception block, called *non-interrupting exception block*, depicted in the following picture:

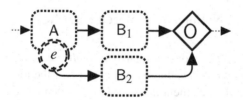

This block is equivalent to the forward-exception block, with the only difference that when an error occurs in the block A, A is not interrupted and continues its execution. In this case, the token semantics is easier since the exception handler is executed in parallel with the sequence flow formed by A and B_1, and no token from A is destroyed. Hence, either the sequence of A and B_1 is executed, or both the sequence and the exception handler B_2 are run in parallel.

All the blocks presented so far present the same lifecycle as activities: in fact, sequence blocks or more complex blocks can be thought as activities that can be decomposed into simpler sub-activities.

10.2 Colored Petri Nets

Colored Petri nets (CPNs) [168, 169, 170] is a well-known extension of classical place/transition (or Petri) nets [223] that was developed for simulating and verifying reactive systems. The formalism of CPNs was introduced as a language for modeling large systems and protocols that can at the same time provide a solid theoretical framework for performing verification tasks. One of the most significant features of CPNs is the existence of primitives for the definition of data types and for describing data manipulation, which allow the creation of compact and parameterizable models.

10.2.1 Data Types

We consider a *type set* $\mathcal{D}$ as a finite set of pairwise disjoint types accounting for the different kinds of objects in the domain of interest. Each type $\mathcal{D} \in \mathcal{D}$ comes with its own (possibly infinite) *value domain* $\Delta_\mathcal{D}$, and with an equality operator $=_\mathcal{D}$. When clear from the context, we simplify the notation and use $=$ in place of $=_\mathcal{D}$. Here are a few examples of data types: strings $\texttt{string} = \langle \mathbb{S}, =_s \rangle$, integers $\texttt{int} = \langle \mathbb{Z}, =_{int} \rangle$, orders $\texttt{Order} = \langle \mathbb{O}, =_o \rangle$ and product types $\texttt{ProdType} = \langle \mathbb{P}, =_p \rangle$ used in some e-commerce application. Our definition of data types is essentially used to symbolically distinguish different value domains. One could see it as an extension of the pure names concept adopted in [227, 228] that allows to distinguish different "kinds" of names.

10.2.2 Preliminary Notions for Colored Petri Nets

We first fix some standard notions related to *multisets*. Given a set A, the *set of multisets* over A, written $A^\oplus$, is the set of mappings of the form $m : A \to \mathbb{N}$. Given a multiset $S \in A^\oplus$ and an element $a \in A$, $S(a) \in \mathbb{N}$ denotes the number of times a appears in S. We write $a^n \in S$ if $S(a) = n$. We also consider the usual operations on multisets. Given $S_1, S_2 \in A^\oplus$: *(i)* $S_1 \subseteq S_2$ (resp., $S_1 \subset S_2$) if $S_1(a) \leq S_2(a)$ (resp., $S_1(a) < S_2(a)$) for each $a \in A$; *(ii)* $S_1 + S_2 = \{a^n \mid a \in A \text{ and } n = S_1(a) + S_2(a)\}$; *(iii)* if $S_1 \subseteq S_2$, $S_2 - S_1 = \{a^n \mid a \in A \text{ and } n = S_2(a) - S_1(a)\}$; *(iv)* given a number $k \in \mathbb{N}$, $k \cdot S_1 = \{a^{kn} \mid a^n \in S_1\}$; *(v)* $|m| = \sum_{a \in A} m(a)$. A multiset over A is called empty (denoted as $\emptyset^\oplus$) iff $\emptyset^\oplus(a) = 0$ for every $a \in A$.

We fix a countably infinite set $V_{\mathfrak{D}}$ of typed variables with a *variable typing function* type : $V_{\mathfrak{D}} \to \mathfrak{D}$.

Given a formula φ expressed in some logical language, we call $Vars(\varphi)$ the set of all variables appearing in φ, and $Const(\varphi)$ the set of all constants appearing in φ. In what follows, with slight abuse of notation we assume that functions type, *Vars* and *Const* are extended to account for sets, tuples and multisets of variables and constants. For example, $Vars(\{x, 1, a, y, z\}) = \{x, y, z\}$ and $Const(\{x, 1, a, y, z\}) = \{1, a\}$.

10.2.3 Definition of Colored Petri Nets

In this section we introduce syntax and semantics of colored Petri nets [171].

A Petri net[223] is a bipartite directed graph, constituted by the three basic types of objects: places (drawn as circles or ellipses), transitions (drawn as rectangles or bars) and directed arcs. In Figure 10.2, one can see a Petri net with three places p_i and five transitions t_j. In every graph of that type directed arcs are connecting transitions to places and places to transitions, while non-graph components, such as output and input functions, define the relationship between the places and transitions, ipso facto completing the basic Petri net definition. To represent a state of the modeled system, Petri net places carry multisets of tokens. Colored Petri nets extend the notion of classical Petri nets by adding types to every places and transitions. Thereby, in colored Petri nets tokens have values of the type assigned to a place they reside in. In Figure 10.2, all places have type integer and there are one token with value 6 that resides in p_1 and one token with value 3 that resides in p_1. Moreover, arcs are inscribed with expressions, which may contain typed variables. For example, the arc from transition t_4 to place p_2 has inscription $x + 1$, where x is a variable of type integer.

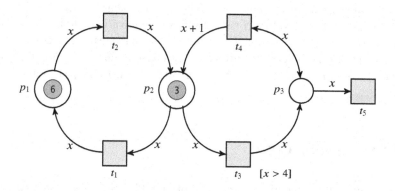

Fig. 10.2: A simple example of colored Petri net

We now give the definition of Colored Petri Nets. CPNs have a color type, which corresponds to a data type or to the cartesian product of multiple data types from $\mathfrak{D}$.

Intuitively, tokens are 'colored' in the sense that a (cartesian product of) datatypes is assigned to each of them. Tokens in places are referenced via *inscriptions* – tuples of variables and constants. We denote by Ω_A the set of all possible inscriptions over a set A.

We use a minimalistic definition of CPN where the input/output behavior of transition is based on pattern matching for retrieving and generating tokens and where the only element left unspecified is the logical language used to define data guards on transitions. For that reason, we assume that a logic $\mathcal{L}$ is given as a blackbox, together with its syntax and semantics: we also assume that the notion of "($\mathcal{L}$-)validity" of an $\mathcal{L}$-formula is well defined.

Definition 10.1 (Colored Petri net) A $\mathfrak{D}$-typed Colored Petri net N is a tuple $N = (\mathfrak{D}, \mathcal{L}, P, T, F_{in}, F_{out}, \text{color}, \text{guard})$, where:
1. P and T are finite sets of places and transitions, s.t. $P \cap T = \emptyset$;
2. $\text{color} : P \rightarrow \mathcal{K}_{\mathfrak{D}}$ is a place typing function, where $\mathcal{K}_{\mathfrak{D}}$ is a set of all possible cartesian products $\mathcal{D}_1 \times \ldots \times \mathcal{D}_m$, s.t. $\mathcal{D}_i \in \mathfrak{D}$, for each $i = 1, \ldots, m$;
3. $F_{in} : P \times T \rightarrow \Omega_{\mathcal{V}_{\mathfrak{D}}}^{\oplus}$ is an input flow, s.t. $\text{type}(F_{in}(p,t)) = \text{color}(p)$ for every $(p,t) \in P \times T$;
4. $F_{out} : T \times P \rightarrow \Omega_{\Delta_{\mathfrak{D}}}^{\oplus}$ is an output flow, s.t. $\text{type}(F_{out}(t,p)) = \text{color}(p)$ for every $(t,p) \in T \times P$;
5. $\text{guard} : T \rightarrow \mathcal{L}$ is a partial guard assignment function, assigning each transition t to a formula $\text{guard}(t) = \varphi(\underline{x})$ in the logic $\mathcal{L}$, s.t. the every variable x in φ is a variable appearing in the input inscriptions of t, i.e. $Vars(\varphi) \subseteq InVars(t)$, where $InVars(t) = \cup_{p \in P} Vars(F_{in}(p,t))$.

We also define $OutVars(t) := \cup_{p \in P} Vars(F_{out}(t,p))$ and $Vars(t) := InVars(t) \cup OutVars(t)$.

The definition from [171] have some common elements, but the are different when coming to way the data carried by tokens are inspected, manipulated and generated.

Guards are used to impose *conditions* (using φ) on tokens flowing through the net. As customary in high-level Petri nets, using the same variable in two different arc inscriptions amounts to checking the equality between the respective components of such inscriptions. For every transition $t \in T$, we also define $^{\bullet}t = \{p \in P \mid (p,t) \in \text{DOM}(F_{in})\}$ as a *pre-set* of t and $t^{\bullet} = \{p \in P \mid (t,p) \in \text{DOM}(F_{out})\}$ as a *post-set* of t.[1]

10.2.4 Semantics of CPNs

We now give the execution semantics of a CPN. Ss a first step we introduce the standard notion of net marking. Formally, a *marking* of a CPN $N = (\mathfrak{D}, \mathcal{L}, P, T, F_{in}, F_{out}, \text{color}, \text{guard})$ is a function $m : P \rightarrow \Omega_{\mathfrak{D}}^{\oplus}$, so that $m(p) \in \Delta_{\text{color}(p)}^{\oplus}$ for every $p \in P$. We write $\langle N, m \rangle$ to denote a CPN N marked with m.

---

[1] DOM(f) denotes a domain of function f.

The firing of a transition t in a marking is defined w.r.t. a so-called *binding* for t defined as $\sigma : Vars(t) \to \Delta_{\mathfrak{D}}$, where . Note that, when applied to (multisets of) tuples, σ is applied to every variable singularly. For example, given $\sigma = \{x \mapsto 1, y \mapsto \mathsf{a}\}$, its application to a multiset of tuples $\omega = \{\langle x, y\rangle^2, \langle x, \mathsf{b}\rangle\}$ results in $\sigma(\omega) = \{\langle 1, \mathsf{a}\rangle^2, \langle 1, \mathsf{b}\rangle\}$.

We now define when a transition can be called *enabled*. Essentially, a transition is enabled with a binding σ if the binding selects data objects carried by tokens from the input places, so that the data they carry make the guard attached to the transition valid in $\mathcal{L}$.

Definition 10.2 A transition $t \in T$ is *enabled* in a marking m, written $m[t\rangle$, if there exists binding σ satisfying the following: *(i)* $\sigma(F_{in}(p, t)) \subseteq m(p)$, for every $p \in P$; *(ii)* $\sigma(\mathsf{guard}(t))$ is $\mathcal{L}$-valid;

When a transition t is enabled, it may fire. Next we define what are the effects of firing a transition with some binding σ.

Definition 10.3 Let $\langle N, m\rangle$ be a marked CPN, and $t \in T$ a transition enabled in m with some binding σ. Then, t may *fire* producing a new marking m', with $m'(p) = m(p) - \sigma(F_{in}(p, t)) + \sigma(F_{out}(t, p))$ for every $p \in P$. We denote this as $m[t\rangle m'$ and assume that the definition is inductively extended to sequences $\tau \in T^*$.

For $\langle N, m_0\rangle$ we use $\mathcal{M}(N) = \{m \mid \exists \tau \in T^*.m_0[\tau\rangle m\}$ to denote the set of all markings of N reachable from its initial marking m_0.

10.2.5 Execution Semantics of CPNs

The execution semantics of a marked CPN $\langle N, m_0\rangle$ is defined in terms of a (possibly) infinite-state transition system where states are labeled by reachable markings and each arc (or transition) corresponds to the firing of a transition in N with a given binding. The transition system captures all possible executions of the net, by interpreting concurrency as interleaving. Formally, let $\langle N, m_0\rangle$ be a marked CPN. Then its execution semantics is described by the transition system $\Lambda_N = (S, s_0, \Rightarrow)$, where:

- S is a possibly infinite set of markings over N;
- $\Rightarrow \subseteq S \times T \times S$ is a T-labelled transition relation between pairs of markings;
- S and $\Rightarrow$ are defined by simultaneous induction as the smallest sets satisfying the following conditions: *(i)* $m_0 \in S$; *(ii)* given $m \in S$, for every transition $t \in T$, binding σ and marking m' over N, if $m[t\rangle m'$, then $m' \in S$ and $m \overset{t}{\Rightarrow} m'$.

Chapter 11
DABs: a Theoretical Framework for Data-Aware BPMN

In this chapter, we present the first application to business processes of the formal verification framework presented in Part I. Specifically, we define a general model of Data-Aware Processes, called DAB, which is a theoretical extension of the BPMN language with full-fledged relational data. We also show how DABs can be translated into RASs, so as to transfer the verification results for RASs described in Part I to this BPMN-oriented model. DABs are similar in spirit to artifact systems concerning the treatment of relational data, but employ a fragment of the BPMN language to express the process schema. We state in Section 11.1 the main contributions that we provide by introducing DABs.

The DAB framework is a theoretical framework that can be seen as the BPMN counterpart of RASs. In the next chapter, we will introduce an operational and implemented framework, called delta-BPMN, that can be seen as the practice-oriented version of DABs.

The content of this chapter was first presented in [49].

11.1 Data-Aware BPMN: Main Contributions

The main question that we intend to answer in this chapter is the following: *how to extend BPMN towards data support, guaranteeing the applicability of the existing parameterized verification techniques and the corresponding actual verifiers?* We answer this question by introducing a BPMN-styled theoretical framework for modeling and verifying data-aware processes (DAPs).

Specifically, this chapter is devoted to introducing a data-aware extension of (a significant fragment of) BPMN, called Data-Aware BPMN (DAB), which supports *case data* (i.e. data relevant to a specific process instance), as well as persistent relational data partitioned into a read-only *catalog* and a read-write *repository*, as explained below.

In DABs the process component is formalized using a *block-structured* version of the standard BPMN language: focusing on block-structured components helps

A. Gianola: *Verification of Data-Aware Processes via Satisfiability Modulo Theories*, LNBIP 470, pp. 213–238, 2023.
https://doi.org/10.1007/978-3-031-42746-6_11

us in obtaining a direct execution semantics, and a consequent modular and clean automatic translation of various BPMN constructs (including boundary events and exception handling): the possibility of having a modular automatic translation will be crucial when we implement this theoretical framework in delta-BPMN, as explained in the next chapter. However, it is important to stress that our theoretical approach for DABs would seamlessly work also for non-structured processes where each case introduces boundedly many tokens. Data are represented as a full-fledged relational database in line with the data- and artifact-centric tradition [47, 99], and hence the theoretical framework of Part I. Consistently with this literature, the running process evolves a set of relations (i.e., the read-write *repository*) comprising data objects that may have been injected from the external environment (e.g., due to user interaction), or borrowed from a read-only relational database with constraints (i.e., the read-only *catalog*). The repository behaves as a working memory and a process log: it contains data that can evolve during the process execution and it may accumulate unboundedly many tuples resulting from complex constructs in the process, such as while loops whose repeated activities insert new tuples in the repository (e.g., the applications sent by candidates in response to a job offer). The catalog, instead, stores background, contextual facts that do not change during the evolution of the system, such as the catalog of product types, the usernames and passwords of registered customers in an order-to-cash process. Case and persistent data are used to express conditions in the process as well as task preconditions; tasks, in turn, change the values of the case variables and interact with the repository via queries and updates.

By leveraging the formal framework of Part I, we encode DABs into RASs. Thanks to this encoding, we can effectively verify safety properties of DABs using directly MCMT on the so obtained corresponding RASs.

Then, using this encoding and the results presented for RASs in Chapter 4, we show that backward reachability is sound and complete when it comes to checking safety of DABs as well. In this context, soundness means that whenever the procedure terminates the returned answer is correct, whereas completeness means that if the process is unsafe then the procedure will always discover it.

In order to guarantee termination, we finally introduce further conditions, expressed as syntactic restrictions over the DAB under study, thus providing a BPMN-grounded counterpart of what imposed in [186] and presented in Section 5.2.1 (e.g., the locality condition). Under these conditions, checking safety for the class of DABs becomes decidable.

In the next sections we first formally define the DAB model (Section 11.2), by presenting the data schema, the process schema and the update logic layer, and we give some examples of DABs inspired by concrete business processes. We then introduce the safety verification problem for DABs (Subsection 11.3.2), we provide a high-level presentation of the encoding of DABs into RASs (Subsection 11.3.3), and we describe the inherited verification results for DABs (Subsection 11.3.4), comprising soundness, completeness and decidability results. To show that our approach goes end-to-end from theory to actual verification, in Section 11.4 we finally conclude the chapter reporting some preliminary experiments demonstrating how MCMT checks safety of DABs.

11.2 Data-Aware BPMN

We start by describing our formal model of data-aware BPMN processes (DABs). Since this model will be then mapped to RASs, during the presentation we will continuously highlight the correspondence existing among some features of DABs and their counterparts in RASs.

We focus here on private, single-pool processes, analyzed considering a single case, similarly to soundness analysis in workflow nets [244].[1] Incoming messages are therefore handled as pure nondeterministic events. The model combines a wide range of (block-structured) BPMN control-flow constructs with task, event-reaction, and condition logic that inspect and modify persistent as well as case data. Given the aim of our approach, recall that if something is not supported in the language, it is because it would hamper soundness and completeness of SMT-based (parameterized) verification.

First, some preliminary notation used in this chapter. We consider a set $S = S_v \uplus S_{id}$ of (semantic) *types*, consisting of *primitive types* S_v accounting for data objects, and *id types* S_{id} accounting for identifiers. Intuitively, the reader can think of id types and primitive types as corresponding to id sorts and value sorts in DB schemata, respectively (cf. Part I). We assume that each type $S \in S$ comes with a domain $\mathbb{D}_S$ (finite when $S \in S_{id}$ and possibly infinite when $S \in S_v$), a special constant $\mathsf{undef}_S \in \mathbb{D}_S$ to denote an undefined value in that domain, and a type-wise equality operator $=_S$. We omit the type and simply write undef and $=$ when clear from the context. We do not consider here additional type-specific predicates (such as comparison and arithmetic operators for numerical primitive types); these will be added in future work. In the following, we simply use *typed* as a shortcut for S-*typed*. We also denote by $\mathbb{D}$ the overall domain of objects and identifiers (i.e., the union of all domains in S). We consider a countably infinite set $\mathcal{V}$ of typed variables. Given a variable or object x, we may explicitly indicate that x has type S by writing $x : S$. We omit types whenever clear or irrelevant. We compactly indicate a possibly empty tuple $\langle x_1, \ldots, x_n \rangle$ of variables as $\mathbf{x}$, and with slight abuse of notation, we write $\mathbf{x} \subseteq \mathbf{y}$ if all variables in $\mathbf{x}$ also appear in $\mathbf{y}$.

11.2.1 The Data Schema

Consistently with the BPMN standard, we consider two main forms of data: *case data*[2], instantiated and manipulated on a per-case basis; *persistent data* (cf. data store references in BPMN), accounting for global data that are accessed by all cases. For simplicity, case data are defined at the whole process level, and are directly visible

---

[1] The interplay among multiple cases is also crucial. The technical report [50] already contains an extension of the framework presented here, in which multiple cases are modeled and verified.

[2] These are called *data objects* in BPMN, but we prefer to use the term *case data* to avoid name clashes with the formal notions.

by all tasks and subprocesses (without requiring the specification of input-output bindings and the like).

To account for persistent data, we consider relational databases. Similarly to what done in Section 3.1, we describe relation schemas by using the *named perspective*, i.e., by assigning a dedicated typed attribute to each component (i.e., column) of a relation schema. Also for an attribute, we use the notation $a : S$ to explicitly indicate its type. In the following definitions, we employ the dot notation R.field to denote specific 'fields' of a relation R such as its name, its attributes, or its id, as they will be defined in the following.

Definition 11.1 (DAB Relation Schema) A *relation schema* is a pair $R = \langle N, A \rangle$, where: *(i)* $N = R$.name is the relation *name*; *(ii)* $A = R$.attrs is a nonempty tuple of attributes.

We call $|A|$ the *arity* of R. We assume that distinct relation schemas use distinct names, blurring the distinction between the two notions (i.e., we set R.name $= R$). We also use the predicate notation $R(A)$ to represent a relation schema $\langle R, A \rangle$. An example of a relation schema is given by $User(Uid$:Int, $Name$:String), where the first component represents the id-number of a user, whereas the second component is the string formed by her name.

11.2.1.1 Data schema

First of all, we define the *catalog*, i.e., a read-only, persistent storage of data that is not modified during the execution of the process. Such a storage could contain, for example, the catalog of product types and the set of registered customers and their addresses in an order-to-cash scenario.

Definition 11.2 (DAB Catalog) A *catalog Cat* is a set of relation schemas satisfying the following requirements:
(single-column primary key) Every relation schema R is such that the first attribute in R.attrs has type in S_{id}, and denotes the *primary key* of the relation; we refer to such attribute using the dot notation R.id.
(non-ambiguity of primary keys) for every pair R_1 and R_2 of *distinct* relation schemas in Cat, we have that the types of R_1.id and R_2.id are different.
(foreign keys) for every relation schema $R \in Cat$ and non-id attribute $a \in R$.attrs $\setminus$ R.id with type $S \in S_{id}$, there exists a relation schema $R_2 \in \mathcal{R}$ such that the type of R_2.id is S; a is hence a *foreign key* referring to R_2.

For additional details on the notions of primary and foreign keys in classical relational databases, see Section 2.7. Notice that in the RAS framework, the catalog corresponds to the (read-only) DB schema of a RAS: however, a catalog is formed of relational symbols and no function symbol, whereas DB schemata usually use an algebraic representation of relations via unary function symbols (cf. Part I). We already remarked in Section 3.1 that these two different representations for full-fledged relational database are essentially equivalent and interchangeable.

From now on, we assume that, whenever a variable x from $\mathcal{V}$ of type $S \in S_{id}$ is considered (where S is the id sort R.id for some relation R in the catalog), either it takes values over the active domain of S or it is equal to undef$_S$ (see Chapters 2 ad 3 for details on 'active domain'). This is also in line with variable assignments in relational databases for RASs (Chapter 3).

Example 11.1 Consider an alternative version of the running example of the book, i.e. a simplified job hiring process in a company. To represent information related to the process we make use of the *Cat* consisting of the following relation schemas:

- *JobCategory*(*Jcid*:jobcatID) contains the different job categories available in the company (e.g., programmer, analyst, and the like) - we just store here the identifiers of such categories;
- *User*(*Uid*:userID, *Name*:StringName, *Age*:NumAge) stores data about users registered to the company website, and who are potentially interested in job positions offered by the company.

Each case of the process is about a job. Jobs are identified by the type jobcatID.

We now define the data schema of a BPMN process, which combines a catalog with: *(i)* a persistent data *repository*, consisting of updatable relation schemas possibly referring to the catalog; *(ii)* a set of *case variables*, constituting local data carried by each process case.

Definition 11.3 (DAB Data Schema) A *data schema* d is a tuple $\langle Cat, Repo, X \rangle$, where *(i)* *Cat* = d.cat is a *catalog*, *(ii)* *Repo* = d.repo is a set of relation schemas called *repository*, and *(iii)* X = d.cvars $\subset \mathcal{V}$ is a finite set of typed variables called *case variables*, such that:

- for every relation schema $R \in Repo$ and every attribute $a \in R$.attrs whose type is $S \in S_{id}$, there exists $R' \in Cat$ such that the type of R'.id is S;
- for every case variable $\mathbf{x} \in X$ whose type is $S \in S_{id}$, there exists $R \in Cat$ such that the type of R.id is S.

We use bold-face to distinguish a case variable $\mathbf{x}$ from a "normal" variable x. It is worth noting that relation schemas in the repository are not equipped with an explicit primary key, and thus they cannot reference each other, but may contain foreign keys pointing to the catalog or the case identifiers. *This is essential toward soundness and completeness of SMT-based verification of DABs.* It will be clear how tuples can be inserted and removed from the repository once we will introduce updates.

Since the repository represents a set of evolving relations of the system, they natively correspond to artifact relations (and hence to artifact components) of the RAS framework (see Section 3.2.2 for details). Similarly, case variables correspond to artifact variables in RASs.

Example 11.2 To manage key information about the applications submitted for the job hiring, the company employs a repository that consists of one relation schema:

Application(*Jcid*:JobcatID, *Uid*:UserID, *Score*:NumScore, *Eligible*:Bool)

NumScore is a finite-domain type containing 100 scores in the range $[1, 100]$. For readability, we use the usual comparison predicates for variables of type NumScore: as we discussed for the RAS version of this example, this is again syntactic sugar and does not require to introduce datatype predicates in our framework. Since each posted job is created using a dedicated portal, its corresponding data do not have to be stored persistently and thus can be maintained just for a given case. At the same time, some specific values have to be moved from a specific case to the repository and vice-versa. This is done by resorting to the following case variables d.cvars: *(i)* **jcid** : jobcatID references a job type from the catalog, matching the type of job associated to the case; *(ii)* **uid** : userID references the identifier of a user who is applying for the job associated to the case; *(iii)* **result** : Bool indicates whether the user identified by **uid** is eligible for winning the position or not; *(iv)* **qualif** : Bool indicates whether the user identified by **uid** qualifies for directly getting the job (without the need of carrying out a comparative evaluation of all applicants); *(v)* **winner** : userID contains the identifier of the applicant winning the position.

At runtime, a *data snapshot* of a data schema consists of three components:
- An immutable *catalog instance*, i.e., a fixed set of tuples for each relation schema contained therein, so that the primary and foreign keys are satisfied.
- An assignment mapping case variables to corresponding data objects.
- A *repository instance*, i.e., a set of tuples forming a relation for each schema contained therein, so that the foreign key constraints pointing to the catalog are satisfied. Each tuple is associated to a distinct primary key that is not explicitly accessible.

11.2.1.2 Querying the data schema

To inspect the data contained in a snapshot, we need suitable query languages operating over the data schema of that snapshot. We start by considering boolean *conditions* over (case) variables. These conditions will be attached to choice points in the process.

Definition 11.4 (DAB condition) A *condition* is a formula of the form $\varphi ::= (x = y) \mid \neg\varphi \mid \varphi_1 \wedge \varphi_2$, where x and y are variables from $\mathcal{V}$ or constant objects from $\mathbb{D}$.

We make use of the standard abbreviation $\varphi_1 \vee \varphi_2 = \neg(\neg\varphi_1 \wedge \neg\varphi_2)$.

We now extend conditions to also access the data stored in the catalog and repository, and to ask for data objects subject to constraints. We consider the well-known language of unions of conjunctive queries with atomic negation, which correspond to unions of select-project-join SQL queries with table filters (as it will be clearer when the operational counterpart of DABs, i.e., the delta-BPMN framework, will be introduced).

Definition 11.5 (DAB Conjunctive Queries) A *conjunctive query with filters* over a data component d is a formula of the form $Q ::= \varphi \mid R(x_1, \ldots, x_n) \mid \neg R(x_1, \ldots, x_n) \mid$

$S(x_1, \ldots, x_n) \mid Q_1 \wedge Q_2$, where φ is a condition with only *atomic* negation, $R \in$ d.cat and $S \in$ d.repo are relation schemas of arity n, and $x_1, \ldots, x_n$ are variables from $\mathcal{V}$ (including d.cvars) or constant objects from $\mathbb{D}$. We denote by *free*(Q) the set of variables occurring in Q that are *not* case variables in d.cvars.

For example, a conjunctive query *JobCategory*$(jt) \wedge jt \neq$ HR lists all the job categories available in the company, apart from HR.

Definition 11.6 (DAB Guard) A *guard* G over a data component d is an expression of the form $q(\mathbf{x}) \leftarrow \bigvee_{i=1}^{n} Q_i$, where: *(i)* $q(\mathbf{x})$ is the *head* of the guard with *answer variables* $\mathbf{x}$; *(ii)* each Q_i is a conjunctive query with filters over d; *(iii)* for some $i \in \{1, \ldots, n\}$, $\mathbf{x} \subseteq$ *free*(Q_i). We denote by *casevars*$(G) \subseteq$ d.cvars the set of case variables used in G, and by *normvars*$(G) = \bigcup_{i \in \{1, \ldots, n\}}$ *free*(Q_i) the other variables used in G.

To distinguish guard heads from relations, we write the former in camel case, while the latter shall always begin with capital letters.

Definition 11.7 A *guard* G over a data component d is *repo-free* if none of its atoms queries a relation schema from d.repo. A *guard* G is said to be *boolean* when its head q is a boolean value.

Notice that *going beyond this guard query language* (e.g., by introducing universal quantification) *would hamper the soundness and completeness of SMT-based verification over the resulting DABs*.

As anticipated before, this language can be seen as a standard (but still quite abstract) query language to retrieve data from a snapshot, but also as a mechanism to constrain the combinations of data objects that can be injected into the process. E.g., a simple guard *input*$(y$:string, z:string$) \rightarrow y \neq z$ returns all pairs of strings that are different from each other. Picking an answer in this (infinite) set of pairs can be interpreted as a (constrained) user input where the user decides the values for y and z. Injected data (like user inputs) can be represented in DABs thanks to the presence of *answer variables ranging over the catalog*: formally, these variables correspond to *existentially quantified data variables* ranging over the read-only DB in the RAS framework. We remind the reader that these variables need to be specifically treated by our versions of the backward reachability procedure, which for this aim employ suitable algorithms for quantifier elimination/cover computation (see Chapters 4 and 7 for details on this).

11.2.2 Tasks, Events, and Impact on Data

We now formalize how the process can access and update the data component when executing a task or reacting to the trigger of an external event.

11.2.2.1 The update logic

We start by discussing how data maintained in a snapshot can be subject to change while executing the process.

Definition 11.8 (DAB Updates) Given a data schema d, an *update specification* α is a pair $\langle G, E \rangle$, where: *(i)* $G = \alpha$.pre is a guard over d of the form $q(\mathbf{x}) \leftarrow Q$, called *precondition*; *(ii)* $E = \alpha$.eff is an *effect rule* that changes the snapshot of d, as described next. Each effect rule has one of the following forms:

(Insert&Set) INSERT $\mathbf{u}$ INTO R AND SET $\mathbf{x}_1 = v_1, \ldots, \mathbf{x}_n = v_n$, where: *(i)* $\mathbf{u}, \mathbf{v}$ are variables in $\mathbf{x}$, case variables or constant objects from $\mathbb{D}$; *(ii)* $\mathbf{x} \in$ d.cvars are distinct case variables; *(iii)* R is a relation schema from d.repo whose arity (and types) match $\mathbf{u}$. Either the INSERT or SET parts may be omitted, obtaining a pure **Insert rule** or **Set rule**.

(Delete&Set) DEL $\mathbf{u}$ FROM R AND SET $\mathbf{x}_1 = v_1, \ldots, \mathbf{x}_n = v_n$, where: *(i)* $\mathbf{u}, \mathbf{v}$ are variables in $\mathbf{x}$ or constant objects from $\mathbb{D}$; *(ii)* $\mathbf{x} \in$ d.cvars; *(iii)* R is a relation schema from d.repo whose arity (and types) match $\mathbf{u}$. As in the previous rule type, the AND SET part may be omitted, obtaining a pure (repository) **Delete rule**.

(Conditional update) UPDATE $R(\mathbf{v})$ IF $\psi(\mathbf{u}, \mathbf{v})$ THEN η_1 ELSE η_2, where: *(i)* $\mathbf{u}$ is a tuple containing variables in $\mathbf{x}$ or constant objects from $\mathbb{D}$; *(ii)* ψ is a repo-free guard (called *filter*); *(iii)* R is a relation schema from d.repo; *(iv)* $\mathbf{v}$ is a tuple of new variables, i.e., such that $\mathbf{v} \cap (\mathbf{u} \cup$ d.cvars$) = \emptyset$; *(v)* η_i is either an atomic formula of the form $R(\mathbf{u}')$ with $\mathbf{u}'$ a tuple of elements from $\mathbf{x} \cup \mathbb{D} \cup \mathbf{v}$, or a nested IF $\ldots$ THEN $\ldots$ ELSE.

We now comment on the semantics of update specifications. An update specification α is executable in a given data snapshot if there is at least one answer to the precondition α.pre in that snapshot. If this is the case, then the process executor(s) can nondeterministically decide which answer to pick so as to *bind* the answer variables of α.pre to corresponding data objects in $\mathbb{D}$. This confirms the interpretation discussed in Section 11.2.1 for which the answer variables of α.pre can be seen as *constrained user inputs* in case multiple bindings are available.

Once a specific binding for the answer variables is selected, the corresponding effect rule α.eff, instantiated using that binding, is issued. How this affects the current data snapshot depends on which effect rule is adopted.

If α.eff is an insert&set rule, the binding is used to *simultaneously* insert a tuple in one of the repository relations, and update some of the case variables – with the implicit assumption that those not explicitly mentioned in the SET part maintain their current values. Since repository relations do not have an explicit primary key, two possible semantics can be attached to the insertion of a tuple $\mathbf{u}$ in the instance of a repository relation R:

(multiset insertion) Upon insertion, $\mathbf{u}$ gets an implicit, fresh primary key. The insertion then always results in the genuine addition of the tuple to the current instance of R, even in the case where the tuple already exists there.

(set insertion) In this case, R comes not only with its implicit primary key, but also with an additional, genuine key constraint defined over a subset $K \subseteq R.\text{attrs}$ of its attributes. Upon insertion, if there already exists a tuple in the current instance of R that agrees with $\mathbf{u}$ on K, then that tuple is *updated* according to $\mathbf{u}$. If no such tuple exists, then as in the previous case $\mathbf{u}$ gets implicitly assigned to a fresh primary key, and inserted into the current instance of R. By default, if no explicit key is defined over R, then the entire set of attributes $R.\text{attrs}$ is considered as a key, consequently enforcing a *set semantics* for insertion.

Example 11.3 We continue the job hiring example, by considering two update specifications of type insert&set. When a new case is created, the first update is about indicating what is the category of job associated to the case. This is done through the update specification `InsJobCat`, where `InsJobCat.pre` selects a job category from the corresponding catalog relation, while `InsJobCat.eff` assigns the selected job category to the case variable **jcid**:

$$\text{InsJobCat.pre} \triangleq getJobType(c) \leftarrow JobCategory(c)$$
$$\text{InsJobCat.eff} \triangleq \text{SET } \mathbf{jcid} = c$$

When the case receives an application, the user id is picked from the corresponding *User* via the update specification `InsUser`, where:

$$\text{InsUser.pre} \triangleq getUser(u) \leftarrow User(u, n, a)$$
$$\text{InsUser.eff} \triangleq \text{SET } \mathbf{uid} = u$$

A different usage of precondition, resembling a pure external choice, is the update specification `CheckQual` to handle a quick evaluation of the candidate and check whether she has such a high profile qualifying her to directly get an offer:

$$\text{CheckQual.pre} \triangleq isQualified(q : \text{Bool}) \leftarrow \texttt{true}$$
$$\text{CheckQual.eff} \triangleq \text{SET } \mathbf{qualif} = q$$

As an example of insertion rule, we consider the situation where the candidate whose id is currently stored in the case variable **uid** has not been directly judged as qualified. She is consequently subject to a more fine-grained evaluation of her application, resulting in a score that is then registered in the repository (together with the applicant data). This is done via the `EvalApp` specification:

$$\text{EvalApp.pre} \triangleq getScore(s : \text{NumScore}) \leftarrow 1 \leq s \wedge s \leq 100$$
$$\text{EvalApp.eff} \triangleq \text{INSERT } \langle \mathbf{jcid}, \mathbf{uid}, s, \text{undef} \rangle \text{ INTO } Application$$

Here, the insertion indicates an undef eligibility, since it will be assessed in a consequent step of the process.

Notice that, by adopting the *multiset insertion semantics*, the same user may apply multiple times for the same job (resulting multiple times as applicant). With a *set insertion semantics*, we could enforce the uniqueness of the application by declaring the second component (i.e., the user id) of *Application* as a key.

If α.eff is a delete&set rule, then the executability of the update is subject to the fact that the tuple **u** selected by the binding and to be removed from R, is actually present in the current instance of R. If so, the binding is used to *simultaneously* delete **u** from R and update some of the case variables – with the implicit assumption that those not explicitly mentioned in the SET part maintain their current values.

Finally, a conditional update rule applies, tuple by tuple, a bulk operation over the content of R. For each tuple in R, if it passes the filter associated to the rule, then the tuple is updated according to the THEN part, whereas if the filter evaluates to false, the tuple is updated according to the ELSE part.

Example 11.4 Continuing with our running example, we now consider the update specification MarkE handling the situation where no candidate has been directly considered as qualified, and so the eligibility of all received (and evaluated) applications has to be assessed. Here we consider that each application is eligible if and only if its evaluation resulted in a score greater than 80. Technically, MarkE.pre is a true precondition, and:

$$\text{MarkE.eff} \triangleq \text{UPDATE } Application(jc,u,s,e)$$
$$\text{IF} s > 80 \text{ THEN } Application(jc,u,s,\texttt{true})$$
$$\text{ELSE } Application(jc,u,s,\texttt{false})$$

If there is at least one eligible candidate, she can be selected as a winner using the SelWinner update specification, which deletes the selected winner tuple from *Application*, and transfers its content to the corresponding case variables (also ensuring that the **winner** case variable is set to the applicant id). Technically:

$$\text{SelWinner.pre} \triangleq getWinner(jc,u,s,e) \leftarrow Application(jc,u,s,e)$$
$$\wedge\, e = \texttt{true}$$
$$\text{SelWinner.eff} \triangleq \text{DEL } \langle jc,u,s,e \rangle \text{ FROM } Application$$
$$\text{AND SET } \textbf{jcid} = jc, \textbf{uid} = u, \textbf{winner} = u,$$
$$\textbf{result} = e, \textbf{qualif} = \texttt{false}$$

Deleting the tuple is useful in the situation where the selected winner may refuse the job, and consequently should not be considered again if a new winner selection is carried out. To keep such tuple in the repository, one would just need to remove the DEL part from SelWinner.eff.

Notice that all these types of updates are in line with the operations that are supported by RASs (see Section 5.3 for details): we notice that the nomenclature for DABs and for RASs is almost identical, apart from DAB conditional updates that corresponds to bulk updates in the RAS framework.

11.2.2.2 The task/event logic

We now substantiate how the update logic is used to specify the task/event logic within a DAB process. The first important observation, not related to our specific approach, but inherently present whenever the process control flow is enriched with relational data, is that update effects manipulating the repository must be executed in an atomic, non-interruptible way. This is essential to ensure that insertions/deletions into/from the repository are applied on the same data snapshot where the precondition is checked, in accordance with the standard *transactional semantics* of relational updates. Breaking simultaneity would lead to nondeterministic interleave with other update specifications potentially operating over the same portion of the repository. This is why in our approach we consider two types of task: *atomic* and *nonatomic*.

Each atomic task/catching event is associated to a corresponding update specification. In the case of tasks, the specification precondition indicates under which circumstances the task can be enacted, and the specification effect how enacting the task impacts on the underlying data snapshot. In the case of events, the specification precondition constrains the data payload that comes with the event (possibly depending on the data snapshot, which is global and therefore accessible also from the perspective of an external event trigger), and the specification effect how reacting to a triggered event impacts on the underlying data snapshot. More concretely, this is realized according to the following lifecycle.

The task/event is initially `idle`, i.e., quiescent. When the progression of a case reaches an `idle` task/event, such a task/event becomes `enabled`. An `enabled` task/event may nondeterministically fire depending on the choice of the process executor(s). Upon firing, a binding satisfying the precondition of the update specification associated to the task/event is selected, consequently grounding and applying the corresponding effect. At the same time, the lifecycle moves from `enabled` to `compl`. Finally, a `compl` task/event triggers the progression of its case depending on the process-control flow, simultaneously bringing the task/event back to the `idle` state (which would then make it possible for the task to be executed again later, if the process control-flow dictates so).

The lifecycle of a nonatomic task diverges in two crucial respects. First of all, upon firing it moves from `enabled` to `active`, and later on nondeterministically from `active` to `compl` (thus having a duration). The precondition of its update specification is checked and bound to one of the available answers when the task becomes `active`, while the corresponding effect is applied when the task becomes `compl`. Since these two transitions occur asynchronously, to avoid the aforementioned transactional issues we assume that the effect operates, in this context, only on case variables (and not on the repository).

11.2.3 Process Schema

A process schema consists of a block-structured BPMN diagram, enriched with conditions and update effects expressed over a given data schema, according to what described in the previous sections. As for the control flow, we consider a wide range of block-structured patterns compliant with the standard. We focus on private BPMN processes, thereby handling incoming messages in a pure nondeterministic

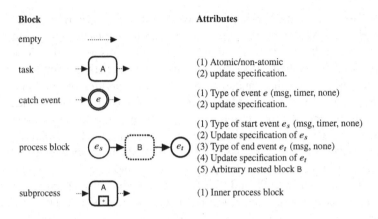

Fig. 11.1: DAB Basic blocks

way. So we do for timer events, nondeterministically accounting for their expiration without entering into their metric temporal semantics. Focusing on block-structured components helps us in obtaining a direct, execution semantics, and a consequent modular and clean translation of various BPMN constructs (including boundary events and exception handling). However, it is important to stress that our approach would seamlessly work also for non-structured processes where each case introduces boundedly many tokens, or in the case where the control-flow backbone of the process is captured using a Petri net, as we will see in Chapter 13.

As usual, blocks are recursively decomposed into sub-blocks, the leaves being task or empty blocks. Depending on its type, a block may come with one or more nested blocks, and be associated with other elements, such as conditions, types of the involved events, and the like. We consider a wide range of blocks, covering basic (cf. Figure 11.1), flow (cf. Figure 11.2), and exception handling (cf. Figure 11.3) patterns. Figure 11.4 gives an idea about what is covered by our approach. With these blocks at hand, we finally obtain the full definition of a DAB.

Definition 11.9 (DAB) A DAB $\mathcal{M}$ is a pair $\langle d, \mathcal{P} \rangle$ where d is a data schema, and $\mathcal{P}$ is a root *process block* such that all conditions and update effects attached to $\mathcal{P}$ and its descendant blocks are expressed over d.

Example 11.5 The full hiring job process is shown in Figure 11.4, using the update effects described in Examples 11.3 and 11.4. Intuitively, the process works as follows. A case is created when a job is posted, and enters into a looping subprocess where it expects candidates to apply. Specifically, the case waits for an incoming application, or for an external message signalling that the hiring has to be stopped (e.g., because too much time has passed from the posting). Whenever an application is received, the CV of the candidate is evaluated, with two possible outcomes. The first outcome indicates that the candidate directly qualifies for the position, hence no further applications should be considered. In this case, the process continues by declaring the candidate as winner, and making an offer to her. The second outcome of the CV

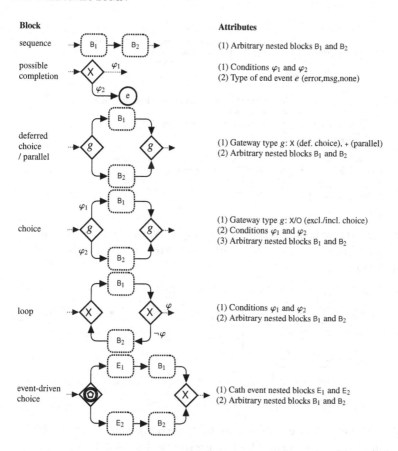

Fig. 11.2: Flow DAB blocks; for simplicity, we consider only two nested blocks, but multiple nested blocks can be seamlessly handled.

evaluation is instead that the candidate does not directly qualify. A more detailed evaluation is then carried out, assigning a score to the application and storing the outcome into the process repository, then waiting for additional applications to come. When the application management subprocess is stopped (which we model through an error so as to test various types of blocks in the experiments reported in Section 11.4), the applications present in the repository are all processed in parallel, declaring which candidates are eligible and which not depending on their scores. Among the eligible ones, a winner is then selected, making an offer to her. We implicitly assume here that at least one applicant is eligible, but we can easily extend the DAB to account also for the case where no application is eligible.

Example 11.6 We provide an additional example of an insurance claim process, depicted in Figure 11.5. We formalize this process as a DAB with an empty repository. Intuitively, the process runs as follows. A case is created when a client sends an insurance claim to an insurance company handling car thefts. When the company

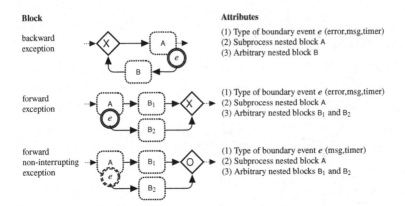

Fig. 11.3: DAB exception handling blocks; for simplicity, we show a single boundary event, but multiple boundary events and their corresponding handlers can be seamlessly handled.

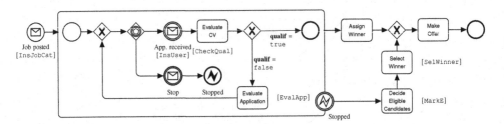

Fig. 11.4: The job hiring process. Elements in squared brackets attach the update specifications in Examples 11.3 and 11.4 to corresponding tasks/events.

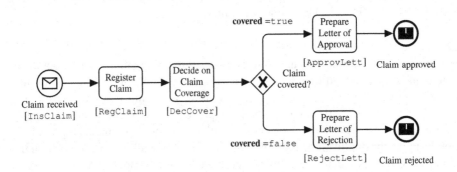

Fig. 11.5: The insurance claim process. Elements in squared brackets attach the update specifications in Example 11.6 to corresponding tasks/events.

receives the claim, it registers it in its information system. Then, the information of the client and of the claim are analyzed, and a decision is taken whether to cover the claim or not. Depending on the decision, the company prepares a letter of approval or of rejection, which is eventually sent back to the client. To take a decision on a received claim, the company requires to check the detailed information about the client and its contract.

Each submitted claim should contain data about the value of the stolen car. In addition, the claim should also contain data about the type of the client as well as the status of the contract (s)he has. This information is maintained by the persistent storage of the information system. We model this persistent storage as a catalog.

According to the catalog, there are three types of clients: Gold, Silver and Bronze. The company policy establishes that, for all the clients, all car thefts until a claim value of 20000€ are covered. Claims for value between 20000€ and 50000€ are covered for Silver and Gold clients only. Finally, claims up to 100000€ are only covered for Gold clients. Notice that the insurance company does not reimburse any claims beyond 100000€.

To represent information related to the process we make use of the catalog Cat_{claim} consisting of the following relation schemas (whose first attribute is the primary key):

- *Claim*(*Cid*:ClaimID, *ClaimAmount*:$\mathbb{Z}$), which stores the information about the possible claim types (i.e., the claimed amounts) that a client can demand.
- *Client*(*Clid*:ClientID, *TypeClient*:String) stores data about the clients registered to the insurance company website, and who can potentially send a claim.
- *Contract*(*Cnid*:ContractID, *ContractClient*:ClientID, *ContractStatus*:String) contains the description of the status of the contracts signed by the clients.

Each case of the process is an instance of an insurance claim. Claim types are identified by the type ClaimID. The process maintains a set of case variables that are used to store the information about the claim under examination: **cid** keeps track of the claim type, **clid** stores the client who sent the claim, **camount** and **cltype** contain the claimed amount of money and the type of the client who is requesting it, respectively; finally, the case variable **status** records the current status of the process, whereas **covered** is a boolean case variable that formalize whether the insurance can cover the claim or not.

We now formally define the update specifications of the process. When a new case is created, the first update is about selecting the ids of the claim type and of the client associated to the case. This is done through `InsClaim`, where `InsClaim`.pre retrieves the claim type id and the client id from the catalog relation *Client*, while `InsClaim`.eff assigns the selected claim and client ids to the case variables **cid** and **clid**, respectively:

$$\texttt{InsClaim.pre} \triangleq getClaim(c, cl) \leftarrow Claim(c, z) \wedge Client(cl, t)$$
$$\texttt{InsClaim.eff} \triangleq \text{SET } \textbf{cid} = c, \textbf{clid} = cl$$

Then, the information about the specific amount of money claimed by the client and about the type of the client are picked from the catalog relations *Claim* and *Client* via the update specification `RegClaim`, and are assigned to the corresponding case variables **camount** and **ctype**. Formally:

$$\texttt{RegClaim.pre} \triangleq getInfo(am, type) \leftarrow Claim(cid, am) \wedge Client(clid, type)$$
$$\texttt{RegClaim.eff} \triangleq \text{SET } \textbf{camount} = am, \textbf{cltype} = type, \textbf{status} = \text{registered}$$

After the information about the claim and the client is registered, the insurance company performs an activity to take a decision about whether the claim can be covered. This decision is based on the data stored in the case variables so far and on the status of the client's contract, which is recorded in the catalog relation *Contract*. In case the contract is still active and the claimed amounts are consistent with the type of the client, the claim can be covered and the case variable **covered** is set to `true`; otherwise, is set to `false`. The update specification attached to this activity is as follows:

$$
\begin{aligned}
\texttt{DecCover.pre} \triangleq\ & isCovered(q) \leftarrow ((\textbf{camount} \leq 100000 \land \textbf{cltype} = \text{Gold} \\
& \land Contract(cn, \textbf{clid}, \text{active}) \land q = \texttt{true}) \lor (\textbf{camount} \leq 50000 \\
& \land Contract(cn, \textbf{clid}, \text{active}) \land \textbf{cltype} = \text{Silver} \land q = \texttt{true}) \\
& \lor (\textbf{camount} \leq 20000 \land Contract(cn, \textbf{clid}, \text{active}) \land \\
& \land \textbf{cltype} = \text{Bronze} \land q = \texttt{true}) \lor q = \texttt{false}) \land \\
& \land \textbf{status} = \text{registered}
\end{aligned}
$$

$$
\texttt{DecCover.eff} \triangleq \text{SET } \textbf{covered} = q
$$

Then, the process execution is split into two branches by an exclusive choice gateway, depending on the value of the case variable **covered**: if **covered** has been set to `true`, the first branch is taken, otherwise the process flows along the second branch. In the former case, the company performs a task that consists of preparing a letter for the claim approval:

$$
\texttt{ApprovLett.pre} \triangleq getStatus(s) \leftarrow \textbf{covered} = \texttt{true} \land s = \text{approvletter}
$$
$$
\texttt{ApprovLett.eff} \triangleq \text{SET } \textbf{status} = s
$$

After this task, the letter is sent to the client and the process terminates in its first end event. In the latter case, a letter for rejection is written and sent to the client, so as to reach the second possible end event of the process. The update specification `RejectLett` for the task where the rejection letter is prepared is analogous to the previous one.

As customary, each block has a lifecycle that indicates the current state of the block, and how the state may evolve depending on the specific semantics of the block, and the evolution of its inner blocks. In Section 11.2.2 we have already characterized the lifecycle of tasks and catch events. For the other blocks, we continue to use the standard states `idle`, `enabled`, `active` and `compl`. We use the very same rules of execution described in the BPMN standard to regulate the progression of blocks through such states, taking advantage from the fact that, being the process block-structured, only one instance of a block can be enabled/active at a given time for a given case. In more details, each block is initially inactive and its state is `idle`. When a process instance, throughout its execution, reaches an `idle` block, it becomes `enabled`. This means that the `enabled` element may be then nondeterministically executed depending on the choice of the process executor(s). When the process instance has completed traversing the block, the block lifecycle state changes from `enabled` to `compl`. The `compl` element then advances the progression of the process instance following what is dictated by the parent block. In the exact same moment, the block changes its state back to idle. For example, the lifecycle of a sequence block S with nested blocks B_1 and B_2 can be described as follows (considering that the transitions of S from idle to enabled and from compl back to idle are inductively regulated by its parent block): *(i)* if S is enabled, then it becomes active, simultaneously inducing a transition of B_1 from idle to enabled; *(ii)* if B_1 is compl, then it becomes idle, simultaneously inducing a transition of B_2 from idle to enabled; *(iii)* if B_2 is compl, then it becomes idle, simultaneously inducing S to move from active to compl. The lifecycle of other block types can be defined analogously.

11.2.4 Execution Semantics

We intuitively describe the execution semantics of a case over DAB $\mathcal{M} = \langle d, \mathcal{P} \rangle$, using the update/task logic and progression rules of blocks as a basis. Upon execution, each state of $\mathcal{M}$ is characterized by an $\mathcal{M}$-*snapshot*, in turn constituted by a data snapshot of d (cf. Section 11.2.1), and a further assignment mapping each block in $\mathcal{P}$ to its current lifecycle state.

Initially, the data snapshot fixes the immutable content of the catalog d.cat, while the repository instance is empty, the case assignment is initialized to all undef, and the control assignment assigns to all blocks in $\mathcal{P}$ the idle state, with the exception of $\mathcal{P}$ itself, which is enabled. At each moment in time, the $\mathcal{M}$-snapshot is then evolved by nondeterministically evolving the case through one of the executable steps in the process, depending on the current $\mathcal{M}$-snapshot. If the execution step is about the progression of the case inside the process control-flow, then the control assignment is updated. If instead the execution step is about the application of some update effect, the new $\mathcal{M}$-snapshot is then obtained by following Section 11.2.2.

11.3 Parameterized Safety Verification of DABs

We now focus on parameterized verification of DABs using SMT-based techniques grounded in the theory of arrays: in this section, we show how to apply these techniques to DABs by first translating them into RASs and then by reducing the verification problem for DABs to the one for RASs.

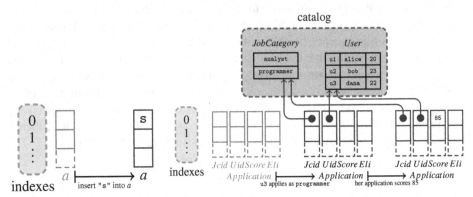

(a) Insertion of value "s" into an empty string array (b) Array-based representation of the job hiring repository of Example 11.2, and manipulation of a job application with a fixed catalog.

Fig. 11.6: Graphical intuition showing the evolution of different array-based systems. The current state of the array is represented in green, whereas consequent states resulting from updates are shown in blue and violet. Empty cells implicitly hold the undef value of their corresponding type.

11.3.1 Array-Based Artifact Systems and Safety Checking: a Brief Summary

We recall that the setting of Array-Based Artifact Systems presented in Chapter 3 bridges the gap between SMT-based model checking of array-based systems [143, 146], and verification of data- and artifact-centric processes [99, 102].

Summarizing the main intuitions behind array-based systems from Section 3.2, we remind the reader that an array-based system logically describes the evolution of arrays of unbounded size. For the sake of completeness and of clarity, we report here again Figure 11.6a, already used in Section 3.2 and intuitively showing a simple array-based system consisting of a single array storing strings. The logical representation of an array relies on a theory with two types of sorts, one accounting for the array indexes, and the other for the elements stored in the array cells. An array changes its content over time, and it is formalized using a *function* variable, called *array state variable*. The interpretation of such a variable in a state is that of a total function mapping indexes to elements: for each index, it returns the element stored by the array in that index. Starting from an initial configuration (formalized by a state formula $I(a)$), the interpretation changes through transitions (formalized by $\tau(a, a')$) when moving from one state to another, reflecting the intended manipulation on the array. In such a setting, the safety verification problem is that of checking whether the evolution induced by τ over a starting from a configuration in $I(a)$ eventually *reaches* one of the *unsafe* configurations described by a state formula $K(a)$.

In Chapter 3, we have extended array-based systems towards an array-based version of the artifact systems, considering in particular the sophisticated model in [186]. In the resulting formalism, called (Universal) RAS, a *relational* artifact system accesses a read-only database with keys and foreign keys (cf. our DAB catalog). In addition, it operates over a set of evolving relations possibly containing unboundedly many updatable entries (cf. our DAB repository). Figure 11.6b gives an intuitive idea of how this type of system looks like, using the catalog and repository relations from Example 11.2. On the one hand, the catalog is treated as a rich, background theory, which can be considered as a more sophisticated version of the element sort in basic array systems. On the other hand, each repository relation is treated as a set of arrays, in which each array accounts for one component of the corresponding repository relation. A tuple in the relation is reconstructed by accessing all such arrays with the same index. The cells of the arrays may point to identifiers in the catalog, in turn related to other catalog relations via foreign keys. In Chapter 4, we focused on parameterized (un)safety of (Universal) RASs, verifying whether there exists an instance of the read-only database such that the artifact system can reach an unsafe configuration, and we showed how to extend the standard backward reachability for successfully solve this problem. In the following subsection, we show how the RAS framework provides a natural foundational and practical basis to formally analyze and verify DABs.

11.3.2 Verification Problems for DABs

First, we need a language to express unsafety properties over a DAB $M = \langle d, \mathcal{P} \rangle$. Properties are expressed in a fragment of the *guard* language of Definition 11.6 that queries repo-relations and case variables as well as the cat-relations that tuples from repo-relations or case variables refer to. Properties also query the control state of $\mathcal{P}$. This is done by implicitly extending d with additional, special case *control variables* that refer to the lifecycle states of the blocks in $\mathcal{P}$ (where a block named B gets variable **B**lifecycle). Given a snapshot, each such variable is assigned to the lifecycle state of the corresponding block (i.e., idle, enabled, and the like). We use $F_{\mathcal{P}}$ to denote the set of all these additional case *control* variables.

Definition 11.10 (DAB Property) A *property* over $M = \langle d, \mathcal{P} \rangle$ is a guard G over d and the control variables of $\mathcal{P}$, such that every non-case variable in G also appears in a relational atom $R(y_1, \ldots, y_n)$, where either R is a repo-relation, or R is a cat-relation and $y_1 \in$ d.cvars.

Example 11.7 By naming *HP* the root process block of Figure 11.4, the property (**HP**lifecycle = completed) checks whether some case of the process can terminate. This property is *unsafe* for our hiring process, since there is at least one way to evolve the process from the start to the end. Since DAB processes are block structured, this is enough to ascertain that the hiring process is *sound*. Property **EvalApp**lifecycle = completed $\land$ *Application*$(j, u, s, \text{true}) \land s > 100$ describes instead the undesired situation where, after the evaluation of an application, there exists an applicant with score greater than 100. The hiring process is *safe* w.r.t. this property (cfr. the **5th** safe property from Section 11.4).

Example 11.8 Let us consider now the business process from Example 11.6. Property **covered** = false ∧ **status** = approvletter describes the undesired situation where, after the evaluation, it has been decided that the claim cannot be covered but a letter of approval has been prepared anyway. The claim process can be shown to be *safe* w.r.t. this property.

We study unsafety of these properties by considering the general case, and also the one where the repository can store only boundedly many tuples, with a fixed bound. In the latter case, we call the DAB *repo-bounded*.

11.3.3 Translating DABs into Array-Based Artifact Systems

Given an unsafety verification problem over a DAB $\mathcal{M} = \langle d, \mathcal{P} \rangle$, we encode it as a corresponding unsafety verification problem over a RAS that reconstructs the execution semantics of $\mathcal{M}$. For the sake of conciseness, we only provide here the main intuition behind the translation, which is fully addressed in the technical report [50]: indeed, the details are quite tedious (and, nevertheless, straightforward) and would detract attention from the main focus of this chapter, which is to provide a foundational framework for verifying data-aware business processes.

We remark that in the course of this chapter, whenever we introduced some feature of DABs, we carefully linked it to its RAS counterpart already. In the translation, d.cat and d.cvars are mapped into their corresponding abstractions in RAS (namely, the RAS read-only DB schema and 'artifact variables', respectively). Specifically, the relations from the DAB data schema are encoded into a corresponding RAS read-only database by employing the equivalent functional representation of typed relations with key dependencies supported by DB schemas (cf. Section 3.1): we will see that this is the systematic way that we exploit for translating relational databases into RASs or into the MCMT database-driven module (a completely analogous translation will be discussed in Chapter 13 for encoding the COA-net catalog into MCMT specifications). d.repo is instead encoded using the intuition of Figure 11.6b: for each $R \in$ d.repo and each attribute $a \in R$.attrs, a dedicated array is introduced: this array is called 'artifact component' in the RAS formalism, and each relation in the repository corresponds to an artifact relation for the corresponding RAS. Array indexes represent (implicit) identifiers of tuples in R, in line with our repository model. To retrieve a tuple from R, one just needs to access the arrays corresponding to the different attributes of R with the same index. Finally, case variables are represented using (bounded) arrays of size 1 ('global arrays', using the nomenclature of MCMT, cf. Section 9.2), i.e., what are called 'artifact variables' in the RAS model. On top of these data structures, $\mathcal{P}$ is translated into a RAS transition formula that exactly reconstructs the execution semantics of the blocks in $\mathcal{P}$. We just provide a small but informative example on how to translate in RASs transitions the execution semantics of the sequence block S with nested blocks B_1 and B_2. For doing that, we use the syntax for MCMT transitions in the database-driven mode (supposing by induction that the MCMT transitions for the nested blocks have been already specified). Let us assume that, besides the other local and global variables, we have declared the following global variables:

```
...
:global Slifecycle
:global B1lifecycle
:global B2lifecycle
...
```

Before the sequence block is enabled, the lifecycle of sub-blocks B_1 and B_2 are in the idle state. Then, the sequence block execution semantics is given by the following three transitions.

```
:comment First Part
:transition
:var j
:guard (= Slifecycle enabled)
:numcases 1
:case
...
:val active
:val enabled
:val B2lifecycle
...
```

In the first one, when S is enabled, it becomes active, simultaneously turning the lifecycle of B_1 from idle to enabled.

```
:comment Second Part
:transition
:var j
:guard (= B1lifecycle compl)
:numcases 1
:case
...
:val Slifecycle
:val idle
:val enabled
...
```

In the second one, when B_1 is compl, it becomes idle, simultaneously turning the lifecycle of B_2 from idle to enabled.

```
:comment Third Part
:transition
:var j
:guard (= B2lifecycle compl)
:numcases 1
:case
```

```
. . .
:val compl
:val B1lifecycle
:val idle
. . .
```

Finally, in the third transition, when B_2 is `compl`, it becomes `idle`, simultaneously inducing S to move from `active` to `compl`, as wanted.

For the other blocks the translation is analogous, but the interested reader should be particularly careful in the case of exception blocks (see [50] for all the details). Regarding the update logic and the interaction between tasks and repository, notice that the insertion/set/deletion/conditional updates faithfully correspond to operations supported by RASs and described in Section 5.3.

With these observations in mind, we define BReach_{DAB} as the backward reachability procedure that: (1) takes as input *(i)* a DAB M, *(ii)* a property φ to be verified, *(iii)* a boolean indicating whether M is repo-bounded or not (in the first case, also providing the value of the bound), and *(iv)* a boolean indicating whether the semantics for insertion is set or multiset; (2) translates M into a corresponding RAS $\widehat{M}$, and φ into a corresponding unsafe formula $\widehat{\varphi}$ over $\widehat{M}$ (Definition 11.10 ensures that φ' is indeed a RAS state formula); (3) returns the result produced by the MCMT backward reachability procedure for RASs BReach_{RAS} on $\widehat{M}$ and $\widehat{\varphi}$.

11.3.4 Verification Results

By exploiting the DAB-to-RAS translation and the formal results for RASs studied in Part I, we are now ready to provide the main technical contributions of this chapter. First and foremost: DABs can be correctly verified using BReach_{DAB}. We make this intuition more precise by adapting the meta-properties from Chapter 4.

Given a DAB $M = \langle \text{d}, \mathcal{P} \rangle$ and a property υ over M, a SAFE (resp. UNSAFE) result is *correct* iff M is safe (resp. unsafe) w.r.t. υ.

Definition 11.11 Given a DAB M and a property υ, a verification procedure for checking unsafety of M w.r.t. υ is: *(i) sound* if, when it terminates, it returns a correct result; *(ii) complete* if, whenever UNSAFE is the correct result, then UNSAFE is indeed returned.

Effectiveness means again that means that all subprocedures in the algorithm can be effectively executed.

Theorem 11.1 BReach_{DAB} *is effective, sound and complete for checking unsafety of DABs that use the multiset or set insertion semantics.*

Proof The theorem is an immediate consequence from Corollary 4.2 for RASs and the translation from DABs to RASs described in the previous subsection. □

Completeness guarantees that whenever a DAB is unsafe with respect to a property, then $BReach_{DAB}$ terminates and detects this. In general, as pointed out in Chapter 4 for RASs, $BReach_{RAS}$ is not guaranteed to terminate, so $BReach_{DAB}$ neither. Hence, $BReach_{DAB}$ is a semi-decision procedure for unsafety.

We study additional conditions on the input DAB for which $BReach_{DAB}$ is guaranteed to terminate, then becoming a full decision procedure for unsafety. The first, unavoidable condition is on the constraints used in the catalog: its foreign keys cannot form referential cycles (where a table directly or indirectly refers to itself). This is in line with the termination result for SASs presented in Section 5.1. To define acyclicity, we associate to a catalog Cat a characteristic graph $G(Cat)$ that captures the dependencies between relation schema components induced by primary and foreign keys. Specifically, $G(Cat)$ is a directed graph such that:

- for every $R \in Cat$ and every attribute $a \in R.attrs$, the pair $\langle R, a \rangle$ is a node of $G(Cat)$ (and nothing else is a node);
- $\langle R_1, a_1 \rangle \rightarrow \langle R_2, a_2 \rangle$ if and only if one of the two following cases apply: *(i)* $R_1 = R_2$, $a_1 \neq a_2$, and $a_1 = R_1.id$; *(ii)* $a_2 = R_2.id$ and a_1 is a foreign key referring R_2.

Definition 11.12 A DAB is *acyclic* if the characteristic graph of its catalog is so.

Theorem 11.2 $BReach_{DAB}$ *terminates when verifying properties over repo-bounded and acyclic DABs using the multiset or set insertion semantics.*

Proof First, notice that Cat is acyclic iff its corresponding DB schema in the translated RAS is acyclic. Hence, a DAB is acyclic iff its translated RAS has an acyclic DB schema. Moreover, repo-bounded implies that, in our translation from DABs to RASs, one can use artifact variables for representing the repository relations of DABs. This is trivial since we do not need (undounded) indexes (taken from some artifact sort) in case of n-ary DABs repo-relations S whose size is bounded by some k, since it is sufficient to associate every tuple in S to $n * k$ corresponding artifact variables. Hence, repo-bounded RASs can be translated into SASs. In view of the previous observations, the theorem is then an immediate consequence from the termination result for SASs stated in Theorem 5.1 and from the translation from DABs to RASs, once noticed that repo-bounded and acyclic DABs can be translated into acyclic SASs.   □

If the input DAB is not repo-bounded, acyclicity of the catalog is not enough: termination requires to carefully control the interplay between the different components of the DAB. While the required conditions are quite difficult to grasp at the syntactic level, they can be intuitively understood using the following *locality principle* (which corresponds to *locality* for RASs): whenever the progression of the DAB depends on the repository, it does so only via a single entry in one of its relations. Hence, direct/indirect comparisons and joins of distinct tuples within the same or different repository relations cannot be used. To avoid indirect comparisons/joins, queries cannot mix case variables and repository relations.

Thus, set insertions cannot be supported, since by definition they require to compare tuples in the same relation. In general, update specifications obeying to the restrictions of Definition 11.2.2.1 cannot directly inquire the repository in their preconditions, but only work over it in the effect. This means that they cannot directly encode the situation of an update specification U that should be executed only if the repository is in a desired state s. However, we can, to some extent, simulate such a blocking update with two consecutive restricted updates. In the first step, the update employs its effects to load from the repository to dedicated case variables $x_{aux,1}, \ldots, x_{aux,k}$ the necessary information to check whether s holds or not. In the second step, the update checks for s in its precondition by inquiring the case variables, and not directly the repository. The entire sequence is then executable if and only if U is executable. Notice that according to the definition of the delete rule, we do not need to explicitly query in the precondition the repo-relation R from which we delete a tuple in its effect.

We now state the main decidability result of this chapter.

Theorem 11.3 *Let M be an acyclic DAB that uses the multiset insertion semantics, and is such that for each update specification u of M, the following holds:*

1. *If u.eff is an* insert&set *rule (with or without an explicit* INSERT *part), u.pre is* repo-free;
2. *If u.eff is a* delete&set *rule, then u.pre is* repo-free *and all case variables appear in the* SET *part of u.eff;*
3. *If u.eff is a* conditional update *rule, then u.pre is* repo-free *and boolean (i.e., it returns either* false *or the empty tuple), so that u.eff only makes use of the new variables introduced in its* UPDATE *part (as well as constant objects in $\mathbb{D}$).*

Then, $BReach_{DAB}$ terminates when verifying repo-free *properties over M.*

Proof The proof is an immediate consequence of Theorem 5.2 and of the translation from DABs to RASs described in the previous subsection. Indeed, we preliminarily notice that acyclic DABs are translated to acyclic RASs. Moreover, if the conditions of the theorem are satisfied, one can easily see that such DABs employ update specifications that correspond via the translation to the strongly local RASs transitions studied in Section 5.3. Finally, we notice that *repo-free* properties over M clearly correspond via the translation to strongly local unsafe formulae for RASs. We then conclude by remembering that Theorem 5.2 states termination of $BReach_{RAS}$ for acyclic RASs with strongly local transitions, when applied to strongly local unsafe formulae. □

Notably, the conditions of Theorem 11.3 represent a concrete, BPMN-like counterpart of the abstract conditions used in Section 5.2.1 (and in [186]) toward decidability.

Specifically, Theorem 11.3 uses two conditions: *(i)* repo-freedom, and *(ii)* the manipulation of *all* case variables at once. We now intuitively explain how these conditions substantiate the aforementioned locality principle. Overall, the main difficulty is that case variables may be loaded with data objects extracted from the repository. Hence, the usage of a case variable may mask an underlying reference to a tuple component stored in some repo-relation. Given this, locality demands that no two case variables can simultaneously hold data objects coming from different tuples in the repository. At the beginning, this is trivially true, since all case variables are undefined. A safe snapshot guaranteeing this condition continues to stay so after an insert and/or set rule of the form in point 1 or after a conditional update rule of the form in point 3 from Theorem 11.3: a repo-free precondition ensures that the repository is not queried at all, and hence trivially preserves locality. Clearly, locality may be easily destroyed by arbitrary delete&set rules whose precondition accesses the repository: a precondition retrieving objects from the repository, can in principle extracts them from different tuples therein. This case can be avoided by imposing repo-freedom. However, this property is not sufficient for guaranteeing locality in case of arbitrary delete&set rules. Indeed, a subtle situation where a repo-free delete&set would destroy locality is the one in which the objects retrieved from (the same tuple in) the repository are only used to assign *a proper subset* of the case variables: the other case variables could in fact still hold objects previously retrieved from a *different* tuple in the repository. Point 2 of Theorem 11.3 guarantees that this never happens by imposing that, upon a set or delete&set operation, *all* case variables are involved in the assignment. Those case variables that get objects extracted from the repository are then guaranteed to all implicitly point to the same, single repository tuple retrieved by the delete rule.

Example 11.9 By considering the data and process schema of the hiring process DAB, one can directly show that it can be easily transformed to an equivalent DAB obeying to all conditions in Theorem 11.3, in turn guaranteeing termination of BReach_{DAB}. For example, rule EvalApp in Example 11.3 matches point 1 since EvalApp.pre is repo-free, so it can be left as it is. An update specification to slightly change is instead SelWinner from the same example. Following the intuition given above, we split it into two non-interrupting update specifications SelWinner_1 and SelWinner_2 as follows. First, we use the effect of SelWinner_1 to load the tuple (jc, u, s, e) from the repo-relation *Application* to dedicated new additional case variables $x_{aux,1}, \ldots, x_{aux,4}$:

$\text{SelWinner}_1.\text{pre} \triangleq getWin1(jc : \text{jobcatID}, u : \text{UserId}, s : \text{String}, e : \text{Bool}) \leftarrow \text{true}$
$\text{SelWinner}_1.\text{eff} \triangleq \text{DEL } \langle jc, u, s, e \rangle \text{ FROM } Application$
$\qquad\qquad \text{AND SET } x_{aux,1} = jc, x_{aux,2} = u, x_{aux,3} = s, x_{aux,4} = e$
$\qquad\qquad \textbf{jcid} = \text{undef}, \textbf{uid} = \text{undef}, \textbf{result} = \text{undef},$
$\qquad\qquad \textbf{qualif} = \text{false}, \textbf{winner} = \text{undef},$

Notice that in the previous update the precondition is repo-free and *all* case variables appear in the SET part, so point 2 of Theorem 11.3 is matched.

In the second step, the update statement SelWinner_2 checks for the validity of the original precondition of SelWinner in its precondition by inquiring the new case variables $x_{aux,1}, \ldots, x_{aux,4}$ (and not directly the repository), and then it performs the original update of SelWinner.

$\text{SelWinner}_2.\text{pre} \triangleq getWin2(\emptyset) \leftarrow x_{aux,4} = \text{true}$
$\text{SelWinner}_2.\text{eff} \triangleq \text{SET } \textbf{jcid} = x_{aux,1}, \textbf{uid} = x_{aux,2}, \textbf{winner} = x_{aux,2},$
$\qquad\qquad \textbf{result} = x_{aux,4}$

Notice that in the previous update the precondition is repo-free, so point 1 of Theorem 11.3 is matched.

11.4 First Experiments with MCMT

We have *manually* encoded the job hiring DAB described in this chapter into MCMT, systematically following the translation rules recalled in Section 13.2, and fully spelled out in [50] when proving the main theorems of Section 11.3.4. Running MCMT Version 2.8 (http://users.mat. unimi.it/users/ghilardi/mcmt/), we have checked the encoding of the job hiring DAB for process termination (which took 0.43sec), and against five safe and five unsafe properties. For example, the **1st unsafe** property describes the desired situation in which, after having evaluated an application (i.e., EvalApp is completed), there exists at least an applicant with a score greater than 0. Formally: **EvalApplifecycle** = completed $\wedge$ *Application*$(j, u, score, e) \wedge score > 0$. The **4th safe** property represents instead the situation in which a winner has been selected after the deadline (i.e., SelWin is completed), but the case variable **result** witnesses that the winner is not an eligible candidate. Formally: **SelWinlifecycle** = completed $\wedge$ **result** = false. MCMT

	prop.	time(s)
safe	1	0.20
	2	5.85
	3	3.56
	4	0.03
	5	0.27
unsafe	1	0.18
	2	1.17
	3	4.45
	4	1.43
	5	1.14

returns SAFE, witnessing that this configuration is not reachable from the initial states. Additional properties (taken from the table on the right) are described in [50].

The table on the right summarizes the obtained, encouraging results, reporting the MCMT running time in seconds. The MCMT specifications containing all the properties to check (together with their intuitive interpretation) are available in [50], and all tests are directly reproducible. Experiments were performed on a machine with Ubuntu 16.04, 2.6 GHz Intel Core i7 and 16 GB RAM.

We stressed again that these experiments were performed over an example manually encoded into MCMT, but exploiting the formal translation from DABs to RASs. We now devote the next chapter to introduce an operational and implemented framework where the translation from DABs into RASs is fully automatized.

Chapter 12
delta-BPMN: the Operational and Implemented Counterpart of DABs

In this chapter, we present an operational framework, called delta-BPMN, that can be seen as a practice-oriented counterpart of DABs and that provides a concrete verifiable language and a proof-of-concept implementation for modeling and verifying data-aware business processes. As we will argue in Section 12.1, although DABs present a more practical flavor than the RAS foundational framework, they are far from being usable in practice: for instance, the (data manipulation) logic layer of DABs is expressed as a precondition/update language that natively matches the update language provided by RASs, but it does not adhere to any standard language (or variant) employed in practice. For this reason, we introduce here a framework where every layer (the process layer, the data layer and the logic layer) is expressed in terms of constructs of well-known *standard languages*.

The content of this chapter was first published in [138].

12.1 From DABs to delta-BPMN

In the previous chapter, we introduced a BPMN-oriented general framework, called DABs, for modeling and verifying data-aware processes. However, the DAB model is still too abstract in the way it represents and manipulates relational data.

When dealing with formalisms integrating processes with data, a fundamental dimension that is worth investigating is about the choice of modeling constructs: it would be essential to employ the same constructs that are offered by process and data modeling standards such as BPMN and SQL, especially in view of the concrete applicability of such integrated formalisms. Unfortunately, the DAB model only partially fulfils this requirement: indeed, while the process component is represented by using (the block-structured fragment of) the BPMN standard, the data manipulation layer is rather abstract and hardly usable in practice. Specifically, the data schema presented in Subsection 11.2.1, although important since inspired by artifact-centric models, presents an abstract language that cannot be straightforwardly encoded in concrete data manipulation languages such as SQL. At the same time, the plethora

A. Gianola: *Verification of Data-Aware Processes via Satisfiability Modulo Theories*,
LNBIP 470, pp. 239–257, 2023.
https://doi.org/10.1007/978-3-031-42746-6_12

of constructs employed to model data-aware processes is not suitable to express the standard languages in their full generality, as verification becomes immediately undecidable if they are not adequately restricted [47]. A last crucial issue is that the vast majority of the literature in this spectrum mainly provides theoretical results that do not directly translate into effective modeling and verification tools.

In this chapter, we tackle these limitations and propose delta-BPMN, an operational and implemented framework for modeling and verifying BPMN models enriched with data, which is based on standard languages like SQL and BPMN. In Section 12.3 we introduce the front-end data modeling and manipulation language PDMML, which relies on the formal framework of DABs, by using a SQL-based dialect to formalize the manipulation of case and persistent data, and show how it can be embedded into a (block-structured) fragment of BPMN that captures the process backbone. In Section 12.2 we will discuss the related work, by comparing PDMML with other concrete, verifiable data-aware process modeling languages existing in the literature.

In Subsection 12.4.1 we show how the delta-BPMN front-end can be realized in Camunda[1], one of the most popular BPMN environments. In Subsection 12.4.2 we also report on the implementation of a translator that, building on the encoding rules abstractly defined in [50], takes a delta-BPMN model created in Camunda and transforms it into the syntax of the 'database-driven module' of MCMT (cf. Chapter 9), to directly perform safety verification over delta-BPMN models. delta-BPMN is currently a prototype and still work in progress: while presenting its features along the chapter, we also report the current status of its implementation.

12.1.1 DABs: a Symbolic Bridge Between RASs and delta-BPMN

From a technical point of view, DABs can be seen as an intermediate model between the model-theoretic framework of RASs and the operational framework of delta-BPMN. DABs and delta-BPMN share the same process component, but the data manipulation layer, although in clear correspondence with the one of DABs, presents in delta-BPMN a more practice-oriented flavor, thanks to the use of an SQL dialect. In this sense, it has been useful and instructive to present DABs after RASs but before delta-BPMN, so as to build a symbolic bridge between the foundational framework and its BPM-oriented implementation.

---

[1] https://camunda.com

12.2 Requirement Analysis for delta-BPMN and Related Existing Tools

The integration of data and processes is a long-standing line of research at the intersection of BPM, data management, process mining, and formal methods. Since our focus is on verification, we circumscribe the relevant works to those dealing with the formal analysis of data-aware processes. This is also crucial because the choice of language constructs is affected by the task one needs to solve - in particular, verifying such sophisticated models requires to suitably control the data and control-flow components as well as their interaction [47, 99].

A second important point is that the vast majority of the contributions in this line of research provide foundational results, but do not come with corresponding operational tools for verification. Hence, all in all, *we consider in this research only those approaches for the integration of data and processes that come with verification tool support*: VERIFAS [186], BAUML [114], ISML [218], dapSL [60], and the delta-BPMN approach considered here, which relies on the DAB formal model as its foundational basis.

We use these approaches to distill a series of important requirements on languages for verifiable data-aware processes, indicating which approaches provide full (+), partial (+/−), or no support (−) for that requirement. The first two requirements concern verifiability, respectively capturing foundational and practical aspects.

RQ 1 The language should be operationally verifiable with a tool.

While the approaches above all come with an operational counterpart for verification, there are huge differences in how this support is provided. VERIFAS comes with an embedded, ad-hoc verification tool (+) that supports the model checking of properties expressed in a *fragment of first-order LTL*. BAUML encodes verification into a form of first-order satisfiability checking over the flow of time (+), defining a fixed set of *test cases* expressing properties to be checked as derived predicates. ISML relies on state-space construction techniques for Colored Petri nets, but in doing so it assumes that the data domains are all bounded (+/−); no specific verification language is defined, leaving to the user the decision on how to explore the state space. dapSL relies instead on an ad-hoc state-space construction that, under suitable restrictions, is guaranteed to faithfully represent in a finite-state way the infinite state space induced by the data-aware process; however, no additional techniques are defined to explore the state space or check temporal properties of interest (+/−). Finally, delta-BPMN, since it is based on DABs, encodes verification of *(data-aware) safety properties* into the state-of-the-art MCMT model checker (+).

The second requirement concerns the analysis of key properties (such as soundness, completeness, and termination) of the algorithmic techniques used for verification. This is crucial since, in general, verifying data-aware processes is highly undecidable [47, 99].

RQ 2 The verification techniques come with an analysis of key properties such as soundness, completeness, termination.

Table 12.1: Requirements coverage (covered +, partially (+/−), not −)

Framework	RQ 1	RQ 2	RQ 3	RQ 4	RQ 5	RQ 6	verification logic
VERIFAS [186]	+	+	−	+	+	y	fragment of LTL-FO
BAUML [114]	+	+/−	+	+	+	n	fixed test cases
ISML [218]	+/−	−	+/−	+	+/−	n	state-space exploration
dapSL [60]	+/−	−	+/−	+	−	n	state-space exploration
delta-BPMN	+	+	+/−	+	+	y	data-aware safety

Since ISML and dapSL do not come with specific algorithmic techniques for verification, no such analysis is provided there (−). BAUML relies on first-order satisfiability techniques that come with semi-decidability guarantees. In [114], it is claimed that for a certain class of state-bounded artifact systems, verification terminates; however, this is not guaranteed, as for that class only decidability of verification is known, not that the specifically employed satisfiability algorithm terminates (+/−). VERIFAS comes with a deep, foundational study on the boundaries of decidability of verification [102]; the study identifies classes of data-aware processes for which finite-state abstractions can be constructed, guaranteeing termination of the verifier when analyzing such classes (+). Finally, delta-BPMN relies on the foundational DAB framework, where soundness, completeness, termination of the algorithmic technique implemented in MCMT are extensively studied (+) (see Section 11.3.4 for these results).

The third crucial requirement is about the type of language adopted, and whether it adheres to accepted standards or is instead rather ad-hoc.

RQ 3 The language relies on well-assessed standards for processes and data.

Recall that, to carry out verification, the features supported by the language need to be carefully controlled. So we do not assess approaches based on their coverage of constructs, but rather focus on which notations they employ. On the one hand, approaches like VERIFAS adopt a language inspired by artifact-centric models but defined in an abstract, mathematical syntax (−). At the other end of the spectrum, BAUML comes with a combination of UML/OCL-based models to specify the various process components (+). In between we find the other proposals (+/−): ISML relies on Petri nets and employs data definition and manipulation languages defined in an ad-hoc way; dapSL instead defines the control-flow implicitly via condition-action rules, and uses a language grounded in the SQL standard for querying and updating the data. delta-BPMN relies on a combination of (block-structured) BPMN and SQL for data manipulation; while standard SQL is employed for data queries and updates, the language has to be extended with some ad-hoc constructs when it comes to actions and (user) inputs (+/−).

In data-aware processes, it is essential to capture the fact that while the process is executed, new data can be acquired.

RQ 4 The language supports the injection of data into the process by the external environment.

All of the listed approaches agree on the need of equipping the language with mechanisms to inject data from the external environment. VERIFAS and BAUML allow one to nondeterministically assign values from value domains to (special) variables, ISML extends this functionality with an ability to guarantee that assigned values are globally fresh (but then it works by assuming a fixed finite domain for such fresh input), whereas dapSL supports all such functionalities using a language of service calls. In delta-BPMN we adopt a data injection approach similar to the one used in VERIFAS.

When executing process cases, one typically distinguishes at least two types of data: volatile data attached to the case itself, and persistent data that may be accessed and updated by different cases at once. This leads to our last requirement.

RQ 5 The language distinguishes volatile and persistent data elements.

While BAUML, VERIFAS, and DAB natively provide distinct notions for case variables and underlying persistent data (+), ISML models conceptually account for token data and separate facts, but such facts are not stored in a persistent storage (+/−), while dapSL models all data as tuples of a relational database (−).

At last, a very important aspect that puts the approaches into two distinct groups, is whether persistent data are managed under a unique access policy, or instead there is a fine-grained distinction based on how the process can access them. This impacts the type of verification conducted, as discussed below. Since supporting or not read-only data simply separates the different approaches, but does not correspond to a qualitative difference, we simply put 'yes' (y) when it is supported and 'no' (n) when it is not.

RQ 6 The language separates read-only persistent data from persistent data that are updated during the execution.

This is an important distinction because it heavily affects the type of verification that must be considered [47, 99]. On the one hand, approaches like BAUML, dapSL, and ISML that do not distinguish read-only from updatable persistent data (n) require to fully fix their initial configuration, and provide verification verdicts by considering all possible evolutions of the process starting from this initial configuration. Contrariwise, approaches like VERIFAS and delta-BPMN that do this distinction (y) in turn focus on forms of parameterized verification where the properties of interest are studied for every possible configuration of the read-only data, certifying whether the process correctly works regardless of which specific read-only data are picked.

Table 12.1 summarizes the different requirements and support provided by the analyzed literature. We take this as a basis to compare the delta-BPMN language and verification infrastructure with the other existing approaches. For completeness, we also indicate in the table which verification properties are considered in each approach.

It is also worth noting that there is a plethora of other approaches falling into the artifact-/data-/object-centric spectrum. For example, Guard-Stage-Milestone (GSM) language [90], the object-aware business process management framework of PHIL-harmonic Flows [183], the declarative data-centric process language RESEDA based on term rewriting systems [233]. In a nutshell, these approaches combine data and processes dimensions, but largely focus on modeling, with few exceptions offering runtime verification of specific properties (e.g., RESEDA allows for a specific form of liveness checking) supported by a tool.

Other relevant works investigate the integration of data and processes with a system engineering approach [200, 117, 86] tailored to modeling and enactment. Of particular relevance is ADEPT [86], which is similar in spirit to delta-BPMN, as it allows to combine a block-structured process modeling language with SQL statements to interact with an underlying relational storage, with the goal of providing execution and analytic services. The main difference with delta-BPMN is that our PDMML language focuses on conservative extensions of (block-structured) BPMN and SQL to obtain a verifiable, integrated model.

12.3 The PDMML Language

To realize the modeling requirements introduced in Section 12.2, we rely on the DAB framework. The main issue there is that while the process backbone relies on (block-structured) BPMN, the definition and manipulation of data is done with an abstract, mathematical language that does not come with a concrete, user-oriented syntax.

To define a delta-BPMN model, we then revisit the data component of the process, introducing a Process Data Modeling and Manipulation Language (PDMML). We do so in two steps: first, we start from BPMN and isolate the main data abstractions that must be represented in our framework, introducing suitable *data definition* operations in PDMML; second, we build on top of the abstract, logical language introduced in Section 11.2.1 and introduce a concrete counterpart for *data manipulation* statements in PDMML, using SQL as main inspiration. In this way, we achieve compliance with **RQ 3**. We then integrate PDMML language for data inspection and manipulation within BPMN blocks, so as to comply with **RQ 3** for both the data and the control-flow aspects.

Notice that, deliberately, PDMML does not come with explicit mechanisms to refer to other process instances from a given instance. This is due to technical reasons related to verification, which will be highlighted in Section 12.4.2.

12.3.1 Sources of Data and their Definition

While BPMN does not introduce any specific language to manipulate and query data, it introduces two main abstractions to account for them: *data objects*, representing *volatile data* manipulated by each case in isolation; and *persistent stores*, representing persistent units of information that are accessed and updated possibly by multiple cases.

Persistent data. The data component of delta-BPMN is completely in line with the theoretical framework provided by DABs (and, clearly, of RASs). We report here for completeness the features of PDMML, stressing here once for all that they bijectively correspond to their counterparts in DABs. To account for **RQ 6**, PDMML allows to define two types of persistent storages with different access policies. More specifically, we use a so-called *repository* $\mathcal{R}$ to store data that can be both queried and updated, and a *catalog store* C with a read access only. The declaration of these two stores is done with a set of statements, each accounting for a relation schema (or *table*) therein. Each table comes with *typed attributes* defining the *names* of the table columns with the respective *(value) types*.

An attribute is declared in PDMML as $A : T$, where A is an attribute name and T is its type. Each type is of one of the following three different forms: *(i)* a *primitive*, system-reserved *type* (such as strings and integers); *(ii)* a dedicated *id type* T_R accounting for the identifiers of table R (like ISBNs for the *Book* table - if they are used as primary key to identify books); *(iii)* a *data type* accounting for a semantic domain (like person names or addresses). The separation between data types and primitive types in PDMML may seem confusing, since in DABs they both collapse into DABs primitive types: however, since PDMML should be thought as a more practice-oriented setting, we prefer here to distinguish system-reserved type from semantic domains. For every catalog table, say, with name R, PDMML also requires to define an attribute with name *id* and a distinguished id type T_R, so as to account for the primary key of that table in an unambiguous way.

Based on these notions, a *catalog* is a set of *catalog tables*, each defined with a statement of the form $R(id : T_R, A_1 : T_1, \ldots, A_n : T_n)$, where: *(i)* R is the *table name*; *(ii)* $id : T_R$ is the explicit table identifier of R with a dedicated (identifier) type T_R; *(iii)* $n + 1$ is the *table arity*; *(iv)* for every $i \in \{1, \ldots, n\}$, T_i is a primitive type, an identifier type of some relation in the catalog or a data type. Each catalog table is equipped with a *table id attribute* of the form $id : T_R$, always assumed to appear in the first position. According to the definition, the other attributes may have, as type, the identifier type of another catalog table. This mechanism is used to define, in a compact way, the presence of a *foreign key* dependency relating two catalog tables. The notion of catalog presented here is equivalent to the one employed for DABs.

Similarly to the case of a catalog, a *repository* is a set of *repository tables*, each defined with a similar statement to that of catalog tables, with the only difference that now there is no explicit table identifier. This means that, while repository tables can reference catalog tables, they cannot reference other repository tables, and thus behave like *free relations*. Conceptually, this is not a limitation, since the idea behind the use of the repository is not to support a full-fledged database (as it is done for the catalog), but to provide a working memory where data taken from the catalog, case variables and external sources are accumulated and manipulated. This approach to model the repository is in line with the foundational framework of [102, 186]. In addition, it enjoys the key properties of these sophisticated scenarios – hence we have to stick with it in the light of **RQ 1**. Again, the notion of repository introduced here is equivalent to DAB repository.

As customary, when defining tables, PDMML requires that each table name is used only once overall (at the catalog *and* repository level). Hence we can use the table name to unambiguously refer to the table as a whole. To disambiguate attributes from different tables, we sometimes use a dot notation, where $R.A$ indicates attribute A within table R. In addition, table aliases can be used within queries towards expressing self-joins.[2]

Volatile data. For modeling volatile, case data in a way that makes them compatible with persistent data, we use typed variables whose declaration signature is similar to the one of attributes. Specifically, a *case variable* with name v and type T is then simply defined in PDMML as a statement #v : T. The definition of the volatile data of a process then just consists of a set of case variable statements.

The collective set of declarations for case variables, catalog relations, and repository relations is called *data model*.

Example 12.1 Consider a mortgage approval process followed by the Customer Service Representatives (CSR) department of a bank.[3] To manage information about available mortgage types, customers' bank accounts, submitted applications, status of their records and possible mortgage approval results, the process relies on multiple sources of data.

Each mortgage application is created by a CSR employee and can be managed throughout the process execution by using process variables. At the same time, certain data values have to be moved from volatile case variables to a persistent repository, and vice-versa. In this process, for example, we use variables #*cid* : CID, #*bid* : BaID, #*bankAmount* : Num to store information about a customer as well as their eligible bank account, and variables #*tid* : MTID, #*duration* : Num, #*amount* : Num to collect data for the mortgage contract.

The information static to the process (i.e., it shall never be updated) is stored in the CSR's read-only database. For example, table *BankAccount*(*BAid* : BankAccountID, *CBA* : CID, *Deposit* : int, *StatusBank* : String) contains information about possibly multiple bank accounts owned by the customers together with the account status information retained in *StatusBank* : String), whereas *MortgageType*(*Mid* : MTID, *Name* : String, *Amount* : Num, *Duration* : Num, *Interest* : Num) contains details regarding various mortgage offers, including information on mortgage duration and the amount of interests to be paid.

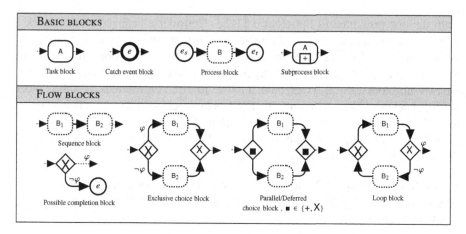

Fig. 12.1: Supported BPMN blocks

12.3.2 The Process Component of delta-BPMN

The control-flow backbone of a delta-BPMN process relies on the recursive composition of block-structured BPMN patterns that adhere to the standard BPMN 2.0 syntax. We focus on block-structured BPMN since this allows us to define a direct execution semantics also for advanced constructs like interrupting exceptions and cancelations, and to exploit this upon verifying the resulting models. This choice is completely in line with the theoretical framework of DABs presented in Section 11.2: we stress again that this is because delta-BPMN should be thought as the operational implemented counterpart of DABs.

Although, conceptually, delta-BPMN supports the same set of blocks as DABs, its current implementation covers the fundamental blocks shown in Figure 12.1. The implementation of the other blocks does not present any additional technical difficulty: their implementation is just ongoing work and will be discussed in the conclusions of this book as future work.

As usual, blocks are classified into leaf blocks (in our case, tasks and events) and non-leaf blocks that combine sub-blocks in a specific control-flow structure. As described in Subsection 11.2.3, each block has a lifecycle, where its states can be idle, enabled, active and compl. The execution rules used for regulating the evolution of each block depending on its type faithfully reconstruct what prescribed by the BPMN standard. We just provide here another example of block different

---

[2] This latter feature is currently not supported by the implementation, but it will be supported soon. The page https://github.com/mrMorningLemon/delta-BPMN provides a continuously updated list of the most recent, newly added features.

[3] For delta-BPMN we consider a new example, that builds on a model from Business Process Incubator (see https://www.businessprocessincubator.com/content/mortgage-approval/ enriched with data by analogy with a similar model from the benchmark in [186].

from the one presented in Subsection 11.2.3. Consider a deferred choice block S with two sub-blocks B_1 and B_2. Its lifecycle starts in state enabled, that can be nondeterministically progressed to state active. This progression simultaneously forces the change of state of B_1 and B_2 from idle to enabled. As soon as one of the two sub-blocks, say, B_1 is selected, it moves to active whereas its sibling block B_2 goes back to idle. As soon as B_1 finishes by reaching state compl, it switches to idle and triggers a simultaneous transition of the parent block S from active to compl. Following this logic, one can analogously and exhaustively define the lifecycle model for each type of block.

Example 12.2 Figure 12.2 shows the control-flow backbone of the mortgage approval process (Example 12.1), represented in delta-BPMN by following the same block decomposition.

The main, open question is how data enter into the definition of blocks. Following the BPMN standard, this is handled in two distinct points: leaf blocks (capturing tasks and events), and (data-driven) choices. Such blocks are annotated with suitable PDMML statements to capture data inspection and manipulation. This is handled next.

12.3.3 Inspecting and Manipulating Data with PDMML

To express how a task/event inspects and manipulates data, we are still consistent with the DAB theoretical framework, but with some significant differences: the data manipulation logic of DABs is a bit too abstract to be employed in a concrete tool. That is why we prefer here to introduce a language, called PDMML that is a dialect of the SQL language, and that can be used in practice in our implementation.

We decorate our tasks/events with three distinct PDMML expressions, respectively defining: *(i) newly declared variables*, to account for external data input; *(ii)* a *precondition*, providing possible bindings for the input variables of the task/event considering the catalog, the repository, as well as the case and newly defined variables; *(iii)* an *effect* that, once a binding for the newly declared variables and for the input variables is picked, determines how the task/event manipulates the case variables and the repository.

An obvious choice to inspect relational data as those present in our catalog and repository is to resort to relational query languages such as SQL. This choice would be in line with **RQ 3**. However, our setting requires to consider two crucial aspects. On the one hand, it is important to coherently employ a single query language to account for different querying needs, such as expressing the precondition of a task or the conditions determining which route to take in a choice. On the other hand, differently from pure SQL, our queries have to consider the presence of case variables, addressing the possibility of simultaneously working over persistent and volatile data, as well as the possibility of injecting data from the external environment. For example, think of a job category that has been chosen by an applicant during the application process (and thus suitably stored in a dedicated case variable) and for which the process should provide all open positions. In this case one would need to use the job category value in the WHERE clause of a dedicated SELECT query accessing the catalog that already contains information about all the positions for the previously selected category. At the same time, one might also want to query only the current state of the case variables, or to ask the user to provide their credit card number when paying a fee.

Newly declared variables. The ability of injecting a data object of type T form the external environment (cf. **RQ 4**) is handled through a *newly declared variable* with the following PDMML statement *decl* ::= (var v : T)*, where v is the name of the newly declared variable. Upon execution, v is bound to *any* value from T. When attached to a task, newly declared variables can be seen as an abstract representation of a user form or a web service result. When attached to an event, they represent the event payload. These variables are essential for performing non-deterministic updates, in line of what done in, e.g., [186]: on the one hand, in the RAS framework they correspond to *existentially quantified data variables* ranging over the read-only database; on the other hand, in the MCMT syntax, they correspond to :eevar variables. These variables are the ones that need to be eliminated by our extended version of backward reachability that we introduced in the previous parts of the book.

Preconditions. Preconditions indicate under which circumstances a task can be executed or an event triggered. They also retrieve data from the catalog, repository, case variables and newly defined variables attached to the same leaf block. To account for these different aspects, PDMML incorporates a hybrid SQL-based query language that can retrieve volatile and persistent data at once. Consistently with the execution semantics of DABs that is, in turn, in line with the customary "variable binding" abstraction employed in formalisms such as Colored Petri nets, the typical usage of queries in our framework is to return a set of answers from which one is (nondeterministically) picked to induce a progression step within the process. Notice that this way of managing query results is customary in the artifact-centric literature [47, 102, 186], and is consistent with Chapter 3.

To define preconditions, we first need to introduce PDMML conditions, defined as:

$$cond ::= x_1 \odot x_2 \mid cond_1 \textbf{ AND } cond_2 \mid cond_1 \textbf{ OR } cond_2$$

Essentially, a PDMML condition is a boolean expression (with negation pushed inwards) over atomic conditions of the form $x_1 \odot x_2$, where x_1 and x_2 are expression terms (whose specific shape is determined by the context in which the condition is used), and $\odot \in \{=, \neq, >, <, \leq, \geq\}$) is a comparison operator. In atomic conditions, we assume component-wise type compatibility of terms (e.g., the two operands in $x_1 \odot x_2$ must have the same type). Notice that, as customary, the atomic condition TRUE (capturing the condition that always succeeds) can be defined as an abbreviation (similarly for FALSE).

Using conditions as atomic building blocks, a PDMML precondition is defined as:

$$pre ::= cond \mid query$$
$$query ::= \textbf{SELECT } A_1, \ldots, A_s \textbf{ FROM } R_1, \ldots, R_m \textbf{ WHERE } filter$$
$$filter ::= cond \mid \text{TUPLE } (\textbf{x}) \textbf{ IN } R \mid \text{TUPLE } (\textbf{x}) \textbf{ NOT IN } R$$
$$\mid filter_1 \textbf{ AND } filter_2 \mid filter_1 \textbf{ OR } filter_2$$

Here, each R_i from the SQL-like *query* can be a repository or a catalog relation, whereas R from *filter* can only be a catalog relation. This is in line with theoretical results for U-RAS and, consequently, for DABs. [4]Terms in *cond* of *pre* can be case variables, constants, or newly defined variables declared in the same leaf block. Instead, terms used in *cond* of *filter* coincide with those from above, but can also use attributes that appear in the **FROM** statement of the contingent *query* expression (i.e., $A_1, \ldots, A_s$). When writing queries, notation $R.A$ can be used to more explicitly refer to attribute A of table R. The language of preconditions defined above can be trivially translated in the language of unions of conjunctive queries with atomic negation presented in the context of DABs (cf. Subsection 11.2.1).

Example 12.3 In the mortgage approval process scenario touched in Examples 12.1 and 12.2, the following query can be used to list bank accounts of the customers who have completed the mortgage application procedure:

```
SELECT BAid, CBA, StatusBank FROM BankAccount
WHERE CBA = #cid AND #status = CompletedApplication
```

Here, $\#status$: String indicates the current status of the process.

Effects. Task/event effects consist of data manipulation PDMML statements operating over case variables and repository tables. In the following, we use term *input variable* to refer to newly defined variables or attributes of the precondition attached to the same leaf block of the effect under scrutiny.

Each case variable $\#v$ can be *updated* using a trivial assignment statement $\#v = u$, where u is either a constant or an input variable. It is assumed that, for each case variable, at most one case variable assignment statement can be written within one update.

One can also model insertion and deletion of tuples into the persistent storage. Since the catalog is read-only, these updates can be performed only on the repository relations.

An *insertion* (statement) on some repository relation R is defined as **INSERT** $v_1, \ldots, v_n$ **INTO** R, where each v_i is either a constant, a case variable or an input variable. This INSERT statement is similar to the corresponding classical DML (data manipulation language) statement in SQL. However, we deliberately avoid using the VALUES clause since we insert one tuple at a time, and so we can rely on the more compact notation where the elements to be inserted are directly indicated close to R.

---

[4] We remark here that the constructs TUPLE (**x**) **IN** R and TUPLE (**x**) **NOT IN** R has not implemented yet.

A *deletion* (statement) is defined as **DELETE** $v_1, \ldots, v_n$ **FROM** R. Here, similarly to the insertion, each v_i is either a constant, a (case) variable, or an input variable, whose type coincides with the type of the i-th attribute in R.

We also allow to perform *conditional updates*. For that, we employ a modified SQL CASE statement directly embedded into the update logic. This statement logically resembles an *if-then-else* expression with multiple *else-if* branches, and in which each condition in the *if*-part is a query. To ensure verifiability as in the context of DABs (cf. Subsection 11.2.2.1) (cf. **RQ 1**), it is necessary for the statement to obey to one limitation: it cannot access any other repository table beyond the one that is being updated. The conditional update statement has the form:

```
UPDATE R SET R.a₁=@v₁,...,R.aₘ=@vₘ WHERE
CASE WHEN F₁ THEN @v₁=u₁¹,..., @vₘ=uₘ¹
     ...
     WHEN Fₖ THEN @v₁=u₁ᵏ,..., @vₘ=uₘᵏ
     ELSE @v₁=u₁ᵉ,..., @vₘ=uₘᵉ
```

This statement is the most sophisticated one in the offered language as it requires the modeler to take care of the following two aspects. First, similarly to the SQL's UPDATE statement, which can modify multiple tuples in a table, ours performs a (conditional) *bulk edit* of elements in *each* tuple of R, and the SET clause specifies (using names of the attributes of R with the R's name in the prefix)[5] what are exactly those elements. The SET clause also uses placeholder variables $@v_j$ that support the conditional update logic: whenever a tuple in R satisfies one of the F_i filters, the corresponding THEN clause will assign concrete values u_j^i to all the placeholder variables mentioned in SET. Second, the modeler has to carefully control the variables and attributes used both in the WHEN and THEN clauses. As we have already mentioned above, each F_i cannot access repository relations but R itself. At the same time, it can reuse elements from the precondition query such as variables and attributes. This, in turn, allows to use F_i for filtering results returned by the precondition query, and thus allowing to carefully select the data that are going to be used in the final update of every single tuple of R. As for the elements appearing in THEN clauses, their values can be constants as well as elements taken from results returned by the precondition query.

Notice that assignments, insertions, deletions and conditional updates are completely analogous to their corresponding counterparts in the update logic layer of the DAB theoretical framework (cf. Subsection 11.2.2): they can be trivially translated into the DAB model. In the following we provide a few examples demonstrating correct and illegal update statements.

Example 12.4 Continuing with the example of the mortgage approval example, we now give the example of a legal conditional update handling the assessment of the eligibility of a mortgage application. To manage key information about the applications submitted for the mortgage approval, the bank employs a repository that consists of one relation schema:

---

[5] This disambiguates the situation where the same relation R is used in the update precondition with some of its attributes both appearing in the SELECT and some of the WHEN clauses.

$$Info(Bank: \texttt{BaID}, StatusB: \texttt{String}, Reliability: \texttt{String})$$

Here, for each application, CSR performs an assessment procedure, during which all customer's bank accounts are checked for reliability. All the accounts with histories that did not include any fraudulent charges, are then marked accordingly in relation *Info*. Technically, we formalize this situation with a conditional update of the form:

```
UPDATE Info SET Info.Reliability=@v WHERE
CASE WHEN Info.StatusB!=fraud THEN @v=Yes
     ELSE @v= No
```

Note that the *when-then-else* clause allows us to perform a bulk update over the repository relation *Info* by changing the reliability status of its entries.

Consider the repository relation *Rejected*(*Bank* : BaID), storing bank accounts that have been already rejected before in the process by another department. The following update statement, that additionally checks if the bank account has already been rejected, is illegal, since the condition of the first case involves the repo-relation *Rejected*:

```
UPDATE Info SET Info.Reliability=@v WHERE
CASE WHEN Info.StatusB!=fraud AND TUPLE (Info.Bank) NOT IN Rejected
THEN @v=Yes ELSE @v=No
```

The overall execution semantics of leaf blocks (e.g., tasks or events) is analogous the one defined for DABs in Subsection 11.2.2.2: we only notice that when the leaf block is `enabled`, beside the binding of the (standard) attributes in the precondition, also a binding for its newly defined variables is provided. In delta-BPMN, we always assume that, in the case of a task having both a precondition and an effect, the task is *atomic* at the level of data updates: this is done, as discussed for DABs, to avoid race conditions with other update specifications potentially operating over the same case variables or repository tables. Notice that race conditions can still occur at the level of the process, when parallel blocks and sequences of tasks/events are employed. Consequently, requiring atomicity for leaf blocks with preconditions and effects does not lead to a loss of generality.

12.3.4 Guards for Conditional Flows

The last place where PDMML statements are needed is in the context of blocks employing choice splits as a way to conditionally route process instances. Specifically, each conditional flow is linked to a PDMML condition whose terms are case variables or constants. Notice that using only case variables is not a limitation, since, as we have seen before, case variables can be filled with data extracted from the catalog/repository, or injected from the external environment.

As shown in Figure 12.1, we assume that each choice split foresees two outputs with complementary guards. This means that the user has to specify only one guard

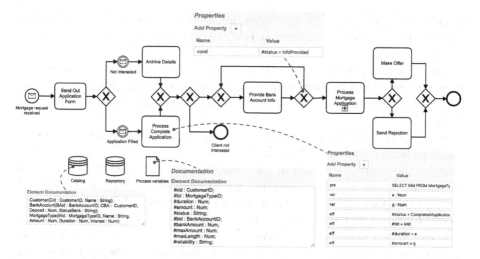

Fig. 12.2: A delta-BPMN model with a few examples of Camunda-based annotations (taken as screenshots from the tool)

φ, while the other guard (indicated as $\neg\varphi$ in the figure) is automatically constructed via syntactic manipulation of φ as follows: De Morgan laws are applied until negation appears just in front of atomic conditions, and then the negated atomic conditions are replaced by their corresponding, complementary conditions (e.g., $\leq$ is substituted by $>$).

We have now completed the definition of PDMML. In the next section we show how PDMML is practically realized in delta-BPMN.

12.4 delta-BPMN in Action

We now put delta-BPMN in action, considering both modeling and verification. For more details and for downloading it, see [137].

12.4.1 Modeling delta-BPMN Processes with Camunda

We discuss how Camunda, one of the most widely employed (open-source) platforms for process modeling and automation, can be directly adapted to model delta-BPMN processes. We in particular employ the Camunda Modeler environment (camunda. com) to create the process control-flow, and its extension part to incorporate PDMML statements. At this stage, it is not essential to recognize the process blocks (and check whether the process control-flow is block-structured): we just annotate the overall process model with the data definitions, the tasks/events with the corresponding PDMML preconditions and effects, and the choice branches with PDMML boolean queries.

An alternative possibility would have been to require the modeler to explicitly insert data object and data store icons in the process model, and annotate those. However, this would clutter the visual representation of the process, creating unreadable diagrams.

More specifically, to declare repository (resp., catalog) relations we use a dedicated persistent store symbol called `Repository` (resp., `Catalog`). The declarations themselves, separated by the semicolon from one another, are put into the documentation box of the element's documentation. For example, Figure 12.2 demonstrates a snapshot of a catalog declaration containing definitions of two relations *Customer* and *MortgageType* from Example 12.1. We deal similarly with case variables: a single data object called `Process variables` is used, whose documentation box contains all case variable declarations with the semicolon being used as a separator (cf. Figure 12.2).

Modeling queries as well as other data manipulation expressions in traditional BPMN 2.0 could be done using annotations. This could be considered as a more traditional approach that, however, as we have already discussed above, can lead to difficulties in managing the processes diagram. Instead, we propose to handle such expressions declaratively within the Camunda extension elements. Given that properties in Camunda are represented as key-value pairs, adding a declaration is rather easy: one needs to use a special data manipulation expression identifier as the key and the actual expression as the value. Consistently with Section 12.3, we use the following reserved identifiers: *(i)* `cond` – a gateway/flow condition identifier; *(ii)* `pre` – a precondition identifier; *(iii)* `var` – a new typed variable declaration identifier; *(iv)* `eff` – an update statement identifier.

Each key is meant to be used only with values of a particular type. Like that, `cond` and `pre` identify queries, whereas `var` and `eff` respectively denote new variable declarations and update statements. All the BPMN elements that admit the aforementioned extensions can have multiple `var` and `eff` identifiers. This is useful as there can be more than one new typed variable declaration as well as multiple case variable assignment statements.

Example 12.5 Task Process Complete Application in Figure 12.2 selects a mortgage type in case a customer has agreed to apply for it. This is done by adding a `pre`-identified property to extension elements of the task with the following query that nondeterministically selects one mortgage type from the *MortgageType* relation:

SELECT *Mid* FROM *MortgageType* WHERE #*status* = FillApp AND $e > 0$ AND $g > 0$

As an effect, this task is supposed to move a chosen mortgage type ID to a dedicated case variable, and decide on the amount of money asked as well as the interest to be paid in case the mortgage offer gets accepted. The latter is done with two newly declared variables e and g, and three `eff`-identified properties with the following case variable assignments: #*tid* = *Mid*, #*duration* = e and #*amount* = g. Note that the last two essentially model a user input and thus realize the data injection mentioned in **RQ 4**.

All the queries identified with `cond` can be used only in blocks containing choice splits (i.e., blocks from Figure 12.1 with φ annotations on the arcs). In Figure 12.2, we show a screenshot of a simple condition assigned to one of the XOR gateways of the loop block.

12.4.2 Encoding delta-BPMN Camunda Processes in MCMT

To make delta-BPMN processes modeled in Camunda verifiable (cf. **RQ 1**) we have implemented a translator that takes as input a `.bpmn` file produced by Camunda following the modeling guidelines of the previous section, and transforms it into the syntax of the state-of-the-art model checker that can verify data-aware processes parametrically to the read-only relations, namely MCMT run in the database-driven mode (cf. Chapter 9).

The translation first checks whether the input model is block-structured, isolating the various blocks. This is done through traversal algorithm that is of independent interest. Each block is then separately converted into a corresponding set of MCMT instructions by implementing, rule by rule, the encoding mechanism sketched in Section 11.3.3 and presented in detail in [50]. This works since the concrete PDMML syntax introduced here for data definition and manipulation faithfully mirrors the abstract, logical language employed there.

For verification, we obviously need also to express which properties we want to check. Every property is currently defined as a *condition* (whose expression terms, in the sense used in Subsection 12.3.3, are case variables or constants), which specifies a "bad", undesired state of the model: we plan to implement more sophisticated properties mentioning also repository and catalog relations, analogously to DAB properties (cf. Definition 11.10).

To add a property, we employ the same mechanism as above that uses Camunda extension elements. More specifically, we add another reserved identifier `verify` which can be used to add property key-value pairs directly to the process. For example, one can write the PDMML condition (#*status*=Archived **AND** *lifecycleMortgage*=Completed) to verify the safety of the model in Figure 12.2, in particular ascertaining whether the mortgage approval process has been finalized with the customer not being interested in the related offer (see the related End event Client not interested in Figure 12.2), thus resulting in her application being archived. Notice that here we use a special variable *lifecycleMortgage* to access the process lifecycle state. In general, one may query the process lifecyle by using a special case variable *lifecycleModelName*, where *ModelName* is the actual process model name. Verification of lifecycle properties for single blocks can be tackled by introducing dedicated case variables, manipulating them in effects according to the lifecycle evolution of the block.

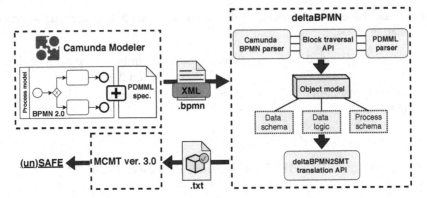

Fig. 12.3: Conceptual architecture of the delta-BPMN framework

It is important to mention that, although this feature is not explicitly reflected in the PDMML language, delta-BPMN provides support for modeling and verification of multi-instance scenarios in which process instances can access and manipulate the same catalog and repository. Formal details are given in [50]. In summary, [50] indicates that unboundedly many simultaneously active process instances can be verified for safety if they do not explicitly refer to each other (i.e., they do not expose their own case identifiers to other instances). Explicit mutual references can instead be handled if the maximum number of simultaneously active process instances is known a-priori.

Figure 12.3 shows the overall toolchain employed for verification. First, a modeler has to produce a delta-BPMN process by enriching a regular block-structured BPMN 2.0 process with a PDMML specification via Camunda extensions using the technique from above. Camunda Modeler then allows to export the delta-BPMN process as an XML-formatted .bpmn file. This file can be then processed by our Java-based tool, called *deltaBPMN*, that employs the following APIs for generating the process specification that can be readily verified by MCMT (http://users.mat.unimi.it/users/ghilardi/mcmt/). In the nutshell, the tool takes two major steps to process the delta-BPMN model. First, it uses the Camunda's BPMN model API to access process components from the input .bpmn file and uses our block traversal API as well as PDMML parser to recognize blocks as well as PDMML statements/declarations and consecutively generate delta-BPMN objects. The latter are specified according to the object model that has been mainly distilled from the DAB formalism and that consists of three major parts: a data schema storing all case variable and relation declarations (from both $\mathcal{R}$ and C), a process schema storing nested supported process block definitions, and a data logic containing update declarations and conditions assigned to blocks. The block traversal API uses a newly developed algorithm for detecting nested blocks that comply to the object model structure. Via the *deltaBPMN2SMT* translation API that internally follows the formal translation from DABs to RASs, the tool then processes the extracted object model and generates a text file containing the delta-BPMN process specification rewritten in the MCMT syntax.

Finally, the derived specification can be directly checked in the MCMT tool that, in turn, will detect whether the specification is safe or unsafe with respect to the *"bad"* property specified in the initial model. Details on MCMT working can be found in Chapter 9; here we just recall that MCMT can be executed in the command line using the following command: `[time] mcmt <filename>`. Here, argument `[time]` is not mandatory, but can be used if one wants to display the MCMT execution time. More information on the model checker installation process, the language for specifying safety properties of delta-BPMN models, advanced execution options and additional details, together with the actual delta-BPMN implementation, can be found on the tool website here: `https://github.com/mrMorningLemon/delta-BPMN`. In addition, as a prototypical example, the mortgage approval example (together with the property to verify described in this subsection) is available as a delta-BPMN process specification on the same website. This example, called `Mortgage.bpmn`, is specified using the Camunda extensions described above, and is ready to be converted by delta-BPMN into a specification file in the `.txt` format that can be directly executed by MCMT. This MCMT specification file, when run by MCMT, returns UNSAFE in secs, as expected: the modeled property to verify was, in fact, a reachable configuration of the system.

12.5 A Brief Discussion on Limitations of DABs and delta-BPMN

We conclude the chapter with some considerations on the limitations we imposed on data schemas for DABs/delta-BPMN and their query languages. Their are fully justified in view of the goal we want to achieve: performing parameterized safety verification. Indeed, these limitations are needed if one wants to leverage the formal framework of RASs presented in Part I, which, in turn, is one of the most powerful and expressive settings for performing parameterized verification of DAPs, as we argued along this book. Thus, full verifiability always comes with a price in terms of limitations on expressiveness.

Nevertheless, these limitations are not so restrictive: we extensively argued throughout the book and showed in several concrete examples that our DAP models are quite expressive and suitable to formalize real-world business processes. This is also confirmed by the benchmark of concrete data-aware business processes that has been analayzed in the experimental section of Chapter 9, which our approach proved to model and verify in a successful way. However, the usability of our approach for modeling concrete and industry-inspired benchmarks of business processes is an open research problem: this is an important future work and it is beyond the scope of this book. We will deepen this discussion in Chapter 14.

Chapter 13
Catalog Object-Aware Nets

In this chapter, we provide the second main application of the formal framework of
U-RASs to the problem of modeling and verification of complex processes enriched
with data. In the previous two chapters, we introduced a formal framework and its
implementation that make use of the BPMN standard language in order to represent
the process component. In contrast, this chapter is devoted to investigating data-aware
extensions of Petri net-based processes toward their safety verification.

Specifically, by taking advantage of the fruitful tradition of employing Petri
nets as the main backbone for processes, we introduce *Catalog and Object-Aware
nets* (COA-nets), an enrichment of colored Petri nets (CPNs) where transitions
are equipped with guards that simultaneously inspect the content of tokens and
query facts stored in a read-only persistent database (i.e., a catalog), and can inject
data into tokens by extracting relevant values from the database or by generating
genuinely fresh ones. This model is particularly tailored to represent the co-evolution
of multiple objects, an essential feature when dealing with real-life processes [116,
246, 218]

The chapter is organized as follows. In Section 13.1, we give the formal definition
of COA-nets and we provide relevant examples. In Subsection 13.1.1, we show the
interesting modeling capabilities of COA-nets: two of the main features of COA-nets
are about the types of object creations supported and the capacity of accommodating
processes with multiple co-evolving case objects, so as to represent and track one-
to-one, one-to-many and many-to-many relationships among them. In Section 13.2,
we show how COA-nets can be encoded into the database-driven mode of MCMT,
i.e., that they can be seen as Universal RASs: this allows us to import the results
for Universal RASs from Chapter 4 and, in Section 13.3, to study parameterized
safety verification of COA-nets using SMT-based techniques. The meta-properties
of these techniques, when applied to the verification of COA-nets, are discussed in
Section 13.4. We conclude the chapter by providing a detailed discussion on how
COA-nets provide a unifying approach for some of the most sophisticated formalisms
in this area, highlighting differences and commonalities.

The content of this chapter is strongly based on [135, 139].

© The Author(s), under exclusive license to Springer Nature Switzerland AG 2023   259
A. Gianola: *Verification of Data-Aware Processes via Satisfiability Modulo Theories*,
LNBIP 470, pp. 259–295, 2023.
https://doi.org/10.1007/978-3-031-42746-6_13

13.1 The COA-net Formal Model

In this section, we present key concepts and notions used for defining catalog-nets. Conceptually, a COA-net integrates two key components. The first is, as customary in the artifact-centric tradition and similarly to (Universal) RASs and DABs, a read-only persistent data storage, called *catalog*, to account for read-only, parameterized data. The second is a variant of CPN, called *v*-CPN [206], to model the process backbone. Places in *v*-CPNs carry tuples of data objects and can be used to represent: *(i)* states of (interrelated) case objects, *(ii)* read-write relations, *(iii)* read-only relations whose extension is fixed (and consequently not subject to parameterisation), *(iv)* resources. As in [206, 116, 218], the net employs *v*-variables (first studied in the context of *v*-PNs [228]) to inject fresh data (such as object identifiers). A distinguishing feature of COA-nets is that transitions can have guards that inspect and retrieve data objects from the read-only catalog. At the end of the section we discuss in more detail all the previously mentioned characteristics using a COA-net in Figure 13.6.

Data types. We recall from Section 10.2 the notion of *type*, and, in line with Chapter 3, we add the type distinction for *id* and *value* objects. We consider a *type set* $\mathfrak{D}$ as a finite set of pairwise disjoint types accounting for the different kinds of objects in the domain of interest. We partition this finite set of types in two disjoint subsets: the subset of *id sorts* $\mathfrak{D}_{id}$ and the subset of *value sorts* $\mathfrak{D}_{val}$. Conceptually, a type in $\mathfrak{D}_{id}$ is called id sort and accounts for *identifiers* of different kinds of objects, while a type in $\mathfrak{D}_{val}$ is called value sort and accounts for *value data types* such as strings, numbers. Each type $\mathcal{D} \in \mathfrak{D}$ comes with its own *domain* $\Delta_{\mathcal{D}}$, and with an equality operator $=_{\mathcal{D}}$: in line with Chapter 3, we require that when $\mathcal{D} \in \mathfrak{D}_{id}$, the domain $\Delta_{\mathcal{D}}$ is *finite*, whereas when $\mathcal{D} \in \mathfrak{D}_{val}$, the domain $\Delta_{\mathcal{D}}$ is possibly infinite. Domains of different types are pairwise disjoint. When clear from the context, we simplify the notation of the equality operator $=_{\mathcal{D}}$ and only use $=$. We assume that each type $\mathcal{D} \in \mathfrak{D}$ comes with a special constant $\mathsf{undef}_{\mathcal{D}} \in \mathfrak{D}$ to denote an undefined value in that domain.

    Catalog. $R(a_1 : \mathcal{D}_1, \ldots, a_n : \mathcal{D}_n)$ is a $\mathfrak{D}$-*typed relation schema*, where R is a relation name and $a_i : \mathcal{D}_i$ indicates the i-th attribute of R together with its data type. When no ambiguity arises, we omit relation attributes and/or their data types. A $\mathfrak{D}$-*typed catalog (schema)* $\mathcal{R}_{\mathfrak{D}}$ is a finite set of $\mathfrak{D}$-typed relation schemas. A $\mathfrak{D}$-*typed catalog instance Cat* over $\mathcal{R}_{\mathfrak{D}}$ is a finite set of facts $R(o_1, \ldots, o_n)$, where $R \in \mathcal{R}_{\mathfrak{D}}$ and $o_i \in \Delta_{\mathcal{D}_i}$, for $i \in \{1, \ldots, n\}$.

    We adopt some natural *constraints* in the catalog relations. First, we assume the first attribute of every relation $R \in \mathcal{R}_{\mathfrak{D}}$ to be its *primary key*, denoted as $\mathrm{PK}(R)$: the type of a primary key needs to be an id sort. Also, the type of such an attribute should be different from the types of other primary key attributes. Then, for any $R, S \in \mathcal{R}_{\mathfrak{D}}$, $R[a] \rightarrow S[id]$ defines that the projection $R.a$ is a *foreign key* referencing $S.id$, where $\mathrm{PK}(S) = id$, $\mathrm{PK}(R) \neq a$ and $\mathcal{D} = \mathcal{D}'$, for $id : \mathcal{D}$ and $a : \mathcal{D}'$. We also assume that every id sort $\mathcal{D} \in \mathfrak{D}_{id}$ determines the primary key of some n-ary $\mathfrak{D}$-typed catalog relation $R_{\mathcal{D}}$, in the sense that every element $s_1 \in \Delta_{\mathcal{D}} \setminus \{\mathsf{undef}_{\mathcal{D}}\}$ is the first component of some tuple $(s_1, \ldots, s_n)$ such that the fact $R_{\mathcal{D}}(s_1, \ldots, s_n)$ is in the catalog instance

Cat. While the given setting with constraints may seem a bit restrictive, it is the one adopted in the most sophisticated settings where parameterization of read-only data is tackled (e.g., [102]).

Example 13.1 Consider a simple catalog of an order-to-delivery scenario, containing two relation schemas. Relation schema *ProdCat*(p : ProdType) indicates the product types (e.g., vegetables, furniture) available in the organisation catalogue of products. Relation schema *Comp*(c : CId, p : ProdType, t : TruckType) captures the compatibility between products and truck types used to deliver orders; e.g. one may specify that vegetables are compatible only with types of trucks that have a refrigerator.

Catalog queries. We fix a countably infinite set $\mathcal{V}_{\mathfrak{D}}$ of typed variables with a *variable typing function* type : $\mathcal{V}_{\mathfrak{D}} \to \mathfrak{D}$. As query language we opt for the union of conjunctive queries with inequalities and atomic negations that can be specified in terms of first-order (FO) logic extended with types. This corresponds to widely investigated SQL select-project-join queries with filters, and unions thereof.

A *conjunctive query (CQ) with atomic negation* Q over $\mathcal{R}_{\mathfrak{D}}$ has the form

$$Q ::= \varphi \mid R(x_1, \ldots, x_n) \mid \neg R(x_1, \ldots, x_n) \mid Q_1 \wedge Q_2 \mid \exists x.Q,$$

where *(i)* $R(\mathcal{D}_1, \ldots, \mathcal{D}_n) \in \mathcal{R}_{\mathfrak{D}}$, $x \in \mathcal{V}_{\mathfrak{D}}$ and each x_i is either a variable of type $\mathcal{D}_i$ or a constant from $\Delta_{\mathcal{D}_i}$; *(ii)* $\varphi ::= y_1 = y_2 \mid y_1 \neq y_2 \mid \varphi \wedge \varphi \mid \top$ is a *condition*, s.t. y_i is either a variable of type $\mathcal{D}$ or a constant from $\Delta_{\mathcal{D}}$. $CQ_{\mathfrak{D}}^{\neg}$ denotes the set of all such conjunctive queries, and *Free*(Q) the set of all free variables (i.e., those not occurring in the scope of quantifiers) of query Q. $C_{\mathfrak{D}}$ denotes the set of all possible conditions, *Vars*(Q) the set of all variables in Q, and *Const*(Q) the set of all constants in Q. Finally, $UCQ_{\mathfrak{D}}^{\neg}$ denotes the set off all *unions of conjunctive queries* over $\mathcal{R}_{\mathfrak{D}}$. Each query $Q \in UCQ_{\mathfrak{D}}^{\neg}$ has the form $Q = \bigvee_{i=1}^{n} Q_i$, with $Q_i \in CQ_{\mathfrak{D}}^{\neg}$. This language is similar in spirit to the query language employed in the DAB data schema (cf. Subsection 11.2.1), but it presents some differences (e.g., here there is no repository relation, but we will see in Subsection 13.2.1 that, in some sense, places can be interpreted, to some extent, as repository relations, or, using the U-RAS nomenclature, artifact relations).

A *substitution* for a set $X = \{x_1, \ldots, x_n\}$ of typed variables is a function $\theta : X \to \Delta_S$, such that $\theta(x) \in \Delta_{\text{type}(x)}$ for every $x \in X$. An empty substitution is denoted as $\langle \rangle$. A *substitution θ for a query Q*, denoted as $Q\theta$, is a substitution for variables in *Free*(Q). An *answer to a query Q* in a catalog instance *Cat* is a set of substitutions $ans(Q, Cat) = \{\theta : Free(Q) \to Val(Cat) \mid Cat, \theta \models Q\}$, where *Val*(*Cat*) denotes the set of all constants occurring in *Cat* and $\models$ denotes standard FO entailment.

Example 13.2 Consider the catalog of Example 13.1. Query *ProdCat*(p) retrieves the product types p present in the catalog, whereas given a product type value veg, query $\exists c.Comp(c, \text{veg}, t)$ returns the truck types t compatible with veg.

COA-nets. We use in the following the standard notions related to multisets presented in Section 10.2. We recall that, given a set A, the set of multisets over A, written

$A^{\oplus}$, is the set of mappings of the form $m : A \to \mathbb{N}$, and given a multiset $S \in A^{\oplus}$ and an element $a \in A$, $S(a) \in \mathbb{N}$ denotes the number of times a appears in S. We write $a^n \in S$ if $S(a) = n$. We also consider the usual operations on multisets defined in Section 10.2. In what follows, with slight abuse of notation we assume that functions type, $Vars$ and $Const$ are extended to account for sets, tuples and multisets of variables and constants. For example, $Vars(\{x, 1, a, y, z\}) = \{x, y, z\}$ and $Const(\{x, 1, a, y, z\}) = \{1, a\}$.

We now define COA-nets, extending v-CPNs [206] with the ability of querying a read-only catalog. As in CPNs, each COA-net place has a color type, which corresponds to a data type or to the cartesian product of multiple data types from $\mathfrak{D}$. Tokens in places are referenced via *inscriptions* – tuples of variables and constants. We denote by Ω_A the set of all possible inscriptions over a set A. To account for fresh external inputs, we employ the well-known mechanism of v-Petri nets [228] and introduce a countably infinite set $\Upsilon_{\mathfrak{D}}$ of S-typed *fresh variables*, where for every $v \in \Upsilon_{\mathfrak{D}}$, we have that $\Delta_{\text{type}(v)}$ is its domain (this domain is finite if the type of v is an id sort, otherwise it provides an unlimited supply of fresh values). We fix a countably infinite set of $\mathfrak{D}$-typed variable $\mathcal{X}_S = \mathcal{V}_{\mathfrak{D}} \uplus \Upsilon_{\mathfrak{D}}$ as the disjoint union of "normal" ($\mathcal{V}_{\mathfrak{D}}$) and fresh ($\Upsilon_{\mathfrak{D}}$) variables.

Definition 13.1 (COA-net) A $\mathfrak{D}$-typed COA-net $\mathcal{N}$ over a catalog schema $\mathcal{R}_S$ is a tuple $(\mathfrak{D}, \mathcal{R}_{\mathfrak{D}}, P, T, F_{in}, F_{out}, \text{color}, \text{guard})$, where:
1. P and T are finite sets of places and transitions, s.t. $P \cap T = \emptyset$;
2. $\text{color} : P \to \mathcal{K}_{\mathfrak{D}}$ is a place typing function, where $\mathcal{K}_{\mathfrak{D}}$ is a set of all possible cartesian products $\mathcal{D}_1 \times \ldots \times \mathcal{D}_m$, s.t. $\mathcal{D}_i \in \mathfrak{D}$, for each $i = 1, \ldots, m$;
3. $F_{in} : P \times T \to \Omega_{\mathcal{V}_{\mathfrak{D}}}^{\oplus}$ is an input flow, s.t. $\text{type}(F_{in}(p, t)) = \text{color}(p)$ for every $(p, t) \in P \times T$;
4. $F_{out} : T \times P \to \Omega_{\mathcal{X}_S \cup \Delta_{\mathfrak{D}}}^{\oplus}$ is an output flow, s.t. $\text{type}(F_{out}(t, p)) = \text{color}(p)$ for every $(t, p) \in T \times P$;
5. $\text{guard} : T \to \{Q \wedge \varphi \mid Q \in \text{UCQ}_{\mathfrak{D}}^{\neg}, \varphi \in C_{\mathfrak{D}}\}$ is a partial guard assignment function, s.t., for every $\text{guard}(t) = Q \wedge \varphi$ and $t \in T$, the following holds:
    a. $Vars(\varphi) \subseteq InVars(t)$, where $InVars(t) = \cup_{p \in P} Vars(F_{in}(p, t))$;
    b. $OutVars(t) \setminus (InVars(t) \cup \Upsilon_{\mathfrak{D}}) \subseteq Free(Q)$ and $Free(Q) \subseteq Vars(t)$, where $OutVars(t) = \cup_{p \in P} Vars(F_{out}(t, p))$ and $Vars(t) = InVars(t) \cup OutVars(t)$.

Here, the role of guards is twofold. On the one hand, similarly, for example, to CPNs, guards are used to impose *conditions* (using φ) on tokens flowing through the net. On the other hand, a guard of transition t may also *query* (using Q) the catalog in order to propagate some data into the net. The acquired data may be still filtered by using $InVars(t)$. Note that in condition *(b)* of the guard definition we specify that, if there are some variables (excluding the fresh ones) in the outgoing arc inscriptions that do not appear in $InVars(t)$, then these are the free variables of Q. Such variables, in turn, are used in the net to propagate data from the catalog via query answers. Moreover, it is required that all free variables of Q are exhaustively covered by the variables in the input and output arcs. This condition essentially forbids to have queries producing answers that are (partially) not going to be used in the net. As customary in high-level Petri nets, using the same variable in two different arc inscriptions amounts to checking the equality between the respective components of such inscriptions. For every transition $t \in T$, we also define $^\bullet t = \{p \in P \mid (p, t) \in \text{DOM}(F_{in})\}$ as a *pre-set* of t and $t^\bullet = \{p \in P \mid (t, p) \in \text{DOM}(F_{out})\}$ as a *post-set* of t.[1]

Semantics. The execution semantics of a COA-net is similar to the one of CPNs. Thus, as a first step we introduce the standard notion of net marking. Formally, a *marking* of a COA-net $N = (\mathfrak{D}, \mathcal{R}_\mathfrak{D}, P, T, F_{in}, F_{out}, \text{color}, \text{guard})$ is a function $m : P \rightarrow \Omega_\mathfrak{D}^\oplus$, so that $m(p) \in \Delta_{\text{color}(p)}^\oplus$ for every $p \in P$. We write $\langle N, m, Cat \rangle$ to denote COA-net N marked with m, and equipped with a read-only catalog instance Cat over $\mathcal{R}_S$.

The firing of a transition t in a marking is defined w.r.t. a so-called *binding* for t defined as $\sigma : Vars(t) \rightarrow \Delta_\mathfrak{D}$. Note that, when applied to (multisets of) tuples, σ is applied to every variable singularly. For example, given $\sigma = \{x \mapsto 1, y \mapsto a\}$, its application to a multiset of tuples $\omega = \{\langle x, y \rangle^2, \langle x, b \rangle\}$ results in $\sigma(\omega) = \{\langle 1, a \rangle^2, \langle 1, b \rangle\}$.

Next, we define when a transition can be called *enabled*. Essentially, a transition is enabled with a binding σ if the binding selects data objects carried by tokens from the input places and the read-only catalog instance, so that the data they carry make the guard attached to the transition true.

Definition 13.2 A transition $t \in T$ is *enabled* in a marking m and a fixed catalog instance Cat, written $m[t\rangle_{Cat}$, if there exists binding σ satisfying the following: *(i)* $\sigma(F_{in}(p, t)) \subseteq m(p)$, for every $p \in P$; *(ii)* $\sigma(\text{guard}(t))$ is true; *(iii)* for every fresh variable $v \in \Upsilon_\mathfrak{D} \cap OutVars(t)$, we have that $\sigma(v) \in \Delta_{\text{type}(v)} \setminus Val(m)$;[2] *(iv)* $\sigma(x) = \theta(x)$, for $\theta \in ans(Q, Cat)$, $x \in (OutVars(t) \setminus InVars(t)) \cap Vars(Q)$ and query Q from $\text{guard}(t)$.[3]

In the definition, point *(iii)* constraints the possible bindings for fresh variables. If $\Delta_{\text{type}(v)}$ of some fresh variable v is the domain of an id sort (i.e., if the type of the variable v is an id sort), it may be the case that the identifiers contained in the catalog for that type are all present in the current marking; in this extreme case, *(iii)* indicates that the transition cannot fire. If instead $\Delta_{\text{type}(v)}$ is a the domain of a value sort, there is always a way to pick a suitable, fresh value for v.

When a transition t is enabled, it may fire. Next we define what are the effects of firing a transition with some binding σ.

Definition 13.3 Let $\langle N, m, Cat \rangle$ be a marked COA-net, and $t \in T$ a transition enabled in m and Cat with some binding σ. Then, t may *fire* producing a new marking m', with $m'(p) = m(p) - \sigma(F_{in}(p, t)) + \sigma(F_{out}(t, p))$ for every $p \in P$. We denote this as $m[t\rangle_{Cat}m'$ and assume that the definition is inductively extended to sequences $\tau \in T^*$.

---

[1] $\text{DOM}(f)$ denotes a domain of function f.

[2] Here, with slight abuse of notation, we define by $Val(m)$ the set of all values appearing in m.

[3] This condition stipulates that the binding needs to "agree" on the result of Q when it comes to the variables of Q that are used in the output inscriptions of t, and have not been already bound by the variables in the input inscriptions of the same transition.

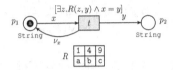

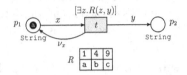

(a) A bounded COA-net.   (b) An unbounded variant of the net in
                                                    Figure 13.1a.

Fig. 13.1: Boundedness in COA-nets with identical catalog instances containing letters from a to z.

For $\langle N, m_0, Cat \rangle$ we use $\mathcal{M}(N) = \{m \mid \exists \tau \in T^*.m_0[\tau]_{Cat}m\}$ to denote the set of all markings of N reachable from its initial marking m_0.

Definition 13.4 (COA-net Boundedness) Given $b \in \mathbb{N}$, place p in a marked COA-net $\langle N, m_0, Cat \rangle$ is called *b-bounded* if $|m(p)| \le b$, for every marking $m \in \mathcal{M}(N)$. The same net is called *bounded with bound b* if every place $p \in P$ is *b-bounded*.

Unboundedness in COA-nets can arise due to various reasons: classical unbounded generation of tokens, but also uncontrollable emission of fresh values with ν-variables or replication of data values from the catalog via queries in transition guards.

Example 13.3 Figure 13.1 demonstrates two almost identical marked COA-nets, with a catalog fixing pairs in a binary relation R whose first component defines the primary key for R, and the second component is a string attribute. The net represented in Figure 13.1a is bounded. This can be seen considering that the guard of t extracts strings stored in the second component of R and compares them to those in place p_1, consequently allowing t to fire only if those values coincide. Moreover, after each firing, the token stored in p_1 is consumed, bringing back to p_1 a token carries a "locally fresh" string value generated using ν_x. Being locally fresh, such a value must be different from any string value present p_1 and p_2. This means that, sooner or later, a string not contained in the second component of R (i.e., different from a, b, and c) will need to be selected when binding ν_x. When this happens, t will not fire anymore. All in all, this means that the marked net will never assign more than one token to p_1, and no more than three tokens to p_2 (where three is indeed the number of distinct string values contained in the second component of R). Differently from the marked net discusses so far, its variant shown Figure 13.1b is unbounded. In this case, the loop relating p_1 and t preserves the bound of one token for p_1, no restrictions are imposed on $\mathsf{guard}(t)$ on the token consumed from p_1. This, in turn, indicates that t can fire unboundedly many times, inflating p_2 with unboundedly many tokens, each carrying one of the three string values a, b, and c extracted from the catalog. This shows an example of unboundedness arising even if the number of values simultaneously present in the current marking stays bounded.

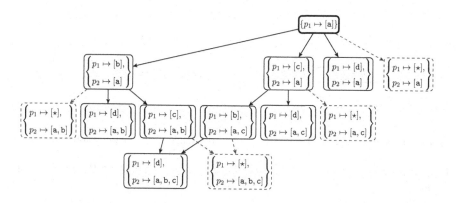

Fig. 13.2: Transition system capturing the execution semantics of the marked net from Figure 13.1a. Symbol $\star$ denotes a string value different from a, b, c, d (there exist infinitely many such $\star$).

Execution semantics. The execution semantics of a marked COA-net $\langle N, m_0, Cat \rangle$ is defined in terms of a possibly infinite-state transition system in which states are labeled by reachable markings and each arc (or transition) corresponds to the firing of a transition in N with a given binding. The transition system captures all possible executions of the net, by interpreting concurrency as interleaving. Technically, let $\langle N, m_0, Cat \rangle$ be a marked COA-net with catalog instance Cat. Then its execution semantics is captured by transition system $\Lambda_N = (S, s_0, \Rightarrow)$, where:

- S is a possibly infinite set of markings over N;
- $\Rightarrow \subseteq S \times T \times S$ is a T-labelled transition relation between pairs of markings;
- S and $\Rightarrow$ are defined by simultaneous induction as the smallest sets satisfying the following conditions: *(i)* $m_0 \in S$; *(ii)* given $m \in S$, for every transition $t \in T$, binding σ and marking m' over N, if $m[t\rangle_{Cat} m'$, then $m' \in S$ and $m \overset{t}{\Rightarrow} m'$.

As pointed out before, we are interested in analysing a COA-net irrespectively of the actual content of the catalog. Hence, in the following when we mention a (catalog-parameterized) marked net $\overline{N} m_0$ without specifying how the catalog is instantiated, we actually implicitly mean the *infinite set of marked nets* $\langle N, m_0, Cat \rangle$ for every possible instance Cat defined over the catalog schema of N.

Example 13.4 Figure 13.2 shows the transition system capturing the execution semantics of the marked net from Figure 13.1a, whose initial marking m_0 assigns to p_1 one token carrying the string value a. For ease of reading, we omit the catalog instance and arc labels. Notice that, although our net is bounded, its transition system contains infinitely many states due to the presence of the v-variable v_x that, in every firing, can be bound to any string value that is not present in current net marking.

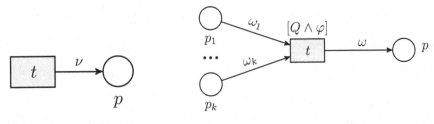

(a) Object generating emitter.   (b) Catalog-based object constructor.

Fig. 13.3: Object creation patterns. In Figure 13.3b, $Free(Q) \neq \emptyset$ and $Vars(\omega) \subseteq Free(Q)$.

13.1.1 Modeling Capabilities

13.1.1.1 Object Creation Patterns

Given that COA-net models can conceptually address two seemingly disjoint dimensions, one may wonder about the modeling capabilities of the COA-net formalism and, in particular, more recurring *modeling patterns* that could be of relevance for domain experts that would like to use COA-nets for representing data- and process-aware information systems. While there are already works that tackle pattern-based modeling approaches using various classes of Petri nets (see, for example, [229, 247]), we focus on specifying patterns that cover generation and management of *multiple* case objects.

When choosing to opt for a setting in which management of case objects is no less important than correct representation of control flow, it is crucial to ensure that such setting lends enough of expressive power for creating, deleting or updating the case objects as well as takes into account their types and relations between each other. In COA-nets, objects are represented as typed tokens. Introducing a new object to a net, apart from using a traditional token generation mechanism, can be done by either using fresh variables or by materializing such object based on results of a query performed on top of a catalog.

The first case is rather limited only to *emitter* transitions and enforces the concept of identity over created objects (that is, every object created with this pattern is *identified* with a unique element taken from the domain of the related variable from $\Upsilon_{\mathfrak{D}}$). The related *object generating emitter* pattern is demonstrated in Figure 13.3a. As an example of its application in practice, one can think of an emitter transition that allows to generate (fresh) identifiers of unboundedly many orders in some order-to-delivery process.

The second *catalog-based object constructor* pattern is shown in Figure 13.3b. Upon firing of transition t, it extracts some relevant data from the catalog using query Q in the guard, and then binds extracted values to variables in ω. This allows to create objects that can potentially coalesce control flow data (taken from some

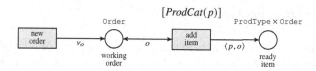

Fig. 13.4: An example of using both patterns from Figure 13.3

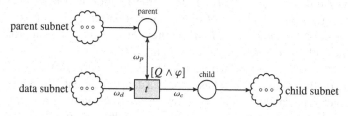

Fig. 13.5: A pattern for creating objects involved in a one-to-many relationship. Here, ω_c contains only variables taken from $Vars(\omega_d)$, $Vars(\omega_p)$ and $Free(Q)$.

of the incoming places of t) with information available in the persistent storage. A simple use case for this pattern can be a direct follow-up of the order creation example. Assuming that our net contains order identifiers, previously generated with emitter new order, and the catalog is the one described in Example 13.1, we can use the former in order to generate new objects specifying an item (of a certain type) being assigned to an order. Figure 13.4 shows that the creation of items is not modeled using an explicit v-variable, but is instead simply obtained by the add item transition which enriches a selected order token with the product type taken from the catalog using the query assigned to add item.

As a side remark, we briefly comment on the overall modeling power of the catalog. In general, it is common to have processes that only alter a portion of all the data they have access to (think, for example, of product types, employees and carriers in an order-to-cash process), or processes that by design can only access some (possibly structured) data in a read-only mode. Given that data objects can also be related to one another, this naturally calls for introducing a static storage to keep track of such read-only relations. In our framework, these relations may be represented with special read-only places (as it is essentially done in [206]). However, using places for read-only relations would not naturally allow one to capture key and foreign key constraints, nor to distinguish the query language used to inspect them from that used for normal places.[4] And even if it were the case, then resulting model will be conceptually too confusing. This is the main reason for having a separate representation.

---

[4] There are also technical results on verification clearly showing that there is a difference between the way read-only and read-write relations can be constrained and queried [55].

13.1.1.2 Object Relationship Patterns

Let us now focus on patterns that help modeling management of relations or, better said, dependencies between case objects. In particular, we show how to address one-to-many relations using the language of COA-nets. We deliberately avoid the trivial one-to-one case as well as the case of many-to-many relations. The latter, however, can be easily represented by simply reifying the relation in a new separate object and producing a consequent pair of one-to-many relations, each of which keeping the new object on the "one" side. In the context of Petri nets, this approach is very much in line with the one recently proposed in [116].

Whenever we want to create an object that is meant to participate in a one-to-many relationship on the "many" side, it has to carry a data of a parent object it is related to. Although such data can be of any type, we suggest to bring its complexity to a bare minimum and use object identifiers whenever possible. Figure 13.5 demonstrates a schematic overview of a generic COA-net for this case. As opposed to object generation patterns, it is crucial to induce the conceptual separation between different subnets that contribute to the creation of case objects and that, at the same time, show their lifecycles. Thus, we use three subnets: two show the lifecycle of the parent (the 'one' side) and child (the 'many' side) objects taking part in the one-to-many relation, respectively stored in *parent* and *child* places; the third subnet, on top of the query Q, is used as an independent data supplier with its own potentially complex workflow. [5] Notice that the last subnet is essentially a combination of object generating emitters and catalog-based constructors. Although it is not explicitly shown in Figure 13.5, the parent subnet considers the parent object lifecycle including the creation step (which can be realized using one of the patterns from Figure 13.3, proviso that newly generated parent objects are duly equipped with unique identifiers as suggested above), whereas the creation of child objects is instrumented with transition t. Notice also that both the catalog query and the data subnet can be avoided. However, that, in turn, requires the modeler to use ν-variables in ω_c. One may also wonder whether given the nature of the catalog storage, dependencies between relations therein should be also taken into account and/or can be reflected in the net model. The answer on this matter becomes evident when looking into the nature of the queries. Strictly speaking, query answers do not carry over any constraints imposed on the source database. Thus, data values that the modeler gets in the net are just copies of those in the catalog.

As an example of the pattern discussed above, one may use the one from Figure 13.4. Here, each newly created item carries a reference to its owning order, and thus models the one-to-many relation between orders and items. Thanks to the multiset semantics of Petri nets, it is still possible to create multiple items having the same product type and owning order. However, it is not possible to track the evolution of a specific item, since there is no explicit identifier carried by item tokens. This can be always changed by adding to the catalog another relation $Item(c : \text{IId}, n : \text{Descr}, p : \text{ProdType})$ that stores information about items by

---

[5] By independence we imply that the data coming from the data subnet are not meant to create any additional dependencies.

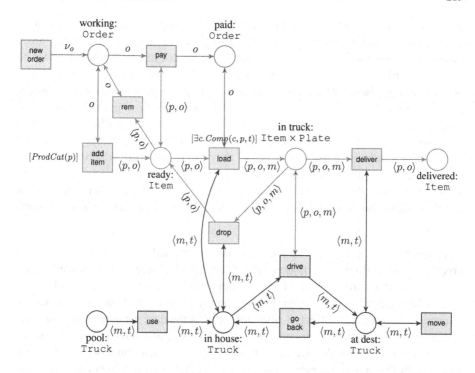

Fig. 13.6: A COA-net (its catalog is in Example 13.1). In the picture, Item and Truck are compact representations for ProdType × Order and Plate × TruckType respectively. The top blue part refers to orders, the central orange part to items, and the bottom violet part to delivery trucks.

capturing their identifiers, short content descriptions and product types, which, in turn provides information for adding identity to items in the net.

Lastly, we would like to comment on one more possible usage of complex objects in COA-nets. Quite often, processes require a presence of resources, both structured and unstructured, which are fixed in the process model domain. Our formalism lends its expressive power to account for both types. Resources should be represented as tokens assigned to dedicated places with the initial marking, and their amount initially present in the net should never change (that is, one shall never create new or destroy any of the already existing resources). A natural example of resources are shipping company employees involved in handling orders.

We conclude with an example that summarizes all the main features of COA-nets.

Example 13.5 Starting from the catalog in Example 13.1, Figure 13.6 shows a simple, yet sophisticated example of COA-net capturing the following order-to-delivery process. Orders can be created by executing the new order transition, which uses a ν-variable to generate a fresh order identifier. A so-created, working order can be populated with items, whose type is selected from those available in the catalog relation *ProdCat*. Each item then carries its product type and owning order. When an order contains *at least one* item, it can be paid. Items added to an order can be removed or loaded in a compatible truck. Unpaid items added to a working order can be always removed, whereas paid ones can be loaded in a compatible truck. The set of available trucks, indicating their plate numbers and types, is contained in a dedicated *pool* place. Trucks can be borrowed from the pool and placed in house. An item can be loaded into a truck if its owning order has been paid, the truck is in house, and the truck type and product type of the item are compatible according to the *Comp* relation in the catalog. Items (possibly from different orders) can be loaded in a truck, and while the truck is in house, they can be dropped, which makes them ready to be loaded again. A truck can be driven for delivery if it contains at least one loaded item. Once the truck is at its destination, some items may be delivered (this is simply modeled non-deterministically). The truck can then either move, or go back in house.

Example 13.5 showcases various key aspects related to modeling data-aware processes with multiple case objects using COA-nets that have been discussed above. Using the pattern from Figure 13.5, we demonstrate that whenever an object is involved in a many-to-one relation from the "many" side, it then becomes responsible of carrying the object to which it is related. This is the case for every item carrying a reference to its owning order and, once loaded into a truck, a reference to the truck plate number. One can also see that the above example manipulates three different object types that have been previously discussed in this section. Unboundedly many case objects representing orders can be genuinely created using the object generating emitter as it is demonstrated in Figure 13.4. The (finite) set of trucks available in the domain is instead fixed in the *pool* place in Figure13.6 by the initial marking, and represents a pool of resources that can change state but are never destroyed nor created. Finally, objects representing items can be arbitrarily created and destroyed using the pattern from Figure 13.5. Since items are in one-to-many relation with orders on the "many" side, their creation is not modeled using an explicit ν-variable, but is instead simply obtained by the add item transition which acquires product types from the catalog using the query in guard(add item). This also demonstrates that, unlike orders and trucks, items do not require any identifiers as the scenario does not need either to track their lifecycle or to relate them to other child objects. Thus, one may also assert that ν-variables are only necessary when the COA-net needs to handle the arbitrary creation of objects that are referenced by other objects or when object identifiers are explicitly required in the modeling scenario.

13.2 From COA-nets to MCMT

We now report on the operational encoding of COA-nets into the verification language supported by the MCMT model checker, showing that the various modeling constructs of COA-nets have a direct counterpart in the database-driven mode of MCMT (cf. Chapter 9), and in turn enabling formal analysis and verification.

Formally, this operational encoding, in fact, implies that COA-nets can be directly modeled as Universal RASs (cf. Section 3.2.2): this consideration will be crucial in order to import all the verification results we developed for U-RASs in Part I. However, we prefer to exhibit an operational, practice-oriented encoding of COA-nets into the MCMT syntax, instead of a formal translation into the theoretical framework of U-RASs, since COA-nets have concrete applications in the context of data-aware business processes modeling and verification: in view of those applications, the support of a tool-based language is certainly more appealing and useful, because it also practically shows how to manually write specification files modeling COA-nets that are ready to be verified by MCMT.

We recall that MCMT is founded on the theory of *array-based systems* [147, 146].

13.2.1 Universal RASs: a Summary

We stressed several times in the course of this book that an array-based system describes the evolution of array data structures of unbounded size. The content of an array a changes over time, and it is represented by a *function* variable, called *array variable*, which defines for each index what is the value stored in the corresponding cell. Its content changes when moving from one state to another, reflecting the intended manipulation of the array. We assume that the reader is now familiar with the notions of state formula, initial formula $I(a)$ and transition formula $\tau(a, a')$. The verification problems we deal with here is the usual one, i.e. the one of *unsafety verification*: it checks whether the evolution induced by τ over a starting from a configuration in $I(a)$ eventually *reaches* an *unsafe* configuration described by a state formula $K(a)$. U-RASs, introduced in Section 3.2.2, are an extension of array-based systems that comprises the artifact-centric model, in the style of [186]. We are in particular interested in applying to COA-nets the results from the sophisticated formalism of U-RASs.

In U-RASs we know that a *relational* artifact system accesses a read-only database with keys and foreign keys (cf. the definition of catalog for COA-nets). In addition, the U-RAS operates over a set of evolving relations possibly containing unboundedly many updatable entries (cf. tokens in places of COA-nets). As in the case of DB schemas for U-RASs, the COA-nets catalog is treated as a rich, background theory for storing read-only data: hence, it can be thought again as a more sophisticated version of the element sort in basic array systems. In U-RASs, each evolving relation (i.e., 'artifact relations') is treated as a set of arrays, where each array accounts for one column of the corresponding evolving relation; a tuple in each evolving relation is identified when accessing with the same index all the arrays corresponding to that relation. Tuples of evolving relations are in some sense similar to tokens carrying data in places of COA-nets. This intuition is instructive since it helps the reader to understand how COA-nets places with tokens carrying data can be equivalently represented, i.e. as artifact relations with tuples storing data.

As shown in Section 4.3, U-RASs can be verified by using the same verification machinery employed with RASs, i.e. the backward reachability procedure BReach_{RAS}, with the proviso of preventively reducing U-RASs to RASs. Unfortunately, this reduction only partially preserves the meta-properties of the RAS verification procedure, but we will see that for the scope of our application to COA-nets, this partial preservation is still significant. Indeed, as it will be discussed below, we will use BReach_{RAS} to formally verify also COA-nets, once suitably encoded into the MCMT syntax. The next section is devoted to showing this encoding: we remind the reader that in order to support the representation of read-only databases (the catalog) and the extension of backward reachability BReach_{RAS}, one needs to adopt the module of MCMT called database-driven mode and extensively described in Chapter 9, which is the one used here too.

13.2.2 Encoding COA-nets into MCMT

In this section, we show how to encode a COA-net $\overline{N}m_0$, where $N = (\mathfrak{D}, \mathcal{R}_\mathfrak{D}, P, T, F_{in}, F_{out}, \mathsf{color}, \mathsf{guard})$ into MCMT specification in the database-driven mode: for details on the database-driven mode of MCMT, see Chapter 9. The translation is split into two phases. First, we tackle the type domain and catalog: we declare them using the MCMT syntax for DB schemas. Then, we present a step-wise encoding of the COA-net elements and the net semantics into the MCMT syntax for U-RASs (cf. Chapter 9).

Data and schema translation. We start by describing how to translate static data-related components. Let $\mathfrak{D} = \{\mathcal{D}_1, \ldots, \mathcal{D}_{n_d}\}$. Each data type $\mathcal{D}_i$ is encoded in MCMT with declaration

```
:smt (define_type Di)
```

For each declared type $\mathcal{D}$ MCMT implicitly generates a special NULL constant indicating an empty/undefined value of $\mathcal{D}$. As it has been already mentioned in Section 13.1, every type has an equality operation defined for it.

To represent the catalog relations of $\mathcal{R}_\mathfrak{D} = \{R_1, \ldots, R_{n_r}\}$ in MCMT, we proceed as follows. Recall that in the catalog every relation schema has $n + 1$ typed attributes among which some may be foreign keys referencing other relations, its first attribute is a primary key, and, finally, primary keys of different relation schemas have different types. With these conditions at hand, we adopt the functional characterization of read-only databases for Array-Based Artifact Systems studied in Section 3.1. For every relation $R_i(id, A_1, \ldots, A_n)$ with $\mathrm{PK}(R) = \{id\}$, we introduce unary functions that correctly reference each attribute of R_i using its primary key. More specifically, for every A_j $(j = 1, \ldots, n)$ we create a function $f_{R_i, A_j} : \Delta_{\mathsf{type}(id)} \to \Delta_{\mathsf{type}A_j}$. If A_j is referencing an identifier of some other relation S (i.e., $R_i[A_j] \to S[id]$), then f_{R_i, A_j} represents the foreign key referencing to S. Note that in this case the types of A_j and $S.id$ should coincide. In MCMT, assuming that $\mathsf{D\_Ri\_id} = \mathsf{type}(id)$ and $\mathsf{D\_Aj} = \mathsf{type}(A_j)$, this is captured using statement

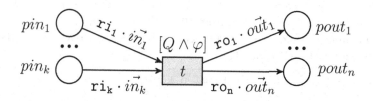

Fig. 13.7: A generic COA-net transition (ri_j and ro_j are natural numbers)

```
:smt (define Ri_Aj ::(-> D_Ri_id D_Aj))
```

All the constants appearing in the net specification must be properly defined. Let $C = \{v_1, \ldots, v_{n_c}\}$ be the set of all constants appearing in N. C is defined as $\bigcup_{t \in T} Const(\text{guard}(t)) \cup supp(m_0) \cup \bigcup_{t \in T, p \in P} Const(F_{out}(t, p))$. Then, every constant $v_i \in C$ of type $\mathcal{D}$ is declared in MCMT as

```
:smt (define vi ::D)
```

As shown in Section 9.3, the code section needed to make MCMT aware of the fact that these elements have been declared to describe a read-only database schema is as follows (notice that the last declaration is required when using MCMT in the database-driven mode):

```
:db_driven
:db_sorts D1,...,Dnd
:db_functions R1_A1,...,Rnr_An
:db_constants v1,...,vnc
:db_relations  //leave empty
```

Here, without loss of generality we assume that n is the index of the last attribute of relation R_{n_r}.

Remark 13.1 The translation of the catalog relations of a COA-net into MCMT is conceptually the same as the one defined for DABs and implemented in delta-BPMN. Indeed, the definitions of the catalog of a DAB and of the catalog of a COA-net are completely analogous and, as briefly mentioned above, both translations rely on the functional characterization of relational databases for Array-Based Artifact Systems studied in Section 3.1. This means, for example, that both an $n + 1$-relation R_1 in the catalog of a DAB and an $n + 1$-relation R_2 in the catalog of a COA-net are translated into a set of n unary functions that map the id-attribute of R_i to the other n attributes of R_i. The implementation in MCMT follows the instructions carefully described in Chapter 9 and it is identical for both DABs and COA-nets.

Places. Given that, during the net execution, every place may store unboundedly many tokens, we need to ensure a potentially infinite provision of values to places p using unbounded arrays. To this end, every place $p \in P$ with $color(p) = \mathcal{D}_1 \times$

$\ldots \times \mathcal{D}_k$ is going to be represented as a combination of arrays $p_1, \ldots, p_k$, where a special index type $\mathtt{P_{ind}}$ (disjoint from all other types) with domain $\Delta_{\mathtt{P_{ind}}}$ is used as the array index sort and $\mathcal{D}_1, \ldots, \mathcal{D}_k$ account for the respective target sorts of the arrays.[6] In MCMT, this is declared as

```
:local p_1 D1      ...      :local p_k Dk
```

Then, intuitively, we associate to the j-th token $(v_1, \ldots, v_k) \in m(p)$ an element $j \in \Delta_{P_{ind}}$ and a tuple $(j, p_1[j], \ldots, p_k[j])$, where $p_1[j] = v_1, \ldots, p_k[j] = v_k$. Here, j is an *"implicit identifier"* of this tuple in $m(p)$. Using this intuition and assuming that there are in total n control places, we represent the initial marking m_0 in two steps (a direct declaration is not possible due to the language restrictions of MCMT). First, we symbolically declare that all places are by default empty using the following MCMT initialisation statement

```
:initial
:var x
:cnj init_p1
     . . .
     init_pn
```

Here, $\mathtt{cnj}$ represents a conjunction of atomic equations that, for ease of reading, we organized in blocks, where each *init_p_i* specifies for place $p_i \in P$ with $\mathtt{color}(p_i) = \mathcal{D}_1 \times \ldots \times \mathcal{D}_k$ that it contains no tokens. This is done by explicitly "nullifying" all components of each possible token in p_i, written in MCMT as

```
(= pi_1[x] NULL_D1)(= pi_2[x] NULL_D2)...(= pi_k[x] NULL_DK)
```

The initial marking is then injected with a dedicated MCMT code that populates (through a transition) the place arrays, initialized as empty, with records representing tokens therein. We come back to the second step of the initial marking encoding after having discussed the transition encoding.

Remark 13.2 The translation of COA-net places into MCMT is completely analogous to the translation of repository relations of DABs into MCMT: indeed, theoretically, both COA-net places and DAB repository relations are translated into 'artifact relations', i.e., sets of artifact components (array variables), of RASs. The main idea behind this is that places contain 'data tuples' as tokens, which correspond to 'data tuples' contained by repository relations in DABs: since the quantity of 'data tuples' in places or repository relations is in principle unbounded, they cannot be represented through a set of variables, but they need a data structure that is unbounded in size. This is the reason of using (a set of) arrays of (possible unbounded) size n, where indexes are used as identifiers of the 'data tuples' of interest. If, instead of unboundedly many tuples, one is interested in considering only bounded information, then a set of variable suffices: this is exactly what happens for COA-net bounded places or for DAB 'case variables', which both correspond to artifact variables of RASs.

---

[6] MCMT has only one index sort, but, as shown in [136], there is no loss of generality in doing that.

Transition enablement and firing. We now discuss how to check for transition enablement and compute the effect of a transition firing in MCMT. To this end, we consider the generic, prototypical COA-net transition $t \in T$ depicted in Figure 13.7. The enablement of this transition is subject to the following conditions:

(FC1) there is a binding σ that correctly matches tokens in the places to the corresponding inscriptions on the input arcs (i.e., each place pin_i provides enough tokens required by a corresponding inscription $F(pin_i, t) = \mathbf{in_i}$), and that computes new and possibly *fresh* values that are pairwise distinct from each other as well as from all other values in the marking;

(FC2) the guard $\mathsf{guard}(t)$ is satisfied under the selected binding.

For simplicity, we assume here that $Q \in CQ_{\mathfrak{D}}^{\neg}$ and it is in Prenex normal form. Whenever $Q \in UCQ_{\mathfrak{D}}^{\neg}$, such that $Q = \bigvee_{i=1}^{n} Q_i$, with $Q_i \in CQ_{\mathfrak{D}}^{\neg}$, one needs to create n-variants of transition t, and suitably modify input and output arcs (together with their inscriptions) as well as transition guards, each of which will contain only one Q_i.

In MCMT, t is captured with a transition statement consisting of a guard G and an update U as follows

```
:transition
:var x,x1,...,xK,y1,...,yN
:var j
:guard G
... U ...
```

Here every x (resp., y) represents an existentially quantified index variable corresponding to variables in the incoming inscriptions (resp., outgoing inscriptions), $K = \sum_{j \in \{1,...,k\}} ri_j$, $N = \sum_{j \in \{1,...,n\}} ro_j$ and j is a universally quantified variable, that will be used for computing bindings of v-variables and updates. In the following we are going to elaborate on the construction of the MCMT transition statement. We start by discussing the structure of G which in MCMT is represented as a conjunction of atoms or negated atoms and, intuitively, addresses all the conditions stated above.

First, to construct a binding that meets condition *(FC1)*, we need to make sure that every place contains enough of tokens that match a corresponding arc inscription. Using the array-based representation, for every place pin_i with $F_{in}(pin_i, t) = ri_i \cdot \mathbf{in_i}$ and $k' = |color(pin_i)|$, we can check this with a formula

$$\psi_{pin_i} := \exists x_1, \ldots, x_{ri_i}. \bigwedge_{\substack{j_1, j_2 \in \{x_1,...,x_{ri_i}\}, j_1 \neq j_2, \\ l \in \{1,...,k'\}}} pin_{i,l}[j_1] = pin_{i,l}[j_2] \wedge \bigwedge_{l \in \{1,...,k'\}} pin_{i,l}[x_1] \neq \text{NULL\_D}_l$$

Here, the first big conjunct is used to check that there are ri_i identical tokens available in the array-based representation of pin_i. Given that variables representing existentially quantified index variables are already defined, in MCMT this is encoded as conjunctions of atoms

```
(= pini_l[j1] pini_l[j2])
```

and atoms

```
    not(= pini_l[x1] NULL_Dl)
```

where NULL_Dl is a special null constant of type of elements stored in pini_l. All such conjunctions, for all input places of t, should be appended to G.

We now define the condition that selects proper indexes in the output places so as to fill them with the tokens generated upon transition firing. To this end, we need to make sure that all the q declared arrays a_w of the system[7] (including the arrays $pout_i$ corresponding to the output places of t) contain no values in the slots marked by y index variables. This is represented using a formula

$$\psi_{pout_i} := \exists y_1, \ldots, y_{ri_i} . \bigwedge_{j \in \{y_1, \ldots, y_{ri_j}\}, w \in \{1, \ldots q\}} a_w[j] = \text{NULL\_D}_w,$$

which is encoded in MCMT similarly to the case of ψ_{pin_i}.

Moreover, when constructing a binding, we have to take into account the case of arc inscriptions causing implicit "joins" between the net marking and data retrieved from the catalog. This happens when there are some variables in the input flow that coincide with variables of Q, i.e., $Vars(F_{in}(pin_j, t)) \cap Vars(Q) \neq \emptyset$. See [136] for the technical details on how to formalize this case.

We now incorporate the encoding of condition *(FC2)*. Every variable d of Q with type$(d) = $ D has to be declared in MCMT as an existential variable as follows

```
    :eevar d D
```

Notice that such variables appear in Q and are used for querying the catalog. As extensively argued in Subsection 1.3.1 and shown in Chapter 4, whenever querying over a relational database is required, the management of such variables becomes one of the most crucial points: these existentially quantified variables get eliminated in the backward reachability procedure used by MCMT whenever it verifies a property. Concretely speaking, in the database-driven module of MCMT, in order to manage such d variables one needs to rely on the advanced quantifier elimination techniques studied in Part II.

In order to represent the guard $Q \wedge \varphi$ in the MCMT syntax, we need to adopt the functional representation of DB schemas (cf. Section 3.1). To do so, we call an *extended guard* a guard $Q^e \wedge \varphi^e$ in which every relation R has been substituted with its functional counterpart and every variable d in φ has been substituted with its array counterpart. Specifically, every relation $R/n+1$ that appears in Q as $R(id, d_1, \ldots, d_n)$ is replaced by the conjunction $id \neq \text{NULL\_D} \wedge f_{R,A_1}(id) = d_1 \wedge \ldots \wedge f_{R,A_n}(id) = d_n$, where D = type$(id)$. The details on how to write this explicitly in MCMT are in the journal article [139]. Variables in φ are substituted with their array counterparts. In particular, every variable $d \in Vars(\varphi)$ is substituted with pinj_i[x] (for some i), which is the array component of the input place pin_j bringing the value bound by the variable d. Given that φ is represented as a conjunction of atoms, its representation in MCMT together with the aforementioned substitution is trivial.

---

[7] This is a technicality of MCMT, as explained in [136], since MCMT has only one index sort.

To finish the construction of G, we append to it the MCMT version of $Q^e \wedge \varphi^e$.

We come back to condition *(FC1)* and show how bindings are generated for v-variables of the output flow of t. As explained in Section 9.3, in MCMT we use a special universal guard :uguard (to be inserted right after the :guard entry) that, for each $j \in \{1, \ldots, n\}$, and for every variable $v \in \Upsilon_{\mathfrak{D}} \cap (OutVars(t) \setminus Vars(\textbf{out}_j))$ previously declared using

```
:eevar nu D
```

and for arrays $p_1, \ldots, p_k$ with target sort D, consists of expression (for all p)

```
(not(=nu p_1[j]))...(not(=nu p_k[j]))
```

This encodes "local" freshness for v-variables, which suffices for our goal. Notice that here j is a universally quantified index variable defined in the MCMT transition statement with :var j. We remark that universal guards are the distinctive feature of U-RASs that distinguishes them from (plain) RASs (cf. Section 3.2.2).

After a binding has been generated and the guard of t has been checked, a new marking is generated by assigning corresponding tokens to the outgoing places and by removing tokens from the incoming ones. Note that, while the tokens are populated by assigning their values to respective arrays, the token deletion happens by nullifying (i.e., assigning special NULL constants) entries in the arrays of the input places. All these operations are specified in the special update part of the transition statement U and are captured in MCMT as follows

```
:numcases NC
...
:case (= j i)
:val v_{1,i}
...
:val v_{k,i}
...
```

There, the transition runs through NC cases. All the following cases go over the indexes y1,..., yN that correspond to tokens that have to be added to places. More specifically, for every place $pout \in P$ such that $|color(pout)| = k$, we add an i-th token to it by putting a value $v_{r,i}$ in i-th place of every r-th component array of *pout*. This $v_{r,i}$ can either be a v-variable nu from the universal guard, or a value coming from a place *pin* specified as pin[xm] (from some x input index variable) or a value from some of the relations specified as (R_Ai id). Note that id should be also declared as

```
:eevar id D_Ri_id
```

where type(id) = D_Ri_id. Every :val v statement follows the order in which all the local and global variables have been defined, and, for array variables a and every case (= j i), such statement stands for a simple assignment $a[i] := v$. For COA-nets, one also has to include a "default" case that essentially encodes a law of inertia for all the tokens that have not been consumed. This is done by repeating local variables in place of v in each :val v statement.[8] Global variables, instead, have same values in all the cases, including the default one.

Finally, let us come back to the initial marking encoding. A special MCMT transition is used to inject the initial marking into the MCMT array-based system. This MCMT transition populates the arrays representing places, all initialized as empty, with entries that correspond to the initial COA-net marking m_0.

This MCMT transition can be executed only if flag init_fl, denoting whether the initial marking assignment has taken place, is TRUE.[9] It works as follows:

```
:transition
:var i1,..., iM
:var j
:guard (=init_fl TRUE)
:numcases NCm0
...
:case (= j i)
:val v₁,ᵢ
...
:val vₖ,ᵢ
...
:val FALSE
...
```

Note that the init_fl flag should be previously declared using the MCMT statement

```
:global   init_fl Bool
```

Same holds for the boolean constants TRUE and FALSE: they are declared using the respective statements

```
:smt (define TRUE ::Bool)
```

and

```
:smt (define FALSE ::Bool)
```

Then, the transition runs through NCm0 cases. All the cases go over the indexes i1,..., iM that correspond to tokens that have to be added to places. More specifically, for every place $p \in P$ such that $m_0(p) \neq \emptyset^\oplus$ and $|\text{color}(p)| = k$, we add an i-th token to it by putting constant $v_{r,i} \in C$ in i-th place of every r-th component array of p. Moreover, every case has to update init_fl, changing its value to FALSE.

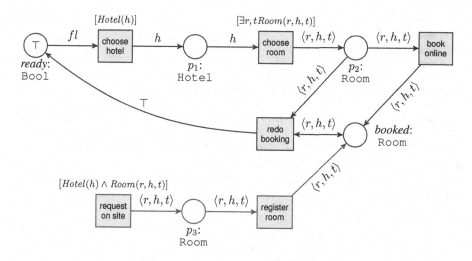

Fig. 13.8: A COA-net representing a hotel booking process with the initial marking containing only one token in place *ready*

13.2.3 Encoding Example

Currently, the encoding presented in the previous section does not have a prototype realizing it. Thus, we demonstrate the feasibility of our approach by manually encoding a COA-net into MCMT [147].

Let us start with a COA-net N that represents a simple, faulty hotel booking scenario.[10] In Figure 13.8, the net is split into two parts, one representing an on-line booking process followed by a customer and the other accounting for bookings done directly on site. In the first process, the customer consequently chooses a hotel and a room in it, and, if the chosen room is not available, can repeat the booking process. The second process instead plays a role of a "booking adversary": it allows to pick any room without verifying the room availability and can always be executed in parallel with the on-line booking process.

Both processes run on a catalog composed of two relations $Hotel(h : \text{HName})$ and $Room(r : \text{RId}, h : \text{HName}, t : \text{String})$. The first relation stores information about all the hotels that can be potentially available for booking, whereas the second relation lists rooms (as well as their types) offered by such hotels.

We now illustrate a few MCMT code snippets acquired by manually translating the booking example. The translation process starts with defining all the static data components such as data types and relation signatures in MCMT:

---

[8] Notice that all local variables have to be indexed with j.

[9] In case a transition is enriched with guard G, then G should contain a conjunct (= init_fl FALSE).

[10] As we will see later, this example encodes unwanted booking behavior.

```
:smt (define-type HName)
:smt (define-type RId)
:smt (define-type Bool)
:smt (define-type String)
:smt (define RoomHotel :: (-> RId HName))
:smt (define RoomType :: (-> RId String))
:smt (define TRUE ::Bool)
:smt (define FALSE ::Bool)
```

Here, `RoomHotel` and `RoomType` are functions used for the functional characterization of the last two attributes of relation *Room*.

To make MCMT aware of the catalog schema used in the example, we add the following block:

```
:db_driven
:db_sorts Hotel Room Bool String
:db_functions RoomType RoomHotel
:db_constants   TRUE FALSE
:db_relations
```

Now we need to encode the places of N. Observe that, while such places as p_3 and *booked* are clearly unbounded, *ready*, p_1 and p_2 will never carry more than one token. To this end, we demonstrate how bounded places can be treated in MCMT by simply resorting to globally declared variables (instead of arrays) for storing token components. Following the translation instructions from the previous section, one gets the following:

```
:local BookedRooms_1 RId
:local booked_2 HName
:local booked_3 String
:local p3_1 RId
:local p3_2 HName
:local p3_3 String
:global p1_1 HName
:global p2_1 Rid
:global p2_2 HName
:global p2_3 String
:global ready Bool
:global init_fl Bool
```

As mentioned above, all the variables needed for representing 1-bounded places are declared using the `:global` keyword. Given that place *ready* can be seen as a flag, we use `Bool`-typed variable `ready` to model it. Then, we write the initialization statement, in which all the places are "nullified", together with all the `eevar` declarations needed later on for encoding transition preconditions:

```
:initial
:var x
:cnj (= init_fl TRUE) (= ready FALSE) (= p1_1 NULL_HName)
     (= p2_1 NULL_RId) (= p2_2 NULL_HName) (= p2_3
        NULL_String)
     (= booked_1[x] NULL_RId) (= booked_2[x] NULL_HName)
```

```
        (= booked_3[x] NULL_String) (= p3_1[x] NULL_RId)
        (= p3_2[x] NULL_HName) (= p3_3[x] NULL_String)
:eevar e HName
:eevar d HName
:eevar f HName
:eevar g RId
:eevar l RId
:eevar m RId
:eevar n String
:eevar o String
:eevar p String
:eevar q Bool
```

This statements are immediately followed by an MCMT transition modeling the initial marking assignment:

```
:transition
:var j
:var x
:guard  (= init_fl TRUE) (= x x)
:numcases 2
:case (= x j)
:val booked_1[j]
:val booked_2[j]
:val booked_3[j]
:val p3_1[j]
:val p3_2[j]
:val p3_3[j]
:val p1_1
:val p2_1
:val p2_2
:val p2_3
:val TRUE
:val FALSE
:case
:val booked_1[j]
:val booked_2[j]
:val booked_3[j]
:val p3_1[j]
:val p3_2[j]
:val p3_3[j]
:val p1_1
:val p2_1
:val p2_2
:val p2_3
:val TRUE
:val FALSE
```

Let us now showcase a net transition. For example, the book online (that deals with unbounded places) is represented with the following code:

```
:transition
:var j
:var x
```

```
:guard  (= init_fl FALSE) (not (= p2_1 NULL_RId))
       (not (= p2_2 NULL_HName)) (not (= p2_3 NULL_String))
       (= booked_1[x] NULL_RId)   (= booked_2[x] NULL_HName)
       (= booked_3[x] NULL_String) (= p3_1[x] NULL_RId)
       (= p3_2[x] NULL_HName) (= p3_3[x] NULL_String)
:numcases 2
:case (= x j)
:val p2_1
:val p2_2
:val p2_3
:val p3_1[j]
:val p3_2[j]
:val p3_3[j]
:val p1_1
:val p2_1
:val p2_2
:val p2_3
:val ready
:val init_fl
:case
:val booked_1[j]
:val booked_2[j]
:val booked_3[j]
:val p3_1[j]
:val p3_2[j]
:val p3_3[j]
:val p1_1
:val p2_1
:val p2_2
:val p2_3
:val ready
:val init_fl
```

The interested reader can go over the complete example encoding here: https://github.com/AlessandroGianola/SMT-based-Data-Aware-Processes-Verification/tree/COA-nets-in-MCMT.

13.3 Unsafety Checking of COA-nets and its Formal Properties

Thanks to the encoding of COA-nets into the database-driven module of MCMT, we can handle the parameterized verification of safety properties over COA-nets.

The purpose of this section is to formalize this verification problem, and to comment on its (meta-)properties, primarily considering algorithmic aspects arising from the encoding into MCMT such as soundness, completeness, and termination. We also discuss (un)decidability issues. In particular, we isolate an interesting class of COA-nets for which verification is decidable. All these considerations are possible because, thanks to the encoding into MCMT, COA-nets can be seen as a particular instance of U-RASs.

13.3.1 Unsafety Properties

We focus our attention on *safety properties*, that is, properties that have to globally hold in each state of the system. As customary, a safety property is verified in the converse, that is, by expressing a corresponding *unsafety property*, and by checking if there exists a reachable state of the system that satisfies it. If so, then the state and the sequence of transitions to reach that state from the initial one witness that the system is indeed not safe.

Definition 13.5 (COA-net Property) An *(unsafety) property* over COA-net N is a formula of the form $\exists \mathbf{y}.\psi(\mathbf{y})$, where $\psi(\mathbf{y})$ is a quantifier-free query that additionally contains atomic predicates $[p \geq c]$ and $[p(x_1, \ldots, x_n) \geq c]$, where p is a place name from N, $c \in \mathbb{N}$, and $Vars(\psi) = Y_P$, with Y_P being the set of variables appearing in the atomic predicates $[p(x_1, \ldots, x_n) \geq c]$.

Here, $[p \geq c]$ specifies that in place p there are at least c tokens. Similarly, $[p(x_1, \ldots, x_n) \geq c]$ indicates that in place p there are at least c tokens carrying the tuple $\langle x_1, \ldots, x_n \rangle$ of data objects. Here, $x_1, \ldots, x_n$ act as a filter that selects the matching tokens in p. Additionally, the same variables may be used to inspect different places as join operators, in turn expressing *co-reference* constraints on tokens present in the respective places. A property may also mention relations from the catalog, provided that all variables used therein also appear in atoms that inspect places.

This can be seen as a language to express *data-aware coverability properties* of a COA-net, possibly relating tokens with the content of the catalog. Focusing on covered markings as opposed as fully-specified reachable markings is customary in data-aware Petri nets or, more in general, well-structured transition systems (such as v-PNs [228]).

Example 13.6 Consider the COA-net of Example 13.5, with an initial marking that populates the *pool* place with available trucks. Property $\exists p, o.[delivered(p, o) \geq 1] \wedge [working(o) \geq 1]$ captures the undesired situation where a delivery occurs for an item *that* belongs to a working (i.e., not yet paid) order. This is expressed by checking for the existence of two tokens that are respectively located in the *delivered* and *working* places, and that co-refer on the same order.

Similarly to what shown in Section 13.2, also properties as of Definition 13.5 admit a direct encoding into the MCMT model checker, as we show next. We start by looking into single components of a property of the form $\exists \mathbf{x}.\psi$ and discuss how each component should be represented in MCMT. As mentioned in Definition 13.5, properties are quantifier-free queries that may contain relations in them proviso that such relations have their variables appearing in atomic place predicates. To this end, the translation of queries without place predicates is "subsumed" by the translation of extended guards presented in Section 13.2 (however, we are going to comment on its peculiarities later on).

We start by translating predicates. An atomic predicate $[p \geq c]$, where $\mathrm{color}(p) = \mathcal{D}_1 \times \ldots \times \mathcal{D}_k$, is represented using the following MCMT statement:

```
(not (= p_1[z_1]   NULL_D1)) ... (not (= p_1[z_c]   NULL_D1))
...
(not (= p_k[z_1]   NULL_Dk)) ... (not (= p_k[z_c]   NULL_Dk))
```

Here, z_i are special existentially quantified *index* variables that can appear only in the property formula and do not need to be explicitly declared anywhere in the MCMT specification. The statement above formalizes the fact that there are at least c tokens in place p (or, similarly, at least c tuples in arrays representing place p) such that each of them has all the components different from NULL.

Analogously, we deal with each atomic predicate of the form $[p(x_1, \ldots, x_n) \geq c]$ and translate it into the following MCMT statement:

```
(= p_1[z_1]   x_1)   ... (= p_n[z_1]   x_n)
...
(= p_1[z_c]   x_1)   ... (= p_n[z_c]   x_n)
```

This statement, as opposed to the statement formalizing predicate $[p \geq c]$, does not need to check that token components are empty. Instead, it formalizes the fact that there are at least c tokens in place p all identical to the token $(x_1, \ldots, x_n)$.

Let us now denote each predicate $[p_i \geq c_i]$ (resp., $[p_i(x_1, \ldots, x_n) \geq c_i]$) statement translation with P_i (resp., P'_i) and the total number of such translations as m (resp. m'). Then, the final translation of property $\exists \mathbf{x}.\psi$ is represented in MCMT as follows:

```
:u_cnj P_i1 P_i2 ... P_im P'_j1 P'_j2 P'_jm' G
```

Here, G is a statement containing the quantifier-free query translation, in which variables in every relation have to be substituted with suitable $p\_j[z_l]$ array components taken from some of the P_i and P'_i statements.

Example 13.7 Consider the COA-net from Section 13.2.3. It is easy to see that it is not always possible to book a room, either on site or on-line, that has not been taken yet (that is, a token with the room identifier has been placed in place *booked*). The property capturing this situation for the on-line component of the net can be written as $\exists r, h, t.[p_2(r, h, t) \geq 1] \wedge [booked(r, h, t) \geq 1]$. In MCMT, proviso that p_2 is 1-bounded and the predicate $[p_2(r, h, t) \geq 1]$ can be substituted with $[p_2(r, h, t) = 1]$, this property is specified as following:

```
:u_cnj (not (= p2_1 NULL_RId)) (not (= p2_2 NULL_HName))
       (not (= p2_3 NULL_String)) (= p2_1 booked_1[z1])
       (= p2_2 booked_2[z1]) (= p2_3 booked_3[z1])
```

Notice that this property encoding is optimized as it suffices to specify that the same token can be found both in p_2 and *booked*.

Similarly, for the on site part of the net the unsafety property is specified as $\exists r, h, t.[p_3(r, h, t) \geq 1] \wedge [booked(r, h, t) \geq 1]$. Its MCMT encoding is as follows:

```
:u_cnj (not (= p3_1[z1] NULL_RId)) (not (= p3_2[z1]
       NULL_HName))
       (not (= p3_3[z1] NULL_String)) (= p3_1[z1] booked_1[z2])
```

```
     (= p3_2[z1] booked_2[z2])  (= p3_3[z1] booked_3[z2])
```

13.3.2 Verification Problem

To express the verification problem of interest in our setting, we follow the line of research extensively studied to formally analyze dynamic systems with read-only relational data [102, 186, 99], focusing our attention on (un)safety properties. Specifically, we will import the results on U-RASs shown in Chapter 4.

Technically, we frame our verification problem as checking whether it is true that *all* the reachable states of a marked COA-net satisfy a desired safety condition, *independently from the content of the catalog*. This captures the fact that the system is *robustly* safe, in the sense that safety does not depend on a specific configuration of the read-only data. In the converse, we take an unsafety property defined as in Definition 13.5, and check whether there exists an instance of the catalog such that the COA-net can evolve the initial marking to a state where that property holds. This is formally captured next.

Definition 13.6 (COA-net Verification Task) Given a property ψ as in Definition 13.5, a marked COA-net $\overline{N}m_0$ is *unsafe* w.r.t. ψ if there exists a catalog instance Cat for N such that the marked fixed-catalog COA-net $\langle N, m_0, Cat \rangle$ can reach a configuration where ψ holds. If this is not the case, then $\overline{N}m_0$ is *safe* w.r.t. ψ.

In the following, whenever we generically mention the term *verification*, we implicitly refer to the verification task of Definition 13.6.

Example 13.8 Consider again the COA-net of Example 13.5, and the property defined in Example 13.6. The COA-net is safe w.r.t. this property, as the property never holds in the executions of the COA-net, irrespectively of the content of the net catalog. This is because an item can be delivered only if it has been previously loaded in a compatible truck; this is in turn possible only if the order to which the loaded item belongs is *paid*.

Example 13.9 In Example 13.7, we have mentioned two properties that we conjecture to be unsafe. MCMT allows to check the corresponding COA-net against both of these properties at once: it suffices to mention them in the specification file and the tool will consider them as one disjunction. This disjunction is shown to be unsafe by MCMT in 0.26 seconds. The tool was run on a machine with macOS High Sierra 10.13.3, 2.3 GHz Intel Core i5 and 8 GB RAM.

13.3.3 Soundness and Completeness

We now consider the usage of MCMT to carry out the verification problem of Definition 13.6. With a slight abuse of terminology, we interchangeably use the term

COA-net to denote the net under study or its MCMT encoding, and likewise for the term *property*.

Proofs of all results in this section are directly obtained by exploiting the close relationship between COA-nets and the foundational framework of U-RASs, which at the basis of the database-driven module of MCMT, implicitly established by the translation defined in Section 13.2.

Specifically, we consider the key (meta-)properties of soundness and complete-ness of the backward reachability procedure BReach_{RAS} encoded in MCMT that we employ here for verifying COA-nets (details on BReach_{RAS} are in Section 4.3).[11] For the sake of clarity, we call this procedure BReach_{COA} when applied to COA-nets, and in our context we assume it takes as input a marked COA-net and an (undesired) property ψ. Given a marked COA-net $\langle N, m_0 \rangle$ and a property ψ, we say that an UNSAFE output of BReach_{COA} is *correct* if there exists an instance of the catalog so that the net can evolve from the initial marking to a configuration that satisfies ψ; we say that a SAFE output is *correct* if such a catalog does not exist.

As in the case of the previous formalism for which we studied verification proce-dures, we formally characterize the (meta-)properties of BReach_{COA} as follows.

Definition 13.7 Given a marked COA-net $\langle N, m_0 \rangle$ and a property ψ, BReach_{COA}, when applied to verify unsafety of $\langle N, m_0 \rangle$ w.r.t. ψ, is:

- *sound* if, whenever it terminates, it produces a correct answer;
- *partially sound* if, whenever it returns SAFE, that output is always correct (in this case, the UNSAFE output can be incorrect);
- *complete* (w.r.t. unsafety) if, whenever $\langle N, m_0 \rangle$ is UNSAFE with respect to ψ, then BReach_{COA} detects it and returns UNSAFE.

In general, BReach_{COA} is not guaranteed to terminate. This is not surprising given the expressiveness of the framework and the type of parameterized verification tackled: they same happen for generic (non-acyclic) SASs, for (Universal) RASs and for generic DABs.

We start by studying BReach_{COA} on COA-nets in their full generality. As we have seen in Section 13.2, the encoding of fresh variables calls for a limited form of universal quantification: specifically, in order to impose that a fresh variable is different from all the values currently present in the net, we need to employ *universal guards*, which are available in U-RASs but not in plain RASs. Indeed, as a side remark, notice that proper freshness goes beyond the features covered by the foundational framework of plain RAS, which in fact does not explicitly consider *fresh* data injection, but only the injection of *possibly fresh* data taken from some (possibly) infinite value domain: in other words, this means that an external user can possibly inject a fresh element from an infinite domain — since there are infinitely many elements, such an element certainly *exists* — but the RAS query language cannot explicitly force the system to pick up such an element. That is why we need to

---

[11] Recall that *Backward reachability* has nothing to do with *marking reachability*. In this work, we deal with reachability of a configuration that satisfies a property which, in turn, is implicitly achieved by covering a marking, which, in turn, assigns to places tokens that carry tuples of data (potentially retrieved from the read-only catalog).

employ U-RASs instead of RASs. Unfortunately, U-RASs cannot be directly verified by BReach$_{RAS}$, but we need first to eliminate the universal quantification by applying the abstraction described in Section 4.4.1. For that reason we can only guarantee that BReach$_{RAS}$ is partially sound when applied to the encoding of COA-nets explicitly using fresh variables, and spurious UNSAFE outcomes can arise.

The phenomenon described above for COA-nets is not surprising. In fact, it is known from previous works (see, e.g., [17]) that when transition formulae employ universal quantification over the indexes of an array, the backward search cannot guarantee that all the indexes are indeed considered. This can lead to potentially spurious situations in which some indexes are simply "disregarded" when exploring the state space. This spurious exploration of the state space, which is similar to what happens in lossy systems, may result in the wrong classification of a SAFE case as being UNSAFE.

With all these considerations in mind, we state the main result about COA-nets.

Theorem 13.1 BReach$_{COA}$ *is effective, partially sound and complete when applied to verify unsafety of COA-nets w.r.t. ψ.*

Proof The theorem follows immediately from Corollary 4.2 and from the encoding of COA-nets and of properties into the database-driven mode of MCMT, i.e. into the theoretical framework of U-RASs. □

To mitigate the presence of potentially spurious results, MCMT is equipped with techniques for debugging the returned result [17]. In particular, MCMT explicitly returns, together with the unsafety verdict, a flag discriminating the case where the produced result is provably correct from the case where the result *may* have been mistakenly obtained due to a spurious exploration of the state space. As we already saw in Chapter 9, when the result may be wrong because of the presence of a spurious trace, MCMT warns the user reporting that the 'stopping failure model' has been adopted (see Section 4.4.1 for details).

A key point is then how to tame partial soundness towards recovering full soundness and completeness, as in the case of RASs. We obtain this for the two special classes of *conservative* and *bounded* COA-nets, described next. Indeed, we discuss how the encoding of these classes falls into the scope of the plain RAS model.

13.3.4 Conservative COA-nets

Conservative COA-nets do not have the ability to inject fresh values into their tokens, but only to manipulate data objects mentioned in the initial marking or in the catalog.

Definition 13.8 (Conservative COA-nets) A COA-net is conservative if no ν-variable is used in its arc inscriptions.

Conservative COA-nets form a subclass of the foundational framework of (plain) RASs (Section 3.2.2), and consequently enjoy all the properties established there. In particular, we inherit that BReach$_{COA}$ is a semi-decision procedure.

Theorem 13.2 BReach$_{COA}$ *is sound and complete when applied to verify unsafety of marked, conservative COA-nets w.r.t. a property* ψ.

Proof This is again a direct consequence of Corollary 4.2 and from the encoding of COA-nets and of properties into the database-driven mode of MCMT: indeed, it is sufficient to notice that the absence of ν-variables ensures that the encoded COA-net is a plain RAS.   □

One may wonder whether studying conservative nets is meaningful. We argue in favor of this by considering some modeling techniques to remove fresh variables from a net while preserving interesting properties.

Avoiding fresh variables

The first technique is to ensure that whenever there is an unnecessary usage of ν-variables, such ν-variables are removed. As we have extensively discussed at the end of Section 13.1, generating a fresh object and inserting it into a token is necessary only if that object can be subsequently used in other tokens as well, thus acting as a reference. This is the case if the object belongs to the "one" side of a many-to-one relationship (e.g., the case of an order that can contain many items), or whenever the object participates to a one-to-one relationship and belongs to the endpoint that has been chosen as reference.

Fixing objects

When the COA-net requires to capture references, ν-variables can still be removed if one limits the scope of verification, by considering a fixed set of "prototypical" objects of a given type instead of the more general case where such objects are created on-the-fly. This is for example what happens in soundness checking of workflow nets, where analysis is limited to a *single* case object and its evolution from the input to the output place of the net.

In the general case, moving from arbitrary creation to a fixed set of elements leads to an under-approximation of the original COA-net. In fact, unsafety carries from the modified to the original net, in the sense that if a property is unsafe for the modified net, then it is unsafe also for the original one. Contrariwise, a property may be judged as safe in the modified net while being unsafe on the original one.

Example 13.10 By inspecting the COA-net of Example 13.5, two observations are in place when it comes to the creation of tokens.
- The creation of orders requires to use a ν-variable to generate fresh order identifiers, which later on are referenced by items so as to track which items belong to which orders.
- The creation of items does not need to appeal to ν-variables, since the only important aspect is to faithfully reconstruct the number of items that belong to

the same order and share category, not to distinguish them. To do so, one can simply rely on the multiset semantics of Petri nets.

To remove the only v-variable present in the net, we can remove the new order transition, and directly use the initial marking to insert one or more order tokens into the *working* place. This allows one to verify how these orders co-evolve in the net. A detected issue carries over the general setting where orders can be arbitrarily created.

Pre-creation of objects

A third technique to eliminate v-variables is similar in spirit to the one just described, but yields a much more sophisticated setting. The idea is the remove ability of the net to create fresh objects, by assuming that all the objects of interest are created at the very beginning. Differently from the previous case, though, we do not explicitly insert these objects in the initial marking, but we assume instead that they are "pre-created" and listed in a dedicated, read-only catalog relation, from which objects are picked and injected in the net. This is more powerful than focussing on a fixed set of objects, since now verification considers all possible configurations of this read-only relation, consequently checking safety where an arbitrary amount of objects is considered.

When the original net contains an emitter transition supporting the unconstrained creation of fresh objects of a given kind (such as in the case of orders for Example 13.5), we can employ this technique to turn the emitter transition into a conservative transition that preserves verification. The general idea on how to do so is shown in Figure 13.9. The original net has an emitter transition that can at any point in time inject a fresh object of type D into a D-typed place p. The corresponding conservative net introduces a new, dedicated unary relation *PreCreated*D, storing the pre-created objects of type D, and modifies the original emitter transition by decorating it with a guard that fetches an object from that relation, and injects that object into p. This approach directly generalizes to the case where tokens in place p contain tuples of objects is handled analogously.

We can intuitively see that this transformation preserves verification through the following line of reasoning. Since the original net supports arbitrary creation of objects, for every n there is a run of the net where exactly n objects are dynamically created and used. To check for unsafety, one such run has to be isolated to show that the system can reach an undesired configuration. Assume this run employs k objects generated through the emitter transition. When carrying out verification of the corresponding conservative net with pre-created objects, there must exist an instance of catalog for which the same run as before is generated. Since relation *PreCreated*D is completely unconstrained, this is indeed possible, as there exists an instance of the catalog that inserts exactly k objects in *PreCreated*D.

Example 13.11 Pre-creation of objects can be applied to the net of Example 13.5, transforming it into a conservative net for which BReach$_{COA}$ is guaranteed to be sound and complete.

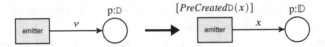

Fig. 13.9: Verification-preserving transformation of an emitter transition injecting fresh objects into a conservative, emitter transition that picks objects from a dedicated read-only catalog relation.

13.3.5 Bounded COA-nets

An orthogonal approach with respect to the one studied in Section 13.3.4 is to analyze what happens if the COA-net of interest is *bounded*. Recall that, as defined in Section 13.1, a COA-net is bounded by b if every reachable marking does not assign more than b tokens to every place of the net. Infinitely many states can still be reached due to the fact that tokens may, along a run, carry infinitely many distinct objects.

In this case, we can straightforwardly "compile away" fresh variables by introducing a place that contains, in the initial marking, enough provision of predefined objects, consuming from that place whenever the net requires a fresh object. This effectively transforms the COA-net into a conservative one, and so Theorem 13.2 applies, leading to the following result.

Corollary 13.1 BReach$_{COA}$ *is sound and complete when applied to verify bounded, marked COA-nets w.r.t a property ψ.*

In Chapter 5, the first two decidability results are obtained when the schema of read-only relations is *acyclic*, that is, its foreign keys never form referential cycles where a relation directly or indirectly points to itself. In particular, by imposing acyclicity and boundedness, we can relate COA-nets to Theorem 5.1.In fact, thanks to boundedness, the content of each place can be stored in a set of predefined variables (whose size would depend on the bound and the arity of the place): this implies that cyclic bounded COA-nets can be equivalently represented as SASs. This, in turn, yields the following.

Theorem 13.3 *The verification problem defined in Definition 13.6 is decidable for acyclic, bounded, marked COA-nets.*

Notice that this decidability result does not imply that BReach$_{COA}$ terminates, as the algorithm and the encoding of COA-nets into data-driven MCMT are not specifically tailored to this particular case. Nevertheless, re-defining the encoding by using predefined variables would not be practical: even if doing so we can theoretically guarantee termination, in the case of a high bound k for the bounded COA-net the use of predefined variables for representing places would make the MCMT specification file unnecessarily long.

It is worth pointing out that Theorem 13.3 covers the case of OA-nets, that is, COA-nets without catalog. Actually, since verifying OA-nets does not require to handle any form of parameterisation, one can relate bounded OA-nets to the notion of bounded, generic transition systems extensively studied in [28, 48], yielding decidability of full model checking for a variety of first-order temporal logics.

Several modeling strategies can be adopted to turn an unbounded COA-net into a bounded one. We briefly illustrate here two, based on prior works.

The first strategy is about explicitly modeling resources that are responsible for the evolution of certain objects [204]. A bound on resources of a certain kind consequently bounds the number of such objects that can coexist in the same state.

The second strategy conceptually relates to multiplicities in data modeling. Whenever there are one-to-many relationships implicitly present in a net, one can ensure that every object participating to the "one" side relates to boundedly many objects on the "many" side by explicitly imposing an upper bound on the multiplicitly attached to the "many" side [203].

We illustrate the application of such strategies in the context of our running example.

Example 13.12 The COA-net of Example 13.5 has two sources of unboundedness: the creation of orders, and the addition of items to working orders.

The creation of unboundedly many orders can be controlled by introducing a suitable resource place, for example a place containing idle managers, each of which gets responsibility over one and only one order at a time. We can then impose that each order is created only when there is an idle manager not working on any other order. More specifically, whenever an order is created and injected in the net, an idle manager is consumed and associated to the order. Whenever an order completely disappears from the net, its responsible manager is returned to the idle manager place. This makes the overall amount of orders unbounded over time, but bounded in each marking by the number of manager resources.

The addition of items to a working order can be bounded by imposing, conceptually, that each order cannot contain more than a maximum fixed number of items.

13.3.6 Discussion on Undecidability of COA-nets

After all the considerations done on soundness, completeness, and decidability, one may wonder whether the intrinsic difficulty in verifying COA-nets comes from the sophistication of the model and/or the fact that verification is parameterized w.r.t. the catalog. We just point out that, even by reducing the modeling capabilities to the acceptable minimum required to capture interesting object-centric processes, unbounded COA-nets remain Turing-powerful.

This is proved in detail in the journal paper [139]. We just report here the main intuition behind this proof. We consider OA-nets, a variant of COA-nets where the catalog is not present at all, and the very simple property of checking whether a designated place is nonempty (which is a particular case of covering).

This problem is decidable for the special case of OA-nets employing just a single type and unary places only. In fact, this setting coincides with that of ν-Petri nets [228], which have decidable coverability.

ν-Petri nets lack the support of object reference, and in turn of one-to-many relationships among objects, since each token can only carry a single data object, not multiple ones. One may consequently wonder whether the decidability status changes by considering the minimal setting in which relationships are supported, namely OA-nets with no catalog and equipped with binary places hosting tokens that carry pairs of data objects.

It turns out that OA-nets of this form are already Turing-powerful, and so make nonemptiness of places undecidable to check. The proof is a simplified version of the one described in [184], which is based on a reduction from the halting problem for Minsky 2-counter automata: this problem is well-known to be undecidable since Minsky 2-counter automata are Turing-powerful.

As a final remark, we notice that this implies, by using the encoding provided in Section 13.2, that verifying safety for generic U-RASs (which is the most general model we consider in this book) is *undecidable* [202].

13.4 Comparison to Other Models

We comment on how the COA-nets relate to the most recent data-aware Petri net-based models, arguing that they provide an interesting mix of their main features.

DB-nets. COA-nets in their full generality match with an expressive fragment of the DB-net model [205]. DB-nets combine a control-flow component based on CPNs with fresh value injection a là ν-PNs with an underlying read-write persistent storage consisting of a relational database with full-fledged constraints. Special "view" places in the net are used to inspect the content of the underlying database, while transitions are equipped with database update operations.

In COA-nets, the catalog accounts for a persistent storage solely used in a "read-only" modality, thus making the concept of view places rather unnecessary. More specifically, given that the persistent storage can never be changed but only queried for extracting data relevant for running cases, the queries from view places in DB-nets, that involve solely relations that are never updated along the run of the net, have been relocated to transition guards of COA-nets. While COA-nets do not come with an explicit, updatable persistent storage, they can still *employ places and suitably defined subnets to capture read-write relations and their manipulation.* More specifically, one can employ an approach presented in [206]. Using this one can define a set of additional relational places P_R, in which every p_i faithfully represents some S-typed relation schema R_i, a set of additional transitions T_{QR}, in which every transition is equipped with a guard that can access a content of some of the relational places and thus models a $UCQ_{\mathcal{D}}^{\neg}$ query. Moreover, such relations can be updated using a set of transitions T_{UR} using the standard token manipulation mechanism: whenever a fact has to be deleted (resp. added), a respective token is consumed (resp. added).

Notice two things here. First of all, using this representation, COA-nets can update only a known number of tuples. Second, as opposed to the formalism used in [206], COA-nets cannot prioritize one enabled transition over another one. This means that, in the case of deletions, one has to update the relation places in a "lossy" manner by introducing additional transitions that would also allow to skip the deletion (this would model cases in which a relation does not have a required tuple), whereas in the case of additions one needs to adopt the multiset semantics, allowing relation places to have potentially multiple instances of the same tuple.

While verification of DB-nets has only been studied in the bounded case, COA-nets are formally analyzed here without imposing boundedness, and parametrically w.r.t. read-only relations. In addition, the MCMT encoding provided here constitutes the first attempt to make this type of nets potentially verifiable in practice.

PNIDs. The net component of our COA-nets model is equivalent to the formalism of Petri nets with identifiers (PNIDs [249]) without inhibitor arcs. Interestingly, PNIDs without inhibitor arcs form the formal basis of the *Information Systems Modelling Language* (ISML) defined in [218]. In ISML, PNIDs are paired with special CRUD operations to define how relevant facts are manipulated. Such relevant facts are structured according to a conceptual data model specified in ORM, which imposes structural, first-order constraints over such facts. This sophistication only permits to formally analyze the resulting formalism by bounding the PNID markings and the number of objects and facts relating them. The main focus of ISML is in fact more on modeling and enactment. COA-nets can be hence seen as a natural "verification" counterpart of ISML, where the data component is structured relationally and does not come with the sophisticated constraints of ORM, but where parameterized verification is practically possible.

Proclets. COA-nets can be seen as a sort of *explicit data* version of a relevant fragment of Proclets [116]. Proclets handle multiple objects by separating their respective subnets, and by implicitly retaining their mutual one-to-one and one-to-many relations through the notion of correlation set. In Figure 13.6, that would require to separate the subnets of orders, items, and trucks, relating them with two special one-to-many channels indicating that multiple items belong to the same order and loaded in the same truck.

A correlation set is established when one or multiple objects $o_1, \ldots, o_n$ are co-created, all being related to the same object o of a different type (cf. the creation of multiple items for the same order in our running example). In Proclets, this correlation set is implicitly reconstructed by inspecting the concurrent histories of such different objects.[12] Correlation sets are then used to formalize two sophisticated forms of synchronization. In the *equal* synchronization, o flows through a transition t_1 while, simultaneously, *all* objects $o_1, \ldots, o_n$ flow through another transition t_2. In the *subset* synchronization, the same happens but only requiring a subset of $o_1, \ldots, o_n$ to synchronize.

---

[12] In the remainder of this section, we assume that if the same creation step is activated multiple times by the same object o, then the whole set of objects created in such multiple activations are considered all part of the same correlation sets.

Fig. 13.10: A table with three Proclet patterns and their corresponding representations in COA-nets. Here P and C respectively stand for parent and child Proclets.

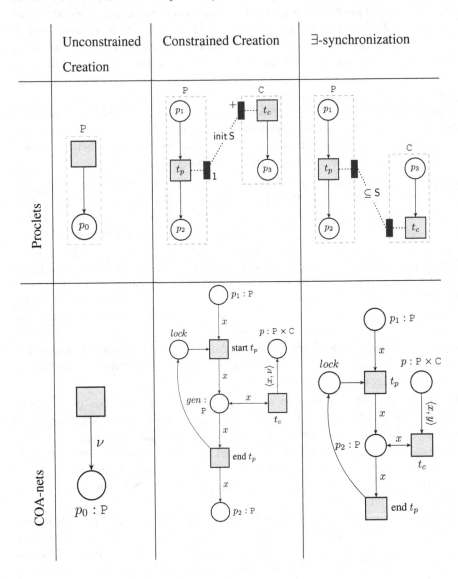

Interestingly, COA-nets can encode correlation sets and the subset synchronisation semantics (see Figure 13.10). A correlation set is explicitly maintained in the net by imposing that the tokens carrying $o_1, \ldots, o_n$ also carry a reference to o. This is what happens for items in our running example: they explicitly carry a reference to the order they belong to. Subset synchronisation is encoded via a properly crafted subnet. Intuitively, this subnet works as follows. First, a lock place is inserted in the COA-net so as to indicate when the net is operating in a normal mode or is instead executing a synchronisation phase. When the lock is taken, some objects in $o_1, \ldots, o_n$ are nondeterministically picked and moved through their transition t_2. The lock is then released, simultaneously moving o through its transition t_1. Thanks to this approach, a Proclet with subset synchronization points can be encoded into a corresponding COA-net, providing for the first time a practical approach to verification. This does not carry over Proclets with equal synchronisation, which would allow us to capture, in our running example, sophisticated mechanisms like ensuring that when a truck moves to its destination, *all* items contained therein are delivered. Equal synchronisation can only be captured in COA-nets by introducing a data-aware variant of wholeplace operation, which we aim to study in the future. We also briefly comment on the constrained creation in Proclets. As defined in [116], this type of creation happens uniquely for a correlation set (that is, two different creations would have two different correlation sets). However, in COA-nets it is possible to create objects asynchronously which can be later correlated (see pattern in Figure 13.5).

Chapter 14
Conclusions

This chapter concludes the book, summarizes the contributions, and discusses future work. In this book, we provided the foundations of Data-Aware Process (DAP) safety verification based on Satisfiability Modulo Theories (SMT) solving and on automated reasoning methods. To do so, we proposed a novel general framework that relies on model-theoretic algebra. In this framework, complex processes enriched with data can be faithfully modeled as symbolic array-based transition systems. These are dynamic systems that evolve over time, where the sets of states and transitions are described symbolically, specifically using logical formulae involving arrays: in such systems, data are formalized using an algebraic representation of relational databases. We verify DAPs against safety properties by employing an extension of the backward reachability procedure. This extension requires the development of sophisticated algorithmic techniques for the treatment of the quantified data variables that are used in transitions. The procedure has been implemented in the state-of-the-art MCMT model checker. We showed how this framework can be successfully applied in the context of BPM to model and verify concrete data-aware business processes: to do so, we introduced different formalisms that on the one hand build on top of standard languages used in practice, on the other hand are able to capture expressive modeling capabilities.

14.1 Overview of the First Part and Relevant Future Work

In the first part, we have studied the problem of SMT-based safety verification for an interesting type of DAPs, i.e., artifact systems. We did so by relying on array-based systems as the underlying inspiring model. We studied safety verification *parametrically* on the read-only database: this means that the read-only database is fixed within a run, but the safety property is checked against *all possible runs* of the system induced by *all possible* read-only database instances over a given DB schema. We have shown how to overcome the main technical difficulty arising from this approach, namely reconstructing quantifier elimination techniques in the rich setting of artifact systems, using the model-theoretic machinery of model completions.

On top of this framework, we have identified three classes of systems for which safety is decidable, which impose different combinations of restrictions on the form of transitions and on the shape of the DB schema.

From the *foundational* point of view, it is an open, non-trivial research question to see whether our framework and similar approaches (e.g., Data Petri nets) can be inter-reduced to each other when we restrict our attention to the three studied decidable fragments. We are also interested in using our theoretical framework as the starting point for a full line of research dedicated to SMT-based techniques for the effective verification of data-aware processes, considering richer forms of verification going beyond safety (such as liveness, fairness, or full LTL-FO), identifying novel decidable classes (e.g., by restricting the structure of the DB and of transition and state formulae) and investigating additional integrity constraints used in database theory. A first attempt that we would like to investigate in order to handle richer forms of verification will be briefly mentioned in Subsection 14.4.2.1. Moreover, studying additional integrity constraints for the DB schemas should extend decidability and model-completability results beyond the case of primary and foreign key dependencies. Finally, it would be interesting to study whether the decidable classes considered here are tight, or whether interesting variations can be found for which decidability is preserved, possibly guaranteeing termination of the backward reachability procedure.

All in all, the formal framework of Part I is deeply rooted in the long-standing tradition of the application of model theory in computer science, as witnessed by notable approaches like the ones in [128, 23, 144, 209, 238, 240, 130, 133]. In particular, this work applies these ideas in a genuinely novel mathematical context and shows how these techniques can be used for the first time to empower algorithmic techniques for the verification of infinite-state systems based on arrays in the style of [146, 80], so as to make such techniques applicable to the timely, challenging settings of DAPs [53]. For additional references on the use of model completeness in computer science, the interested can read our survey [51]. We hope that this book will trigger further interest for the formal verification community to widen the application of model-theoretic techniques in this context.

14.2 Overview of the Second Part and Relevant Future Work

In Part II, we developed efficient techniques for handling the quantifiers introduced during the computation of preimages in the backward reachability procedure. Specifically, we proved that the problem of eliminating quantifiers in model completions required by our machinery is equivalent to the well-known problem of computing covers, which has been studied before in the literature of symbolic model checking. In Chapter 7 we presented for the first time a *correct* and *efficient* procedure for computing covers for the theory of equality and uninterpreted symbols (i.e., $\mathcal{EUF}$):

this procedure is based on a constrained variant of the well-established Superposition Calculus.

In Chapter 7, we also specialized this calculus to the case of interest of our applications to DAP verification, showing it becomes a tractable problem. Finally, we extended the calculus to deal with a significant case of non-empty DB theory that is useful in practice.

In this respect, an interesting future direction is to develop efficient algorithms for computing covers to further theories axiomatizing integrity constraints used in database applications. Practical algorithms for the computation of covers for richer DB theories (e.g., the ones falling under the hypotheses of Proposition 4.5) still need to be designed. Symbol elimination of function and predicate variables should also be combined with cover computations.

Combined cover algorithms (along with the perspectives in [157]) are crucial also in the context of DAP verification: they are needed when dealing with complex DB (extended)theories that can be seen as combination of different theories. In Chapter 8 we showed that covers exist in the combination of two convex universal theories over disjoint signatures in case they exist in the component theories and in case the component theories also satisfy the equality interpolating condition. We proved that the last condition is in some sense needed for cover transfer. In order to prove our result on combined covers, Beth definability property for primitive fragments turned out to be the crucial ingredient to extensively employ. In case convexity fails, we showed by a counterexample that covers might not exist in the combined theory. The last result raises the following research problem: even if in general covers do not exist for the combination of non-convex theories, under which conditions can one decide whether covers exist and, if so, how can one compute them?

DAP applications suggested also a different line of investigations, which led us to consider so-called 'tame combinations', where we need cover algorithms for DB theories combined with (fragments of) arithmetic theories. For significant DB theories, and in practical cases where only very limited arithmetic is used, combined cover computation can be efficiently handled. Our algorithm for covers in tame combinations has been implemented in version 3.0 of MCMT.

In general, we believe that this algorithm can be exploited in various model-checking applications, especially when uninterpreted domains are extended with arithmetic capabilities. A final future research line could consider cover transfer properties to non-disjoint signatures combinations, analogously to similar results obtained in [129, 130] for the transfer of quantifier-free interpolation. Indeed, the main challenge here seems to consist in finding sufficient conditions for the existence of covers in combination of non-convex theories: in fact, we know from Section 8.4 that the non-convex version of the equality interpolation property [45] is not enough for this purpose.

We concluded Part II by providing a description of the database-driven mode of MCMT for verifying safety of Universal RASs, and an experimental evaluation of that tool against a benchmark of concrete data-aware business processes inspired from the DAP literature. The results shown there are promising: most of the tested examples were successfully verified in less than 1 second. We aim at building on the encouraging results reported here toward an extensive experimental evaluation of our approach, by enlarging the experimental setup and extending the capabilities of the tool to incorporate forms of verification that go beyond safety.

Concerning implementation, we plan to further develop MCMT to incorporate in it the plethora of optimizations and sophisticated search strategies available in infinite-state SMT-based model checking. A natural next step in this respect is to study how the computation of over-approximations, abstractions and invariants (a capability that MCMT already supports but that should be adapted to the "db_driven" mode) and well-established techniques for SMT-based model checking like CEGAR [196, 15] and IC3 [39, 163, 40] can be used to speed up the verification of artifact systems.

14.3 Conclusions for the Third Part and Relevant Future Work

In Part III, we focused our attention on the BPM applications of the formal framework introduced in Part I.

14.3.1 Data-Aware BPMN and delta-BPMN

In Chapter 11, we have introduced a data-aware extension of BPMN, called DAB, balancing between expressiveness and verifiability. We have shown that parameterized safety problems over DABs can be correctly tackled by translating them into RASs and exploiting the SMT-based and automated reasoning techniques presented in the first two parts: in particular we applied the backward reachability procedure implemented in the MCMT model checker.

We have then identified classes of DABs suitably controlling the data components and the way the process manipulates it, guaranteeing termination of backward reachability. We have also shown that a realistic example of DAB can be actually verified by MCMT with promising performances.

DABs should be thought of as an intermediate formalism between RASs and more practice-oriented models and languages. In this spirit, in Chapter 12 we have introduced a SQL-based language for modeling and manipulating volatile and persistent data, and demonstrated how it can be incorporated into the existing BPMN standard, resulting in a language for modeling data-aware BPMN that we called delta-BPMN. We showed how these delta-BPMN processes can be modeled with Camunda using its native extension capabilities. We also reported on an implementation of a prototype that takes delta-BPMN models produced in Camunda and automatically translates them into the syntax of MCMT that, in turn, allows for their immediate verification.

There are plenty of avenues for future work. We enumerate the most important ones, considering methodological, foundational, and experimental aspects.

From the methodological point of view, the conditions we have introduced to guarantee termination of DABs can be seen as modeling principles for data-aware process designers who aim at making their processes verifiable. The applicability of such principles to real-life processes is an open question, calling for genuine, further research on empirical validation on real-world scenarios, as well as on the definition of guidelines helping modeling and refactoring of arbitrary DABs into fully verifiable ones. Frameworks for the empirical validation of data-aware process models have been recently brought forward [222], and can be in fact extended also considering the verifiability factor.

From the foundational perspective we are interested in equipping DABs with datatypes and corresponding rigid predicates, including arithmetic operators, as done in [102] for artifact systems. This is promising especially considering that there are plenty of state-of-the-art SMT techniques to handle arithmetic, and the general framework from Part I already supports them. The extension of DABs with arithmetic is then quite easy to achieve, but this would break the decidability result that we presented: in fact, when dealing with (unbounded) arithmetic, the locality principle does help anymore. At the same time, we want to attack the main limitation of our approach, namely that guards and conditions are actually existential formulae, and the only (restricted) form of universal quantification available in the update language is that of conditional updates. Universal guards in transition formulae could be very useful in specifications: for example, they would allow us to specify a branch in a job hiring process that is followed only if *no* applicant satisfies a certain condition. This extension is again straightforward, if one considers the general framework of U-RASs. However, as we commented several times along this work, the use of universal guards may introduce spurious unsafe traces, compromising some of the theoretical results we got for DABs.

An orthogonal, challenging question is how, and to what extent, some of the most recent techniques developed for temporal model checking of artifact-centric systems [102] can be incorporated in our approach, allowing us to prove more sophisticated properties beyond safety: this is again connected to the more general question, mentioned in the previous sections, on how to attack different verification tasks in the U-RAS framework.

We stress that DABs and delta-BPMN focus on private BPMN processes. Natural future work is to extend their scope towards collaborative processes and choreographies. The literature already contains notable examples of approaches combining BPMN with data when dealing with multiple interacting processes, but, as highlighted several times, the focus of these works so far has been mainly on modeling and enactment [200, 199, 198] and not on verification.

Finally, the operational counterpart of DABs given by delta-BPMN is still ongoing work and, as commented in Chapter 12, some capabilities still need to be implemented: for example, there are blocks of the process component (e.g., the exception handler blocks) that are covered by the DAB model but are not supported by delta-BPMN yet. Moreover, we know that Camunda also allows to extend its user interface with additional third-party functionalities: we intend to develop a fully integrated environment for modeling and verification of delta-BPMN processes. We also plan to investigate in more detail the usability aspects of our proposal. Indeed, its usability for concrete benchmarks of industrial-inspired business processes is an open research problem. Specifically, interesting use cases are still missing. This does not only hamper empirical research on how data-aware processes are modeled in practice, but also the possibility of carrying out extensive experimental evaluations. In particular, the community lacks benchmarks written using the integration of standard process-centric languages such as BPMN with standard languages for expressing the sophisticated types of data objects we support. We believe that this is one of the most important open challenges that the BPM community needs to address in the future, and we are already working in this direction. We are currently setting up a concrete benchmark completely written using our SQL-based language and the BPMN standard that could be then fully adopted (including process- and data-specific metrics) within the RePRoSitory platform [83], and that we intend to use for evaluating the performance of delta-BPMN.

We also hope that cutting-edge research on the automated discovery of multi-perspective processes will eventually produce sophisticated models to be fed to our verification machinery.

14.3.2 COA-nets

In Chapter 13, we have brought forward an integrated model of processes and data inspired by Colored Petri Nets that balances between modeling power and the possibility of carrying sophisticated forms of verification parameterized on read-only, immutable relational data. We have approached the problem of verification not only foundationally, but also systematically by showing a direct encoding into MCMT, so as to import all the theoretical results for U-RASs: in order to show the feasibility of the encoding, we encoded in MCMT a simple example of COA-net, for which unsafe configurations were tested in fractions of a second. We have also shown that this model directly relates to some of the most sophisticated models studied in this spectrum, attempting at unifying their features in a single approach.

Given that MCMT is based on SMT, our approach naturally lends itself, as for DABs, to be extended with numerical data types and arithmetic. It would be also interesting to study the impact of introducing "data-aware wholeplace operations", essential to capture the most sophisticated synchronization semantics, so-called "equal synchronization", defined for Proclets [116]. We think that this is possible if one uses the capabilities of U-RASs in their full generality, i.e., by employing proper universal guards (and not only the limited form we use here for freshness).

We also tried to discuss how certain formal restrictions imposed on the general formal model of COA-nets can be interpreted conceptually. In the future, it would be important to perform a further systematic investigation on modeling capabilities of COA-net subclasses for real examples. As remarked above, we are currently working on the definition of a benchmark for testing delta-BPMN: it seems interesting to consider the translation of this benchmark into corresponding imperative data-aware formalisms, including COA-nets. To facilitate the translation process, we plan on implementing a tool that would allow us to perform it automatically. However, we already know that this would require a preliminary study on additional heuristics improving MCMT's performance for imperative models.

14.4 Additional Open Directions

As argued several times, the main contribution provided by this work is to pave the way for the use of SMT solving and for the development of automated reasoning methods in order to model and verify data-aware processes. This idea originated several independent research directions that all have in common the use of SMT-based techniques for solving problems intrinsically involving the interplay of processes and data. We present five of these open directions that have been recently proved to be particularly promising.

14.4.1 Verification of Artifact Systems Under Ontologies

The first direction we are investigating concerns the study of (safety) verification for variants of artifact systems where, instead of managing a database, they operate over a description logic (DL) ontology that stores background, incomplete information about the artifacts. In [58, 59], we presented an attempt to attack this problem, by studying artifact systems where the underlying DL ontology is specified in (a slight extension of) RDFS [42], a schema language for the Semantic Web formalized by the W3C. In spirit, this approach is reminiscent of previous works studying the verification of dynamic systems (in particular, Golog programs) operating over a DL ontology, such as [76, 254]. We intend to deepen this investigation by considering (possibly richer) artifact systems operating over other significant DL ontologies.

14.4.2 Safety Verification of (Data-Aware) Multi-Agent Systems

The aim of the second direction we mention is the automatic safety verification of multi-agent systems (MASs) [177, 178, 179], parameterized on the number of concrete agents. The problem of verifying whether a given MAS is safe consists of establishing whether none of its possible executions can lead to bad states. In a declarative setting, a set of states is usually captured by a "state" formula existentially quantifying over agents. As the studied verification is parameterized, it only describes the finite set of possible agent *templates*, while the actual number of concrete agent instances that will be present at runtime, for each template, is unbounded and cannot be foreseen: in case the MAS is proved to be safe, this outcome needs to be *independent* of the actual number of concrete agents.

This problem lies at the intersection of parameterized verification and of verification of multi-agent systems. In [119, 118], we presented a first attempt to attack this problem using infinite-state model checking based on SMT, relying on the general framework introduced in Part I: specifically, in [119] we illustrate the theoretical foundations of our approach to MASs, whereas in [118] we detail the core implementation of SAFE [5], a web tool that makes our results operational. This tool provides an intuitive user interface that allows to directly encode PMASs into MCMT, so as to be immediately verified.

From the foundational perspective, *data-aware* extensions of this setting can be directly incorporated, along the line studied in this book. For instance, this will allow us to model and check for safety extended models of MASs that can be interpreted as suitable extensions of U-RASs, where agents are given *read and write* access to private and public databases, hence allowing us to model complex systems in which data is stored and exchanged, possibly involving arithmetic. From a practical perspective, these extensions can be easily added to SAFE: it would be enough to enrich SAFE with the aforementioned modeling capabilities, to automatically translate MAS specifications into MCMT specifications and then to exploit the database-driven mode of MCMT.

14.4.2.1 Verification of DAP Linear-Time Properties via LTLfMT

In this book, we only focused on *safety* verification of Data-Aware Processes, and we did not consider checking temporal properties that go beyond safety, such as *liveness* [29].

We recently started investigating SMT-based techniques for attacking the satisfiability problem of first-order extensions of Linear Temporal Logic (LTL). LTL and LTL over finite traces (LTLf) are common languages to express temporal properties in the fields of formal verification and AI. Specifically, LTLf has recently been successfully employed in AI and BPM [91], since reasoning over finite traces is more natural in real-world scenarios. However, in DAP modeling the propositional nature of LTLf is a severe limitation. In these contexts, as repeated several times, specifying actions and constraints that depend on the content of a relational database requires, at least, the expressiveness of first-order logic and the use of first-order theories as customary in SMT. In order to obtain the expressiveness needed to model and reason about these scenarios, in [124] we introduced and studied LTLf Modulo Theory (LTLfMT), a logic that extends LTLf by replacing propositional symbols with first-order formulas interpreted over an arbitrary first-order theory, in the spirit of SMT. We provided a semi-decision procedure for LTLfMT satisfiability based on tableaux methods, which we implemented in the BLACK tool [125, 126], a recent SAT and SMT-based state-of-the-art satisfiability checker for temporal logics. A preliminary experimental evaluation assesses the applicability of our approach.

A notable fact is that the first-order temporal properties that we can check in this framework open the possibility to express and verify sophisticated conditions on the evolution of concrete business processes enriched with real data, going beyond safety verification [155]. We intend to follow this path by introducing general DAP models for which full-fledged linear temporal properties expressed via LTLfMT can be effectively verified.

14.4.2.2 Conformance Checking for DAPs

A parallel research line in the DAP context where the use of SMT solving seems to be very fruitful is given by *conformance checking*. Conformance Checking [62] is a key process mining [245] task for comparing the expected behavior described by a process model and the actual behavior recorded in a log as sequences of action or events. The problem of how to perform this task in an effective way has been extensively studied for pure control-flow processes, but only few approaches have tried to solve it by also considering also the interaction with data [192]. In [120, 121] we tried to attack this challenging problem by considering processes that combine the data and control-flow dimensions. In particular, we adopted Data Petri Nets as the underlying formalism for representing DAPs, and showed how SMT-based techniques can be effectively employed for computing *data-aware alignments*, one of the most significant conformance metrics. For this purpose, we introduced an operational framework called CoCoMoT (Computing Conformance Modulo Theories) that uses state-of-the-art SMT solvers like Yices and Z3 as the underlying algorithmic backbone. We are convinced that the high flexibility and expressivity provided by SMT solvers can be effectively applied to solve other conformance checking tasks and, possibly, can be promoted to be among the most successful tools to employ in process mining.

14.4.2.3 Verification of Reinforcement Learning Agents in Structured Environments

The last research direction that is worth investigating is at the intersection of AI and Machine Learning (ML), and concerns the *verification of learning agents*. Designing agents that are both *adaptive* and *trustworthy* is a long-standing problem: these two problems are usually attacked separately. While trustworthiness is the goal of formal verification, adaptiveness is instead tackled by using ML settings. Reinforcement Learning (RL) [242] is one of these ML settings and has emerged as one of the most important techniques for equipping agents with learning capabilities used to maximize a reward while operating in an unknown environment. The application of techniques from formal methods and knowledge representation in an RL-based framework has so far typically revolved around guaranteeing that a single agent [92, 159, 160] or multiple agents [158] ensure temporal specifications of interest *in the limit* (i.e., after the learning phase). They do so in a generic context where no assumption is made on the structure of the state space. We are interested in a different setting, i.e., the one where learning agents act in so-called 'structured environments' [156]. These are environments where agents come with an explicit *structure*, for example relational data representing what the agents know about the world (in the style of [47, 53]). Our interest is to investigate such systems both *during and after the learning process*. This is for example relevant for BPM applications, where the states are process states and there are some constraints that must not only be satisfied in the limit but also during learning. This requires to incorporate at once background knowledge on the process itself in the form of (safety) constraints that should always be respected, preconditions and effects dictating how states can evolve into other states (and, conversely, which transitions do not exist at all), and finally also on goals that should be satisfied in the limit. We are currently studying how to combine automated reasoning and reinforcement learning techniques to formally verify the behavior of agents interacting in such structured environments.

14.5 Final Considerations

All in all, we believe that the expressive frameworks and the powerful techniques based on SMT solving and automated reasoning in general provide a very effective *theoretical and methodological basis* for solving problems that intrinsically combine dynamic features with static, data-oriented dimensions. Our conviction is that SMT provides a *universal framework* to attack a multitude of problems that can be described in symbolic terms. In the BPM spectrum, as we already showed [120], this means going beyond verification and tackling a wide spectrum of reasoning tasks for data-aware processes along their entire lifecycle.

Correction to: Verification of Data-Aware Processes via Satisfiability Modulo Theories

Alessandro Gianola

Correction to:
A. Gianola: *Verification of Data-Aware Processes via Satisfiability Modulo Theories*, **LNBIP 470,**
https://doi.org/10.1007/978-3-031-42746-6

The online version of this book has been revised after publication: The abstracts have been updated to match the ones originally submitted by the author.

The updated version of the book can be found at
https://doi.org/10.1007/978-3-031-42746-6

References

1. BPMN 2.0. https://www.omg.org/spec/BPMN/2.0/About-BPMN/.
2. cvc5. https://github.com/cvc5/cvc5.
3. MathSAT5. https://mathsat.fbk.eu/.
4. The Yices SMT Solver. https://yices.csl.sri.com/.
5. SAFE: the Swarm Safety Detector. http://www.safeswarms.club, 2020. Accessed: 2020-09-01.
6. P. A. Abdulla, K. Cerans, B. Jonsson, and Y.-K. Tsay. General decidability theorems for infinite-state systems. In *Proceedings of LICS '96*, pages 313–321, 1996.
7. P. A. Abdulla and G. Delzanno. Parameterized verification. *International Journal on Software Tools for Technology Transfer*, 18(5):469–473, 2016.
8. P. A. Abdulla, G. Delzanno, N. B. Henda, and A. Rezine. Regular model checking without transducers (on efficient verification of parameterized systems). In *Proceedings of TACAS 2007*, volume 4424 of *LNCS*, pages 721–736. Springer, 2007.
9. P. A. Abdulla, G. Delzanno, and A. Rezine. Parameterized verification of infinite-state processes with global conditions. In *Proceedings of CAV 2007*, volume 4590 of *LNCS*, pages 145–157. Springer, 2007.
10. P. A. Abdulla, F. Haziza, and L. Holík. Parameterized verification through view abstraction. *International Journal on Software Tools for Technology Transfer*, 18(5):495–516, 2016.
11. S. Abiteboul, R. Hull, and V. Vianu. *Foundations of Databases*. Addison-Wesley, 1995.
12. S. Abiteboul and V. Vianu. Models for data-centric workflows. In *In Search of Elegance in the Theory and Practice of Computation - Essays Dedicated to Peter Buneman*, pages 1–12, 2013.
13. F. Alberti, A. Armando, and S. Ranise. ASASP: Automated symbolic analysis of security policies. In *Proceedings of CADE 2011*, volume 6803 of *LNCS (LNAI)*, pages 26–33. Springer, 2011.
14. F. Alberti, R. Bruttomesso, S. Ghilardi, S. Ranise, and N. Sharygina. SAFARI: SMT-based abstraction for arrays with interpolants. In *Proceedings of CAV 2012*, volume 7358 of *LNCS*, pages 679–685. Springer, 2012.
15. F. Alberti, R. Bruttomesso, S. Ghilardi, S. Ranise, and N. Sharygina. An extension of lazy abstraction with interpolation for programs with arrays. *Formal Methods in System Design*, 45(1):63–109, 2014.
16. F. Alberti, S. Ghilardi, E. Pagani, S. Ranise, and G. P. Rossi. Brief announcement: Automated support for the design and validation of fault tolerant parameterized systems - A case study. In *Proceeding of DISC 2010*, volume 6343 of *LNCS*, pages 392–394. Springer, 2010.
17. F. Alberti, S. Ghilardi, E. Pagani, S. Ranise, and G. P. Rossi. Universal guards, relativization of quantifiers, and failure models in Model Checking Modulo Theories. *Journal on Satisfiability, Boolean Modeling and Computation*, 8(1/2):29–61, 2012.
18. F. Alberti, S. Ghilardi, and N. Sharygina. Booster: An acceleration-based verification framework for array programs. In *Proceedings of ATVA 2014*, volume 8837 of *LNCS*, pages 18–23. Springer, 2014.
19. F. Alberti, S. Ghilardi, and N. Sharygina. Decision procedures for flat array properties. In *Proceedings of TACAS 2014*, volume 8413 of *LNCS*, pages 15–30. Springer, 2014.
20. F. Alberti, S. Ghilardi, and N. Sharygina. A framework for the verification of parameterized infinite-state systems. *Fundamenta Informaticae*, 150(1):1–24, 2017.
21. A. Artale, A. Kovtunova, M. Montali, and W. M. P. van der Aalst. Modeling and reasoning over declarative data-aware processes with object-centric behavioral constraints. In *Proceedings of BPM 2019*, volume 11675 of *LNCS*, pages 139–156. Springer, 2019.
22. F. Baader, D. Calvanese, D. L. McGuinness, D. Nardi, and P. F. Patel-Schneider, editors. *The Description Logic Handbook: Theory, Implementation, and Applications*. Cambridge University Press, 2003.
23. F. Baader, S. Ghilardi, and C. Tinelli. A new combination procedure for the word problem that generalizes fusion decidability results in modal logics. *Information and Computation*, 204(10):1413–1452, 2006.

© The Editor(s) (if applicable) and The Author(s), under exclusive license to Springer Nature Switzerland AG 2023
A. Gianola: *Verification of Data-Aware Processes via Satisfiability Modulo Theories*, LNBIP 470, pp. 297–317, 2023.
https://doi.org/10.1007/978-3-031-42746-6

24. F. Baader and T. Nipkow. *Term Rewriting and All That*. Cambridge University Press, United Kingdom, 1998.
25. L. Bachmair and H. Ganzinger. Rewrite-based equational theorem proving with selection and simplification. *Journal of Logic and Computation*, 4(3):217–247, 1994.
26. L. Bachmair, H. Ganzinger, C. Lynch, and W. Snyder. Basic paramodulation. *Information and Computation*, 121(2):172–192, 1995.
27. L. Bachmair, H. Ganzinger, and U. Waldmann. Refutational theorem proving for hierarchic first-order theories. *Applicable Algebra in Engineering, Communication and Computing*, 5:193–212, 1994.
28. B. Bagheri Hariri, D. Calvanese, G. De Giacomo, A. Deutsch, and M. Montali. Verification of relational data-centric dynamic systems with external services. In *Proceedings of PODS 2013*, pages 163–174, 2013.
29. C. Baier and J.-P. Katoen. *Principles of model checking*. MIT Press, 2008.
30. H. Barbosa, C. Barrett, M. Brain, G. Kremer, H. Lachnitt, M. Mann, A. Mohamed, M. Mohamed, A. Niemetz, A. Noetzli, A. Ozdemir, M. Preiner, A. Reynolds, Y. Sheng, C. Tinelli, and Y. Zohar. CVC5: A versatile and industrial-strength SMT solver. In *Proceedings of TACAS 2022*, LNCS. Springer, To appear.
31. C. Barrett, P. Fontaine, and C. Tinelli. The SMT-LIB Standard: Version 2.6. Technical report, Available at: http://smtlib.cs.uiowa.edu/language.shtml, 2018.
32. C. W. Barrett and C. Tinelli. Satisfiability modulo theories. In *Handbook of Model Checking.*, pages 305–343. 2018.
33. P. Baumgartner and U. Waldmann. Hierarchic superposition with weak abstraction. In *Proceedings of CADE 2013*, volume 7898 of *LNCS (LNAI)*, pages 39–57. Springer, 2013.
34. M. M. Bersani, F. Marconi, M.Rossi, M. Erascu, and S. Ghilardi. Formal verification of data-intensive applications through model checking modulo theories. In *Proceedings of SPIN 2017*, pages 98–101. ACM, 2017.
35. M. Bílková. Uniform interpolation and propositional quantifiers in modal logics. *Studia Logica*, 85(1):1–31, 2007.
36. R. Bloem, S. Jacobs, and A. Khalimov. *Decidability of Parameterized Verification*. Morgan & Claypool Publishers, 2015.
37. M. Bojańczyk, L. Segoufin, and S. Toruńczyk. Verification of database-driven systems via amalgamation. In *Proceedings of PODS 2013*, pages 63–74, 2013.
38. A. R. Bradley. Sat-based model checking without unrolling. In *Proceedings of VMCAI 2011*, volume 6538 of *LNCS*, pages 70–87. Springer, 2011.
39. A. R. Bradley. SAT-based model checking without unrolling. In *Proceedings of VMCAI 2011*, volume 6538 of *LNCS*, pages 70–87. Springer, 2011.
40. A. R. Bradley. IC3 and beyond: Incremental, inductive verification. In *Proceedings of the 24th International Conference on Computer Aided Verification (CAV)*, volume 7358 of *LNCS*, page 4. Springer, 2012.
41. A. R. Bradley and Z. Manna. *The Calculus of Computation - Decision Procedures with Applications to Verification*. Springer, 2007.
42. D. Brickley and R.V. Guha. RDF Schema 1.1. W3C Recommendation, World Wide Web Consortium, 2014. Available at https://www.w3.org/TR/rdf-schema/.
43. D. Bruschi, A. Di Pasquale, S. Ghilardi, A. Lanzi, and E. Pagani. Formal verification of ARP (address resolution protocol) through SMT-based model checking - A case study. In *Proceedings of IFM 2017*, volume 10510 of *LNCS*, pages 391–406. Springer, 2017.
44. R. Bruttomesso, A. Carioni, S. Ghilardi, and S. Ranise. Automated analysis of parametric timing-based mutual exclusion algorithms. In *Proceedings of NFM 2012*, volume 7226 of *LNCS*, pages 279–294. Springer, 2012.
45. R. Bruttomesso, S. Ghilardi, and S. Ranise. Quantifier-free interpolation in combinations of equality interpolating theories. *ACM Transactions on Computational Logic*, 15(1):5:1–5:34, 2014.
46. J. R. Burch, E. M. Clarke, K. L. McMillan, D. L. Dill, and L. J. Hwang. Symbolic model checking: 10^20 states and beyond. *Information and Computation*, 98(2):142–170, 1992.

47. D. Calvanese, G. De Giacomo, and M. Montali. Foundations of data-aware process analysis: A database theory perspective. In *Proceedings of PODS 2013*, pages 1–12, 2013.

48. D. Calvanese, G. De Giacomo, M. Montali, and F. Patrizi. First-order μ-calculus over generic transition systems and applications to the situation calculus. *Information and Computation*, 259(3):328–347, 2018.

49. D. Calvanese, S. Ghilardi, A. Gianola, M. Montali, and A. Rivkin. Formal modeling and SMT-based parameterized verification of data-aware BPMN. In *Proceeding of BPM 2019*, volume 11675 of *LNCS*, pages 157–175. Springer, 2019.

50. D. Calvanese, S. Ghilardi, A. Gianola, M. Montali, and A. Rivkin. Formal modeling and SMT-based parameterized verification of multi-case data-aware BPMN. Technical Report arXiv:1905.12991, arXiv.org, 2019.

51. D. Calvanese, S. Ghilardi, A. Gianola, M. Montali, and A. Rivkin. From model completeness to verification of data aware processes. In *Description Logic, Theory Combination, and All That*, volume 11560 of *LNCS*, pages 212–239. Springer, 2019.

52. D. Calvanese, S. Ghilardi, A. Gianola, M. Montali, and A. Rivkin. Model completeness, covers and superposition. In *Proceedings of CADE 2019*, volume 11716 of *LNCS (LNAI)*, pages 142–160. Springer, 2019.

53. D. Calvanese, S. Ghilardi, A. Gianola, M. Montali, and A. Rivkin. Verification of data-aware processes: Challenges and opportunities for automated reasoning. In *Proceedings of ARCADE 2019*, volume 311. EPTCS, 2019.

54. D. Calvanese, S. Ghilardi, A. Gianola, M. Montali, and A. Rivkin. Combined Covers and Beth Definability. In *Proceedings of IJCAR 2020*, volume 12166 of *LNCS (LNAI)*, pages 181–200. Springer, 2020.

55. D. Calvanese, S. Ghilardi, A. Gianola, M. Montali, and A. Rivkin. SMT-based verification of data-aware processes: a model-theoretic approach. *Mathematical Structures in Computer Science*, 30(3):271–313, 2020.

56. D. Calvanese, S. Ghilardi, A. Gianola, M. Montali, and A. Rivkin. Model completeness, uniform interpolants and superposition calculus (with applications to verificaton of data-aware processes). *Journal of Automated Reasoning*, 65(7):941–969, 2021.

57. D. Calvanese, S. Ghilardi, A. Gianola, M. Montali, and A. Rivkin. Combination of uniform interpolants via Beth definability. *Journal of Automated Reasoning*, 66(3), 2022.

58. D. Calvanese, A. Gianola, A. Mazzullo, and M. Montali. SMT-based safety verification of data-aware processes under ontologies (preliminary results). In *Proceedings of DL 2021*, volume 2954, pages 1–15. CEUR Workshop Proceedings, 2021.

59. D. Calvanese, A. Gianola, A. Mazzullo, and M. Montali. SMT safety verification of ontology-based processes. In *Proceedings of AAAI 2023*, volume 37(5), pages 6271–6279. AAAI Press, 2023.

60. D. Calvanese, M. Montali, F. Patrizi, and A. Rivkin. Modeling and in-database management of relational, data-aware processes. In *Proceedings of CAiSE 2019*, LNCS, pages 328–345. Springer, 2019.

61. A. Carioni, S. Ghilardi, and S. Ranise. MCMT in the land of parametrized timed automata. In *Proceedings of VERIFY 2010*, pages 47–64, 2010.

62. J. Carmona, B. F. van Dongen, A. Solti, and M. Weidlich. *Conformance Checking - Relating Processes and Models*. Springer, 2018.

63. P. Caspi, D. Pilaud, N. Halbwachs, and J. Plaice. Lustre: A declarative language for programming synchronous systems. In *Proceedings of POPL 1987*, pages 178–188. ACM Press, 1987.

64. R. Cavada, A. Cimatti, M. Dorigatti, A. Griggio, A. Mariotti, A. Micheli, S. Mover, M. Roveri, and S. Tonetta. The nuxmv symbolic model checker. In *Proceedings of CAV 2014*, volume 8559 of *LNCS*, pages 334–342. Springer, 2014.

65. A. Champion, A. Mebsout, C. Sticksel, and C. Tinelli. The kind 2 model checker. In *Proceedings of CAV 2016*, volume 9780 of *LNCS*, pages 510–517. Springer, 2016.

66. C.-C. Chang and J. H. Keisler. *Model Theory*. North-Holland Publishing Co., Amsterdam-London, third edition, 1990.

67. A. Cimatti, E. M. Clarke, E. Giunchiglia, F. Giunchiglia, M. Pistore, M. Roveri, R. Sebastiani, and A. Tacchella. Nusmv 2: An opensource tool for symbolic model checking. In *Proceedings of CAV 2002*, volume 2404 of *LNCS*, pages 359–364. Springer, 2002.

68. A. Cimatti, A. Griggio, B. J. Schaafsma, and R. Sebastiani. The mathsat5 SMT solver. In *Proceedings of TACAS 2013*, volume 7795 of *LNCS*, pages 93–107. Springer, 2013.

69. E. Clarke, A. Biere, R. Raimi, and Y. Zhu. Bounded model checking using satisfiability solving. *Formal Methods in System Design*, 19(1):7–34, 2001.

70. E. M. Clarke and E. A. Emerson. Design and Synthesis of Synchronization Skeletons using Branching-Time Temporal Logic. In *Proceedings of Logic of Programs 1981*, volume 131 of *LNCS*, pages 52–71. Springer, 1981.

71. E. M. Clarke, E. A. Emerson, and A. P. Sistla. Automatic verification of Finite-State Concurrent Systems using Temporal Logic Specifications. *ACM Transactions on Programming Languages and Systems*, 8(2):244–263, 1986.

72. E. M. Clarke and O. Grumberg. Avoiding the state explosion problem in temporal logic model checking. In *Proceedings of PODC '87*, pages 294–303. ACM, 1987.

73. E. M. Clarke, O. Grumberg, and D. E. Long. Model checking and abstraction. *ACM Transactions on Programming Languages and Systems*, 16(5):1512–1542, 1994.

74. E. M. Clarke, O. Grumberg, and D. A. Peled. *Model checking*. MIT Press, 2001.

75. E. M. Clarke, T. A. Henzinger, H. Veith, and R. Bloem, editors. *Handbook of Model Checking*. Springer, 2018.

76. J. Claßen, M. Liebenberg, G. Lakemeyer, and B. Zarrieß. Exploring the boundaries of decidable verification of non-terminating golog programs. In *Proceedings of AAAI 2014*, pages 1012–1019. AAAI Press, 2014.

77. C. Combi, B. Oliboni, M. Weske, and F. Zerbato. Conceptual modeling of processes and data. In *Proceedings of ER 2018*, volume 11157 of *LNCS*, pages 236–250. Springer, 2018.

78. S. Conchon, A.Goel, S. Krstic, A. Mebsout, and F. Zaïdi. Invariants for finite instances and beyond. In *Proceedings of FMCAD 2013*, pages 61–68, 2013.

79. S. Conchon, D. Declerck, and F. Zaidi. Cubicle-W: Parameterized model checking on weak memory. In *Proceedings of IJCAR 2018*, volume 10900 of *LNCS (LNAI)*, pages 152–160. Springer, 2018.

80. S. Conchon, A. Goel, S. Krstic, A. Mebsout, and F. Zaïdi. Cubicle: A parallel SMT-based model checker for parameterized systems - Tool paper. In *Proceedings of CAV 2012*, volume 7358 of *LNCS*, pages 718–724. Springer, 2012.

81. S. Conchon, A. Mebsout, and F. Zaïdi. Certificates for parameterized model checking. In *Proceeding of FM 2015*, volume 9109 of *LNCS*, pages 126–142. Springer, 2015.

82. D. C. Cooper. Theorem proving in arithmetic without multiplication. In *Machine Intelligence*, volume 7, pages 91–100. Edinburgh University Press, 1972.

83. F. Corradini, F. Fornari, A. Polini, B. Re, and F. Tiezzi. Repository: a repository platform for sharing business process models. In *Proceedings of BPM (PhD/Demos)*, volume 2420, pages 149–153. CEUR Workshop Proceedings, 2019.

84. F. Corradini, C. Muzi, B. Re, L. Rossi, and F. Tiezzi. Animating multiple instances in BPMN collaborations: From formal semantics to tool support. In *Proceedings of BPM 2018*, volume 11080 of *LNCS*, pages 83–101. Springer, 2018.

85. W. Craig. Three uses of the Herbrand-Gentzen theorem in relating model theory and proof theory. *Journal of Symbolic Logic*, 22:269–285, 1957.

86. P. Dadam, M. Reichert, S. Rinderle-Ma, A. Lanz, R. Pryss, M. Predeschly, J. Kolb, L. T. Ly, M. Jurisch, U. Kreher, and K. Göser. From ADEPT to aristaflow BPM suite: A research vision has become reality. In *Proceedings of BPM Workshops*, volume 43 of *LNBIP*, pages 529–531. Springer, 2009.

87. G. D'Agostino and M. Hollenberg. Logical questions concerning the mu-calculus: Interpolation, lyndon and los-tarski. *Journal of Symbolic Logic*, 65(1):310–332, 2000.

88. E. Damaggio, A. Deutsch, R. Hull, and V. Vianu. Automatic verification of data-centric business processes. In *Proceedings of BPM 2011*, volume 6896 of *LNCS*, pages 3–16. Springer, 2011.

89. E. Damaggio, A. Deutsch, and V. Vianu. Artifact systems with data dependencies and arithmetic. *ACM Transactions on Database Systems*, 37(3):22:1–22:36, 2012.

90. E. Damaggio, R. Hull, and R. Vaculín. On the equivalence of incremental and fixpoint semantics for business artifacts with Guard-Stage-Milestone lifecycles. In *Proceedings of BPM 2011*, volume 6896 of *LNCS*, pages 396–412. Springer, 2011.

91. G. De Giacomo, R. De Masellis, M. Grasso, F. M. Maggi, and M. Montali. Monitoring business metaconstraints based on LTL and LDL for finite traces. In *Proceedings of BPM 2014*, volume 8659 of *LNCS*, pages 1–17. Springer, 2014.

92. G. De Giacomo, L. Iocchi, M. Favorito, and F. Patrizi. Foundations for restraining bolts: Reinforcement learning with LTLf/LDLf restraining specifications. In *Proceedings of ICAPS 2018*, pages 128–136. AAAI Press, 2019.

93. G. De Giacomo, X. Oriol, M. Estañol, and E. Teniente. Linking data and BPMN processes to achieve executable models. In *Proceedings of CAiSE 2017*, volume 10253 of *LNCS*, pages 612–628. Springer, 2017.

94. M. de Leoni, P. Felli, and M. Montali. A holistic approach for soundness verification of decision-aware process models. In *Proceedings of ER 2018*, volume 11157 of *LNCS*, pages 219–235. Springer, 2018.

95. R. De Masellis, C. Di Francescomarino, C. Ghidini, M. Montali, and S. Tessaris. Add data into business process verification: Bridging the gap between theory and practice. In *Proceedings of AAAI 2017*, pages 1091–1099. AAAI Press, 2017.

96. L. de Moura and N. Bjørner. Z3: an efficient SMT solver. In *Proceedings of TACAS 2008*, volume 4963 of *LNCS*, pages 337–340. Springer, 2008.

97. G. Delzanno. An overview of MSR(C): A CLP-based framework for the symbolic verification of parameterized concurrent systems. *Electronic Notes in Theoretical Computer Science*, 76:65–82, 2002.

98. G. Delzanno, J. Esparza, and A. Podelski. Constraint-based analysis of broadcast protocols. In *Proceedings of CSL '99*, volume 1683 of *LNCS*, pages 50–66. Springer, 1999.

99. A. Deutsch, R. Hull, Y. Li, and V. Vianu. Automatic verification of database-centric systems. *ACM SIGLOG News*, 5(2):37–56, 2018.

100. A. Deutsch, R. Hull, F. Patrizi, and V. Vianu. Automatic verification of data-centric business processes. In *Proceedings of ICDT 2009*, pages 252–267, 2009.

101. A. Deutsch, R. Hull, and V. Vianu. Automatic verification of database-centric systems. *SIGMOD Record*, 43(3):5–17, 2014.

102. A. Deutsch, Y. Li, and V. Vianu. Verification of hierarchical artifact systems. In *Proceedings of PODS 2016*, pages 179–194, 2016.

103. A. Deutsch, Y. Li, and V. Vianu. Verification of hierarchical artifact systems. *ACM Transactions on Database Systems*, 44(3):12:1–12:68, 2019.

104. M. Dumas. On the convergence of data and process engineering. In *Proceedings of ADBIS 2011*, volume 6909 of *LNCS*. Springer, 2011.

105. M. Dumas, M. La Rosa, J. Mendling, and H. A. Reijers. *Fundamentals of Business Process Management, Second Edition*. Springer, 2018.

106. B. Dutertre. Yices 2.2. In *Proceedings of CAV 2014*, volume 8559 of *LNCS*, pages 737–744. Springer, 2014.

107. B. Dutertre and L. De Moura. The yices smt solver. Technical report, Computer Science Laboratory, SRI International, 2006.

108. E. A. Emerson and V. Kahlon. Model checking guarded protocols. In *Proceedings of LICS 2003*, pages 361–370. IEEE, 2003.

109. E. A. Emerson and K. S. Namjoshi. On reasoning about rings. *International Journal of Foundations of Computer Science*, 14(4):527–550, 2003.

110. H. B. Enderton. *A mathematical introduction to logic*. Academic Press, 2nd edition edition, 2001.

111. J. Esparza, A. Finkel, and R. Mayr. On the verification of broadcast protocols. In *Proceedings of LICS '99*, pages 352–359, 1999.

112. J. Esparza, P. Ganty, J. Leroux, and R. Majumdar. Verification of population protocols. *Acta Informatica*, 54(2):191–215, 2017.

113. M. Estañol, M.-R. Sancho, and E. Teniente. Verification and validation of UML artifact-centric business process models. In *Proceedings of CAiSE 2015*, volume 9097 of *LNCS*, pages 434–449. Springer, 2015.

114. M. Estañol, M.-R. Sancho, and E. Teniente. Ensuring the semantic correctness of a BAUML artifact-centric BPM. *Information and Software Technology*, 93:147–162, 2018.

115. R. Fagin. Probabilities on finite models. *Journal of Symbolic Logic*, 41(1):50–58, 1976.

116. D. Fahland. Describing behavior of processes with many-to-many interactions. In *Proceedings of PETRI NETS 2019*, volume 11522 of *LNCS*, pages 3–24. Springer, 2019.

117. D. Fahland, A. Meyer, L. Pufahl, K. Batoulis, and M. Weske. Automating data exchange in process choreographies (extended abstract). In *Proceedings of EMISA 2016*, volume 1701, pages 13–16. CEUR Workshop Proceedings, 2016.

118. P. Felli, A. Gianola, and M. Montali. A SMT-based implementation for safety checking of parameterized multi-agent systems. In *Proceedings of PRIMA 2020*, volume 12568 of *LNCS*, pages 259–280. Springer, 2020.

119. P. Felli, A. Gianola, and M. Montali. SMT-based safety checking of parameterized multi-agent systems. In *Proceedings of AAAI 2021*. AAAI Press, 2021.

120. P. Felli, A. Gianola, M. Montali, A. Rivkin, and S. Winkler. CoCoMoT: Conformance checking of multi-perspective processes via SMT. In *Proceedings of BPM 2021*, volume 12875 of *LNCS*, pages 217–234. Springer, 2021.

121. P. Felli, A. Gianola, M. Montali, A. Rivkin, and S. Winkler. Data-aware conformance checking with SMT. *Information Systems*, 117, 2023.

122. A. Finkel and P. Schnoebelen. Well-structured transition systems everywhere! *Theoretical Computer Science*, 256(1):63–92, 2001.

123. A. Gacek, J. Backes, M. Whalen, L. G. Wagner, and E. Ghassabani. The jkind model checker. In *Proceedings of CAV 2018*, volume 10982 of *LNCS*, pages 20–27. Springer, 2018.

124. L. Geatti, A. Gianola, and N. Gigante. Linear temporal logic modulo theories over finite traces. In *Proceedings of IJCAI 2022*, pages 2641–2647. ijcai.org, 2022.

125. L. Geatti, N. Gigante, and A. Montanari. A sat-based encoding of the one-pass and tree-shaped tableau system for LTL. In *Proceedings of TABLEAUX 2019*, volume 11714 of *LNCS*, pages 3–20. Springer, 2019.

126. L. Geatti, N. Gigante, and A. Montanari. BLACK: A fast, flexible and reliable LTL satisfiability checker. In *Proceedings of OVERLAY 2021, co-located with GandALF 2021*, volume 2987 of *CEUR Workshop Proceedings*, pages 7–12. CEUR-WS.org, 2021.

127. S. Ghilardi. An algebraic theory of normal forms. *Annals of Pure and Applied Logic*, 71(3):189–245, 1995.

128. S. Ghilardi. Model theoretic methods in combined constraint satisfiability. *Journal of Automated Reasoning*, 33(3-4):221–249, 2004.

129. S. Ghilardi and A. Gianola. Interpolation, amalgamation and combination (the non-disjoint signatures case). In *Proceedings of FroCoS 2017*, volume 10483 of *LNCS (LNAI)*, pages 316–332. Springer, 2017.

130. S. Ghilardi and A. Gianola. Modularity results for interpolation, amalgamation and superamalgamation. *Annals of Pure and Applied Logic*, 169(8):731–754, 2018.

131. S. Ghilardi, A. Gianola, and D. Kapur. Compactly representing uniform interpolants for EUF using (conditional) DAGS. Technical Report arXiv:2002.09784, arXiv.org, 2020.

132. S. Ghilardi, A. Gianola, and D. Kapur. Computing uniform interpolants for EUF via (conditional) DAG-based compact representations. In *Proceedings of CILC 2020*, volume 2710, pages 67–81. CEUR Workshop Proceedings, 2020.

133. S. Ghilardi, A. Gianola, and D. Kapur. Interpolation and amalgamation for arrays with maxdiff. In *Proceedings of FOSSACS 2021*, volume 12650 of *LNCS*, pages 268–288. Springer, 2021.

134. S. Ghilardi, A. Gianola, and D. Kapur. Uniform interpolants in EUF: algorithms using dag-representations. *Log. Methods Comput. Sci.*, 18(2), 2022.

135. S. Ghilardi, A. Gianola, M. Montali, and A. Rivkin. Petri nets with parameterised data - modelling and verification. In *Proceedings of BPM 2020*, volume 12168 of *LNCS*, pages 55–74. Springer, 2020.

136. S. Ghilardi, A. Gianola, M. Montali, and A. Rivkin. Petri nets with parameterised data: Modelling and verification (extended version). Technical Report arXiv:2006.06630, arXiv.org, 2020.

137. S. Ghilardi, A. Gianola, M. Montali, and A. Rivkin. delta-BPMN. `https://github.com/mrMorningLemon/delta-BPMN`,`https://doi.org/10.6084/m9.figshare.19178546.v2`, 2021. Software.

138. S. Ghilardi, A. Gianola, M. Montali, and A. Rivkin. Delta-BPMN: A concrete language and verifier for data-aware BPMN. In *Proceedings of BPM 2021*, volume 12875 of *LNCS*, pages 179–196. Springer, 2021.

139. S. Ghilardi, A. Gianola, M. Montali, and A. Rivkin. Petri net-based object-centric processes with read-only data. *Information Systems*, 107, 2022.

140. S. Ghilardi, A. Gianola, M. Montali, and A. Rivkin. Relational action bases: Formalization, effective safety verification, and invariants (extended version). *CoRR*, abs/2208.06377, 2022.

141. S. Ghilardi, A. Gianola, M. Montali, and A. Rivkin. Safety verification and universal invariants for relational action bases. In *Proceedings of IJCAI 2023*, To appear.

142. S. Ghilardi, E. Nicolini, S. Ranise, and D. Zucchelli. Combination methods for satisfiability and model-checking of infinite-state systems. In *Proceedings of CADE 2007*, volume 4603 of *LNCS*, pages 362–378. Springer, 2007.

143. S. Ghilardi, E. Nicolini, S. Ranise, and D. Zucchelli. Towards SMT model checking of array-based systems. In *Proceedings of IJCAR 2008*, volume 5195 of *LNCS (LNAI)*, pages 67–82. Springer, 2008.

144. S. Ghilardi, E. Nicolini, and D. Zucchelli. A comprehensive framework for combined decision procedures. *ACM Transactions on Computational Logic*, 9(2):8:1–8:54, 2008.

145. S. Ghilardi and S. Ranise. Goal-directed invariant synthesis for model checking modulo theories. In *Proceedings of TABLEAUX 2009*, volume 5607 of *LNCS*, pages 173–188. Springer, 2009.

146. S. Ghilardi and S. Ranise. Backward reachability of array-based systems by SMT solving: Termination and invariant synthesis. *Logical Methods in Computer Science*, 6(4), 2010.

147. S. Ghilardi and S. Ranise. MCMT: A model checker modulo theories. In *Proceedings of IJCAR 2010*, volume 6173 of *LNCS (LNAI)*, pages 22–29. Springer, 2010.

148. S. Ghilardi and S. J. van Gool. Monadic second order logic as the model companion of temporal logic. In *Proceedings of LICS 2016*, pages 417–426, 2016.

149. S. Ghilardi and S. J. van Gool. A model-theoretic characterization of monadic second order logic on infinite words. *Journal of Symbolic Logic*, 82(1):62–76, 2017.

150. S. Ghilardi and M. Zawadowski. *Sheaves, games, and model completions*, volume 14 of *Trends in Logic—Studia Logica Library*. Kluwer Academic Publishers, Dordrecht, 2002.

151. S. Ghilardi and M. W. Zawadowski. A sheaf representation and duality for finitely presenting heyting algebras. *Journal of Symbolic Logic*, 60(3):911–939, 1995.

152. S. Ghilardi and M. W. Zawadowski. Undefinability of propositional quantifiers in the modal system S4. *Studia Logica*, 55(2):259–271, 1995.

153. S. Ghilardi and M. W. Zawadowski. Model completions, r-Heyting categories. *Annals of Pure and Applied Logic*, 88(1):27–46, 1997.

154. A. Gianola. *SMT-based Safety Verification of Data-Aware Processes: Foundations and Applications*. PhD thesis, Free University of Bozen-Bolzano, 2022.

155. A. Gianola and N. Gigante. LTL modulo theories over finite traces: modeling, verification, open questions. In *Proceedings of OVERLAY 2022, co-located with AIxIA 2022*, volume 3311 of *CEUR Workshop Proceedings*, pages 13–19. CEUR-WS.org, 2022.

156. A. Gianola, M. Montali, and M. Papini. Automated reasoning for reinforcement learning agents in structured environments. In *Proceedings of OVERLAY 2021*, volume 2987, pages 43–48. CEUR Workshop Proceedings, 2021.

157. S. Gulwani and M. Musuvathi. Cover algorithms and their combination. In *Proceedings of ESOP 2008*, volume 4960 of *LNCS*, pages 193–207. Springer, 2008.

158. L. Hammond, A. Abate, J. Gutierrez, and M. J. Wooldridge. Multi-agent reinforcement learning with temporal logic specifications. In *Proceedings of AAMAS 2021*, pages 583–592. ACM, 2021.

159. M. Hasanbeig, D. Kroening, and A. Abate. Towards verifiable and safe model-free reinforcement learning. In *Proceedings of OVERLAY 2019*, volume 2509. CEUR-WS.org, 2019.

160. M. Hasanbeig, D. Kroening, and A. Abate. Deep reinforcement learning with temporal logics. In *Proceedings of FORMATS 2020*, volume 12288 of *LNCS*, pages 1–22. Springer, 2020.

161. T. Henzinger and K. L. McMillan R. Jhala, R. Majumdar. Abstractions from Proofs. In *Proceedings of POPL 2004*, pages 232–244. ACM, 2004.

162. G. Higman. Ordering by divisibility in abstract algebras. *Proceedings of the London Mathematical Society*, 3(2):326–336, 1952.

163. K. Hoder and N. Bjørner. Generalized property directed reachability. In *Proceedings of SAT 2012*, volume 7317 of *LNCS*, pages 157–171. Springer, 2012.

164. J. E. Hopcroft and J.-J. Pansiot. On the reachability problem for 5-dimensional vector addition systems. *Theoretical Computer Science*, 8:135–159, 1979.

165. S. Houhou, S. Baarir, P. Poizat, and P. Quéinnec. A first-order logic semantics for communication-parametric BPMN collaborations. In *Proceedings of BPM 2019*, volume 11675 of *LNCS*, pages 52–68. Springer, 2019.

166. J. Hsiang and M. Rusinowitch. Proving refutational completeness of theorem-proving strategies: The transfinite semantic tree method. *Journal of the ACM*, 38(3):559–587, 1991.

167. R. Hull. Artifact-centric business process models: Brief survey of research results and challenges. In *Proceedings of OTM 2008*, volume 5332 of *LNCS*, pages 1152–1163. Springer, 2008.

168. K. Jensen. *Coloured Petri Nets - Basic Concepts, Analysis Methods and Practical Use - Volume 1*. EATCS Monographs on Theoretical Computer Science. Springer, 1992.

169. K. Jensen. *Coloured Petri Nets - Basic Concepts, Analysis Methods and Practical Use - Volume 2*. EATCS Monographs on Theoretical Computer Science. Springer, 1994.

170. K. Jensen. *Coloured Petri Nets - Basic Concepts, Analysis Methods and Practical Use - Volume 3*. Monographs in Theoretical Computer Science. An EATCS Series. Springer, 1997.

171. K. Jensen and L. M. Kristensen. *Coloured Petri Nets - Modelling and Validation of Concurrent Systems*. Springer, 2009.

172. A. John, I. Konnov, U. Schmid, H. Veith, and J. Widder. Counter attack on byzantine generals: Parameterized model checking of fault-tolerant distributed algorithms. Technical Report arXiv:1210.3846, arXiv.org, 2012.

173. D. Kapur. Shostak's congruence closure as completion. In *Proceedings of RTA '97*, volume 1232 of *LNCS*, pages 23–37. Springer, 1997.

174. D. Kapur. Nonlinear polynomials, interpolants and invariant generation for system analysis. In *Proceedings of SC-Square 2017 (co-located with ISSAC)*, volume 1974. CEUR Workshop Proceedings, 2017.

175. A. Karbyshev, N. S. Bjørner, S. Itzhaky, N. Rinetzky, and S. Shoham. Property-directed inference of universal invariants or proving their absence. *Journal of the ACM*, 64(1):7:1–7:33, 2017.

176. R. M. Karp and R. E. Miller. Parallel program schemata. *Journal of Computer and System Sciences*, 3(2):147–195, 1969.

177. P. Kouvaros and A. Lomuscio. Parameterised verification for multi-agent systems. *Artificial Intelligence*, 234:152–189, 2016.

178. P. Kouvaros and A. Lomuscio. Parameterised verification of infinite state multi-agent systems via predicate abstraction. In *Proceedings of AAAI 2017*, pages 3013–3020, 2017.

179. P. Kouvaros, A. Lomuscio, E. Pirovano, and H. Punchihewa. Formal verification of open multi-agent systems. In *Proceedings of AAMAS 2019*, pages 179–187, 2019.

180. L. Kovács and A. Voronkov. Interpolation and symbol elimination. In *Proceedings of CADE 2009*, volume 5663 of *LNCS (LNAI)*, pages 199–213. Springer, 2009.

181. T. Kowalski and G. Metcalfe. Uniform interpolation and coherence. *Annals of Pure and Applied Logic*, 170(7):825–841, 2019.

182. J. B. Kruskal. Well-quasi-ordering, the Tree Theorem, and Vazsonyi's conjecture. *Transactions of the American Mathematical Society*, 95:210–225, 1960.

183. V. Künzle, B. Weber, and M Reichert. Object-aware business processes: Fundamental requirements and their support in existing approaches. *International Journal of Information System Modeling and Design*, 2(2), 2011.

184. S. Lasota. Decidability border for petri nets with data: WQO dichotomy conjecture. In *Proceedings of PETRI NETS 2016*, volume 9698 of *LNCS*, pages 20–36. Springer, 2016.

185. R. Lazic, T. C. Newcomb, J. Ouaknine, A. W. Roscoe, and J. Worrell. Nets with tokens which carry data. *Fundamenta Informaticae*, 88(3):251–274, 2008.

186. Y. Li, A. Deutsch, and V. Vianu. VERIFAS: A practical verifier for artifact systems. *Proceedings of the VLDB Endowment*, 11(3):283–296, 2017.

187. L. Libkin. *Elements of Finite Model Theory*, chapter Fixed Point Logics and Complexity Classes. Texts in Theoretical Computer Science. An EATCS Series. Springer, 2004.

188. P. Lipparini. Locally finite theories with model companion. In *Atti della Accademia Nazionale dei Lincei. Classe di Scienze Fisiche, Matematiche e Naturali. Rendiconti, Serie 8*, volume 72. Accademia Nazionale dei Lincei, 1982.

189. M. Ludwig and U. Waldmann. An extension of the Knuth-Bendix ordering with lpo-like properties. In *Proceediings of LPAR 2007*, pages 348–362, 2007.

190. L. L. Maksimova. Interpolation theorems in modal logics and amalgamable varieties of topological Boolean algebras. *Algebra i Logika*, 18(5):556–586, 632, 1979.

191. L. L. Maksimova. Interpolation theorems in modal logics. Sufficient conditions. *Algebra i Logika*, 19(2):194–213, 250–251, 1980.

192. F. Mannhardt, M. de Leoni, H. A. Reijers, and W. M. P. van der Aalst. Balanced multiperspective checking of process conformance. *Computing*, 98(4):407–437, 2016.

193. K. L. McMillan. *Symbolic Model Checking*. Kluwer Academic Publishers, Norwell, MA, USA, 1993.

194. K. L. McMillan. Interpolation and SAT-Based Model Checking. In *Proceedings of CAV 2003*, volume 2725 of *LNCS*, pages 1–13. Springer, 2003.

195. K. L. McMillan. Applications of Craig Interpolation to Model Checking. In *Proceedings of CSL 2004*, volume 3210 of *LNCS*, pages 22–23. Springer, 2004.

196. K. L. McMillan. Lazy Abstraction with Interpolants. In *Proceedings of CAV 2006*, volume 4144 of *LNCS*, pages 123–136. Springer, 2006.

197. G. Metcalfe and L. Reggio. Model completions for universal classes of algebras: necessary and sufficient conditions. Technical Report arXiv:2102.01426v1, arXiv.org, 2021.

198. A. Meyer, L. Pufahl, K. Batoulis, D. Fahland, and M. Weske. Automating data exchange in process choreographies. *Information Systems*, 53:296–329, 2015.

199. A. Meyer, L. Pufahl, K. Batoulis, S. Kruse, T. Lindhauer, T. Stoff, D. Fahland, and M. Weske. Automating data exchange in process choreographies. In *Proceedings of CAiSE 2014*, volume 8484 of *LNCS*, pages 316–331. Springer, 2014.

200. A. Meyer, L. Pufahl, D. Fahland, and M. Weske. Modeling and enacting complex data dependencies in business processes. In *Proceedings of BPM 2013*, volume 8094 of *LNCS*, pages 171–186. Springer, 2013.

201. Microsoft Research. The Z3 Prover. https://github.com/Z3Prover/z3.

202. M.L. Minsky. *Computation: Finite and Infinite Machines*. Prentice-Hall, Englewood Cliffs, NJ, 1967.

203. M. Montali and D. Calvanese. Soundness of data-aware, case-centric processes. *International Journal on Software Tools for Technology Transfer*, 18(5):535–558, 2016.

204. M. Montali and A. Rivkin. Model Checking Petri Nets with Names Using Data-Centric Dynamic Systems. *Formal Aspects of Computing*, 28(4):615–641, 2016.

205. M. Montali and A. Rivkin. DB-Nets: on the marriage of colored Petri Nets and relational databases. *Transactions on Petri Nets and Other Models of Concurrency*, 12:91–118, 2017.

206. M. Montali and A. Rivkin. From db-nets to coloured petri nets with priorities. In *Proceedings of PETRI NETS 2019*, volume 11522 of *LNCS*, pages 449–469. Springer, 2019.

207. G. Nelson and D. C. Oppen. Simplification by cooperating decision procedures. *ACM Transactions on Programming Languages and Systems*, 1(2):245–257, 1979.

208. G. Nelson and D. C. Oppen. Fast decision procedures based on congruence closure. *Journal of the ACM*, 27(2):356–364, 1980.

209. E. Nicolini, C. Ringeissen, and M. Rusinowitch. Satisfiability procedures for combination of theories sharing integer offsets. In *Proceedings of TACAS 2009*, volume 5505 of *LNCS*, pages 428–442. Springer, 2009.

210. E. Nicolini, C. Ringeissen, and M. Rusinowitch. Combining satisfiability procedures for unions of theories with a shared counting operator. *Fundamenta Informaticae*, 105(1-2):163–187, 2010.

211. R. Nieuwenhuis and A. Oliveras. Fast congruence closure and extensions. *Information and Computation*, 205(4):557–580, 2007.

212. R. Nieuwenhuis and A. Rubio. Theorem proving with ordering and equality constrained clauses. *Journal of Symbolic Computation*, 19(4):321–351, 1995.

213. R. Nieuwenhuis and A. Rubio. Paramodulation-based theorem proving. In *Handbook of Automated Reasoning (in 2 volumes)*, pages 371–443. MIT Press, 2001.

214. A. Nigam and N. S. Caswell. Business artifacts: An approach to operational specification. *IBM Systems Journal*, 42(3):428–445, 2003.

215. A. M. Pitts. On an interpretation of second order quantification in first order intuitionistic propositional logic. *Journal of Symbolic Logic*, 57(1):33–52, 1992.

216. A. Pnueli. The Temporal Semantics of Concurrent Programs. *Theoretical Computer Science*, 13:45–60, 1981.

217. A. Pnueli, J. Xu, and L. Zuck. Liveness with (0,1, infty)- counter abstraction. In *Proceedings of CAV 2002*, volume 2404 of *LNCS*, pages 107–122. Springer, 2002.

218. A. Polyvyanyy, J. M. E. M. van der Werf, S. Overbeek, and R. Brouwers. Information systems modeling: Language, verification, and tool support. In *Proceedings of CAiSE 2019*, volume 11483 of *LNCS*, pages 194–212. Springer, 2019.

219. J. P. Queille and J. Sifakis. Specification and verification of concurrent systems in cesar. In *Proceedings of Symposium on Programming 1982*, volume 137 of *LNCS*, pages 337–351. Springer, 1982.

220. R. Rado. Universal graphs and universal functions. *Acta Arithmetica*, 9:331–340, 1964.

221. M. Reichert. Process and data: Two sides of the same coin? In *Proceedings of OTM 2012*, volume 7565 of *LNCS*, pages 2–19. Springer, 2012.

222. H. A. Reijers, I. T. P. Vanderfeesten, M. G. A. Plomp, P. Van Gorp, D. Fahland, W. L. M. van der Crommert, and H. D. D. Garcia. Evaluating data-centric process approaches: Does the human factor factor in? *Software and System Modeling*, 16(3):649–662, 2017.

223. W. Reisig. *Understanding Petri Nets - Modeling Techniques, Analysis Methods, Case Studies*. Springer, 2013.

224. C. Richardson. Warning: Don't assume your business processes use master data. In *Proceedings of BPM 2010*, volume 6336 of *LNCS*, pages 11–12. Springer, 2010.

225. A. Robinson. *On the metamathematics of algebra*. Studies in Logic and the Foundations of Mathematics. North-Holland Publishing Co., Amsterdam, 1951.

226. A. Robinson. *Introduction to model theory and to the metamathematics of algebra*. Studies in logic and the foundations of mathematics. North-Holland, 1963.

227. F. Rosa-Velardo and D. de Frutos-Escrig. Name creation vs. replication in petri net systems. *Fundamenta Informaticae*, 88(3):329–356, 2008.

228. F. Rosa-Velardo and D. de Frutos-Escrig. Decidability and complexity of petri nets with unordered data. *Theoretical Computer Science*, 412(34):4439–4451, 2011.

229. N. Russell, W. M. P. van der Aalst, and A. H. M. ter Hofstede. *Workflow Patterns: The Definitive Guide*. MIT Press, 2016.

230. T. Rybina and A. Voronkov. A logical reconstruction of reachability. In *Perspectives of Systems Informatics, 5th International Andrei Ershov Memorial Conference, PSI 2003, Revised Papers*, pages 222–237, 2003.

231. S. Schmitz and P. Schnoebelen. The power of well-structured systems. In *Proceedings of CONCUR 2013*, volume 8052 of *LNCS*, pages 5–24. Springer, 2013.

232. A. Schrijver. *Theory of linear and integer programming*. Wiley-Interscience series in discrete mathematics and optimization. Wiley, 1999.

233. J. C. Seco, S. Debois, T. T. Hildebrandt, and T. Slaats. RESEDA: declaring live event-driven computations as reactive semi-structured data. In *Proceedings of EDOC 2018*, pages 75–84, 2018.

234. K. Segerberg. *An Essay in Classical Modal Logic*, volume 13 of *Filosofiska Studier*. Uppsala Universitet, 1971.

235. V.Yu. Shavrukov. Subalgebras of diagonalizable algebras of theories containing arithmetic. *Dissertationes Mathematicae*, CCCXXIII, 1993.

236. M. Sheeran, S. Singh, and G. Stålmarck. Checking safety properties using induction and a sat-solver. In *Proceedings of FMCAD 2000*, volume 1954 of *LNCS*, pages 108–125. Springer, 2000.

237. B. Silver. *BPMN Method and Style*. Cody-Cassidy, 2nd edition edition, 2011.

238. V. Sofronie-Stokkermans. Interpolation in local theory extensions. *Logical Methods in Computer Science*, 4(4), 2008.

239. V. Sofronie-Stokkermans. On interpolation and symbol elimination in theory extensions. In *Proceedings of IJCAR 2016*, volume 9706 of *LNCS (LNAI)*, pages 273–289. Springer, 2016.

240. V. Sofronie-Stokkermans. On interpolation and symbol elimination in theory extensions. *Logical Methods in Computer Science*, 14(3), 2018.

241. D. Solomakhin, M. Montali, S. Tessaris, and R. De Masellis. Verification of artifact-centric systems: Decidability and modeling issues. In *Proceedings of ICSOC 2013*, volume 8274 of *LNCS*, pages 252–266. Springer, 2013.

242. R. S. Sutton and A. G. Barto. *Reinforcement learning: An introduction*. MIT press, 2018.

243. C. Tinelli and M. T. Harandi. A new correctness proof of the Nelson-Oppen combination procedure. In *Proceedings of FroCoS 1996*, pages 103–119, 1996.

244. W. M. P. van der Aalst. Verification of workflow nets. In *Proceedings of ICATPN '97*, volume 1248 of *LNCS*, pages 407–426. Springer, 1997.

245. W. M. P. van der Aalst. *Process Mining - Discovery, Conformance and Enhancement of Business Processes*. Springer, 2011.

246. W. M. P. van der Aalst. Object-centric process mining: Dealing with divergence and convergence in event data. In *Proceedings of SEFM 2019*, volume 11724 of *LNCS*, pages 3–25. Springer, 2019.

247. W. M. P. van der Aalst, C. Stahl, and M. Westergaard. Strategies for modeling complex processes using colored petri nets. *Transactions on Petri Nets and Other Models of Concurrency*, 7:6–55, 2013.

248. S. J. van Gool, G. Metcalfe, and C. Tsinakis. Uniform interpolation and compact congruences. *Annals of Pure and Applied Logic*, 168(10):1927–1948, 2017.

249. K. M. van Hee, N. Sidorova, M. Voorhoeve, and J. M. E. M. van der Werf. Generation of database transactions with petri nets. *Fundamenta Informaticae*, 93(1-3):171–184, 2009.

250. V. Vianu. Automatic verification of database-driven systems: a new frontier. In *Proceedings of ICDT 2009*, pages 1–13, 2009.

251. A. Visser. Uniform interpolation and layered bisimulation. In P. Hájek, editor, *Gödel 96: Logical foundations on mathematics, computer science and physics – Kurt Gödel's legacy*. Springer Verlag, 1996.

252. W. H. Wheeler. Model-companions and definability in existentially complete structures. *Israel Journal of Mathematics*, 25(3-4):305–330, 1976.

253. G. Yorsh and M. Musuvathi. A combination method for generating interpolants. In *Proceedings of CADE 2005*, volume 3632 of *LNCS*, pages 353–368. Springer, 2005.

254. B. Zarrieß and J. Claßen. Decidable verification of golog programs over non-local effect actions. In *Proceedings of AAAI 2016*, pages 1109–1115. AAAI Press, 2016.

Printed in the United States
by Baker & Taylor Publisher Services